Gower Handbook of Training and Development

Third Edition

Gower Handbook of Training and Development

Third Edition

Edited by Anthony Landale

Gower

First edition published 1991
Second edition published 1994
This edition published by
Gower Publishing Limited
Gower House
Croft Road
Aldershot
Hampshire GU11 3HR
England

Gower
Old Post Road
Brookfield
Vermont 05036
USA

British Library Cataloguing in Publication Data
Gower handbook of training and development. – 3rd ed.
   1. Employees – Training of – Handbooks, manuals, etc.
   I. Landale, Anthony   II. Handbook of training and development
   658.3'124

ISBN 0 566 08122 9

Library of Congress Cataloging-in-Publication Data
Gower handbook of training and development / edited by Anthony
   Landale. – 3rd ed.
      p.   cm.
   ISBN 0-566-08122-9 (hardback)
      1. Employees–Training of–Handbooks, manuals, etc.   2. Personnel
   management–Handbooks, manuals, etc.   I. Title: Handbook of
   training and development.
   HF5549.5.T7G557   1999   99-18669
   658.3'124–dc21   CIP

Typeset in Times by IML Typographers, Chester and printed
in Great Britain at the University Press, Cambridge.

Contents

PART ONE   TRAINING AND DEVELOPMENT AND THE LEARNING ORGANIZATION

Introduction – levels of learning – the nature of learning – what organizations need to do – conclusion – further reading

The context of change – the need for new skills – planning for change – strategic decision making – learning and change – skills management systems – learning cultures – further reading

The initial challenge – the context for vision and values – values as guides – starting a vision and values process – conclusion – further reading

PART FOUR   IT RELATED LEARNING

List of figures

List of tables

Notes on contributors

DIANE BAILEY (*Designing effective training*) is Managing Director of DBA Training Design Consultancy – a long-standing 'virtual' organization run from Rochdale, Lancashire in the UK. She was, from 1978–1982, Controller of Training Research and Development for the Distributive Industry Training Board. Her national remit in that role involved Diane and her team of 45 people in planning, designing and implementing training and development in all areas relevant to the 2.5 million people working in distribution.

In 1982 she established DBA and has run it since then. DBA operates in both the public and the private sector and tackles a range of training and development projects for organizations of all sizes. One of DBA's specialisms is the design and development of training materials of all types including Self-Study and Distance Learning packages. Diane is an established author.

TOM BARRY (*Vision and values*) started his career in sales and management before working with two well-known management training and development companies. At MaST International he was a consultant and then at Blessing/White he became European Managing Director before leaving to start his own business, The Blueprint Organisation.

Tom's current interests at Blueprint are twofold. Namely, to combine his professional interest in organizational strategy and values, employee motivation and change management with the strong commercial practice needed to grow all aspects of a successful business. He enjoys building long-term client relationships and some of his clients include Lloyds/TSB, Sun Microsystems and Reed Business Information.

Tom is a frequent speaker at seminars and conferences, and has written widely about the subject of organizational and individual values. He can be contacted on 0181 748 2400.

SHARON BARTRAM and **BRENDA GIBSON** (*Identifying training needs*) have worked in partnership as SBG Associates since 1991. Their considerable experience in learning, training and development enables them to build practical solutions with their clients. Their manuals on *Training Needs Analysis, Evaluating Training* and *Activities for Developing Training Skills*, also published by Gower, are good examples of what they do. Sharon is a member of the Institute of Personnel and Development and Brenda has a Masters Degree in Management Learning from Lancaster University.

TREVOR BENTLEY (*Performance management*) is a partner in **the space between**. He works primarily as an executive coach and brings a human touch into the most bottom-line focused organizations. He teaches and writes widely in the field of humanistic management and is well known both in the UK and Australia for his facilitation skills, writing and training. His most recent work is in helping senior executives in building long-term effective business relationships and in moving organizations towards partnerships with their stakeholders. His new book *The Human Touch* is to be published in the year 2000. He can be contacted on e-mail at – *trevor@thespacebetween.com* or by phone on 01452 813908.

DAVID BIRCHALL (*Technology supported learning*) is head of the Henley Research Centre where he has responsibility for a number of major EC and UK Government funded projects. An engineer by background, he has researched and taught in the areas of technological change, technology and management learning and is a founder member of the Future Work Forum at Henley. He is responsible for Henley's initiatives on IT and Management Learning and is responsible for GroupWare and CD-ROM projects. He was formerly Director of Henley's MBA programme and had responsibility for the launch of the distance learning MBA. A recent book, published by FT Pitman, is *Creating Tomorrow's Organisation – Unlocking the Benefits of Future Work* which deals with many aspects of new style organization.

GEORGE BOAK (*Personal development plans*) is an experienced independent training consultant. He has worked closely with managers from a wide range of companies on aspects of management and personal development. Over the past 15 years he has carried out extensive work with individualized learning contracts and personal development plans to help practising managers and professionals identify and target specific areas for development of their skills in the workplace. He is the author of *A Complete Guide to Learning Contracts* (published by Gower, 1998) and *Mental Models for Managers* (with David Thompson, Century Publishing Random House, 1998). He is a visiting lecturer at Newcastle Business School and at the University College of Ripon and York St John. He can be contacted on *george@gbco.demon. co.uk*

PETER BRAMLEY (*Evaluating training and development*) is author of *Evaluating Training Effectiveness* and has also published a number of papers on evaluation issues. Until 1998 he was a lecturer in the Department of Organisational Psychology at Birkbeck College, London, where his responsibilities included teaching master's courses on training and development, organizational change and the consulting process. Currently he is running his own international consulting business which includes running workshops for organizations that want to evaluate their own events.

DAVID CLUTTERBUCK (*Mentoring: developing two for the price of one*) pioneered developmental mentoring in the UK in the 1980s, when the first edition of his book *Everyone Needs a Mentor* appeared. A founder director and now trustee of The European Mentoring Centre, David and his team at Clutterbuck Associates now consult around the world, helping companies develop mentoring schemes and providing professional external mentors for executives and directors. He continues to research and develop understanding about the principals and practice of mentoring. Other relevant books on mentoring, co-authored with David Megginson, are *Mentoring in Action* and *Mentoring Executives and Directors* (forthcoming). In addition, *Learning Alliances* brings together best practice and current theory on mentoring, coaching, counselling and other 'helping to learn' behaviours.

IAN CUNNINGHAM (*Development through Self-Managed Learning*) chairs Strategic Developments International Ltd. and the not-for-profit Centre for Self-Managed Learning. He is a Visiting Professor at Middlesex University and he is on the Adjunct Faculty of the Fielding Institute, California.

Ian describes himself as primarily a 'development assistant'. In this role he works with organizations at various levels including assisting with organization-wide change, with teams (on their development) and on individual mentoring and coaching of managers, directors and CEOs. He also writes, researches and organizes self-managed learning programmes as well as running workshops in areas such as mind-body integration.

GEOFF DAVIES (*Drama-based training*) is a drama and management consultant with a long and successful experience in the use of drama and related techniques in education and training. He is the author of a best-selling education book and a series of stories for children. Following a career in teaching, he has run a centre for teachers, worked on the development of interactive training techniques and been a senior lecturer in a Further Education College before forming Action in Management, AiM. He has a national reputation as a trainer of teachers and is an associate lecturer at Newcastle, Sunderland, Durham and Teesside Universities.

ANDY DICKSON (*High performance teams*) is a management training consultant with Impact Development Training Group based in Windermere, UK – a company specializing in developing high performing teams as well as other areas of organization and people development.

Impact's experience of team development spans nearly 20 years with senior management, departmental, cross-cultural, virtual, project and sports teams throughout the world. Andy has worked for UK and American based specialists in experiential team development and his work has taken him to the USA, Australia and mainland Europe. He can be contacted on 015394 88333.

CHRIS ELGOOD (*Games and simulations*) specializes in creating and presenting management games and is the author of *The Handbook of Management Games and Simulations*, published by Gower and now in its 6th edition. Born in 1932 and with a background in both lecturing and the training and development function he now runs his own consultancy, Chris Elgood Associates. He is also Honorary Visiting Fellow (Management Learning) The University of Bradford Management Centre.

ALAN GEORGE (*The manager as trainer*) has a special interest in helping managers meet learning needs, whether their own or those of their teams. He is a member of the Institute of Personnel and Development and has degrees from Cambridge and Sussex. He is Managing Director of Calibre Learning Ltd, a consultancy that has worked for 15 years on training design and delivery. He has authored a large number of open learning packages and his company now also provides Web-based training as a flexible and interactive resource. He welcomes feedback on the ideas in his chapter via *info@calibre-learning.co.uk* or via Calibre's Web site – *www.calibrelearning.co.uk*

NORRIE GILLILAND (*Developing your people through Investors in People*) is Principal of Mycadi, Glasgow-based human resource consultants. His book *Developing Your Business Through Investors in People* was published by Gower in 1996 and quickly featured among their best-sellers. His second book *How to Train Your People to Whack The Competition* was published by Gower in 1998.

MICHAEL GREGG (*Using psychometrics in management development*) is a Principal Consultant for Development Dimensions International in Europe involved in all aspects of selection and assessment. He has a Masters in Occupational Psychology and a PhD in Occupational Psychology.

With over 17 years of experience in Occupational Psychology, he has developed a large portfolio of clients and has consulted in most recognized areas of the discipline. These include OD, job/competency analysis, individual assessment, selection using biodata, scored application forms, structured interviews and assessment centres, senior management development, placement and training using accomplishment records to development workshops, management skills training, and Level A/B occupational testing courses (BPS approved).

Michael is also acknowledged as an expert in the field of personality assessment in the workplace and holds a BPS practising certificate and certificates of competence at both Level A and Level B and has an advanced working knowledge of psychometrics and the tools used for analysis.

KEN GRIFFITHS (*Learning for change*) is a management trainer and business consultant in the North West of England, specializing in helping small and medium-sized companies to develop the potential of their workforce through effective training. He spent 25 years with IBM United Kingdom, eventually becoming Chief Instructor (Marketing Training) at a time when the company was embarked on an extensive re-engineering programme. He is co-author of *A Learning Approach to Change* (Gower, 1998).

VAL HAMMOND (*Foreword*) heads Roffey Park Management Institute, one of the longest established management training centres in Europe.

Roffey Park specializes in the people aspects of management development and this reflects Val's own interests and research specialisms. After 20 years professional and managerial experience in diverse sectors – law, advertising, film-making, information technology and petroleum – Val joined the research team at Ashridge, where she spent 14 years, predominantly as Director of Research. She joined Roffey Park as Chief Executive in 1993.

ROGER HANCOCK (*Drama-based training*) is an experienced teacher, inspector and trainer. Before co-founding Action in Management he was General Adviser (Drama and Dance) for Newcastle upon Tyne. He has extensive experience of supporting schools and other agencies in the development of new teaching and management approaches, organizing courses, conferences and other events and assessing the in-service needs of teachers. His brief also included the support and development of health education across the city. In the latter years in his post he had responsibility for assisting a group of schools in managing the range of educational and organizational change introduced in the late 1980s.

JULIE HAY (*TA at work and assessment and development centres*) is Chief Executive of training consultancy A D International. She has many years managerial and consultancy experience within industry, government and the public sector. She is a regular presenter at international conferences and is the author of numerous articles and books on individual and organizational development, trainer training, people skills, assessment and development centres and transformational mentoring. She is the author of the highly successful *Gower Assessment and Development Centre* (published by Gower, 1997), a three-volume photocopiable resource containing all you need to run your own centres. Julie can be contacted at ADI on 07000 234683, fax 07000 234689, or e-mail *julie@adinternational.com*

BINNA KANDOLA (*Going forward with competencies*) is co-founder of Pearn Kandola, a leading practice of occupational psychologists. He is a specialist in managing diversity, equal opportunities and assessment and development, and the author of several books. Over the past 15 years he has worked with clients on a wide variety of projects; these include the first assessment centre in the UK for selecting dealers for a major financial services company; competency analysis of executive officers within a government agency; and conducting a diversity audit for a major computer manufacturer. He is particularly interested in the use of competency techniques for developing fair selection methods.

SUE KNIGHT (*NLP at work*) is founder of The Sue Knight Partnership, an international business consultancy offering tailor made in-house programmes and a range of NLP based open programmes leading to certification. The company also provides one to one high performance coaching. Sue Knight is author of the books *NLP at Work, NLP Solutions, Introducing NLP* and *Personal Selling Skills*, and has pioneered the use of NLP in business. She can be contacted by telephone on 01628 667868, by fax on 01628 667865 or e-mail on *support@sueknight.co.uk*, and via her web page www.sueknight. co.uk

ANTHONY LANDALE (*The art of facilitation*) is currently editor-in-chief of *Management Skills & Development* magazine having been the editor from 1992–1998. He is a regular contributor to the *Guardian*'s management page and to the management press and is a freelance trainer specializing in areas including facilitation, coaching and personal development. Additionally he is a qualified counsellor with his own private practice.

MARTIN LEITH (*Large group interventions*) and Mo Cohen developed thenew.org (*www.thenew.org*) to help organizations embrace new ways of thinking, working and serving. He specializes in bringing together diverse and often very large groups of people to address complex strategic issues. Martin has worked with many organizations including Guinness (in Ireland), Shell (in The Netherlands and Oman) and West Herts Community Health NHS Trust (in the UK). He teaches creativity on the MA Change Management course at the University of Brighton.

BOB LITTLE (*Multimedia and CBT*) A former management trainer and writer of open learning materials, Bob Little is currently editor of *Management Skills & Development* magazine, as well as *TACT Tile*, the newsletter of the Association for Computer Based Training (TACT).

One of the UK's foremost writers on all aspects of human resources, including all aspects of computer based training, Bob regularly contributes to publications including the IT and management training press.

LEX MCKEE (*Accelerated learning*), a passionate musician, artist, and author, has been delivering direct training since 1982. He has helped boost the intellectual capital of individuals and groups from many of the UK's top 100 organizations.

The hallmark of his delivery is a symbiotic relationship between training and entertainment, an approach he calls 'Entrainment'. Learning, he believes, is a short-term experience unless surrounded by a positive experiential environment, and true Accelerated Learning must include the harnessing of the emotional and subconscious mind. Lex has formed The Registry of Accelerated Trainers, an organization that recognizes and accredits competence in accelerated training methods. The Registry will be responsible for researching, validating, and implementing the latest proven accelerated learning tools and techniques. He can be contacted on 01494 536981.

ED MOORBY (*Employee development – budgeting and financial control*) has over 30 years' experience of employee development. As the senior executive for the employee development function at both the Prudential Corporation and TSB Retail Bank he has managed multi-million pound budgets and capital expenditure. Since leaving the bank his career has included being President of the European Institute for Vocational Training, international consultancy in financial services and four years as the IPD's chief examiner for employee development. He is author of *How to Succeed in Employee Development*. In 1998 he completed a doctorate which involved a study of the relationship between high achievement behaviour and brain processes.

ALAN MUMFORD (*Learning styles and the learning organization*) has experience in management development, including periods with John Laing & Sons, IPC Magazines, ICL and The Chloride Group.

In 1983 he was appointed Professor of Management Development at International Management Centres and is now Visiting Professor there. His main work is in improving management performance, especially through effective learning processes with senior managers and directors and developers in a variety of organizations including Ford of Europe, Pilkington, Unilever and Unison (the UK's largest trade union). He has worked with organizations in Australia, South Africa and the United States. His publications include *The*

Manual of Learning Styles, 3rd edition (1992), *How Managers Can Develop Managers*, published by Gower (1993) and *How to Choose the Right Development Method*, published by Honey (1997).

JOHN NIXON (*Counselling skills*) works as a coach, counsellor and facilitator. His consultancy practice provides a range of personal and management development services to commercial and corporate organizations as well as one-to-one career management and outplacement. With extensive experience in advertising and marketing, much of his work is in the ethical use of counselling psychology within the sales and marketing functions. His focus is increasingly with line managers and staff whose employers are looking for major changes in customer facing attitudes, processes and skills.

EDDIE OBENG (*The future of management development and education*) is Founder Director of Pentacle The Virtual Business School and was previously at Ashridge Management College as Director of Project Management and Strategy Implementation and also Executive Diector of Operations and Information, having begun his career with Shell. Eddie works with a wide range of organizations in both the public and private sectors to improve the performance of both managers and the business, and offers a new approach to developing business management skills to help organizations manage change and implement strategy. Eddie is author of *All Change! The Project Leader's Secret Handbook, Putting Strategy to Work, Making Re-engineering Happen, New Rules for the New World, SoundBytes, Achieving Organisational Magic* and *CyberSense*. He is also a major contributor to the *Financial Times Handbook of Management*. He can be contacted on *www.pentaclethevbs.com* or by phone on 0044 (0) 1494 678 555.

IAIN POLLOCK (*Using National Occupational Standards in training and development*) is a T & D Manager with a large accountancy practice. Previously he had worked in consultancy in the UK and USA for several years, advising clients on HR and OD matters. Before this he worked in the HR function of a large oil company in the UK and USA. He has experience in compensation and benefits, training and development, industrial relations and organization development as well as management of HR functions. He has conducted numerous projects including human resource IT systems development, TQM processes, BPR and benchmarking. He has also designed and delivered many skills development training programmes including team working, leadership, communication and creating creative solutions.

CHRIS SENIOR (*Lifelong learning and CPD*), a chartered engineer, has wide experience gained in industry and government of the training and development of a range of professional staff. As senior executive at the Engineering Council he is responsible for setting standards and promoting action on continuing professional development throughout the engineering profession, working in partnership with professional institutions, employers and universities and contributing to national and international projects and initiatives. He works also as a professional development consultant.

Particular interests focus on developing strategies for individuals and employers to gain real benefit from continued learning. He led the establishment of the Inter-Professional Group on CPD and is a Fellow of the Institute of Personnel Development.

MATTY SMITH (*Technology supported learning*) originally trained as a teacher, and has 20 years' teaching experience. Matty became interested in the use of computers to support learning towards the end of the 1980s. In 1996, following three years as the Operations Manager of the Doctoral Programme, Matty moved into a research position, funded through the Ford Motor Company, looking at the effective use of IT in support of distributed learners, with special reference to LotusNotes and the Internet. Particular areas of interest are in online facilitation skills, evaluation of learning that occurs through technology and developing effective training programmes for those wanting to use the technology to support both teaching and learning.

COLIN STEED (*Web-based training*) has over 25 years' experience in the IT training industry. Having spent ten years in British Airways IT department at Heathrow, where he was responsible for training computer operations staff, he joined the major IT conference organizers Infotech in 1978. After three years organizing high-level IT conferences at Infotech he founded Training Information Network in 1981. Training Information Network produced directories of training courses and in 1982 he launched the first magazine in the IT training field, *IT Training*, which he edited until it was sold in 1998. Additionally, he launched *Management Training* magazine (subsequently renamed as *Management Skills & Development*). He was instrumental in founding and setting up the Institute of IT Training in 1995 and is now editor of *IT Skills* magazine.

MORRY VAN MENTS (*Role-play*) originally studied physics at Birmingham University, and then served in the Air Force as a Technical Education Officer. On leaving the Air Force he joined the BBC and became a studio manager for 'The Archers'.

With experience in the private and public sector he became Director of Continuing Education at Loughborough University where he became intrigued with the problems of teaching adults. He was looking for a way of actively involving them and using their experience. Simulation and gaming was the answer. He used them extensively in his courses at first, then became Secretary, Chairman, and finally President of SAGSET (the Society for the

Advancement of Education and Training in Education and Training). He is also past Vice-Chair of the (UK) Universities Council for Adult and Continuing Education (UCACE). He is now a freelance education and training consultant.

VAUGHAN WALLER (*Open learning*) is Marketing Manager of CC Information Systems, specialists in multimedia hardware and support for technology based training. He is also Chairman of TACT, The Association for Computer Based Training.

With a background in electronic engineering, Vaughan has over ten years' experience working in the technology based training field. In that time, he has been involved in the entire gestation of the industry from its early experiments with tape-driven microfiche to the latest online technology.

He can be contacted on his e-mail address: *vaughanw@cc-information-systems.co.uk*

MICHAEL WATERS (*Personal development*) is Lead Consultant for Personal Development with one of the UK's major educational consultancies (KAS) and a leading authority on personal development within the educational world. He is a sought-after trainer and a frequent contributor to business, management and educational publications. He is author of *The Element Dictionary of Personal Development* (published by Element, 1996).

KRYSTYNA WEINSTEIN (*Action learning*) first encountered action learning while at Manchester Business School and has been running AL programmes since the mid-1980s as an independent consultant. She is a member of the International Foundation for Action Learning and produces their quarterly newsletter. As an ex-journalist/editor she still writes on 'frivolous' subjects as well as management development and applies the principles of AL in writing the programmes that she runs.

SIR JOHN WHITMORE (*Performance coaching*) is a respected writer and practitioner of coaching in UK and Europe. His best-selling book, *Coaching for Performance* is acclaimed as a milestone in thinking on leadership in business.

An early career in professional motorsport is Sir John's sporting pedigree. Among his notable successes are winning the British and European Saloon Car Racing Championships in 1961 and 1965.

He trained with Tim Gallway, the originator of The Inner Game and began his career running training programmes for business and sports people in coaching techniques, teambuilding and other areas of personal development. He is a founder of Performance Consultants with David Hemery and David Whitaker, two like minded Olympic gold medalists and coaches.

RICHARD WILLIAMS (*Learning for change*) is an independent consultant and expert witness specializing in the field of personal injuries litigation. He first worked as a research and development engineer for a shipbuilding and engineering group. He then spent 25 years with IBM United Kingdom as a systems engineer, salesman, instructor and later as Manager of Entry Marketing Education during a period of intensive change in the company. He is co-author of *A Learning Approach to Change* (Gower, 1998).

MIKE WILLS (*The training process*) has designed and implemented training processes, strategies and other related projects for blue chip companies such as Xerox, Lucas Industries and Rover Group in Europe, North America and South East Asia, meeting standards of organizations such as the US Navy and Airforce. The second edition of his book, *Managing the Training Process*, has recently been published by Gower. His Web site (*http://ourworld.compuserve.com/homepages/mikewills*) covers all aspects of training and development.

PAT YOUNG (*The art of facilitation*) has been facilitating groups and individuals for over 13 years. He has trained in many aspects of facilitation including group process facilitation at the University of Surrey, where he was awarded a post graduate diploma (1987–1989), and group dynamics as an apprentice to Sheila Ernst IGA. He is an accredited member of the IDHP. His experience includes facilitating the Post Graduate Diploma in Humanistic Psychology and Facilitation at the University of Surrey, as well as diploma and advanced diploma counselling courses at Sandwell College and Birmingham Counselling Centre. He was an associate facilitator on the University of Surrey's open programme for personal and professional development and facilitated the first IDHP Certificate course in Group Dynamics. He has worked as a consultant since 1987 specializing in facilitator training, group and team dynamics and individual coaching. He is currently a Director of Learning Edge Ltd.

Foreword by Val Hammond

Chief Executive, Roffey Park Management Institute

Currency for the millennium

As the dawn of the new millennium, a notable trend in business has been the huge resurgence of interest in training and development. No longer is the organizational training budget the first casualty of hard times. The profession is alive and thriving, though it has seen some notable changes, not least of which is the demand for greater value. Organizations simply do not have money to waste on ineffective development and individuals are less prepared to take time out from work for a 'jolly'. Now everybody wants to see some perceptible change. Training and development have always been a partnership between the individual, the organization and the training provider. Each in turn has taken the lead role. Providers began by offering their brochures and catalogues, allowing people to choose from their available wares. Then organizations came to the fore when they began to explain to providers what they wanted for their employees. Interestingly, the key partner now is the individual who is often responsible for his/her own development.

Employees in all sectors are increasingly recognizing that they no longer have a 'job for life' – almost the only currency they have is their experience and the training and development they can take with them. It is now a positive personal statement to have a strong track record of development.

But other factors are also driving the resurgence. The trend to continuing professional development is encouraging many managers to think more clearly about keeping their skills up-to-date. Likewise government initiatives, such as Investors in People and National Vocational Qualifications, are laying down the tracks for future development. These factors are helping to create an ongoing learning climate – and the market is becoming less cynical of these initiatives as organizations and individuals continue to sign up for them.

Change is also afoot within organizations. As well as general quality improvement programmes, many employers are attempting to create multi-skilled employees fit for any eventuality. By equipping people with greater skills – including those at the very top – organizations are attempting to create a body of expertise which can safeguard against the uncertainties of the future.

Allied to this is a move to 'real-time' development. In the past, employees may have signed up for training in order to achieve a far-off goal such as a future promotion. The late 1990s has seen a move to 'just-in-time' training – we all want development now to help us cope with situations we are currently facing.

Change of focus

Training and development was once the poor relation of personnel – a secondary department. But it is now a valued profession in its own right, with its own qualifications, its own skill base and in many cases its own career ladder. Indeed being a part of this profession is now something that many aspire to.

It is not only the profile of trainers and developers which has changed dramatically, so too has their role. Many now act as internal consultants or counsellors, helping people to understand their strengths and their development needs.

Everyone has moved round the table. With trainers taking a supportive, consulting role, line managers are increasingly absorbing the nuts and bolts of training. For trainers and line managers alike, new skills need to be learned, particularly those of facilitation – a word once condemned as jargon but which is now an established component of the business vocabulary. Updating their own skills and finding calm for themselves – away from the pressures of the workplace – will continue to be important priorities for developers.

As part of their changing role, trainers and developers now need to be more knowledgeable about training providers. Indeed, a key aspect of their role is that of matchmaker and deal-maker, rather than administrator. Keeping abreast of providers is no easy feat. But trainers will need to continue to develop and experiment in the quest for value, utilizing new techniques and different technologies.

Two other factors are coming to the fore. One is the flexibility of training provision. The development needs of part-time or flexi-workers create new demands. The challenge for training providers is to recognize the new constraints that people work under and to find more innovative ways of reshaping the development experience into a programme which can be delivered at the individual's convenience.

The second factor is that training programmes are increasingly featuring an international element. This reflects the reality of the global marketplace. It is impossible to think about training people for just the local geographic environment. We all have to think more internationally than we ever did before. Training providers are also competing in a global market, which means that organizations can now seek out the best providers in the world for their chosen development solution.

Competitive edge

For an organization, the competitive advantage that comes from training and development is not restricted to equipping people with relevant skills. It also impacts upon the recruitment and retention of employees. Interestingly, job candidates are now opting to work in organizations where they know the quality of the training and development is high. Senior managers are beginning to recognize this. No longer can they avoid the importance of training and development for their employees. No longer can they play to complacency and avoid their own development. Part of this is to do with their role. At one level, senior managers exist to get the job done and to achieve the required return on investment. But their role is also to provide an environment in which people can give of their best – and this has to be a developmental environment.

As all HR issues, particularly training and development, move up the business agenda, the challenge now for trainers is to demonstrate tangibly to their boardroom colleagues that development is not just a motivational tool, it is also a key asset which really adds value to individuals and to the organization. It is the printing press for the currency of the new millennium.

If you are aiming for appropriate and effective development this handbook will provide a useful starting point.

Introduction

> Education can no longer be confined to schools. Every employing institution has to become a teacher.
>
> Peter Drucker

This latest edition of the *Handbook of Training and Development* provides a fascinating insight into the challenges which organizations and employees are facing and what strategies and resources are available for today's training professional.

All 38 chapters in this edition are new and many of the contributors, whilst being best-selling authors or established industry figures, are appearing for the first time in this form. However, as you would expect, this is evolution rather than revolution. There may be substantial new content that reflects the growing enthusiasm for, say, personal development and technology-based training, but the effective trainer need not be concerned that his or her skills are in danger of being overlooked. Rather, the opposite is true; this handbook builds on the foundations that previous editions have laid down while, at the same time providing insights into some of the latest trends and developments in the industry.

It is my belief that there has never been a better time to be a training manager, a training consultant or a training and development professional. I say this because, after many years witnessing the lip service organization paid to 'people development', it is now crystal clear that in today's changing world an organization's very survival depends upon how they support their people to learn and keep on learning.

There is also more commitment from the employees themselves. Indeed, employees are articulating, in a way businesses have never heard before, that they have their own aspirations and expectations of work that extend way beyond the monthly pay cheque. This sea change may have been catalysed by the breakdown of the traditional contract of employment but the consequence for training and development is surely welcome. From the employers point of view performance may be the key priority but for the employee the perspective is employability – and the common language here is training and development.

A broader role

Of course, the training function has been far from immune to the recent changes that have swept through business. Bottom line results and the transfer of hard skills will always be a part of the agenda but increasingly there is also a requirement to empower others. The consequence for today's trainer is that they are likely to find they have a broader range of roles or at least the choice to get involved with business management at a different level. So while the remit of a current day trainer will include traditional presentation it may well also require a range of consultancy, coaching, and facilitation skills.

This is a rich mix and offers tremendous opportunities for training practitioners. The voice of the training and development function now demands to be heard at every stage of the business cycle from planning to review; it is also central to any change strategy and is key to the development of each individual manager and every team project. In fact, from the assessment process a person goes through when they are recruited into a company to the counselling that they might receive when they leave, it is apparent that training and development has a central role to play.

The new business imperative on employee development also makes T & D a profession with far more kudos than in the days when it had the reputation as a sinecure for those whose careers had run out of steam. But with the status comes challenges and responsibilities too. With managers under constant pressure to review and improve performance it is incumbent on trainers and training management to have a range of response strategies that can be tailored to individual and team needs.

Model trainers

It is my contention that in order to provide the level of support required trainers must work continuously on their own development. The only credible authority they possess comes from keeping their skills up-to-date and in being authentic in who they are. Furthermore, trainers also have to be effective in imparting their knowledge and experience. This means being able to adapt their style to whatever situation they are in and being cognisant of the learner's needs. In this respect they will be more than IT literate, they will be champions of IT as a means through which employees can access learning. They will also have trained in the latest learning technologies such as NLP and accelerated learning.

In effect, trainers have to be able to 'walk their talk'. Business managers are looking to the T & D professionals for essential support and trainers have to be able to model the skills that they expect others to learn. For example, if you are a trainer in an organization that is giving more development responsibility to line management, you need to know both what development opportunities there are within the business as well as being able to coach and mentor managers as they pick up the role for the first time. As a coach you might use counselling skills or transactional analysis as the basis of your style. And you need to be confident and genuine in the support you are providing.

Of course, nobody can be an expert at everything and trainers are no exception to this rule. They will have their own interests, strengths and specialisms. However, it is important that for those people for whom training and development is a responsibility that they understand the principles involved and know, if necessary, where to go to find out more.

This handbook is one of the key resources that can help in this respect – helping training professionals to get to the heart of the subjects in which they are interested in a relatively short time. Of course, there are some for whom the material provided here will be too brief. With this in mind I encourage readers of this handbook to view these chapters as a starting point in their own explorations about learning. For those who find that what is provided here only begins to whet their appetite then they will be pleased to see that every contributor has given a recommended further reading list at the end of their chapter.

There may also be some readers who wonder about the structure of this handbook or who would have wished for chapters not included here. There are certainly arguments for structuring this book in a different way, but I hope it is at least easy to find your way around the vast range of material on offer – and if you would have preferred to see, for example, the chapter on costing T & D at the front of the handbook then I would remind you of the cyclical nature of training and how close endings are to new beginnings. As for those chapters that you would have liked to see included, but which are not here, I accept that we have had to make some hard choices. However, what is included does, I believe, represent the heart of today's training and development agenda.

Anthony Landale

Part One

Training and development and the learning organization

As mentioned in the Introduction, the ways in which organizations support their employees to learn is becoming a prerequisite not just for business success but perhaps for business survival.

In this section of the handbook you will find a range of contributions that address this imperative towards learning as a continuous process. The chapters cover both organizational and individual perspectives and provide insight and practical advice for training and development professionals.

It is my advice that the reader of this handbook starts either by reading those chapters in which they have immediate interest or gravitates to writers whom they know or who they might have heard about. Whether your interest is in change, teams, standards or any of the other subjects outlined here you will find material that will provoke your interest and challenge your thinking.

Chapter 1

The business of learning

Ian Cunningham

This chapter highlights the central role of learning for organizational success. It specifically focuses on different levels at which people learn and the various dimensions of learning. It concludes with a checklist of questions that managers can use to provoke thought or initiate discussions about the development of a learning organization.

Introduction

Learning has become a big deal. Chief executives readily extol the virtues of becoming a learning organization and company reports abound with claims about how important learning is and how much they are investing in human resource development. Meanwhile governments and organizations are busily promoting the idea of lifelong learning and even the notion of a learning society.

The implications are clear. Research evidence tells us that learning in organizations is fundamental to organizational success and survival (de Geus, 1997; Cunningham, 1998). Reg Revans has long promoted the equation that the rate of learning in an organization must be greater than or equal to the rate of change facing the organization (Revans, 1980) – now it appears his thinking has become mainstream.

Levels of learning

Most people use the term 'learning' to describe both a process and an outcome. That is, in order to know something or to acquire a skill we have to go through a process of learning. This process produces a change: we now know something we did not know before or we can now do something we could not do before. So learning is associated with personal change. However, learning is also seen as an outcome of this change. People are said to possess particular learning.

One problem with the 'learning as outcome' position is the way in which certification and accreditation distort learning processes. The educational system especially engages in a crude grading approach which ranks people vertically. Marks and grades are given on the basis of some aggregate performance without providing the sophistication of, for example, the best 360 degree feedback methods. The latter provide horizontal assessments – they show the strengths and weaknesses that we all have and do not engage in pass/fail or marking exercises.

Hence, well run 360 degree feedback processes help the person to see future learning needs and provide a basis for a person to make their own choices about what they should do. In contrast the current educational grading processes categorize people, and can induce a sense of failure in those who do not jump through the hoops successfully and a sense of arrogance in those who 'do well'. Furthermore, for both categories the outcomes are potentially detrimental to learning. Failures are put off future learning and the arrogant successes may not see the need to continue learning.

Neither of the uses of the term learning (process and outcome) require a process called training. Many organizations, for example, W H Smith, are recognizing this by using titles such as 'Learning and Development Manager'. As Paul Kirk, MD of Rover Power Train, in the UK explains: 'Training is something that is done to you; learning is something you have to do for yourself'. So the emphasis, via such ideas as the learning organization, has become more focused on creating effective learning environments and support structures. From our own research using in-depth interviews of people in a variety of organizations it seems that training contributes at most 10 to 20 per cent of what makes a person effective.

There is also evidence (Cunningham, 1998) that poor training has been a negative factor in promoting effective learning. Didactic, authoritarian training courses can put people off learning and sometimes people learn things that are inappropriate and unhelpful in their work. The problem can also be compounded by people's personal experiences of education in school, college or university. We have researched people's positive and negative experiences of learning – and education comes out as by far the most mentioned negative experience followed by training courses. Many people in organizations associate the notion of learning with unpleasant experiences in education and are, therefore, put off by the word.

This latter point often raises the need to have learning masquerade under the banner of 'development'. Note that I use the two terms interchangeably. However, there are writers and theorists who suggest that development is different. They see it as requiring a person to go through a series of stages, for example from crude learning of facts in a rote mode to sophisticated, holistic learning which has a spiritual dimension. These stage models are often based on theorists from child development such as Piaget and Kohlberg (see Crain, 1992 for a fuller exploration of these issues).

Given that this piece is on learning, I will leave aside the notion that development should be used as a different concept and revert to Gregory Bateson's model (1973) in which he proposes three levels of learning.

In Bateson's theory, 'Learning Zero' is a mere reflex response. We may be awakened by an alarm clock and this produces a change in behaviour (from sleep to waking). However, it is a change that is not a new behaviour and it is triggered by habit. 'Learning One' encompasses most of what is the focus of learning in organizations. It is often conceived as being 'added on' to the person, or as if it can be accumulated ready for use like charging a battery. The competencies orientation is an example. It is only with 'Learning Two' that learning constitutes a change in the person, and in how that person thinks about what they are doing in their work and life. It involves a shift of assumptions after which both the person and their behaviour are different. It is also at this level that basic habits and patterns of behaviour change.

Let us take an example. People often complain about their problems of time management. A standard training approach might be to offer hints and tips as to how to use time better. It might also focus on providing electronic organizers or even paper based systems. This 'Learning One' mode may fail however if the person has, for instance, an ingrained habit of procrastinating. However, at 'Learning Two' we might address those very habits by encouraging the person to reflect on their procrastination and change the behaviour that causes the problem.

Hence 'Learning Two', in Bateson's theory, is a more in-depth approach to learning. It is worth noting that working at this level does not necessarily undermine 'Learning One' methods. Once a person has cured their procrastination habit, time management techniques may be of great value. Working at the 'Learning Two' level is, however, consistent with a learning to learn approach. It ideally results in the person learning to change for themselves. Hence they can learn whatever is needed to be effective in their work – and they are not thrown by changes in the organization or its environment.

The nature of learning

Learning produces change in people, but such change may not always be positive. A person could learn at work how to defraud their employers or how to engage in a whole range of antisocial behaviours. Hence we have to consider what constitutes good learning. One dimension of good learning has come to be recognized as its holistic dimension. People do not just need to learn new knowledge and skills; learning has an emotional and a moral dimension too. Research shows that effective top managers are highly emotionally sophisticated (Evans and Bartolomé, 1980; Cunningham, 1998) and indeed what Goleman (1995) has called EQ (as a measure of emotional sophistication) is more important than IQ in predicting a successful career.

Learning also has a social dimension. People in organizations learn with, and from, each other. This is essential. It is at the heart of ideas about the learning organization. It is also apparent from research conducted by a range of organizations including Sussex University and the Institute for Research on Learning (see Brown and Duguid, 1991; Cunningham, 1998). What these studies show is that collectively generated learning is crucial for organizational effectiveness.

Research evidence also shows the extent to which learning is both planned and unplanned. It seems that by setting goals and attempting to work to these, people can be more successful in their learning – and they can make better use of unplanned learning opportunities.

This latter point also links to the fact that learning can be both conscious and unconscious. Often, even planned learning can be associated with unconscious learning. When people set clear goals to which they are personally committed this seems to focus the unconscious mind such that learning takes place outside of the person's consciousness. When the person comes to check their progress against their learning goals they can be surprised at changes that have taken place.

Sometimes this learning can result from errors and mistakes. The person may dwell on a mistake at the time and as a result find that they do not repeat it in future. They may not have made a conscious decision about how to act but their unconscious mind provides the guidance.

People also learn in different ways: there is not one universal right way in which to learn. Kolb (1984) and Honey (1997) (see, for example, Chapter 7 of this handbook) have popularized the idea that there are different learning styles. Whether their models are right or wrong does not matter; what these and other authors have done is to demonstrate that many educational and training assumptions about learning are fallacious, especially when they assume a 'one size fits all' mode.

Educational and training approaches also go astray when they assume that people's learning can be controlled. People are self managing and will make their own choices about what they learn. One of the strangest assumptions can be that 'what is taught equals what is learned'. CEOs will often say 'I want my people trained to be more self motivating.' The fact that this is a nonsense seems to escape them. People will learn from events what they choose to learn. Harangued by the CEO they may learn to dislike the person, to reduce their estimation of the company and so on. The message delivered is not necessarily the message received.

What organizations need to do

Creating and sustaining a culture that supports learning is a crucial requirement for organizations. One way in which I have found it helpful to engage
top managers in a dialogue about this is to have a rough agenda or checklist
with which to initiate discussion. The following is an example of such a list.

Does the organization:

- Recognize that change is happening continually – and that people therefore have to learn continually?
- Support learning as a strategic value?
- Build in plans and resources for new learning into any major change it
  initiates?
- Look on development and training expenditure as an investment (for
  which it wants a pay-off) – not a cost to be written off?
- Encourage people to own their own learning and to recognize that it is
  their responsibility to manage their own development? (Alongside this
  the organization needs to recognize that it has a responsibility to staff to
  support them in their own development.)
- Encourage mentoring relationships for all who want them?
- Give people elbow room in their jobs so that they can develop and apply
  new learning?
- Reward learning? (This may not be monetary; public praise is a reward.)
- Encourage the coaching of staff at all levels? Do managers model it by
  demonstrating exemplary coaching of people who report to them?
- Encourage an 'asking' culture in general – if people do not know something relevant to their needs are they encouraged to learn by asking others
  e.g. more senior people?
- Provide opportunities for front line staff who deal with customers to get
  their experience of the needs of the market heard – so that others can
  learn about these needs?
- Encourage sharing across internal (e.g. departmental) boundaries – facilitating networking and using cross-functional teams for projects?
- Recruit people who are good learners – and ensure that the ability to
  learn is a criterion in selection?
- Ensure that all new staff have an induction programme that is tailored to
  their needs – and that new people are encouraged to ask questions, even if
  the questions seem stupid or banal to existing staff?
- Ensure that appraisals are oriented to people's development and that
  future learning is a key focus of the appraisal interview.
- Supplement vertical structures (e.g. appraisals) with horizontal ones,

specifically where there is a need to involve the peer group in developing learning?
- Insist that staff have personal development plans or learning contracts which are genuinely stretching – and demand learning of relevance for the organization?
- Demand that anyone applying for promotion must produce their current development plan or learning contract in order to be considered for promotion – and ask them about the document in their promotion interview?
- Use technology that is learner friendly; for example computer systems that encourage people to learn new (and better) ways of doing things?
- Recognize the needs of part-time staff? (If they have a commitment to the organization, they also need development.)
- Avoid relying on training and the production of manuals to solve all learning issues?
- Provide workshops on coaching to help develop coaching capability in the organization?
- Encourage people to think creatively about their careers and not to expect easy promotions but, for instance, to consider developmental sideways moves and secondments?
- Recognize that people may struggle to learn new ways of working – and be sympathetic to this while at the same time not letting people off the hook if they really do need to learn and change?
- Help people to learn from mistakes; recognize that if someone gets something wrong that it is likely that they need to *learn* to get it right?
- Recognize that learning is not always painless – it can be uncomfortable for people to realize that they have to make fundamental changes in their behaviour in order to perform effectively?
- Appreciate that learning is not only about new knowledge and skills? (Some of the most important learning is about developing qualities such as courage, sensitivity and perseverance.)
- Avoid quick fixes? Does it recognize that significant learning can take time?
- Urge all staff to see it as their duty both to continue their own learning and to support others in their learning?
- Provide a written commitment to support learning in contracts of employment?

This checklist can, at first sight, look daunting, especially for organizations that have done little to foster a learning culture. However, it is possible to develop a strategy which phases in some of these actions over time. Also, many of them can be done at the same time and can be mutually reinforcing. One example gives a flavour of what can be achieved.

Birmingham Midshires Building Society in the UK has recently transformed itself from an old-fashioned, poorly-performing organization to one that has won awards for customer service and has become financially stable. Some of the actions that it has phased in over the last five years include:

- ceasing to have a traditional HR function and replacing it with a business-focused people development team;
- creating full time coaches for teams and for individuals;
- using 360 degree feedback, starting at the top, as a basis for directors and managers to write development contracts. Successful completion of the contract provides the basis for the decision on the level of salary increment the person gets (lack of progress on learning and development means no salary increment). This scheme has started with the CEO and is being cascaded down the organization;
- creating a learning network of 'champions for learning';
- capturing and sharing best demonstrated learning practice;
- supporting the use of self-managed learning sets to provide mutual assistance in learning for middle managers;
- ceasing 'sheep dip' training and producing more focused and flexible training;
- providing access to learning resources for people across the organization;
- recruiting people because they are good learners.

All this shows that it can be done. The challenge for development professionals is to take a strategic view and have the courage to grasp these new opportunities.

Conclusion

This chapter has outlined how central learning has become to organizational survival and success. However, despite all the promotion of learning it is still sometimes associated with didactic, authoritarian models of education and training. Many people for this reason are put off by the very word itself.

The challenge for development professionals is to help change attitudes to learning and to encourage people to learn. This also implies opening the minds of employees to how and where they learn and the need to take learning out of the classroom.

For those whose responsibility it is to promote learning within organizations the most important step to take is to recognize that learning needs to happen, continuously, at every level of the organization. Creating and sustaining a learning culture has become a high priority for organizations and the discussion as to how such a culture can be engendered needs to be on every organizational agenda.

Further reading

Argyris, C. (1977), 'Double Loop Learning in Organisations', reprinted in D. A. Kolb, I. M. Rubin, and J. M. McIntyre (1980) (eds), *Organizational Psychology: Readings on Human Behavior in Organizations*, Englewood Cliffs: Prentice-Hall.

Bateson, G. (1973), *Steps to an Ecology of Mind*, London: Paladin.

Brown, J. S. and Duguid, P. (1991), 'Organizational Learning and Communities-of-Practice' in *Organization Science*, **2**, (1), (February) 40–57.

Crain, W. (1992), *Theories of Development*, Englewood Cliffs: Prentice-Hall.

Cunningham, I. (1998), *The Wisdom of Strategic Learning*, (2nd edn), Aldershot: Gower.

de Geus, A. (1997), *The Living Company*, Cambridge, Mass: Harvard Business School Press.

Evans, P. and Bartolomé, F. (1980), *Must Success Cost So Much?*, London: Grant McIntyre.

Goleman, D. (1995), *Emotional Intelligence*, London: Bantam.

Honey, P. (1997), *The Best of Peter Honey*, Maidenhead: Peter Honey Publications.

Kolb, D. (1984), *Experiential Learning*, Englewood Cliffs: Prentice-Hall.

Revans, R, (1980), *Action Learning: New Techniques for Management*, London: Blond and Briggs.

Chapter 2

Learning for change

Ken Griffiths and Richard Williams

> The centre of gravity in business success is already shifting from the exploitation of a company's physical assets to the realisation of the creativity and learning potential of all the people with whom it has contact – not just its employees. Education and training are therefore being seen less as issues of cost and more as pre-conditions for competitive success.
>
> Extract from the executive summary, *Tomorrow's Company,*
> *an RSA Inquiry* (1995)

The context of change

Manifestations of change surround us in today's world. Even if we do not understand all of them, we accept the constant diversifying, merging and restructuring of organizations as commonplace. Among the thousands of enterprises around the world currently embarking on major change programmes there will almost certainly be at least one of your major competitors. Some of the triggers for such programmes have been government legislation, aggressive competition, advances in technology, changing demographics of the workforce and changes in customer needs. Whether these organizations achieve their change objectives, however, will depend on the skills that their employees develop to meet the conditions of the new world.

In this chapter we will take a look at the evidence that supports the case for learning as a key determinant of success; consider models of change that highlight the need for quality planning and decision making before focusing on the requirement for needs analysis and skills management systems. Finally, we conclude with some pointers for leadership concerning what constitutes a learning culture and how it can be fostered.

The need for new skills

The priority that needs to be placed on people in a change process cannot be stressed enough. During the 1980s General Motors reputedly spent some $60 billion on robotics and extensive computer systems in an attempt to match the efficiency and effectiveness of the leading Japanese car manufacturers. They failed; not because the technology was inadequate – on the contrary, it was probably the best that money could buy at the time – they failed because they did not match their investment in technology with a corresponding one in the people that were going to have to operate it as part of their jobs.

People are the determinant factor in situations such as this: they need training and time to learn and develop the skills required to master new technology if any significant change is to occur. Equally important, they need to be convinced of the personal benefit of learning new techniques and working with the latest equipment. In other words, they need to know 'what's in it for them'.

In April 1994, a large UK insurance company was fined £300 000 by LAUTRO – the Life Assurance and Unit Trust Regulatory Office – 'for putting the public at risk by failing to ensure its salesforce was properly trained'. This penalty followed on from the company's own suspension of its pensions sales force for a month's vigorous retraining and reassessment. Less than half the sales force returned to work. Most had either failed or did not resit the qualifying exams. Over a year later it was reported that another large UK insurance company had made a provision of £100 million against its exposure to the problem of mis-selling personal pension schemes. The industry exposure is now estimated at over £10 billion.

These cases, however, represent only one side of the coin. There are success stories too. In the High Street there are outlets that can provide a pair of glasses in an hour with precision-ground prescribed lenses produced by technicians using high performance technology. This typically took a week or more a few years ago. In the same High Street there are other outlets that produce a set of colour photographs, plus an extra set of prints if wanted, in an hour, again using high performance technology. A few years ago this process used to take at least three working days.

While high performance technology was a key factor in these examples it would count for nothing unless its operators really knew how to use it. We believe the prime lesson is an obvious one. Successful change depends on effective training and development, and on getting it right first time. While this dependency is not absolute in every case, the contribution made by an effective training programme is substantial enough to make the difference between failure and success.

Planning for change

Any change needs a clear case for action. If staff understand why there is a problem and what needs to be done, they are more likely to co-operate and offer ideas than if orders are dictated from above. The case for action will normally include:

- a description of the 'A' point – where we are now
- the reason this is unsatisfactory
- a description of the 'B' point – the desired outcome
- the actions needed to get from A to B.

Unfortunately, life is rarely so easy. Obeng (1997) says the world is changing faster than most organizations can learn to adapt to it. He calls the type of project implied by the above 'Painting by Numbers': a closed project, where we know what to do and how to do it.

Suppose we know only one of these, or worse still, neither. Obeng's description is shown in Figure 2.1.

	KNOW WHAT TO DO	DON'T KNOW WHAT TO DO
KNOW HOW	CLOSED 'Painting by Numbers'	SEMI-OPEN 'Making a Movie'
DON'T KNOW HOW	SEMI-CLOSED 'Going on a Quest'	OPEN 'Lost in the Fog'

Figure 2.1   Project types

The implications for learning are different in each case, as are the implications for leadership. Because of increasingly rapid change, projects often move out of the comfortable 'closed' box. Organizations typically react to this by throwing planning to the wind, or planning only as far as they can see. The former approach leads to confusion and waste; the latter to short-termism. In each case, employees have no picture of where the organization is heading nor the part they should play. Covey (1989) describes seven habits to cultivate and increase personal effectiveness. His advice includes the need to clarify goals and to find time to plan. This is even more important at a time of change, not less.

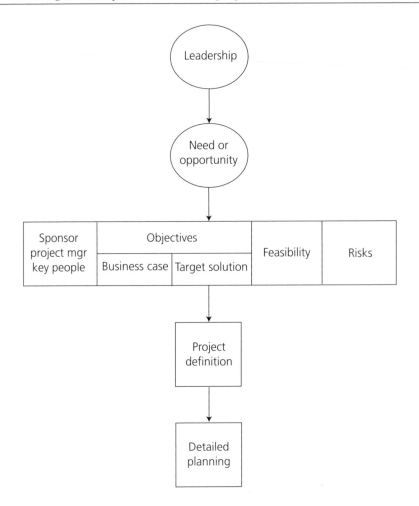

Figure 2.2   The project model

Whatever the project type, we have found the planning model shown in Figure 2.2 to be highly effective. This model is explained in detail in Griffiths and Williams (1998). Briefly, at the outset:

- some need or opportunity must exist (a 'case for action')
- leadership from the top is essential
- key people need to be involved (sponsor, project leader, key users and implementers)
- objectives are known, with a business case and a feasible target solution
- risks and assumptions are identified.

The next step is to define what is 'within' the project and what is 'without'. This step is the one most frequently missed, especially in 'semi-open' projects. The painters are so eager to paint that they forget to agree on the picture. A short project definition workshop (PDW) between key players would correct this by producing a clear and agreed project specification. This is an important document for communication both inside and outside the team. It will include deliverables, milestones, review processes and a management control system robust enough even to handle changes of direction inherent in a semi-open project. Once this is all done, then and only then, should detailed work start.

Strategic decision making

Even with 'Lost in the Fog' projects, there is help. Matheson and Matheson (1998) distinguish between being smart – making good strategic decisions – and acting smart – carrying out those decisions. Based on techniques developed to improve research and development (R & D) decision making, they underline the crucial need for good strategic decision making in business. Efficient execution cannot turn a bad decision into a good one. The PDW technique goes some way towards confirming and refining a project decision, before resources are committed, but Matheson and Matheson start even earlier, describing six dimensions of decision quality:

- appropriate frame
- creative, 'doable' alternatives
- meaningful, reliable information
- clear values and trade-offs
- logically correct reasoning
- commitment to action.

R & D decisions are inherently foggy. Their timescale is long, markets and pay-offs are uncertain, there may be internal competition for scarce resources, and the development route may lead into uncharted territory. Decisions are usually made by a form of beauty contest, where competing advocates strive to outdo the cases of their peers. Many strategic business decisions are made in a similar way. Consequently the business fails to look at all viable alternatives. It makes inconsistent evaluations based on inadequate information, unclear value measures or faulty logic, and thus fails to gain commitment within the firm.

A frequent cause of poor strategy is a failure to 'frame' the decision. Matheson and Matheson quote Hammer and Champy's statement (1993) 'The changes that will put a company out of business are those that happen outside the light of its current expectations'. They refer to the example of

Xerox which in the 1970s found that its Asian competitors could sell copiers profitably in the USA below Xerox's manufacturing cost. By adopting bench-marking and learning about quality improvement from their Japanese partner, Xerox rode the storm. During the same decade, its Palo Alto Research Center (PARC) was working on original inventions such as the personal computer, the user-friendly interface, the computer network and laser printing. Xerox was so busy trying to make money the old way that it failed to capitalize on PARC's excellent lab work. Other companies, then unknown (Apple, Adobe, 3Com and others), saw the potential and reaped the benefits.

Learning and change

So, the issue around change is for companies to make the right decisions and then to link people development to the business strategy. It is our experience that when you start with business results, job performance and education needs will naturally follow on. Firms that send staff on courses without reasoned business justification are potentially wasting their money.

Let us expand on this process of developing learning needs, which is relatively straightforward and absolutely crucial.

It follows a hierarchical process of expansion and refinement, beginning at the highest level with the business needs and their requirements. *Business requirements* are defined by executive management and expanded into *performance requirements* that are defined by line management, then developed into *education requirements* by education management. The requirements should be seen as reference points, and be clearly defined and measurable where possible, so that outcomes can be assessed at each stage of the training programme and any necessary corrections made.

The needs analysis process will highlight the size of the skills gaps – the difference between the skills identified in the performance requirements, and the current skills as reflected in the skills management system (see later). Training and development (T & D) then need to decide whether to design a new training programme, to adapt an existing one, to buy one in, or to out-source all of it. They should recommend a specific solution, a cost, and a schedule. At the same time, line management should investigate likely savings, and should be prepared to underwrite them. If this proves difficult they should consider consulting such bodies as Investors in People UK, the British Quality Foundation, or the European Foundation for Quality Management for guidance.

The outcome from this analysis can be a report that includes:

● *The business requirements:* prioritized to focus the readers' attention on the prime drivers, together with recommendations for gathering feedback on whether the training contributed to the planned business outcomes.

- *The performance requirements:* including required skill profiles, standards of performance, number of people required, career opportunities, and feedback to evaluate whether students were able to use new knowledge and skills in their jobs.
- *The education requirements:* who and where the learners are, their current skills, knowledge, and attitude level; what additional skills, knowledge, and attitudes they need, and by when; the number, calibre and timing of any new hires; the availability and suitability of existing courses and other learning events; feedback on student reactions to the training and what knowledge and skill they gained.
- *Critical success factors:* including potential 'show stoppers' identified during the analysis.
- *Return on investment:* where it is called for, and including as many alternatives as possible in the analysis.
- *Recommendations:* these should include a training solution, and suggested commitments by executive management such as providing subject matter experts, personal involvement with the training, supplying keynote speakers on induction courses, and actioning the next step.

Needs analysis is discussed in greater detail in Chapter 10.

Skills management systems

As part of this process the HR or training department has vital work to do in setting up a skills management system. Without such a system skills profiles, skills gaps, people development and career planning will be difficult to track and administer once an organization grows beyond a certain size.

We all have job-related skills, knowledge and experience that can be codified and expressed as a skills profile. Such profiles show the skill levels for the most important skills of a particular job. The skill levels could have the following meanings:

Level 0 – none. Level 1 – bag-carrier. Level 2 – sometimes calls for help. Level 3 – self-sufficient. Level 4 – advises others.

The job skills can also be weighted to indicate their relative importance, so that job skill #1 has a weighting of 4, #2 a weighting of 3 and so on. Thus, an expert having a level of 4 in all four job skills would score $(4 \times 4) + (4 \times 3) + (4 \times 2) + (4 \times 1) = 40$ units.

Furthermore, we can assign ranges to the various scores as follows:

Trainee   =   0 – 15 units
Qualified =   16 – 25 units
Senior   =   26 – 35 units
Expert   =   36 – 40 units

But how do we go about getting skills profiles in the first place and, having got them, how do we turn them into a skills management system? Experience shows that the people best qualified to develop a skills profile initially are the employees themselves, and they usually make a thorough job of it. The input to the system should be designed so that people can easily record their skills, knowledge, and experience, against the core skills of their job. There should also be room to record previous experience, academic qualifications and training courses already attended. In fact, it is almost impossible to decide what to leave out. Most of the information about what people think about themselves has value. Line management then has the chance to adjust the information one way or the other based on their assessment. The end product is a skills inventory of the organization – a human assets register.

Now that we have a skills inventory we can do quite a lot with it. For example, we can ask questions such as, 'Which people have good, or better, skills in leadership and can speak acceptable French?'. Or, 'How many units do we have in job skill #3?'. We can compare the current skills inventory with previous years, a form of human balance sheet. We can, if other companies employ a similar methodology, also compare ourselves with others, including our competitors. Our human assets register then becomes a tool that allows us to measure not only our own progress, but our progress relative to other organizations.

Learning cultures

Knowing what the skills base of an organization is allows managers to make more realistic business decisions and implement appropriate plans. However, there is another part of the equation: the culture of the organization itself. Some change situations might be quite simple to resolve, however with the pace of change it is increasingly likely that managers will find themselves beyond the 'Painting by Numbers' scenario described earlier.

The strategic decision makers must not exclude themselves from the development cycle or they will lead their people into the 'fog'. The core skills and attitudes that they need to develop are critical and include:

● decision analysis and disciplined decision making
● discounted cash flow analysis
● creating alternatives
● alignment

- comfort with uncertainty
- systems thinking
- value maximization culture.

Furthermore they also have a responsibility in developing the organizational culture so that it fosters learning. One of the key issues here is to look at how mistakes and failure are treated. Most organizations have an ingrained culture where blame is the norm and we can see, after just a few moments thought, what consequences this has for employees.

In such cultures people will hide their errors to avoid punishment and staff will collude to hide mistakes; they know that if they are honest they will get punished. Thus the best hiders and colluders are rewarded by praise and promotion and there is little learning from each other or from honest mistakes, except learning how to manipulate the system.

Another aspect of such cultures is how they foster the forming of cliques. Trust and teamwork is non-existent except within these cliques and in the worst situations key information is hidden so that others err or look stupid. Because of all the above, quality and service levels are static or in decline.

In contrast in a blame-free, or 'open', culture:

- errors are admitted because quality and service are more important
- learning and improvement are natural
- sharing information and teamwork are natural
- behaviour reinforcement is largely positive
- trust is high
- expectations are high
- staff help each other out without being asked or ordered to.

Clever leaders use great imagination to motivate their staff. To encourage an open culture they reward desired habits like information sharing. They also think of a wide variety of incentives. People are motivated in a hundred ways, only one of which is money. Staff also look for leadership. Mahen Tampoe's *Liberating Leadership* (1998) describes a survey of 1000 respondents, from staff to directors in most industries and occupations, which asked them to rank 35 leadership behaviours they had encountered. Most important were treating mistakes as learning opportunities, promoting other people's self-esteem, practising what he or she preached and demonstrating personal integrity. Least important were inspiring fear, making sure things were done their way and telling people what to do.

The implications for leaders are clear. The world is changing and with it employee expectations. In response, management skills and habits need to change fundamentally. The implications for training and development are equally stark. The old days of running an unchanging syllabus are over. Trainers need to offer a variety of learning experiences, inside and outside the classroom, not just in routine job skills, but in opportunities to learn. The new world is a challenging but hugely exciting one, where even trainers can learn too.

Further reading

Amos, E., Spiller, J., Storey, D. and Wade, R. (1997), *The Middle Market – How They Perform: Education, Training and Development*, Foundation for Manufacturing and Industry.

Covey, S. (1989), *The Seven Habits of Highly Effective People*, New York: Simon & Schuster.

Eccles, A. (1994), *Succeeding with Change*, Maidenhead: McGraw-Hill.

Griffiths, K. and Williams, R. (1998), *A Learning Approach to Change*, Aldershot: Gower.

Hammer, M. and Champy, J. (1993), *Reengineering the Corporation*, London: Nicholas Brealey.

The Industrial Society (1997), *Learning Organisations* (Report – Managing Best Practice no. 33), London: The Industrial Society.

Matheson, D. and Matheson, J. (1998), *The Smart Organisation*, Maidenhead: McGraw-Hill.

Obeng, E. (1997), *New Rules for the New World*, London: Capstone.

Tampoe, M. (1998), *Liberating Leadership*, London: The Industrial Society.

Chapter 3

Vision and values: practical guidance for training and development professionals

Tom Barry

In the face of rapid structural and cultural changes today's organizations are demanding new and different levels of contribution from their workforce. However, while organizations are demanding more focus and commitment, the employees themselves are setting their own agenda, including ways in which they can get a sense of personal progress and balance at work.

This chapter will look at these seemingly conflicting priorities and consider what a critical issue this is to the progress and success of an organization. Specifically it will look at the relevance of vision and values to today's business, how the success of any values process is via individuals and the practical steps you can take to define, communicate and commit staff to the process.

Throughout the chapter there is practical guidance provided for training and development professionals who have a central role to play in one of the most powerful and uniting examinations that a business can undertake.

The initial challenge

Whether you like it or not most large organizations have a publicly stated vision and a set of values and considering their supposed potential, it is no surprise that boards often spend long hours defining and articulating them. Typically, board members also find the exercise extremely worthwhile and rewarding and are usually keen to share their discoveries. They consequently want to launch programmes and initiatives to help others revitalize their businesses.

But then something happens. Or more precisely, nothing happens. The enthusiasm of the creative process gets lost in the latest margin figures from the manufacturing plant. The company's commitment to change unsupportive behaviours is overtaken by the need to sack the financial controller in a hurry.

The vision and values the company has laboured so long to create fall to the bottom of the in-tray.

What happens when the employees get to hear of the board session that created the vision and values? If they are feeling generous, they might put it down to the chief executive's 'latest idea'. Alternatively, they might ignore it and use the unforgettable acronym discovered in an American manufacturing company a few years ago: BOHICA. Bend Over, Here It Comes Again!

Certainly those plaques that hang from office walls that announce the vision and values are seen by most as glib platitudes. With equal certainty, however, while it is easy to predict such a cynical reception, the contribution of a vision and set of values to the success of today's organization and the employees within it cannot be dismissed – the board *are* right!

This contradiction highlights one of the most challenging hurdles the training and development professional must overcome, an attitudinal one that the vision and values do not relate in any way to the daily lives of the business's employees. Of the many hurdles you will face in the whole process, this can be the most challenging.

The context for vision and values

The importance that is attached to vision and values is a result of increasing change facing organizations. Communications have made business global and immediate, forcing us to deal with more in less time. The use of technology has increased dramatically, doing away with jobs and ways of working that were core only five years ago. Competition now has a longer reach, is fiercer and is coming from all directions.

Many organizations have responded to the pressures with 're-engineering' tactics. Such an approach was meant to clear lines of communication, break departmental barriers and clear 'dead wood'. However, it often translated into 'slash and burn' – gutting organizations in order to make them lighter, more flexible and responsive. It was also a plan dependent on employees at all levels accepting ambiguity, holding themselves accountable for outcomes, and managing their own careers and morale. In short, giving more and asking for less.

Furthermore, as Professor Paul Turner summarized in his Inaugural Professorial Lecture at Nottingham Business School in the UK, there were implications for management too. 'Overall, the rapid change demanded new types of management techniques other than the traditional command and control, management by objectives type of approach.' In effect, organizations lost the traditional levers of control over their employees at the very time when front line staff were becoming the differentiating factor in a company's success.

Meanwhile, many employees were making radical changes in their own expectations and aspirations. A new generation emerged that wanted *both* a stimulating and demanding work life *and* a fulfilling and a rewarding home life. Coopers and Lybrand's findings (October 1997) from graduates at a range of top business schools in the UK and USA proves that this search for 'Both ... And' comes from those with the most traditional expectations.

So, if employees are changing, business is changing and the way of working in an organization is changing, what is there to replace the 'traditional levers of control'? It is this background which forces vision and values to the forefront of any training and development strategy.

Values as guides

The timeliness and relevance of vision and values is to provide both organizations and individuals with a sense of 'destination' and a set of 'guidelines' at a time of perpetual transition. Phillip J. Caroll, erstwhile CEO of Shell Oil defined the issue: 'If Vision is our destination, then Values are the guides that will get us there'. Some practical examples might help you recognize their relevance to your own business.

When your core market of magazine publishing is being redefined by the Internet, what are those essential tenets of the way you do business that you want to keep and those that you want to drop? When your roadside recovery business is under threat from cars that do not break down as often as before, do you continue to value the technical expertise that built the business? In short, how do you set out to define the new guides for the business to replace or build on those that are no longer relevant? And what is the practical role that training and development has in helping create and deliver this process?

This chapter will provide some practical guidelines later that can help start this process but training and development professionals should not underestimate their task. Why? Because it is one that has to start from the boardroom, it has to be continuously linked to the practicalities of a changing business and it always has the potential to emerge as another BOHICA initiative. However, it is also a process that allows you to make training and development sit firmly at the heart of the business in the minds and practice of all employees.

Starting a vision and values process

It would be nice to take you straight into 'a six point plan for success' and have you believe that a vision and values process is both easy to create and simple to implement. However, it is a mistake, all too commonly made, to think that it is so easy.

What the vision and values process has to produce is two results:

1. The *tangible, written outputs and plans* to align the business in practical ways to its future stated intent. Easy to see, touch and do something with!
2. The *intangible, unwritten intentions* to do things differently in a way that will require a change in behaviour, by many people, over a long period of time.

A step-by-step guide is presented below to produce the first set of results. However, the guide also warns you not to start this process until you truly understand and can manage the implications of the second set of results. The cynicism mentioned at the start of this chapter has its roots not in failure, but in the success of producing the first set of results but not following through with the second set.

Step one: creating the right background and helping others to understand that success is dependent on individual values and discretionary effort

Re-engineering in many businesses, for all its productivity and efficiency gains, has also resulted in increased stress, increased workload, decreased feelings of job security and decreased motivational levels. This clearly was not the result expected. It also affected levels of trust in the business, employee loyalty, career opportunities and personal satisfaction in the company. The paradox is simple but confusing to many. Downsizing 'survivors' are asked for increased creativity, flexibility and innovation and are asked to do this at the same time as their workloads and stress levels are increasing and their motivation is slowing down. This is the ground of the attempted transition from vision and values to practical implementation, and it illustrates the paradox. The incorporation of individuals into this transition has operated under the title of 'empowerment', yet it is a word that signifies to many a failure of bold expectations. Why? The answer is laid out clearly by Chris Argyris in his article in the *Harvard Business Review* (Argyris, 1998).

In examining successful vs. unsuccessful attempts to empower workers in any meaningful sense, Argyris has given a simple yet effective piece of insight by distinguishing between *external* and *internal* commitment.

When an organization tries to implement change by defining vision, strategy, work process and individual job requirements in a rigid top-down fashion, the highest level of commitment that can be achieved is one best thought of as 'contractual compliance'. With little control over work, employees can only act on that which is narrowly expected of them. This is *external* commitment, and it characterizes strategies that sacrifice motivation for a simple co-operation.

Motivation, enthusiasm, innovation and trust can only come about through a strategy that aims at *internal* commitment and it is here that a values process has its role. If senior management wants the dynamic, creative, focused individual to match the flatter, more versatile organization, the individual can only be asked to make such a commitment based on their own motivations and agendas. Individuals must be able to define tasks, define the behaviour required to perform the tasks, take part in defining performance goals, and define the importance of the goal. It is all good common sense but not good common practice. Why? Blocking this more viable use of the word 'empowerment' is the command-and-control culture, in which anxious management becomes wary of, and hostile to, what they see as excessive expectations of empowerment on the part of employees. Managers feel their control challenged in a way that makes good intellectual sense but has little practical comfort.

Highlighting the distinction between internal and external commitment helps us understand some key criteria for success in implementing vision and values. Values are an attempt to harness internal commitment, to generate discretionary effort that can only be put into practice through a strategy that comes from the individual. However, if the core values of an organization are to be aligned with the motivations of the individual, then surely we must take a final, obvious step before implementing vision and values. In our motivational strategy and method we must acknowledge and include the fact that along with organizational values, there are individual values.

Nowhere is the significance of the acknowledgement and inclusion of individual values better seen than in the recently emerging work/life debate. Given the cloud of individual disillusionment – demands made of employees, the extent to which they are stretched – their priorities and values are now increasingly focused on those aspects of their lives completely divorced from work. Ambition in the workplace is now taking a back seat to the priorities of home, the family, personal development and most other spheres of life which have been weathered by working in today's economy.

While to some the work/life debate may appear to be a 'soft' HR issue, it has as its centre the discretionary effort needed if vision and values are to become a practical, profitable reality. The way to get internal commitment rather than external commitment is to give employees personal reasons to do what the company wants them to do.

It is this facet of the individual that today's company needs to tap. Unfortunately, it is this facet of the individual that now risks being left unused. The key is to capture the self-interest of the individual and build a bridge between the values of the business and those of the individual. Radical culture change and workplace anarchy is not necessary. The method of building this bridge is incredibly simple.

Step two: creating your organization's values and helping individuals find the vital link to your business

There are three discrete stages to work to if you have decided to lead your business into the process of creating and implementing organizational values. It is advisable to create a plan listing all three and then a plan to examine the implications for the people and the business.

1. Defining your organizational values

Setting the ground rules
Defining your values looks simple and honest enough on paper. However, it is the process of facilitating and managing the key people in the business through that process that is one of the aspects that makes a difference between initial success and initial failure.

- Choose your facilitator carefully, whether from inside your business or from elsewhere. To borrow the American expression, 'the ticket to the ball game' these days is for a facilitator to have an excellent working knowledge of the subject. But that is not enough. The overriding consideration you should look for in choosing your facilitator is his or her commercial experience, an ability to empathize with the key team and an equal ability to challenge them to test their answers.

- Think it through. If you accept that your vision is where you want to get to and your strategy the chosen route to that point, then your values must be tested time and time again in this critical phase against the commercial realities of what you are trying to achieve. Do not let the CEO introduce the values of another company because he or she 'likes the feel of them'. Only let the CEO do that if he or she can prove that by doing so, it will further the commercial interests of *all* the stakeholders in, and partners to, the organization.

- Test the state of organizational readiness to enter a process like this. The correct timing is critical. From experience there are two questions that you will need to answer: Has the business got its strategy in place and agreed by the key team? What sense of urgency do the business and the key individuals have?

    The extent to which the strategy is in place and agreed is a crucial predictor of success. This is particularly so in the defining stage but more importantly for the later second and third stages. To put it bluntly, if people are not clear about whether they have got a job or not or who their boss is or colleagues are, then there is no impetus to define the future guidelines of the organization.

This is a common source of frustration for the board. Why? Because by the the time they have finalized the strategy, they are itching to move on to the next phase, but the majority have not yet seen it or understood its implications.

- Test the organizational and personal energy to complete the process. If the previous question is important, this question is crucial. It will help you clarify whether there is any organizational energy to complete the process and more importantly, whether there is any personal energy to tap into. John P. Kotter's *Leading Change; Why Transformation Efforts Fail* talks of creating a 'sense of urgency' to prompt deep and sometimes personal reasons to define values.

An organization with a clear future, stable markets and few competitive pressures will obviously not have the same urgency as the companies described earlier. Agree what the organizational urgency is before you start, then test the personal urgency of your key team. An example is a group of individuals on the board of a large advertising agency. Their personal urgency was to prove to themselves that they could do a better job for their already successful business. Take advantage of these deep-rooted individual reasons. They bring power and urgency to process.

Conducting the process
The 'process' revolves around a workshop of one or two days' duration.

- *Form a group of opinion leaders* This might be your board, or it might include a wider group of other personnel. Their status is secondary to their sense of urgency, and to their willingness to contribute, challenge and to be challenged in a rigorous way.

- *Get people thinking* Having established your group, get people thinking well before the workshop itself. Ask them to write down the picture of the organization five years hence. Then, from a list of possible current and future values, have them prioritize these values in importance in reaching that state of five years hence. This 'future state' thinking ensures that they come to the workshop with some key dilemmas already clear in their minds. One of their dilemmas will always be to find the correct balance between the values that guided the organization to its present day and those that you will need to take it forward. The example of the publisher struggling to come to terms with the Internet (a good sense of urgency there!) was of a group unwilling to alter the importance it gave to 'accuracy' over 'speed'. Is speed more important in *how* they do things or will accuracy always be the most important? Or are they both equally vital?

- *Use the available technology*   There are dilemmas that technology can help you solve. Using software designed to let everyone vote at the same time, and anonymously, each value is defined and prioritized against each other to answer the question 'Which value will get us to our destination quicker?'. For to value everything is to value nothing. The process of defining and prioritizing calls upon the skilled facilitation mentioned earlier. It can be an exhausting process squeezing exact definitions out of a group of individuals who often want to *do* more than to *think* but it is a critical stage. Half-formed definitions in this stage emerge as weak and confusing guides when others in the organization get to see them later.

- *Create an importance/satisfaction matrix*   Exactness is also critical here and the importance/satisfaction matrix allows you to discover the key areas to focus on in the organization straight away. Having already ranked the importance of each value, ask the board to score their current level of satisfaction with the organization's performance against each value. The scores can be plotted into this matrix. The result gives immediate attention to those areas in need or urgent repair and distinguishes those areas where the organization needs only to maintain its current performance (see Figure 3.1).

High importance Low satisfaction **OPPORTUNITIES TO ACT ON**	High importance High satisfaction **STRENGTHS TO BUILD ON**
OPPORTUNITIES EMERGING Low importance Low satisfaction	**MAINTAIN ONLY** Low importance High satisfaction

Figure 3.1   Importance/satisfaction matrix

It is this clear linking of values to the business agenda that is vital to achieve. Values will only have a chance of delivering their potential to the organization if you can make the connection and test them against the current activities. For example, if the 'customer comes first' is of high importance to your future, then what is the current state of your performance in delivering that value? Generate examples of procedures and decisions that support or go against each value. Help them link each value to their specific behaviour as a board or as individuals. Test their future intentions and look for gaps in the business plans that do or do not support the newly defined values. If they do not calibrate themselves against each value and behave accordingly, there is little chance anyone else will.

2. Communicating your organizational values

The completion of the workshop above is only the start of a process that puts training and development at the centre of events. Your communication of the values will eventually involve corporate communications and marketing but your initial role is twofold:

- Take the values created in the board workshop and test them with your employees to ensure you have reached a correct, working definition. Set up a number of employee focus groups of 8–10 people and work with them to test the results you have come up with. Remember that you are testing for interpretation and relevance to them, not asking them to create a fresh set of values. Use as many open questions as possible, record the groups and play them back again afterwards. I suggest you create questions around the following themes:
  - Detailed definition of each value *from* the individuals including what this value means to them in their place of work, what this value means to customers and suppliers and some specific behavioural examples of this value.
  - The relevance of each value *to* the individuals in their job today and their future.
  - Examples of advancing and hindering policies and practices.

  In doing this, you are leading the initial process of communication and involvement and shaping up the values' working definitions and their relevance to the business. This is a stage of validating what you have got and going back to the original board group to show and recalibrate the results. It is also a stage where you will learn a lot about how each value looks in action to the front line people who make the difference. It can be a frustrating time as the days tick by. Board members will be asking 'what's happening?' and you will not yet have linked any training or development initiative to the values. It might be frustrating, but it is critical not to enter your next role too soon.

- Use all available media to communicate the values. Work with marketing to sell the values into the business, communicate the value of values to the business again and again and illustrate how the company is currently benefiting from its existing values and needs to support its desired values.

   At the same time be aware of the traps. Do not expect individuals to change their behaviour at this stage. Do not overpromise what values can do for the business or the speed in which it will all happen. And do not be dispirited by the inevitable cynicism of the few.

3. Make your organizational values come alive for each of your employees

Until now, your role as a training and development professional has been one of organization and influence. This phase allows you to bring all your professional skills together to create a process to make the organizational values both meaningful and exciting for each individual in your business.

It is also a phase that occurs naturally from the successful completion of the above two. Rather than detail the process of this phase, you will need to make a checklist against which you can calibrate your progress.

- Establish a series of workshops for all employees to attend in groups up to 25 or 30. Fix a tight timescale . . . and stick to it.
- Have a board member introduce each workshop. It signals the importance and helps everyone understand how values benefit the business.
- Mix workshop participants across all ages, functions and seniority. Organizational values provide guidelines for all employees to behave in a consistent way. They will all learn new and different interpretations of each value.
- Help each person clarify and discuss what each organizational value means to him or her. The second stage 'communicating your organizational values' will have already started that process so this becomes a formal confirmation and not a surprise.
- Let each person take stock of their own individual values and visualize how they can link those to the organizational values. Argyris's internal commitment comes from the realization that there is a personal reason to follow the organizational values.
- Help each person clarify in practical ways how to put that overlap into practice. Have them focus on what they need to do differently, on what to stop and on what to start to support the organizational values.
- Give time for discussion and planning for specific activities that each individual will start after the workshop. Help them build a plan with

milestones that demonstrates when and how they will contribute to acting on the organizational values.

- Ask people to discuss 'what could go wrong?'. By letting people see the downside of the process, they will avoid the pitfalls from the start. The biggest pitfall is overpromising to oneself and to the organization that things change overnight. They will not, but consistency of follow through makes up for many a broken enthusiastic promise!
- Have people commit to a partner to measure success after the workshop. One of the greatest prompters in ensuring that the momentum is kept up is for people to have a partner to coach, listen, challenge and celebrate after the workshop. Do not be too worried about who pairs with whom. It is a *process* partnership to keep up energy and enthusiasm.
- Link all other training and development processes into the organizational values. Test your induction, appraisal and development processes; they will often lag behind what you are looking to achieve and measure and may reward the wrong behaviours.

Conclusion

This chapter has set out some practical guidance for training and development for professionals who are on the path of clarifying and implementing organizational vision and values. Properly positioned, clearly defined and then implemented in the two distinct stages of communication and individual commitment, this is a process that is one of the most powerful and uniting examinations a business can undertake.

It is not a short-term process, however, and what is not covered is the continuation of the project into the business in one year's time, in two years' time and beyond. There is a prize there worth working for and it is a prize that will be directly attributed to the energies of training and development.

Further reading

Argyris, C. (1998), 'Empowerment: The Emperor's New Clothes', *Harvard Business Review*, May–June.

Barry, T. (1998), 'Get A Life', *Management Skills and Development*, March.

Bowles, M. (1997), 'The Myth of Management: Direction and Failure in Contemporary Organisations', *Human Relations*, July.

Collins, J. C. and Porras, J. I. (1996), 'Building Your Company's Vision', *Harvard Business Review*, September–October.

Coopers and Lybrand (1997), IPD Harrogate Conference.

George, J. M. and Jenkins, R. (1997), 'Experiencing Work: Values, Attitudes and Moods', *Human Relations*, April.

Goffee, R. and Jones, G. (1996), 'What Holds the Modern Company Together', *Harvard Business Review*, November–December.

Handy, C. (1996), *Beyond Certainty*, London: Arrow Business Books.

Hendry, C. and Jenkins, R. (1997), 'Psychological Contracts and New Deals', *Human Resource Management Journal*, **7**(1).

Hinings, C. R., Thibault, L., Slack, T. and Kikulis, L. M. (1996), 'Values and Organisational Structures', *Human Relations*, July.

Hutton, W. (1996), *The State We're In*, London: Vintage.

Kotter, J. P. (1995), 'Leading Change, Why Transformation Efforts Fail', *Harvard Business Review*, March/April.

Oliver, J. (1998), 'Losing Control', *Management Today*, June.

Orpen, C. (1997), 'The Downside of Downsizing: Managing an Organisation to its Right Size', *Strategic Change*, **6**.

Porter, M. E. (1985), *Competitive Advantage*, New York: The Free Press, McMillan.

Porter, M. E. (1990), *The Competitive Advantage of Nations*, London: MacMillan Press.

RSA Inquiry (1995), 'Tomorrow's Company: The Role of Business in a Changing World'.

Turner, P. (1998), 'Achieving and Maintaining the Human Advantage in Organisations: the Role of HR 1979–1997 and Beyond', Nottingham Business School Inaugural Lecture, 2 June.

Chapter 4

High performing teams

Andy Dickson

If one word were to be used to summarize the main change in the working practices of organizations in the latter stages of the twentieth century it would surely be 'team'. The challenge for both team leaders and trainers, however, is to ensure that their teams both understand what the term involves and how to work together to achieve their team objectives.

This chapter will take a practical look at teamworking in organizations and will look in some detail at the levels of team development which trainers and team leaders need to keep in mind. At each level of activity the author will also highlight what the trainer's main focus should be.

Finally, this chapter will provide real world examples of the different types of high performing teams and will highlight what sort of training and development can be used to achieve higher performance.

Teamworking in organizations

Maslow's hierarchy of needs (Maslow, 1970), provides us with a clear understanding of why people have been, and still are, drawn to work together. Once we have met our survival-related needs Maslow's model suggests that people will then want to meet their needs of safety, social relationships and self-esteem – all of which can be satisfied through teamworking.

As far back in time as you care to go you can find examples of people working in teams to achieve success and there are certainly parallels between old tribal behaviours and the working patterns we see in today's business environments. The tribes may have different names – Microsoft and Apple, sales and production, Jeff's team and Jane's team but the dynamics have changed very little.

As for the drivers for teamworking in today's commercial organizations these can be found in the increase in global competition, the pressing demands of shareholders and the explosion in technology. Expectations for quality products and service are higher than ever and organizations are under constant pressure to improve working practices. In this context teamworking is simply a response by companies to harness the power of their people.

However, high performing teams are complex animals and every team is different. Much of this is due to the unique make-up of each team in its reason for existing and the people within it. To help make sense of high performing teams, how they work and how they perform, I am now going to look at three levels of team activity that people working with teams need to keep in mind: purpose, strategy and implementation.

These three levels overlap. Some of the issues discussed in purpose, for example, clearly move into strategy and implementation. This is because a team is what it does and how it does it, whatever its intentions. Team identity is inextricably linked to how team members behave and vice versa.

Level one: purpose

This level is fundamental. A high performing team must know why it exists and what its purpose is. Without the answers to these basic questions it is difficult for a team to perform and indeed you can see this happening when teams lose their way or drift from their original purpose.

A high performing team must demand answers and clarify its mission if it is in doubt about its purpose. A well-defined mission includes a well-defined statement of intent which is understood by all team members and may or may not be broadcast outside the team. If it is to be seen by other parties, it must be clear and concise and understandable to any stakeholder reading it.

The team's mission or task should also be clearly in line with the organization's mission and objectives and should be accompanied by clear team targets, goals or objectives. A clear objective should be stated as 'to achieve .... by ....'

Furthermore, each objective must have clear success criteria that are clearly measurable. If there is any doubt the team must clarify its objectives so that team members understand what they are trying to achieve, how they will know they have achieved it and by when. It is likely that team objectives will change and so a regular review of objectives should be made to ensure the team is on course for success and is dealing positively with change. To help a team clarify their objectives team members should know:

● What the organization's needs are which relate to their existence and the part they play in its ultimate success.
● Who the interested parties/stakeholders are in the process and what expectations they have.

The trainer's focus

In most cases the most appropriate and effective way of dealing with each of the above uncertainties is through guided facilitation. At the purpose level the trainer's primary task is to help build and maintain a conducive environment. This will stimulate the team to think creatively and help them explore their purpose. The trainer should also challenge the team to explore all stakeholder expectations which includes defining clearly the purpose and success criteria for each stakeholder. If clarity is required it is likely that stakeholders will need to be questioned to find out their expectations and measures of success.

It is important to remember that it is often the lack of 'purpose' level information which leads to under performing teams. The trainer's facilitation at this level is critical in enabling the team to develop clear goals and objectives with associated success criteria.

Level two: strategy

This is probably the most complex level and it falls into two sections – first, the selection of people, skills and structure and second, the issue of values, strategy, attitude and commitment all of which form the team culture.

1. Selection and construction of team

Understanding the make-up of the team is a critical factor for success. Having the correct skills is of course a basic requirement, especially in teams which are dependent on technical or functional requirements such as IT, engineering or accountancy. Selecting the right skills of people should also be balanced with their personal approach to working in a team including their personal preferences and preferred team role.

The work of a number of researchers can be taken into account here and there are tools available to help the process of selection. Other than a straightforward interview process an assessment event may prove useful where individuals can be seen in action and their contribution to a team observed. It can happen that brilliant individuals do not necessarily make ideal team players and it may be more appropriate to select a team player with less brilliant functional skills.

For those who want to explore team roles both Belbin® and Margerison and McCann® have developed non-psychometric models which help individuals identify their personal strengths in a team situation. Each of these models identifies a number of team roles seen as being vital to a successful team. Team members can have their strengths in one or two main areas or be spread across a variety of characteristics. In both cases it is stressed that the importance is to have a balance of team roles to ensure a team which will be effective in agreeing direction, co-ordinating, creating ideas, paying attention to detail, looking outside the team, implementing strategy and reviewing performance. Too many of one team role, or certain combinations, can be detrimental to team performance.

In Belbin's later work he also recognizes different kinds of task as requiring different combinations of team roles. Successful high performing teams will constantly review their personnel and make sure that there is a good fit of people with the required set of skills and characteristics. Furthermore, high performing teams are not scared of changing team members if the performance of the team is below par.

The trainer's focus

At this first strategy level the trainer/facilitator has a number of tasks to keep in mind. First, there may be a need for the trainer to help the team leader to develop job specifications and effective recruitment and interviewing procedures. This might include liaison with the HR/personnel department or might require the trainer, if they are knowledgeable enough, coaching the managers involved in successful recruitment procedures including the use of psychometrics and interview techniques. Alternatively, the trainer might he involved in the development and running of assessment centres to help build the team. Belbin's team roles that help to identify which team members play which roles and who fills in as a second if key players are not available is a good tool here. Psychometric profiles such as Myers Briggs Type Indicator (MBTI) can also be useful in helping team members and the trainer/facilitator to appreciate their interpersonal preferences and understand the dynamics within the team. With this in mind the trainer should be prepared to act as coach both for individuals and the team.

Another aspect of the trainer's work at this stage could be to carry out a training needs analysis in order to see what development team members might need in order for them to become more effective in their roles.

2. Team culture

The second part of strategy is the way in which the selected team works together. Here, there are more intangibles and the process must be carefully handled. Once team members are in place and they are clear about their mission and objectives it is important for individuals to get to know each other and develop relationships between themselves and other team members to create a real sense of team. Below are a number of factors that need to be taken into account when building an effective team culture.

Trust and respect   Team members need to understand each other's strengths and weaknesses. This should not be confused with liking each other. This process of building appreciation helps develop a bond between team members which is the bedrock of effective teamworking. This is the time that the team culture is formed and it is a crucial stage.

Ground rules   In the case of new teams this is the foundation for the future and the ideal time to establish and agree working practices. There is much evidence that suggests that this is also the best time to focus on the team dynamics. Some companies do this in-house while others use external specialists who are expert at building and developing teams.

Values   Establishing team values is an essential and critical step in the development of a high performing team. Without this, team members will have no firm reference as to how to work together and behave. In some cases, teams find it useful to look at the values of other teams to select the kind of things that may be important to them. Experience suggests it is useful to provide some input and then facilitate the ensuing discussion. It is extremely important after the discussion that team members then have some time to reflect and then agree to a summary of the values. Any disagreement must be treated carefully; if team members move forward with different values there is a danger of misunderstanding and a mismatch of behaviours later on. This values stage actually becomes a fundamental part of the team's identity. It is the way the team wants to work together and determines how it will be perceived by others. Anyone crossing these values is likely to get their fingers burned.

Leadership   Part of the values discussion will be about leadership and leadership style. For a high performing team to be successful it is important that team members are able to contribute to the processes so far described. If leadership does not facilitate this and is too prescriptive in style it is unlikely that the team will achieve the desired level of 'buy-in' to its mission and strategy. However, it is also important that the level of leadership provided is strong enough to give direction and structure to the process of team development and that the leader is able to gain the motivation and commitment of the team. The leader or co-ordinator must therefore ensure a good balance between task achievement, team needs and individual development.

Communication and feedback   Communication within the team is vital. The team members must get used to giving open and honest high quality feedback. The most common model used for this is the Johari (1970) window which encourages individuals to disclose information about themselves so that they in return can receive high quality feedback. Alongside these factors are what Tuckman (1965) has described as the four stages of team development (see Figure 4.1).

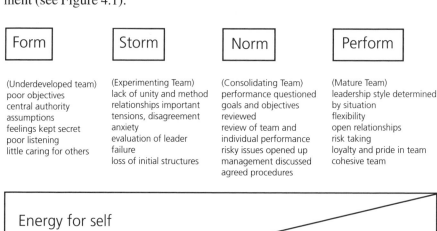

Figure 4.1   Team development (adapted from Tuckman, 1965)

1. *Team development: forming*   This is part of the formative stage. Typically team members are, at first, wary of each other and communication is limited. It is the skill of the facilitator to draw out the thoughts and ideas of team members to begin developing the team. Experience shows that in initial discussions team members stick to safe comments. As time moves on, this 'ritual sniffing' stage can move quickly into a heightened level of communication where team members who still do not know each other very well are more ready to stand up for what they think is right.

2. *Team development: storming*   When team members do not know each other well this can easily lead to misunderstanding and an uncomfortable stage which Tuckman (1965) describes as 'storming'. It is, despite external appearances, an essential stage in team development and without it, it is difficult for a team to truly move on. It has to be said that the storming phase can take various guises and is not always an extreme event. The storming phase must be handled carefully by the facilitator as often, to team members or observers, it is seen as a negative stage from which they back away or draw negative conclusions rather than a positive step in team development.

3. *Team development: norming* Following this stage, team members accept that 'difference of opinion' is inevitable and also a positive attribute. It is often at this stage that the ground rules or values are addressed so that the team can make the most of team members' strengths.

4. *Team development: performing* This is when the team utilizes its combined strengths to optimize team performance using their new understanding of each other.

Continuous improvement Finally, there is the issue of continuous improvement and the accepted best practice here is through the use of Kolb's (1976) learning cycle. Real experience is reviewed by critical appraisal of team performance. This is followed by a period of summarizing and agreeing on future best practice.

The trainer's focus

The trainer has to be especially sensitive at this level – remembering it is their task to serve the team as it goes through the various stages of its development. Some of the ways in which the trainer can help serve the team are as follows:

- Most people will be more engaged in the process of teambuilding when they have some theoretical framework to help them understand what is going on. In this respect the trainer can present the various theories on teams to give the team an insight into how teams work, how they develop and how they communicate. The more information they have, the more they can make sense of, and rationalize, what is actually happening.

- In helping the team to develop trust the trainer/facilitator might consider engaging the team members in stressful/challenging situations where individual team members have to rely on each other.

- In the same way the trainer/facilitator might encourage the team to explore their strengths and weaknesses and to find ways to value each individual contribution.

- Another approach which is often successful is to facilitate the team through an exploration of both individual and team values in order to establish a set of shared team values.

- It will be important for the team to explore what is important to them about how they work together. Ideally they should establish a common working practice which they all 'buy-in' and commit to. The trainer/facilitator will need to challenge the team if there is no 'buy-in'.

Only if team members agree – or agree to disagree – are they likely to be able to work successfully later on.

● Open and honest communication channels are essential for effective teamworking. The trainer/facilitator will need to ensure there are agreed and clear guidelines for giving and receiving feedback.

● The team will need to have a strategy for successfully integrating new team members. It is the trainer's task to raise their awareness about how they will manage this process.

Level three: implementation

Following level two on strategy the team is now ready to move on to the detailed plan of action. The team has a clear mission, objectives, values and working practice. Now it is a question of carrying out the plan, operating to the refined working practice, behaving in line with the agreed values and applying themselves to the challenges ahead.

During the implementation stage, however, there are a number of factors to take into account:

Reviewing performance   Reviewing performance and continuous improvement is vital. It is also important that the team is conscious of what is happening outside of their work so that they can implement their plans for change as and when it happens.

Feedback   At this stage, more than any other, it is key that communication is clear and everyone is kept informed. Clear feedback must be given between team members to maintain high standards of performance. Note must also be taken of the feedback from all outside parties so that the team can measure its performance against stakeholder expectations.

Celebrating success   One often overlooked characteristic of a high performing team is its commitment to rewarding and celebrating success. This can take many forms and can take place at agreed strategic milestones or ultimate goal attainment.

The trainer's focus

At the implementation stage the trainer is concerned with helping the team to perform effectively. The tasks here include:

● Establishing intermediate goals and success criteria.
● Ensuring the team regularly reviews performance and has a strategy for change, if it is required.

- Establishing a process of continuous improvement where the momentum and ideas for change come from within the team.
- Introducing a process for reviewing team and individual performance.
- Acting as a coach to help guide the team towards their objectives.
- Helping the team to identify performance gaps, and helping individuals develop the necessary skills to fill them.
- Challenging any acceptance of under performance at either individual or team level.
- Finally the trainer/facilitator will want to help the team to celebrate their successes.

In essence there is an ongoing training and development role required for high performing teams and carefully planned and targeted training and development is seen as an investment rather than a cost by successful teams. Such development of the team and individuals takes into consideration the need to address the requirements of both the team and the individuals within it.

Types of team and their development

As we know a variety of teams operate in modern businesses. Highlighted here are some of the most popular team types and the ways in which they operate and how they have used training and development.

The teamworking culture

In many cases, an organization decides to embrace a new culture which is all about the whole organization buying into a team approach. In these cases it can require fundamental changes of attitude and behaviour for the workforce. It is unfortunate that there have been many instances where this wholesale introduction of teamworking has gone hand in hand with other efficiency drives such as downsizing or relocation. When this happens it is no surprise to find the reaction to teamworking being less than enthusiastic. Carried out in the correct way however, the introduction of a teamworking culture can be extremely effective and produce excellent results for customers, company and employees alike. Important characteristics of successful implementation include:

- Buy-in from the top.
- Inspirational leadership.
- Clarity of direction and mission.
- A willingness to involve people at different levels and to listen to their ideas.

- An opportunity for employees to state their case and help shape working practice.
- A willingness for more responsibility further down the organization.
- Recognition that good ideas may come from all levels in the company.
- Clear communication and active listening.
- Clear lines of feedback both up and down.
- A process of 'buy-in and agreement' for all levels.
- Demonstrable improvements which show behavioural commitment to change at all levels.

Examples of such practices were seen by employees of Rover in the late 1980s and early 1990s. The commitment to turn round a company which had become notorious in the world's motor industry for bad working practices into a highly prized brand name was in fact the result of the success of implementing a learning culture built on teamworking at all levels.

Other examples of such practice can be found in many of the privatized utilities in the early 1990s. Many chose teamworking as a way to become more efficient and provide improved service to customers and shareholders alike. For example, Manweb, the electricity supplier, who cover the diverse areas of the Liverpool conurbation and the bleak mountainsides of North Wales, adopted teamworking at this time and turned an inefficient regional electricity company into a highly successful multi-service utility with a share price higher than any other electricity distributor. They cascaded teamworking using an integrated training package of cross-functional events including customer service, innovation and outdoor problem solving. Their successful approach broke down many of the old stereotypes of the electricity board and significantly improved service for customers.

Project teams

In some cases the use of teamwork is applied specifically to a project team. It is often true that such teams are constructed specifically to achieve a given task within a target time. In these situations the purpose of the team is very clear, as are the expected deliverables. Team members are often handpicked for their specific skills and ability to deliver. One of the biggest problems a project team has to cope with is the limited amount of time they have to bond and establish a team culture and accepted working practices. Often the project team is in need of external facilitation to act as a catalyst to speed up this essential process before implementing the required strategy.

The British Lions rugby team in their preparations for playing against South Africa in 1997 is an interesting example. Integrated carefully with their rugby training, the team from the four home nations used a series of team development exercises including outdoor activities to build trust and support between team members. They also developed a set of shared values known as the Lions' laws which became the accepted working practice for the squad of players and managers. Despite being 5–1 outsiders the Lions won the series 2–1.

International and cross-cultural teams

In the global marketplace companies need to work in teams made up of various nationalities, cultures and languages. This provides its own problems as communication and cultural norms can be potential barriers to successful teamworking.

In many cases companies employ forms of team development to bring their people together to establish personal relationships, develop trust and a common understanding, despite language and cultural barriers. Merck, the American pharmaceutical giant is one example of a company that applied such teamworking practices. As part of their drive for cross-cultural teamworking they brought together people from 21 different countries, speaking 14 different languages. The aim was to break down cultural barriers and introduce teamworking. To achieve this, much of their work used interactive, experiential projects where the need for the spoken word was less important. This form of interactive teamworking is very successful in such cases; it develops a basic level of trust which often creates a solid foundation for more detailed discussions later where more patience is displayed by team members as a result of the early time spent together. The international business schools INSEAD and IMD also use interactive team development programmes to develop the networking abilities of participants on their management programmes. Such programmes speed up their ability to work together despite cultural and language differences.

Virtual teams

Much of the virtual nature of teams is due to the increase in multi-site, multi-teamworking where individuals may have allegiance to a variety of teams on a variety of projects. A major problem with virtual teams is often communication and co-ordination. Often team members are geographically separated and are chosen for their skills and not their seniority. It may be that an employee finds themselves co-ordinating a team which includes senior players within it. When you consider that people may belong to a number of teams and have a variety of reporting structures and appraisal responsibilities, it becomes more understandable why employees can become confused as to where their priorities lie.

Training can play an especially useful role in addressing this issue as for example in the case of a major UK communications company which used a highly interactive experiential programme in the mid-1990s to replicate virtual teamworking. This dynamic and exciting methodology helped team members to highlight the benefits and problems they could expect to encounter in virtual teamworking and through facilitation team members were able to clarify their working practice and iron out difficulties they might encounter.

Senior teams

Many senior teams suffer from 'been there, done that, development is not for me'. It is often difficult for team members at this level to admit that things could be better or admit to problems. And this also makes it difficult for out-siders to suggest an intervention as this may be seen as undermining the team or be taken as a criticism. More enlightened senior teams, however, realize that there is always room for improvement and see that team development is an ongoing issue which needs regular maintenance, especially at their level.

Senior teams often benefit from a longer term integrated approach which incorporates performance coaching. This, combined with opportunities to take the team away from their normal environment and concentrate on team dynamics, is an effective way of maintaining the effectiveness of a high per-forming senior team.

One of many high profile examples of a senior team attending to their own development issues were the directors of Sun Microsystems UK who went off on a sailing boat off the northwest of Scotland together to see how they could work more effectively as a team rather than as a highly talented group of indi-viduals.

Summary

For many organizations, high performing teams are simply the most natural way of getting the best performance from their human resource. However, just because we know the potential of teams to perform does not mean that they will necessarily achieve the desired results. Indeed, teams not only need to understand their own development issues, they need to be guided and helped along the way, and in this respect training and development have a critical role to play. Trainers who are working with teams and team leaders need to develop a range of core skills including excellent facilitation skills, coaching and presentation skills. They also need to accept the differences in every team, work with the recognizable patterns and be prepared to help the teams find their own solutions to the problems they encounter.

Further reading

Adair, J. (1987), *Effective Team Building*, London: Pan Books.

Belbin, M. (1981), *Management Teams – Why They Succeed or Fail*, London: Heinemann.

Eales-White, R. (1995), *Building Your Team*, London: Kogan-Page.

Hastings, C., Bixby, R. and Chaudry-Lenton, R. (1986), *The Superteam Solution*, Aldershot: Gower.

Jerome, P. (1995), *Recreating Teams During Transitions*, London: Kogan-Page.

Katzenbach, J. (1998), *Teams At The Top*, Cambridge, Mass: Harvard Business School Press.

Kolb, D. (1984), *Experiential Learning*, Englewood Cliffs: Prentice-Hall.

Leigh, A. and Maynard, M. (1995), *Leading Your Team*, London: Nicholas Brealey Publishing.

Maslow, A. (1970), *Motivation and Personality*, New York: Van Nostrand.

Parker, G. (1996), *Team Players and Teamwork*, Englewood Cliffs: Prentice-Hall.

Pokras, J. (1996), *Building High Performance Teams*, London: Kogan-Page.

Syer, J. and Connolly, C. (1997), *How Teamwork Works*, Maidenhead: McGraw-Hill.

Tuckman, B. (1965), 'Development Sequence in Small Groups', *Psychological Bulletin*, **63**.

Wilson, G. (1996), *Self-Managed Teamworking*, London: Pitman.

Chapter 5

Lifelong learning and continuing professional development (CPD)

Chris Senior

This chapter outlines the imperatives of lifelong learning and highlights what is driving it, what its focus is and how it is delivered. It considers the latest initiatives in continuing professional development (CPD), defines the different policies that are in operation and provides models and case studies that illustrate the processes involved.

Introduction

> We are in a new age – the age of information and of global competition. Familiar certainties and old ways of doing things are disappearing. The types of jobs we do have changed as have the industries in which we work and the skills they need. At the same time new opportunities are opening up as we see the potential of new technologies to change our lives for the better. We have no choice but to prepare for this new age in which the key to success will be continuous education and development of the human mind and imagination.

Thus starts the government consultative document *The Learning Age* (DfEE, 1998). For a government to produce such a comprehensive statement in its first year in office is a clear sign that the time of lifelong learning has arrived.

However, continuous learning is not new. Individuals, companies, communities and countries have always needed to adapt to changing situations. The achievements of societies, professions and organizations have arisen from building on the experiences of others. Advances in, for example, medicine and engineering, have been built on the experiences of previous professionals and the research activities of universities.

Yet much of this learning was responsive and ad hoc. It also focused on the learning of a small part of the population – those who were skilled in a trade or educated to professional levels. A number of factors have forced learning to be more central for individuals, organizations, and governments. The increased pace of change, whether of technology, working practices, employment structures, or individual aspirations has resulted in a recognition that learning should be structured and better managed. Competitive pressures, both between companies and between countries have also played a part; there is no escape from global influences where competitive advantage comes from knowledge and the ability to exploit it effectively. Countries benchmark themselves against international levels of education and skills. Individuals who are not competent in some way, and who are not continually adapting to changing employment situations, soon fall behind.

So learning has moved towards being a central driver for ensuring survival and enhancing excellence, and increasingly is recognized as a strategic tool to support business success, personal career advancement, and national image. It also has wider contributions, such as helping to promote active citizenship, enabling people to play a full part in their families and their communities.

The focus of lifelong learning

The importance of lifelong learning is also recognized internationally. Since the early 1990s there have been worldwide conferences on the subject and a European Initiative for Lifelong Learning has been established. A number of countries have developed national strategies for promoting learning and, as reflected in the UK, these stress the importance of all people having access to learning opportunities, with the aims of personal growth, economic success, and social coherence.

The context of lifelong learning is broad and attempts to define it tend to emphasize the visionary and motherhood aspects. At its simplest it can be defined as any learning undertaken by individuals throughout their lives. It covers formal education and training, but it also covers informal learning through, for example, self-study and reading; and it recognizes that, in practice, most effective learning is through the day-to-day demands and experiences of work, and social interactions.

The main focus of lifelong learning is on post compulsory education – on the need for individuals to have access to learning opportunities at work, at home, and into retirement. A commitment to improvement and growth is central, complemented by the processes of assessing capabilities and interests, identifying needs, seeking and carrying out a range of learning activities, reflecting on experience and reviewing progress. Hence a central requirement of initial education is to develop these learning skills.

Individual commitment is central but must be supported by action from others. Employers need to encourage and guide their employees through coaching, mentoring and appraisal systems, as well as providing opportunities for training and development. But, it is outside of employment that there are difficulties for individuals in finding support and guidance. Career advice for adults is not easily available and information on courses and other learning opportunities is difficult to access. Libraries, a potentially valuable source of learning and information, are closed on Sundays. Those who are out of work, self-employed, or returning to work need guidance on a range of issues. These include how to identify and prioritize their needs, how to seek out and use appropriate sources of learning, and how to fund their learning.

There is a long tradition in the UK of adult education provided by universities and colleges. This has aimed at providing short courses on a range of liberal arts subjects. Libraries and museums were established to promote education and access to information. In the 1980s the government set up an initiative to encourage further and higher education to provide courses for industry and commerce. This has continued through a greater recognition of the role of educational institutions in the areas on continuing vocational education. Tax relief for individuals to follow some education and training courses has been extended, in particular for courses leading to vocational qualifications. This funding support is, however, limited in comparison with other countries.

In the UK there have not been clear national policies on lifelong learning. Until the mid-1990s there were separate government departments for education and training. The 1998 consultative document is essentially the first to tackle the subject in any coherent way and it proposes some potentially useful initiatives. Individual learning accounts is one of these and could provide individuals with a system of financial contributions from government and employers. The University for Industry is another and could provide a valuable signposting service, linking providers and learners.

Another encouraging sign has been the increasing recognition of the need for continuity from initial education in school into higher education and employment. Debate on the national curriculum has highlighted the importance of core skills such as communication and teamworking and one positive development has been the review of the National Record of Achievement, a requirement for all school leavers. This has been redesigned for versions to be used in schools, in higher education and in adult life.

Continuing professional development (CPD)

For many people the major drivers for lifelong learning have been their professional bodies. Traditionally most of these have provided a range of opportunities for their members to keep up-to-date with services including journals, conferences, meetings, research, and information sources such as libraries. Increasing levels of redundancies among professional staff have also highlighted the need to enhance members' employability and professional institutions and trade unions now provide a range of education and training courses, as well as guidance and support services to members.

However, the most significant development by professional bodies over recent years has been the establishment of policies for the continuing professional development (CPD) of their members. The starting point for this is the need for their members to keep up-to-date in terms of rapidly changing professional expertise required, and the need for this to be broadened and enhanced with new competencies. There is concern that all members need to take active steps to develop their professional competence throughout working life. It is not sufficient to do this simply on an ad hoc basis. CPD has become a focus for debate within institutions about the needs for their members not just to continue learning, but for institutions to regulate their members' CPD in some way.

CPD is generally defined as: 'the systematic maintenance, improvement and broadening of knowledge and skill and the development of personal qualities necessary for the execution of professional duties throughout the practitioners' working life'.

This definition highlights three crucial elements of CPD:

1. that it is systematic or planned
2. that it is about broadening and deepening knowledge, skill and expertise in addition to updating it
3. that it is about a lifelong commitment to continuing professional competence.

In fact, CPD is also defined simply as: 'Commitment to professional competence'. Here, the focus is explicitly on the attitude of members to act as professionals through continuous learning to achieve high standards of professionalism.

The driving force for CPD is, essentially, the need for a profession to show to the public that members are keeping themselves competent as professionals. It is part of the quality assurance system of a profession. The need to gain the confidence of government and employers has encouraged professional bodies to try to regulate their members' CPD. Policies vary from being purely voluntary, through obligatory, to mandatory as follows:

- With a voluntary system the decision to undertake CPD is the choice of the individual. An institution sets guidelines recommending what should be done. It does not set penalties for non-compliance. Members can accept or reject the guidelines.
- An obligatory system places responsibility for compliance on the individual. An institution gives guidelines for CPD but does not set penalties for non-compliance. However, compliance may be taken into

account if members upgrade their membership, or in cases where their competence is in question.
- In a mandatory system the responsibility is both corporate and individual. An institution sets standards for CPD and members must comply. If they do not, they will be subject to some form of discipline which may include being expelled from membership.

Most professions have, in the past, treated CPD as a voluntary activity with action focused on promoting the benefits of CPD to members in terms of enhanced employability, and on providing support through information and guidance. Some, for example the Chartered Institute of Marketing, have provided some additional recognition to those who meet certain CPD criteria.

In practice, most institutions now treat CPD as an obligation of membership, monitoring members through sample surveys. In professions where there is a requirement for membership in order to practise (e.g. actuaries, doctors), the CPD obligation is essentially mandatory. In other professions (e.g. lawyers) CPD was introduced as mandatory for new members and is being extended to all.

The approach taken by professional bodies has been a combination of action to stress the benefits of CPD and sanctions to regulate members' CPD. The actual requirements expected of members include the following:

- No specific requirement but general encouragement and support; there may be financial incentives to attend specific courses.
- Requirement to attend courses and be competent in specific areas.
- Members to carry out a minimum amount of CPD each year; usually defined as hours, but in some cases translated into a points system.
- Members to provide evidence of carrying out CPD; usually in terms of keeping records and plans.

The focus of CPD

Many professional institutions have, in the past, focused on measures of CPD based on the amount of input in terms of hours spent. This has placed most value on formal activities, such as courses. Other, less formal activities, such as reading, projects, workshops, research, and experience both within and outside employment have been encouraged, but present difficulties in measurement terms.

This focus is changing, however, to a recognition that the only valid measure of CPD is the results and outputs, towards using the learning and taking further development action. Professionals need to have evidence, not primarily of the CPD carried out, but of the professional competence being maintained, or developed. The aim is that of continuing professional competence with CPD as important evidence of commitment to this. This focus on outputs requires specifications of the competencies required in jobs and professional roles. These profiles may be defined by employers, and professional bodies or they may be based on the occupational standards produced nationally. In lifelong learning and CPD they provide signposts for individuals to use in identifying needs and planning action.

Engineering is one profession which has reviewed its requirements for professional formation towards a focus on output measures. New members for registration are required to provide evidence, in the form of action plans, for their commitment to CPD and thereafter there is an obligation for all members, through a code of practice on CPD as follows.

1. *Self-management* – Take responsibility for and manage CPD.
    - identify and prioritize development needs and opportunities
    - use appropriate guidelines and competence benchmarks (e.g. from profession, employer)
    - plan and carry out development action using a range of appropriate opportunities
    - record development achievements
    - evaluate achievements and review against needs.

2. *Demonstration of commitment* – Demonstrate commitment to maintaining professional competence through self-managed CPD.
    - note professional institution and any legal/commercial requirements for evidence of CPD
    - be aware of potential for uses of evidence in appraisal/employment/recruitment
    - be aware of useful sources and forms of evidence
    - have available and, if required, provide suitable evidence.

3. *Learning support* – Support the learning and development of others.
    - be prepared to act as a mentor
    - encourage employers to support professional development
    - share professional expertise and knowledge
    - provide support for the learning of others
    - contribute to the activities of a professional body.

The last point highlights a central issue of CPD – namely that learning should be a shared activity. There is a danger in lifelong learning to focus on the individual. In practice real achievement in professional and business life depends on team activities, on shared information and values, and on shared learning. Innovation and growth depends on the synergy of people committed to continuous improvement. Learning for staff should be measured by its contribution to the performance of the teams and organizations in which they work.

Framework for CPD

The first part of the code above summarizes the practical action to be carried out by individuals. However, CPD is a partnership between the key players – individuals, employers, professional bodies and academic and other providers. Their roles can be seen through a model framework for CPD. The model shown in Figure 5.1 was developed for the construction industry.

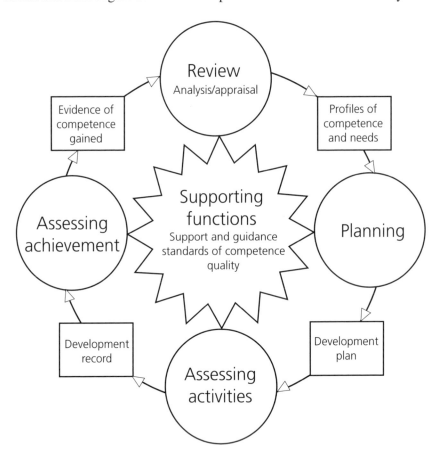

Figure 5.1   Model framework for CPD

This framework has four processes which individuals carry out. Each of the processes results in an output which records an individual's experiences and demonstrates achievements. The outputs provide evidence of carrying out the processes and can be used to measure quality. Three supporting functions underpin and facilitate the processes.

The framework is a development cycle. Those undertaking it should be more competent, as well as being more adept at managing their learning. There is no correct place to begin the cycle although many will logically enter at the review process.

The practical steps that individuals and employers need to take in progressing CPD are summarized with reference to Figure 5.1.

1. *Review*   Individuals review their personal and professional experiences in a structured way. This enables them to identify their interests and competencies and match these against future needs and opportunities. Individuals will note:

    ● Achievements and targets in their current job.
    ● Any requirements from a professional or regulatory body.
    ● Personal interests and commitments.
    ● Career aspirations.
    ● Changing employment opportunities.

    Sources of help in this process include:

    ● Their employer and any relevant system of appraisal.
    ● Any competence standards from employers, profession or occupational body.
    ● Colleagues, their manager, a mentor.

    This review results in a profile of an individual's personal and professional competencies; together with priority areas for their development.

2. *Planning*   Having identified their areas of competence individuals need to formulate a personal development plan. It should be flexible. Some learning will be planned, but much will be opportunistic. However, a systematic approach will help ensure that learning needs are achieved.

    The Institute of Personnel Development (IPD) recommends a framework for a plan which covers the following:

    ● Where do I want to be? What do I want to be doing?
    ● What do I want/need to learn?
    ● What will I do to achieve this?
    ● What resources or support will I need?
    ● What will my success criteria be?
    ● Target dates for review and completion.

    The choice of learning activity will depend on the particular personal and employment situation. Attendance at courses of more than a day or two may be difficult for people working in small organizations or who are self-employed.

3. *Development activities*   Successful learners use a wide variety of experiences as sources of learning. The demands and challenges of day-to-day work provide valuable opportunities for gaining new experience and expertise. The aim should be to integrate learning with work and vice versa.

    Learning activities may include:

    ● On the job experience.
    ● In-house and external courses.
    ● Distance learning programmes and self-directed study.
    ● Lectures, seminars, conferences.
    ● Projects, research, secondments.
    ● Coaching, tutoring, mentoring.
    ● Relevant voluntary work.
    ● Reading books and journals; writing papers.
    ● Gaining qualifications.

4. *Record and assess achievements*   An important outcome of development is a record of the activities undertaken and the learning achievements. This forms part of the continuous process of reflection and improvement. However, records can provide important evidence of the learning activities and of their achievements. Wherever possible, external assessment will be useful to benchmark learning against professional or national targets. Formal assessment as part of an academic, professional or academic qualification would be especially valuable.

    The IPD recommends that a record should include:

    ● Activity dates.
    ● What did you do?
    ● Why?
    ● What did you learn from this?
    ● How have/will you use this?

5. *Supporting functions*   In practice individuals faced with the pressures of demanding jobs and a changing employment market need help to manage their learning effectively. Essential support can be provided here by both professional bodies and employers.

    Professional bodies can provide:

    ● Information on the requirements for CPD in terms of the obligations of their members, and evidence needed.
    ● Framework of professional competencies.
    ● Guidelines and good practice on CPD.

- Planning and recording documents; increasingly these are competence based.
- Guidance through help lines and mentoring services.
- Workshops on managing learning.
- Information on sources of suitable learning opportunities.
- Provision of learned society activities.

Employers can provide:

- A culture of continuous improvement.
- Clear definitions of responsibility with job targets.
- An appraisal system to link individual interests with business needs.
- A structured system of training plans and budgets.
- Support to individuals through coaching and mentoring.
- Realistic resourcing for training in terms of time and money.
- National recognition of commitment to learning through the Investors in People standard.
- Information and guidance on sources of learning.
- Links with colleges, universities and other providers.

Conclusion

Lifelong learning and CPD have become part of the fabric of individual and organizational life but there is still much to be done to translate the rhetoric into reality. In particular many individuals lack the necessary competencies to manage their learning and employers have a long way to go before they can claim to have developed learning cultures at work. What we can see already, however, is the greater focus that many CPD schemes are placing on the outputs and the benefits of learning. This will continue and will enable greater recognition and transfer of learning.

This is a fast moving arena and one that is critical for training management. There are key roles for professional bodies, universities and others to support individuals and employers through activities such as networking, mentoring, career development workshops, information and guidance. For those who are looking at CPD as a way to promote lifelong learning, or simply as good practice, the codes of practice and models outlined here will provide a useful starting place. Further sources of information are provided below.

There are many books, reports, and sources of information on lifelong learning and CPD. In particular:

Government departments   the DfEE is the lead department in respect of lifelong learning and national skills development policies. It publishes policy documents, reports, and sponsors research. The DTI is a source of information on business, innovation and competitiveness.

Professional bodies   provide a wealth of information covering their specific professional area. As well as learned society activities, courses, journals, conferences, institutions provide guidance on CPD practice; this includes planning and recording documents; often these are computer based.

Colleges and universities   provide courses on a wide range of subjects; often these are run in partnership with an employer to meet particular needs. Learning can be assessed and accreditation given in terms of nationally recognized academic and vocational qualifications.

Career development providers   there are many commercial sources of material suitable for individuals to manage their careers, including tools for assessing interests and abilities.

Research/initiatives   there are many projects and initiatives concerned with lifelong learning, sponsored by universities and professional bodies in partnership with employers. A national campaign for learning is supported by many organizations.

National training organizations   provide a national focus for occupational standards and training activities for specific employment areas.

TECs/LECs   Training and Enterprise Councils provide advice and information on local provision of training, and on any funding available. They link with the Investors in People standard.

Further reading

The Learning Age (1988), DfEE consultation paper, London.

Using Standards to Raise Performance: a User's Guide (1996), Construction Industry Standing Conference, London.

For Life – a Vision for Learning in the 21st Century (1997), RSA Report, London.

Broadening Horizons, Making the Most of Progress File (1998), DfEE, Sheffield.

Lifelong Learning – a Survival Concept for the 21st Century (1994), European Lifelong Learning Initiative, London.

Standards and Routes to Recognition (1997), The Engineering Council, London.

Ball, C., Davies, H., Flatley, C. and Hardy, C. (1994), *Promoting Lifelong Career Development*, Cambridge: CRAC.

Gear, J., McIntosh, A. and Squires, G. (1994), *Informal Learning in the Professions*, University of Hull.

Loriman, J. (1997), *Continuing Professional Development – a Practical Guide*, Stevenage: Institute of Electrical Engineers.

Markula, Markku (1998), *Passion to Learn*, IACEE Report, Helsinki.

Norton, B. and Burt, V. (1997), *Practical Self Development: a Step by Step Approach to CPD*, Corby: Institute of Management.

Pedler, M., Burgoyne, J. and Boydell, T. (1991), *The Learning Company, a Strategy for Sustainable Development*, Maidenhead: McGraw-Hill.

Spurling, A. (1995), *Towards an Unknown Land*, Cambridge: CRAC.

Tomlinson, H. and Holmes, G. (1996), *Continuing Professional Development in Five Professions*, Leeds Metropolitan University.

Watkins, J., Drury, L. and Bray, S. (1996), *The Future of the UK Professional Associations*, University of Bristol.

Winfield, G. (1998), *Professional Bodies and Output-Based Models for Continuing Professional Development*, University of Warwick.

Woodward, I. (1996), *Continuing Professional Development Issues in Design and Delivery*, London: Cassell.

Chapter 6

Using National Occupational Standards in training and development

Iain Pollock

In this chapter I intend to give you my reasons for using National Occupational Standards (I shall refer to them as standards and explain what they are later) and why I believe that they can be of use to you, the training and development (T & D) manager.

As a former T & D manager, I think I can do this in a manner which will not only be relevant but understandable. I shall give a brief explanation of why standards were designed, what a standard looks like and what they can be used for. Then I shall examine the practical purposes to which standards can be applied in T & D activities, with particular emphasis on the issue of measuring the impact of training. Finally, I shall guide you to the places and people who can assist you to find out more about how to use standards.

Let me be very honest with you. A few years ago if you had asked me what you could do with standards I would have told you in no uncertain terms. I had no use for them. The company I worked for had their own internal standards (although they did not call them that) which dovetailed nicely into the rest of their human resource (HR) systems, including T & D. The considered views of outsiders were of no interest to us. We believed that the standards which outsiders created were too generic to be of use. It was a valid position for that company at that time.

Now I have broadened my experience and can appreciate where and why standards can be of use and freely admit that I now believe my old company could have used them to great effect all those years ago. Perhaps reading this chapter will convince you too.

What are standards?

Some years ago academic research into education methods concluded that the, then, accepted way of educating people was not working. The argument was framed thus. If you expose any population to the same amount and level of educational input, all things being equal, each person will advance their ability by a similar amount. However, while everyone improves, the least able will not close the gap on the most able. Some of the population, the most able, may reach proficiency but the majority will not. Yet surely the purpose of education is to have everyone in the population reaching proficiency. If this is true, then the system did not achieve its goal.

The alternative method proposed was that education should aim to help everyone reach, in a given population, what was termed 'mastery' in the subject. This would be achieved by giving each person individualized learning opportunities and assessing the individual's performance against a target. So far so good, but what relevance did this have for the world of T & D?

The answer lay in the notion of mastery and the means by which we decided whether an individual had achieved it. This research formed the basis of the movement to design National Occupational Standards in the UK.

Standards are based upon competence and allow us to measure the level of competence attained by each person. They are therefore focused on outcomes and achievements – not theoretical knowledge – and can be applied to any occupation or subgroup within an occupation. In the UK, but also increasingly in other countries, standards form the basis of the (Scottish) National Vocational Qualification (S/NVQ) system. The award of an S/NVQ confirms the level of competence at which a person is performing against the standards for their occupation.

This is not 'rocket science' although standards have a very particular style of expression. If you read one, and understand the principles applied, then you will find all the others easily understandable. A standard always has:

- The element of competence which describes the activity.
- A description of the criteria by which success in that activity will be judged.

If it is to become a qualification it will probably have:

  - The range of circumstances in which those activities should be carried out.
  - The knowledge and understanding which underpins the activity.
  - The type of evidence one would need to produce in order to confirm that someone is competent.
  - The personal qualities, sometimes referred to as competencies, which would help someone achieve the standard.

Here is an example of just one standard: Improve training and development programmes.

Element 1 – Identify potential improvements to training and development programmes

Performance criteria   (what does the person have to do?):

1. All information on training and development programmes required for their improvement is gathered and reviewed.
2. Potential improvements to training and development programmes are clearly identified.
3. The objective of the potential improvements are clearly specified.
4. The feasibility of implementing potential improvements is accurately determined and reviewed with all relevant people.
5. Potential improvements are prioritized according to their cost and benefit.
6. Proposals for the introduction of improvements are presented to the relevant people in a manner which promotes effective decision making.

Range   (what types of information should the person have access to and provide?):

●   Information that is reviewed: results of evaluation, suggestions, recommendations, proposals.
●   Proposals presented to: practitioners, colleagues, clients.
●   Objectives of improvements considered: improvements in learners' development and achievement, cost effectiveness, improved effectiveness, improved efficiency.
●   Improvements considered as a result of: weakness with current systems and practices, newly available methods, newly available technology.
●   Improvements considered to: current programmes, own practice, others' practice.

Evidence requirements   Performance evidence (what has to be done):

1. Review of the results of evaluation and other information.
2. Proposals for improvements and other information.
3. Presentation of proposals.

Knowledge evidence   (what the person must know to do the job competently):

1. Organization's training and development aims and objectives.
2. Organization's structure.
3. Organization's resources.
4. Presentation skills.
5. Likely obstacles to change.
6. Methods to promote and facilitate commitment to change.
7. How to prepare plans which are capable of implementation.
8. How to prioritize, summarize and design presentations.
9. Current government legislation and policy relating to training and development.

10. Employment and equal opportunities legislation and good practice.
11. Relevant national and organizational debates relating to training and development.
12. Relevant national and organizational debates concerning learning.
13. Relevant national and organizational debates relating to quality improvement.

Finally, candidates are required to provide evidence of identifying improvements of at least two distinct training and development programmes.

If you have to judge whether one of your staff is performing competently in improving training and development programmes, the standard gives an excellent jumping off point. It defines the activity, tells you what has to be achieved and how competence will be assessed or measured. What more could you want as a measuring device for the value of training? It must be admitted that, in the past, one of the main complaints against standards was that they were written in stilted language and presented to their audience in a non user-friendly way. The Qualifications and Curriculum Authority (QCA), however, have now relaxed the rigid linguistic and presentation rules so that, as old standards are rewritten and new ones created, they are becoming much easier to understand and use.

What do people use standards for?

Now that I have whetted your appetite, you may be thinking about going out and creating your own standards. Stop right there. Standards can only be created by an Industry Lead Body (ILB) or National Training Organization (NTO) – for example the Chemical Industries Association, the Law Society, the Construction Industry Training Board, Skillset – not by individuals or individual companies. These standards are nationally recognized and apply across their industry or sector in a consistent manner. The ILBs and NTOs monitor the consistency and applicability of the standards written for their industries and ensure that the achievement of the associated qualifications, NVQ, SVQ, GNVQ, are properly assessed.

You may ask, why will the standards in my industry be useful to me? Are they not too generic to apply to the particular circumstances which my company has to cope with? Perhaps and perhaps not. The first question to address is whether or not your company is using any kind of standard against which you recruit, train, assess, develop and advance your employees. If the answer is 'yes', as it was in my case years ago, it may be that standards offer you little. If the answer is 'no' then I contend that standards, at the very least, give you an excellent starting point for the creation of a logical, consistent suite of HR systems. There is also a middle point and that is where my experience has now led me to believe that I could have benefited from being more open minded in using standards when I was a training and development manager. Let us take these scenarios one by one.

My company has a set of internal standards and they work for us   If you are in this enviable situation then the existence of standards may well be of no concern for you other than as a means by which your company monitors whether it is keeping in line with the way your industry is progressing. Your most effective role could be to participate in your ILB's or NTO's continuing activities in developing and refining your industry's standards and giving of your expertise to help others in less fortunate circumstances. On the other hand, it may be well worth your while investigating opportunities where standards could be applied specifically to your T & D activities.

My company has no internal set of standards   For people in your position the existence of standards is a godsend. Standards offer a starting point from which you can work on many aspects of T & D, not least how to create for yourself a system for measuring effectiveness. They can provide a ready-made framework upon which you can base your HR systems and policies. Even if you are only concerned with T & D, standards offer a basis by which you can assess how staff competence measures up to what is demanded in the industry. I believe that in most large companies internal standards will exist and they will work, to a greater or lesser extent, for the benefit of the company. In small and medium sized enterprises (SMEs), however, my experiences indicate that the resources just do not exist to devote the time and money to creating company specific standards. So they either have none, and therefore have sporadically consistent HR systems and policies, or they use standards. If you are in the former camp try standards.

My company has internal standards but I am unsure what they mean   This was my situation in the past. In my experience it meant that the company had decided what it required some time ago. If this is where you find yourself, then your HR systems may be well integrated and staff assessed against well thought out objectives. But how relevant are these objectives in today's changing and changed business world? Have the internal standards been constantly examined and updated to ensure their viability? If not, then standards can be a terrific starting point for such a review and not just in a narrow T & D sense. They can cut out much hard work by offering an insight into what your industry believes to be the most important competencies for its workforce. Standards will save you time; you do not need to start from scratch.

The major question in all of these scenarios is what level of objectivity can you claim for any standards which you employ? The beauty of the standards I am speaking of is that they are not slanted toward a particular company culture but reflect, in the purest sense, the things which the individual must do to prove that they are competent at a particular activity. There is an argument about the generic nature of standards, about how they cannot cover the needs of individual companies. In my opinion the fact that standards are generic is a strength. For example, when a standard speaks of 'relevant people' it enables you to specify who those are for your company. When they speak of 'all information' they allow you to decide what is relevant for your situation. Standards do not box you in; they offer a flexible framework which you can mould to suit your needs.

What use are standards in training and development?

I do not know about you but I have been asked, or told, many times by management or clients that they need to know how they can measure the value of training interventions. Indeed, I had one manager, and now have one colleague, who devoted significant time and energy trying to devise a means of measuring the effectiveness of training. There is a plethora of writing on the subject and a number of complex models which delve into the depths of statistical analysis to offer us the means by which we can convince sceptical line managers of the value of training, especially so-called soft skills training.

I used to offer, design and deliver programmes which met the specific individual need. In my strategy I calculated that if my T & D interventions improved staff skills and solved day-to-day problems for the managers simultaneously, then the managers would stop whining about the costs and time and, even if they were not supportive of T & D, they would at least tolerate training. It worked for me but what if it had not? I was lucky because my then employer had the cash to afford the luxury of a well-funded T & D programme. Many of you may not be so fortunate, so what can you do?

You will not be surprised to discover that I believe one answer is to use standards. They are the perfect means by which to assess a person's ability to perform an activity competently. All of the statistical models in the world cannot tell you whether or not a person can lead a team in a satisfactory manner. With luck they tell you if the performance is better than when last observed. Standards can tell us if the person can lead a team; because the person has to prove that they are capable of leading a team. The standards give us a series of measures by which we can gauge their ability and therefore enable us to say that the person is, or is not, competent to the level which we desire.

Let us look again at the standard reproduced in this chapter. It is but one piece of a portion of the Standards in Personnel Management. The unit where it appears, 'Improve training and development programmes', has three component parts. They cover 'identifying', 'planning the introduction of' and 'implementing' improvements to training and development programmes. They cover ten pages and are the result of painstaking work to define exactly what is required for an individual to carry out these activities competently.

This is not something any of us could just sit down and write – I know from personal experience that it took many months to come up with the agreed standards. Yet, what many of us try to do when we attempt to define measures of peoples' performance and potential is to create things from scratch. Why bother to reinvent the wheel? If you can identify or devise training or experiential events which will educate a person to improve training and development programmes then these standards will not only allow you to measure their subsequent performance, they will also allow you to measure the effectiveness of the training.

Does this mean that you will need to begin offering S/NVQs and have to cope with all of the bureaucracy these allegedly impose? No. S/NVQs are becoming ever more popular but they do not necessarily suit everybody.

I believe that for the SME, S/NVQs are an excellent and cost-effective means of training staff and assessing their performance. It means you do not have to have complex in-house T & D systems. Certainly you pay for the person to attempt the qualification, but it is less costly than having to develop your own systems, and if you end up with a more competent workforce, then the return on investment will surely be worthwhile. For the T & D manager, S/NVQs offer an ideal solution to the problems of either designing and delivering programmes and/or choosing training providers and assessing the worth of the intervention. By its very nature an S/NVQ measures the worth of the training provided when the staff member is assessed for competence. Wherever the gaps are in their portfolio of proof of competence, there are the gaps in the training provision.

Some other companies, large and small, while accepting the principles of standards still wish to impose their style, language and culture upon them. They employ firms to write and install competency frameworks for them. This process is the same as when one writes standards, but the product will be company specific and, possibly, more detailed than a standard. The underlying principles remain however; namely to provide a means by which the company can assess and improve the competence of the workforce and a means by which the individual can assess their own competence and improve their performance and career prospects. The value to the T & D function is that the framework will provide a means of measuring the value of the training programmes offered. Sometimes this is merely a spin-off but it exists and should be used. It saves you time, allows you to take the debates about the value of training programmes, and gives you a series of measuring tools which can win that debate with the line manager.

Let's face it, if you can approach a line manager with a clear description of an activity at which his or her staff must be competent, if you can demonstrate

that some training is required to bring people to an acceptable level of competence, and if you can then demonstrate that your staff have achieved that level
of competence then the line manager will probably be convinced of the value
of the proposed training? In fact one of the reasons the line manager may not
be convinced is because we, as HR, are sometimes a little too timid to enter
into the debate. But that is a subject for another chapter in another book.

Where can you find out more?

There are a host of organizations that can give you further information about
the standards that apply to your industry or sector.

If you know the NTO for your industry or sector they are the best place
to begin. If not, then the next best place to enquire is the Qualifications and
Curriculum Authority or Scottish Qualifications Authority, who will be able
to put you in touch with your NTO. Others who can help include TECs and
LECs, the CBI and the Department for Education and Employment. If you are
a member of an industry or sector group which meets regularly, say for
benchmarking purposes, your colleagues may have some contact numbers for
you. Here are some of the main organizations' telephone numbers.

QCA	0171 387 9898
SQA	0141 248 7900
DfEE	0114 275 3275
TEC National Council	0171 735 0010
Investors in People	0171 467 1900
NTO National Council	0114 261 9926
Scottish Council of NTOs	0131 228 4010

However you decide to pursue your new-found interest in standards it should
not take more than a couple of calls to get to an individual who can give the
requisite information.

Just remember, standards can help us all. They are a tool, available to make
our lives in T & D easier. They may not suit our purposes perfectly but if we
use them sensibly, who knows, even creatively, they can save us time and
money.

Further reading

Anderson, L. W. and Sosniak, A. (1994), *L. Bloom's taxonomy – a forty year
retrospective*, Chicago, Illinois: The National Society for the Study of
Education.

Burke, J. (1988), *Competency Based Education and Training*, London: Falmer Press.

Holyfield, J. and Moloney, K. (1996), *Using National Standards to Improve Performance*, London: Kogan Page.

Jessup, G. (1991), *Outcomes – NVQs and the Engineering Model of Education and Training*, London: Falmer Press.

Chapter 7

Learning styles and the learning organization

Alan Mumford

What we know about managerial learning

The idea that organizations should be capable of encouraging, and making available to others, learning by their individual members has emerged as one of the energizing ideas about organizations in the 1990s. The attention, one may almost say the excitement, generated amongst human resource practitioners by the concept of the learning organization has a number of roots. One has been that the concept of the learning organization, and the practices associated with it, gives management developers access to levels of the organization to which they may not previously have had entry. Another is that management developers are historically overexcited by discoveries in their field. Whether it is case studies, management by objectives, outdoor training or action learning, they seem ever ready and willing to take on new ideas. This may have its positive aspect but the consistent inability to recognize the fact that particular methods of development may be suitable for some purposes but not others (Mumford, 1997) is less commendable.

Recently there has been a gradual but consistent move towards using normal work in the development of managers rather than relying on methods such as courses detached from the reality of managerial experience. In its best forms, the learning organization encourages its members to look at everything they do at work as a potential learning opportunity. For example, people often claim that they learn from both successes and mistakes in their work – but they also say that mistakes are covered up or punished rather than treated explicitly and deliberately as useful learning. An organization that provides an environment in which both mistakes and successes are so reviewed is at least partially on the way to becoming a learning organization.

Nor do we have to express these issues in quite such stark terms as successes or mistakes. I was involved recently with a company which had, 18 months previously, acquired another business and was looking at a further acquisition. When I asked them whether they had learned a lot from the first acquisition they replied: 'Oh yes, a tremendous amount'. But when I then pressed them on where the information about the previous acquisition had been captured, and therefore how accessible it was to those involved in the new acquisition, there was a stunned silence. An example like this illustrates the point that a learning organization captures and uses experience, knowledge, skills and insights in many different forms. (Honey and Mumford, 1996)

Creating effective learning environments

We know at least three things about managerial learning which ought to impact on our approach in trying to create effective learning environments:

1.   All learning is individual.
2.   Much learning is, however, achieved through interaction with others.
3.   Most managerial learning occurs in and around the job although courses sometimes provide splendid injections.

In his book *The Fifth Discipline*, which created much of the interest in the learning organization, Peter Senge said: 'Individual learning does not guarantee organisational learning. But without it no organisational learning occurs' (Senge, 1990). Unfortunately, neither the writing of Senge and his followers, nor that of most other writers on the learning organization, carry through with this obvious yet crucial comment. The subsequent sequel, *The Fifth Discipline Fieldbook*, for example, has two pages on learning processes – but over 100 on the so-called systems approach. Nor do other writers pay much attention to the role of individual learners – they ascend quickly into the rarefied atmosphere of the learning organization, all too often proposing values far removed from the rather more prosaic reality of most managers.

It may seem unfair to criticize Senge, who after all also says that a learning organization is one in which 'people are continually learning how to learn'. The problem is that this is nowhere addressed in his book. The individual learner is the base of the attempt to create a learning organization. This can be expressed as a learning pyramid shown in Figure 7.1.

One use of this model is to emphasize that a learning organization is created through effort at different levels (again, to be fair to Senge, he has given a great deal of emphasis to what he calls team learning although I prefer the term group learning). Unfortunately, the learning organization literature wholly ignores one-to-one learning relationships; yet such relationships are crucial in the effective creation of a complete integrated learning environment but are especially important to management development people who want to try and influence the creation of their own learning organization.

The learning pyramid

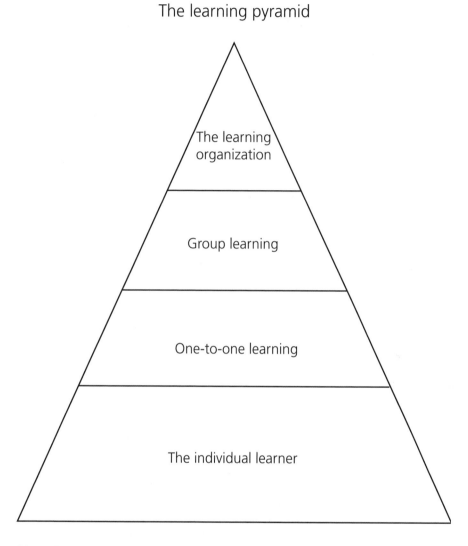

Figure 7.1   The learning pyramid

If we want to talk to other people about learning in the organization, it would seem desirable that we have some sort of model (no doubt many would prefer to avoid the word 'theory') about how learning occurs. Even better, we would also have some idea of our own preferred approach to learning and that of anyone we are trying to help.

The idea and practice of the learning cycle, and the great discovery of individual preferences about learning, also ought to be deployed. This is a practical example of how to use an aspect of management development with which many people have become very familiar over the last 15 years and which can improve our capacity to introduce something new. Attempts to introduce the learning organization ought to take account of individual learning style preferences in two ways: first, by recognizing that no single process either of learning, or of ways of introducing learning as an issue, is likely to be equally attractive to all individuals. Second, by designing interventions in the knowledge that we have our own different learning preferences and that we will be faced with people who may have their own different preferences.

Learning style preferences

All trainers will have had the experience that individuals, despite having apparently the same needs, learn differently from the same experience. Not only do they learn different things; they actually have strongly operational preferences about the ways in which they like to learn. So one individual faced with, for example, outdoor training will describe it as the most stimulating learning experience of his or her life, whereas another on exactly the same course with apparently the same needs for teamwork and leadership will describe it as irrelevant. Some individuals learn a great deal by observing the actions of others at meetings, and modelling effective behaviours. Others at the same meeting with the same participants have no such interest. Some individuals respond very well to the idea of keeping a regular learning log or diary – others see no point in such a process.

David Kolb was the person who developed the first diagnostic tool, called the Learning Styles Inventory, to help identify which individuals had which preferences (Kolb, 1984). With my colleague, Peter Honey, I developed a different tool – the Learning Styles Questionnaire (LSQ) and this is now used in more than 30 countries. The technical details of the LSQ, and ideas on its use are provided in a technical guide (Honey and Mumford, 1992; 1995). For most trainers the practical use of the LSQ has been to provide better for differences in preferred ways of learning through the more effective design of courses and through the recognition of the different needs of participants.

In a more general development context, the LSQ has been found to be particularly helpful in drawing up individual development plans which can specifically recognize the likelihood of an individual learning effectively from any particular activity. Individuals can then either choose to avoid activities which they are likely to find frustrating, or alternatively – and more desirably – can see that they need to develop those styles in which they are less strong in order to become better all-round learners. There is now considerable literature, referred to in the technical guide, on how people have used the LSQ.

The proposition in this chapter is that just as the LSQ can be used in identifying preferences about learning amongst individuals, it serves the same purpose, perhaps even more powerfully, in identifying the likely approach of trainers or tutors to what they are predisposed to offer. If trainers favour learning in a particular way, the likelihood is that they will offer learning to others in the same kind of way. This may seem a remarkably obvious conclusion. I find, however, that on the Learning To Learn Workshops that I run, it is often in practice, a great revelation to trainers! They recognize fully and consciously for the first time the impact that their own preferences have on what they provide, how they provide it and how others respond to it. This chapter extends this discovery to the likely approach that trainers and developers may take to the learning organization, and the likely responses of others to those who wish to initiate such a process.

The four learning styles

Honey and Mumford identify four learning styles, which initially we express through 'General Descriptions'. These are deliberately expressed as managerial and professional behaviours, not initially as explicit statements about the ways in which individuals will learn. The original reason for this was that since we saw learning as being mainly focused on the work that managers and professionals do, it seemed more helpful to encourage people to consider learning by thinking of their most frequent behaviours, rather than specific statements about learning behaviours which most of them would not recognize. This original design feature in fact becomes even more useful in the context of the learning organization, since the 'learning in and around the job' focus is even more appropriate in that context. The four learning styles are summarized below:

Activists like new experiences, crises, being thrown in at the deep end, being involved with other people and fighting fires. They enjoy business games and role-playing exercises. They do not like solitary work or being asked to review experiences to see what they have learned from them.

Reflectors like collecting information through reading, or through observing others in action. Whereas activists quite enjoy being thrown in at the deep end, reflectors like to think, organize and plan before taking action. (They therefore tend to be effective at finding out which is the deep end!) They provide information within a learning group, both about the facts the group should be considering, and feedback from observation about how the group itself is operating. They do not enjoy situations where they are forced into the limelight in things like role-plays, or where their work or learning activities seem to them to be unduly rushed.

Theorists prefer things to be offered to them as part of a system, a model, a concept or theory. They like checking the theory and perhaps disagreeing with it, and will often claim to prefer events which intellectually stretch them. They like structure and clear purpose. They are much less attracted to situations which emphasize emotion and feeling. They dislike what they perceive as shallow, gimmicky or unsupported ideas or techniques. They dislike being involved with participants or tutors who they see as of lower intellectual calibre.

Pragmatists insist on a direct link between what they are asked to learn and what they may be able to do in their job. If a technique seems relevant they like the chance to try it out. They respond well to learning activities with high face validity such as action learning and some simulations. They dislike learning experiences centred on things which seem unlikely to be practised in their own organization. If statements of general theory or practice are offered, particularly if drawn from organizations different from their own, they may reject the experience.

Individual learning style preferences can tell us something about the likely reaction of particular individuals to specific behaviours and practices designed to create a learning organization. For example, a learning organization would be one in which all experiences are reviewed so that learning is squeezed from them. The acquisition case earlier in this chapter illustrates the issue of learning styles. If the individuals involved were all strong theorists concerned with creating models and structures, or strong activists basically concerned just with driving the acquisition through, then the desired reviewing and reflecting behaviour is much less likely to occur. Of course, there are issues here about broadening the basis of selection of teams so that there is a balance of learning styles.

Managers responsible for trying to help create learning organizations could also use learning styles information to assess likely reactions to a learning organization. The reaction of line managers to the idea of a learning organization, and even more to the particular behaviours and practices necessary to create it will be substantially affected by what they prefer to do as learners – not just by general propositions that learning is a good thing, or that a learning organization is desirable. Some line managers will favour some aspects of effective learning organization practices, others will not. Learning style preferences explain some aspects of this:

● Activists may well respond enthusiastically to the idea of learning from real work rather than being sent away on courses. They are much less likely to follow through with review sessions about what is being learned, how it is being learned or with whom the learning is being shared. They are less likely to want highly organized structured plans for creating the learning organization. They are less likely to give substantial time to formal processes designed to create the learning organization or to review its effectiveness. They are most likely to be suspicious of the term itself, seeing it perhaps as 'theoretical' or 'typical' flavour of the month personnel jargon.

- Reflectors will be particularly enthused about the opportunities for creating and collecting data. They will see this in general terms in relation to managerial experiences, but also in terms of responding to questionnaires about the learning organization (or for example the Learning Styles Questionnaire results). They will like comparing results individually or between units. In contrast to Activists they will want to spend time in deciding what a learning organization actually means and how good the existing organization is in learning terms. There is some risk that they will spend more time reviewing and analysing information than in acting on it, for example in setting up the disciplines and processes necessary for a learning organization.

- Theorists are likely to be interested in the term, but they will want to debate different interpretations of it. What are the differences between the definitions of Senge, Pedler and Honey and Mumford? How crucial are concepts such as 'double loop learning' and 'defensive routines'? They are quite likely to be attracted to the idea of a systematic attempt to create a learning organization – and may therefore be particularly attracted to Senge's approach because it is very much a systems approach. They are quite likely to go for a 'big bang' approach in any area for which they are responsible, rather than setting up pilot exercises in particular units, or taking up particular features of a learning organization and working through them slowly and perhaps pragmatically over time.

- Pragmatists will be encouraged if the particular theme of the learning organization towards which they are turned by initiators is actually using current reality as a learning experience. They would, for example, seize eagerly on the acquisitions case given earlier, and be quite enthusiastic about filling a flip chart with similar situations in their own organization from which more effective learning could have been produced. They would be less happy with any work on the learning organization which leaves them with a diagnosis of the present situation, without any indications of what they can do as a result. Moreover, what they should do must be expressed in very direct and practical terms.

The link between a learning organization and individual learning styles is both important and convenient. It is important because it is a way of understanding better the likely reaction of individuals to the whole idea, and this in turn will help in offering guidance on how to learn more effectively within such an organization. It is convenient because the Learning Styles Questionnaire is already widely used and may therefore provide an already familiar base for such understanding. The next step, of course, is for individual learners to help others to learn – which is primarily what the learning organization is intended to achieve as well.

Of course, the learning organization will make use of these differences in Learning Style Preferences, not only to predict how individuals may respond to the idea, but to try and create more effective learning partnerships. Individuals can be assisted to recognize each other's strengths and weaknesses in learning terms and thereby accept the desirability of joint effort to stimulate effective learning in an organization. For example, the strengths of a strong activist, driving ahead quickly to get things done, can be matched with a strong reflector who will try and ensure that the results of quick action are reviewed, so learning can be applied throughout the organization. Learning Styles also can be used to create project teams or task forces, using a mix of people who, again, will work together to ensure that the team and the organization as a whole creates more effective learning.

Further reading

Honey, P. and Mumford, A. (1992), *Manual of Learning Styles*, Maidenhead: Honey.

Honey, P. and Mumford, A. (1995), *Learning Styles Questionnaire Facilitator Guide Organisation Design and Development*, USA: King of Prussia.

Honey, P. and Mumford, A. (1996), *How to Manage Your Learning Environment*, Maidenhead: Honey.

Kolb, D. (1984), *Experiential Learning*, Englewood Cliffs: Prentice-Hall.

Mumford, A. (1997), *How to Choose the Right Development Method*, Maidenhead: Honey.

Senge, P. (1990), *The Fifth Discipline: The Art and Practice of the Learning Organization*, New York: Doubleday.

Senge, P. (1994), *The Fifth Discipline Fieldbook*, London: Nicholas Brealey.

Chapter 8

The manager as trainer

Alan George

As line managers are increasingly expected to take on development responsibilities, so trainers find themselves needing to instruct, coach and guide managers along the way. This chapter provides the rationale for managers learning the requisite training skills and indicates those developmental opportunities that training consultants can encourage managers to use.

Introduction

The first question I want to address in this chapter is this: why should a manager want to be a trainer? The answer depends on what we mean by 'training'. If we extend the term to include anything that contributes to the development of the staff they manage, then the case is hard to refute. In fact, effective managers have always found their own ways of encouraging their staff to develop; it can be seen as the management function that adds most value to their team's productivity.

New managers soon discover that their own success depends on having well motivated and competent staff. The challenge for many is to know how to develop this motivation and build competencies.

In this chapter we start by considering in what sense a manager can be a trainer. We shall then next look at the behaviours you would expect to see in a manager who is thinking creatively about the development of his or her staff.

Work-based training opportunities present themselves every day. So how can managers organize their own work and that of their team members to grasp these opportunities? A range of activities will be considered in this chapter including: coaching, delegating, mentoring, work shadowing and secondment, and group development activities such as team meetings and project work. There will also be a brief look at the opportunities in bringing training to the desktop through open and flexible learning and the use of

Web-based learning. The chapter concludes with some suggestions of how managers can be encouraged to develop the skills they will need to fulfil this role.

In what sense can a manager be a trainer?

Managers have their own work to complete as well as managing their team. This involves maintaining their professional practice and keeping in touch with the processes that they manage as well as dealing with budgets and maintaining relations and communications with other parts of the organization.

Yet, it is the management of people that remains at the centre of the role. Most managers would, for example, want to be closely involved in the recruitment and selection of their team members, even if they have the support of training and HR professionals in doing so. In smaller organizations more and more of the personnel functions are assumed by the manager with the help of occasional external inputs.

Managers are also responsible for the training and development of their personnel. In fact, managers who take this responsibility seriously have some distinct advantages over trainers – the most obvious being to identify their staff's training needs. Through their managing of operations they can monitor on a day-to-day basis the matching of tasks with competencies. Although under-performance may stem from other factors including, for example, bad management, a proportion of it comes from lack of training. The consequences of this lack will be evident to the manager as they observe how people tackle assignments.

The area where some managers score less well than trainers is in establishing robust relationships with their staff and providing staff development opportunities. Some managers kill off motivation in their concern for competence. Others rarely improve performance because they do not want to rock the boat. The closeness of working relations, particularly in small organizations, can sometimes mean that poor performance is tolerated by both managers and their teams. It can also work the other way round, particularly with small project teams. Pulling together to achieve clearly defined goals, the manager and team members can recognize skill gaps and systematically fill them.

However, it is a fact that most managers need some help in creating learning relationships with their staff. With help a manager can take an increasingly holistic view of the development of his or her staff. They can become a trainer and a developer, not just attending to skills needs of individuals but also working on the increased productivity of their teams in a number of other dimensions.

Where the environment is right, managers will see new assignments as an opportunity for all those involved, to learn and develop the new skills and knowledge that they need. A significant proportion of this learning can be generated within the workplace by managers who know how to act as staff developers. Managers can also use staff appraisal as the springboard for planned development during the ensuing months or year ahead.

How do you know a developmental manager when you see one?

Trainers who are looking for the distinctive features of the developmental manager need only look for those characteristics they would expect to find in other areas of effective management – vision matched with planning. The developmental manager has a deep commitment to get the best out of all his or her staff. This can only be achieved if matters are not left to chance. The latest fashionable idea will quickly be spotted by staff and assigned to the bin with other failed initiatives.

At a formal level, developmental management will manifest itself in a number of ways:

- Some form of written statement on staff development so that everyone knows the value that is attached to learning at work.
- A system for planning and communicating learning goals which the department or organization needs to meet if it is to maintain and improve the quality of what it does.
- Some clear linkage between periodic appraisals and development planning.
- A shared and equitable plan for the allocation of training budgets.
- Up-to-date individual records of any significant training that has been completed.

If this formal framework is established it becomes possible for many other procedural and cultural changes to occur. To achieve this, a manager will need to be encouraged to:

- Give time to each staff member so that they know what standards of work are being achieved.
- Treat appraisal as an opportunity to recognize achievement and motivate staff to new learning and improved performance.
- Remember what it was like not to know how to do something.
- Constantly practise and improve management skills in coaching and work-based training.

- Promote open dialogue on important issues that relate to what is being learnt in all aspect of the business.
- Ensure that knowledge is managed and used, not wasted and lost.

Work-based training opportunities

Here is a brief summary of the main opportunities that a trainer might point out as available to the developmental manager:

Coaching

Coaching can be described as 'helping or enabling an individual or a small group in the workplace, to acquire knowledge or develop a skill or skills which are needed to improve job performance' and should become a natural first option for managers. A manager can use coaching for:

- skills development, such as using a software package;
- performance development, such as prioritizing work assignments;
- behavioural development, such as working more effectively with a colleague.

Coaching is something people in the workplace and elsewhere do informally from time to time when someone comments, 'I'm not sure how to do this; can you help?' Unfortunately people will only ask for help if they work in a climate where it is safe to admit that you do not know. The power relationship that exists between some managers and their staff may make this a high-risk activity for the person who needs coaching. Coaching skills may therefore need to be assessed and improved through training.

The skills that managers need to develop include:

- Listening skills to establish what the learner already knows and assess how motivated they are to learn.
- Facilitation skills to help keep the focus on the learner so that the member of staff does the work and the manager supports them.
- Instructional skills to make clear presentations and demonstrations on how to perform tasks.
- Challenging skills to help the learner reassess performance.
- Feedback skills to enable the learner to develop their own sense of how well they are doing; this includes praising wherever it is justified.
- Assessing skills to test understanding and performance.

For futher information on coaching, see Chapter 23.

Delegation

Delegation creates excellent opportunities for managers to provide structured learning for their staff. Effective delegation also makes a major statement to staff about the levels of trust that exist in the organization. From the manager's point of view delegation may be the only way of getting the job done and staying sane; but it has to be done in a considered and consistent way. Last minute crisis delegation is likely to backfire with recriminations, such as 'I might as well have done it myself', or 'I don't know why she didn't do it herself'.

The skills that managers need to develop to use delegation as a staff development opportunity include:

- *Task assessment* – what competencies does the task call for? How important/urgent is the work?
- *Person assessment* – who has the potential to handle the work? What will they learn in doing it?
- *Contracting* – drawing up a clear set of objectives, lines of responsibility and deadlines for the work.
- *Giving feedback* – when to intervene, when to offer feedback and how to do it in a positive way.
- *Assessing* – reviewing the delegated task outcomes and the process the person used to achieve them.

Managers need to decide the extent and the limits of the delegation and talk them through with the person given the delegated work. The manager may:

- Agree a plan with the person being delegated the work which includes a definition of key stages when progress will be reviewed.
- Encourage the person being delegated the work to prepare their own plan for approval. It might be agreed that they will only report during the work, by exception, if an unforeseen obstacle or problem has arisen.
- Allow the person being delegated the work a free hand to complete the task in their own way to meet agreed objectives and standards. The manager should not consult them until the work is completed.

The choice of which level will depend on the complexity and duration of the work and the experience and competence of the person being delegated the work.

If the delegation is to be used to develop learning in the workplace, the manager needs to make sure that they discuss the learning outcomes of the activity, not just the results. What has the person being delegated the work learnt about their present level of competence? Where do they and the manager need to plan further training and development? The opportunity can also be used to praise people for their successes and efforts.

Mentoring

Mentoring can be described as 'an agreement between an experienced and a less experienced colleague, where the more experienced provides help and support to improve the mentee's job performance'. Mentoring can provide continuing and customized support for members of the team. For the manager who wants to achieve sustained growth of key members, mentoring schemes are well worth considering. However, it is not usual for the manager to act as mentor for their own staff. The ideal relationship would involve a degree of organizational distance between the mentor and the mentee, to increase confidentiality, objectivity and to free the dialogue from 'historical' assumptions and other personal baggage.

So the manager's main role may be:

● To identify situations where mentoring is feasible and desirable.
● To explain the mentoring scheme to participants and prepare them to get the most benefit.
● To help mentees define the type of help they are looking for.
● To help them identify suitable mentors in other parts of the organization or outside the organization.
● To monitor the progress and outcomes of the scheme.

Mentoring schemes may be set up for staff who are taking on new responsibilities or who need specific support to handle difficult assignments. Mentor schemes have also been a very effective support for equal opportunities initiatives. Indeed the manager who wants to develop his or her competency in training and developing staff should consider finding a mentor for themselves; a manager in another department who has experience of working in this way would be a suitable person.

As with coaching, the success of the process depends on developing and adhering to a contract. This needs to specify:

● learning objectives
● issues of confidentiality
● what help the mentor is able to offer
● what the mentee will do as their part of the contract
● frequency of meetings
● measures of attainment of objectives
● review dates
● closure of the contract.

For further information on mentoring, see Chapter 24.

Work shadowing and secondment

Good practice within the organization needs to be captured and disseminated; work shadowing can be a very effective way of doing this. Placing a new or inexperienced person for a while with someone who performs well should create plenty of opportunity for learning on the job. Of course, the manager needs to make sensible choices in setting up work shadowing. They need to select the staff member who will be shadowed, not just for their expertise, but also for the willingness to help a less experienced person. Again, it is important that the purpose of the work shadowing is fully discussed and agreed between all parties, so that an informal contract can be drawn up.

Secondment has the advantage of broadening staff experience and vision, by putting them in touch with practice in other parts of the organization or outside the organization. Longer secondments sometimes lead to changes in a career plan. Either the individual finds new work opportunities outside or they come back looking for ways of using the new things they have learnt. Managers therefore need to take care of the exit and re-entry of secondees. Often real learning opportunities are lost by putting the returning secondee back into the same slot or, worse still, one that makes no use of their new skills and knowledge.

Group development activities

As the manager acquires more confidence in the role of trainer/developer, he or she can begin to make more constructive use of the occasions when staff work together. This might start by a re-examination of the way team briefing meetings are run. Why not encourage supervisors and staff to take responsibility for researching a problem and proposing several solutions, with their own preferred option?

Making such events more interactive and more focused on everyone's learning will help establish greater trust and understanding. People who have attended training sessions can make short presentations supported by a paragraph or two of good ideas they picked up. People who have tackled the task of defining a new working practice can describe how it is to be applied.

Project work has its own momentum and energy; having clearly specified goals and working to deadlines in a small team can be very satisfying. A manager who wants to develop his or her staff can use the selection of team members and the definition of roles to exploit the diversity of competencies and experience in the group. Whatever project management procedure or software is used, time should also be set aside at intervals for process reviews. These provide space to ask how well the group is working, defining and solving problems and using its resources to the best advantage.

Training at the desk, or in the learning centre

With the advent of Web-based communications over company intranets or via the Internet, training is now being made available to staff at their own workstations. All the advantages of multimedia and computer-based training can now be delivered online to work-based learners. Web-based learning also gets over a number of the constraints of open learning or CD-ROM packages; it is live and can for example include direct feedback from a physically remote tutor. Learners can raise questions and communicate via e-mail with the tutor or with one another.

Managers who plan to use this type of learning as part of their training and development strategy will need to:

- Find a good source of Web-based material.
- Select programmes that match most closely organizational and departmental development goals.
- Ensure that their IT networks and PCs have the capacity to handle online material.
- Induct their staff in this new way of learning.
- Monitor progress.

Issues that the manager may need to address include:

- Reconciling work commitments with training commitments.
- Legitimizing this kind of training so that others do not interrupt or claim priority for other assignments.
- Recognizing that not all people like to learn in this way.

Some of these difficulties can be resolved by setting up a learning centre with a series of PC workstations, so that staff can leave their normal place of work and book in for a training session.

Getting the best out of training

In addition there are training courses provided within or outside the organization, which the trainer can bring to the attention of the developmental manager. But even when the manager does opt for this route he or she still has the responsibility of ensuring that this investment results in appropriate learning. Some organizations set up procedures which require managers to discuss with their staff any proposed attendance at training courses. The results of this discussion can be recorded on a form, a copy of which can be sent to the training provider. In this way the learning objectives of the participant can be explored and matched with those of the provider's published programme.

Sometimes the problems associated with getting value out of training are further upstream at the point when a workshop or course is chosen. Managers should take advice on this from professional trainers wherever they have access to them. Some training needs can only be met by sending staff outside the organization to 'open' courses. Other needs are so specific to the organization or involve so many staff that it is better, and probably cheaper, to commission a trainer to come and run a customized event. As with any other purchase, it is wise to seek professional advice before making major investments.

The manager also has a responsibility to evaluate the outcomes of the course. The most obvious way of doing this is to have a post-course discussion with the member of staff and to encourage them to share what they have learnt wherever appropriate.

How and when to get help

Trainers and training managers reading this chapter may have a range of reactions. Some of this chapter's content may seem very much part of the day-to-day practice in your organization, but there may be other issues where closer communication and support might provide new opportunities for staff development.

If you are a manager and work in a small company where there is no trainer, you might approach your local Training and Enterprise Council (TEC) and ask for access to their lists of approved trainers. In some cases you may also get other forms of support from your TEC. You may also have access to a professional body that can provide training, or you may have colleagues who can recommend a local provider.

In larger organizations you will have access to a training and development department. Talk to them about the advantages that you see in developing a learning environment for your staff. They should be delighted to respond to your approach; trainers often feel they have to struggle to get access to managers like you!

Further reading

Bentley, T. (1997), *Bridging the Performance Gap*, Aldershot: Gower.
Downes, S. (1995), *Learning at Work*, London: Kogan-Page.
George, A. (1997), *Train and Develop Your Staff*, Aldershot: Gower.
Hayes, J. (1996), *Developing the Manager as Helper*, London: Routledge.
Honey, P. (1994), *101 Ways to Develop Your People Without Really Trying*, Maidenhead: Peter Honey Publications.
MacLennan, N. (1995), *Coaching and Mentoring*, Aldershot: Gower.

Part Two

Best practice for training and development

Training and development (T & D) clearly has to be aligned with business planning but the individual processes and approaches that contribute to meeting the T & D objective are numerous.

In this section of the handbook you will find chapers that highlight the many varied disciplines and strategies that make up the territory of T & D. This includes everything from training needs analysis and programme design through to culture-changing T & D initiatives.

The breadth of contributions in this section of the handbook is indicative of the challenges that face training professionals. The skills that many trainers and managers have built up are not enough on their own. The challenge for the trainer is to be able to adjust and focus those skills to meet the changing needs of the business and the individual employee.

Chapter 9

The training process

Mike Wills

When people talk about the training process they usually mean the day-to-day activities that make up the annual training cycle. Concentrating on the process is the best place to start if you want a quick and significant improvement in training efficiency.

There are, however, several dangers in considering the training process in isolation. The most obvious is that the training provided may have little or no relevance either to business requirements or to the development needs of the people. Another danger is that maintaining the process can become an end in itself. Then training becomes inflexible and insensitive to change.

Of course, it is very easy to say that effective training has to be aligned with a company's business directions and values; that the training department has to provide courses which support the company's goals; and that anyone who is involved in managing the training process has to have a clear idea of where the business is going. All this assumes that those involved in running the business have a clear idea of where they are going. Unfortunately, this is not always the case. And when the foundation is not firm the training process is unable to support the business.

This means that for effective training we have to start with business basics.

Getting the basics right

Not every company uses the same method to ensure that the business is built on firm foundations, but the following is a summary of current thinking on the subject.

Alignment

The key to getting the basics right is making sure that everybody has the same understanding of the current situation and that everyone is pulling in the same direction for the future. Without alignment no company can make progress and no training department can provide effective training.

Philosophy

A philosophy is a statement of what the company stands for. It is a set of values and beliefs by which actions can be judged. A philosophy makes it clear which behaviours are appropriate and which are unacceptable. The following is a typical example:

> *We succeed through satisfied customers*
> *We value our employees*
> *We aspire to deliver quality and excellence in all that we do*
> *We require premium return on assets*
> *We use technology to deliver market leadership*
> *We are responsible members of society*

Mission

A mission is a statement of what a company or organization is here to do. A mission should describe what is done for whom in such a way that it can not be confused with anybody else's mission. An example of a mission for a training department might be: 'To provide sales training for XYZ's UK-based sales staff'.

Communicating the mission to every employee ensures that everybody knows what business they are in. It also helps to highlight any duplication or gaps in a company's structure. If you think a company's mission is so obvious that it hardly warrants the effort of defining it, be prepared for a shock. Try asking a selection of people what they think their department's mission is.

Assessment

The mission is about maintaining today's processes, but training and surviving in today's business environment is also about encompassing change.

Change always has its roots in the past and yet has to start in the present. There is not much point in deciding where you are going if you do not know where you started from.

Assessment is very much about understanding where the company is today, and determining the reasons for both success and failure.

Vision

A vision is a 'picture' of where the organization wants to be in the future. By describing the future in emotional rather than measurable terms, a vision can exert a strong pulling force which helps keep the organization aligned.

An example of a vision is: 'Every household will have their own wind-driven generator'. Describing events in pictorial terms, and from a future viewpoint where success has already been achieved, greatly enhances the probability of a vision coming to fruition. A vision provides a basis for deciding which actions should be taken.

Goals

Goals are quantitative figures, such as sales, profit and market share, that are established by top management. Goals put the flesh on the vision. Without goals the vision will remain only a dream.

Policies

A policy is a medium- to long-range course of action comprising a goal and a strategy (a 'what' and a 'how'). A strategy is the means of achieving the goal. Without the means a policy is only a slogan like 'Work Harder' or 'Think Smarter'. Imploring people to improve without providing the means cannot, and does not, work.

Be careful of how the word 'policy' is used, as it is often used interchangeably with 'philosophy' which has quite a different meaning.

Policy deployment

Policy deployment is the process of ensuring that the company's policies for quality, cost and delivery (QCD) are understood throughout the company. The way the system works in practice is that the policy is communicated across the organization as well as being cascaded down through the line managers.

Cross-functional communication of policies is very important because it binds the functions together in pursuit of the company goals. It helps functions co-operate instead of selfishly pursuing their own objectives at the expense of others. It is this subtle but important distinction that separates policy deployment from management by objectives (MBO). As a policy cascades down, all line managers are expected to translate the 'what' in the light of their own responsibilities, and to identify 'how' they will achieve the goals. As a result of this, the 'how' at one level becomes the 'what' at the next level down.

Policy deployment is a cyclical process. Progress against the goals should be checked, the reasons for any deviations (both positive and negative) diagnosed and the policies modified in the light of the diagnosis.

The company's attitude towards training

So far we have talked about the company getting its own house in order. A company that has already gone to this amount of trouble is very likely to be committed to training, but it would be a mistake to take this commitment for granted. If it is taken for granted, it often turns to apathy or resistance. It is also not worth going any further without obtaining a high level of commitment to training. However, senior management commitment to training is not enough by itself. The training department has to get its own house in order and the organization has to be aware of the importance that is attached to training.

The process for getting the basics right for any department is the same as for the whole company. This is no less true for the training function. As previously stated, training has to be aligned with the business direction of the company. If the company has got its basics sorted out, and communicated them effectively, the training function should be in no doubt as to which business directions and values should be supported.

Where there is a risk of fragmentation or misalignment of the training effort it is vital that all the key players within the training community agree on the following areas.

Training mission

Where there is more than one training organization within a company it becomes imperative that the 'coverage' provided by each training department is understood and well defined. This helps to avoid duplication and prevents training needs falling between the cracks. An example of a training department's mission could be: 'To provide sales and customer care training for all the sales representatives who work in the corporation's telecommunications division'.

Notice that this mission states what types of training are provided for which population of students. It can be inferred from the statement that this training department does not do technical training, but provides sales and customer training for telecommunications staff wherever they are located. If this is not true then the mission statement would have to be modified.

Training philosophy

The training philosophy is a statement of a company or organization's attitude towards training. It has to define clearly the importance that is attached to training. It has to be communicated, with conviction, to every employee. If the philosophy is just a set of words without the backing of real and practical commitment, the authors of the policy will soon be 'found out'.

Training policy

In the same way that a business policy has a goal and the means to attain the goal, a training policy should also have targets and measures. For example, having all employees oriented to the company's philosophy, ethics, values, principles and business priorities is a goal. Having new employees attend induction and quality training within three months of joining the company is the measure that will achieve the goal.

Following the principles of policy deployment, these measures now become the goals of the new employees' managers and of the training department. The managers will have to provide the means for releasing new employees for training within three months. The training department has to take measures to ensure the availability of training.

Training standards

The training policy will incorporate many of the training standards, such as:

- Hours of functional training per employee.
- Additional hours of training for managers.
- Minimum level of training before starting a new job.
- The amount and timing of induction training.

There are many other standards that also have to be agreed and met for the training process to run smoothly. The following are just a selection:

- trainer-to-student ratio
- trainer training
- trainer accreditation
- face-to-face percentage
- delivery-to-preparation ratio
- cost per student-day
- cost per trainer-day
- classroom standards
- administrative standards
- course development standards.

Definition of training

While it is essential to have a training philosophy, policy and standards, it is impossible to judge whether our training is in accordance with these if there is no clear definition of training. For example, a company might have a target to give each of its employee's five days of training every year. Depending on what is considered to be training, one company might say it is providing three days of training and another company might claim nine days – even though both companies' employees have received exactly the same amount of training and development!

An amazing number of activities might be considered as training. The following is just a selection:

- classroom (trainer led)
- distance learning
- computer-based training
- on-the-job training
- external courses
- large-scale workshops
- attendance at seminars
- attending exhibitions
- attending conferences
- attending communications meetings
- evening classes
- further education
- assignments
- participating in quality circles
- reading articles and books.

Some of the above activities, such as classroom training and computer-based training, would always be considered as training. Activities such as exhibitions, conferences, assignments and reading would not usually be classified as training.

Clearly, on-the-job training should be considered as training, but surely not all of the time spent under supervision should qualify for the employee's 'hours of training'. The conclusion we came to was that the time spent on producing usable output should not be included in the training time.

Without a definition of training, deciding whether an activity should be recognized as training becomes very subjective. The working definition of training that I use is: 'Training is the transfer of defined and measurable knowledge or skills'. From this definition it can be seen that training activities should have objectives and a method for checking whether these objectives have been met.

Having agreement on a definition of training is more important than which of the many good definitions you decide to use. This allows you to be aligned within your own company, and to make sensible comparisons with other companies.

If you have not already done so, this would probably be a good time to consider which activities in your company should be considered as training. The French Ministry of Work, Employment and Professional Training considers that training activities are those activities which are paid for by employers and take place in accordance with a programme which:

- has predetermined objectives
- specifies the teaching methods
- specifies the personnel to be used
- has an implementation plan
- assesses the results
- is given in premises separate from the production area unless it includes practical training
- can include correspondence courses, safety and security training and training outside of work hours.

The ministry specifies no set minimum duration for a training activity and any duration of course can be included in the minimum statutory time per worker (1.2 per cent) if the training agency agrees. However, in practice, the state does not often allow a training activity lasting less than a day to be included.

Training as part of the business

A useful approach for understanding the training process is to consider it as a system whose boundaries interact with the rest of the business (see Figure 9.1). Training needs are identified, training is provided to meet the needs, the output is compared to the requirements and any necessary changes are made to the system to obtain the desired output.

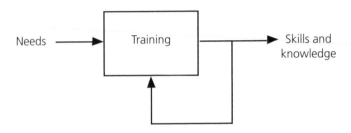

Figure 9.1   Training as a system whose boundaries interact with the business

However, while this approach helps you understand how training processes operate, it also puts training at the centre of the universe. The effect of this training-centred approach is that the business will see training either as a panacea for all problems or as having no direct relevance to the business. Neither of these impressions will help you manage the training process effectively.

A better approach is to extend the boundaries of the system so training is an integral part of the business (Figure 9.2).

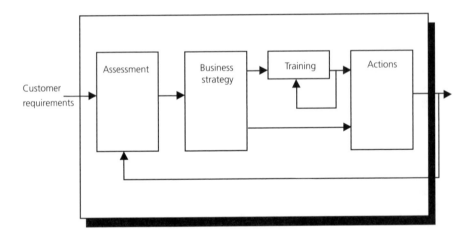

Figure 9.2   Training as part of the business system

Companies which have made this degree of progress have taken the first step towards being a 'learning organization'. There are many definitions of a learning organization but the one I like (based on Pedler, Burgoyne and Boydell) is: 'A learning organization is one which facilitates the learning of all its members and continuously transforms itself to achieve superior competitive performance'.

The training process

Having established where training fits into the business, we can now take a look at the training process itself. The fundamental elements of any process are as follows.

Accountability and responsibility

No process will work efficiently unless somebody 'owns' or is accountable for the process. The accountable person is the person whose telephone rings when something goes wrong with any part of the process. This person is like the captain of a ship, ultimately accountable for everything that happens on board even though the crew is responsible for carrying out most of the tasks.

The training manager is the 'owner' of the training process. This makes the training manager accountable for every step as well as the entire training process. Being accountable for every step is tough, because the responsibility for carrying out many of the individual steps lies with other people. It is the training manager who has to make sure nothing falls down the cracks between the steps of the process.

Identifying the stakeholders

A stakeholder is a person who has a vested interest in the outcome of the process. Stakeholders often have a positive or negative impact on the outcome of a process, even though they might not take a direct part in it. This is especially true if the process involves 'treading on their turf'. This makes it vital for you to involve stakeholders during the early stages of process design. Managing directors, heads of departments, and human resource managers are all stakeholders in the training process.

Defining and documenting the training process

Definition of a process involves establishing the beginning and end points of your process. Although defining the boundaries is, to some extent, arbitrary, the following guidelines should help you decide:

- The beginning of your process is where you take over control from someone else.
- The end of your process is where you hand over control to another person.

The easiest way of documenting a process is to tape some sheets of flip-chart paper together and use 'Post-it' notes to represent the steps of the process. You already have the beginning and end points, so these can be stuck on to the sheets straight away. Stick additional steps on the sheets until you have a series of related steps that connect the end point to the beginning point. Make sure you use a verb and a noun to describe each step in the process. This clarifies what is involved in each step and separates one step from another. 'Select course' is different to 'Develop course' which in turn is different to 'Deliver course'.

A brief overview of the steps of the training process follows.

- *Identify needs*   The process starts off by identifying the business needs and turning these needs into training requirements.
- *Evaluate needs*   A check is made to ensure that the requested, or mandated, training is suitable for the people concerned. A check is also made to make sure that training can meet the identified need. In the cases where training is not a suitable approach the need has to be analysed further so that alternatives to training can be suggested.
- *Select courses*   Given that the business need is one where training can make a contribution, the next step is to identify suitable courses. The choice will be between using an existing company course, buying an external course, and developing a new course.
- *Develop courses*   If no suitable courses are available, new courses have to be developed and piloted.
- *Determine workload*   At this stage you should be able to make your first estimate of the resources you will need to meet the training need.
- *Select trainers*   Before a course can be delivered suitable trainers need to be identified. If you do not have sufficient trainers to meet the expected workload, you will need to start the process of recruiting new trainers.
- *Develop trainers*   It is likely that the trainers you select to run new courses will need further development of their own skills and knowledge. If you are developing people to be trainers, you will need to put them through a programme of training and experiences before you allow them to train unassisted. Depending on the level and frequency of the courses, this could take from three months to a year.
- *Certify trainers*   If a course is new to the trainers, they should undergo a programme of observation and practice to ensure that they reach the required standard before they are allowed to deliver the course by themselves.
- *Identify location and resources*   Before advertising the dates of the proposed courses it is best to make sure that appropriate locations and resources are available.

- *Finalize budget*   By this stage you should have enough information to know how much it is going to cost to meet the training need. Negotiations over the actual budget are started.
- *Finalize training plan*   After budget negotiations are complete you will need to make adjustments to the training plan. Often there will be more demand for a course than there are places available so it will be necessary to prioritize the candidates. Prioritizing should still be done even if sufficient places are available, because the people most in need of the course will still get trained if budgets are cut later in the year.

  The training plan is built up throughout the early steps of the training process and it is at this stage that the finalized plan can be put together ready for presentation to senior management.
- *Pre-course administration*   Once the training plan has been agreed the course administrator has to ensure that the identified people get to the right course, at the right time.
- *Prepare course*   Before the courses can be delivered the trainers need to prepare themselves, the materials and the training rooms. The trainees also need to prepare themselves for the course.
- *Deliver course*   Although course delivery is the culmination of all the efforts that have been put into the previous steps, it should be remembered that, as far as the rest of the organization is concerned, this is only the start of the change process.
- *Validate training*   Validation is the process of ensuring that the course meets and continues to meet its stated objectives. Tests, observations and student feedback are all data that have to be analysed to determine whether the objectives are being met.
- *Post-course administration*   As soon as the training has been completed attendance on the course should be noted on the students' training records.
- *Transfer learning*   The students then have to use the knowledge and practise the skills to ensure that the learning is transferred into the business.
- *Evaluate training*   As with any process, the training process should have a method of ensuring that it has had the desired effect.
- *Revise courses*   The courses then need to be revised to incorporate the changes identified during evaluation.

Checkpoints

If you are managing this process you need to establish checkpoints to keep the process on track, under control and producing the required outputs. Checkpoints can occur at the beginning, during and at the end of the process. Checks at the beginning answer the question of whether the correct outputs will be produced. Checks during the process answer the question of whether the correct outputs are being produced. Checks at the end answer the question of whether the correct outputs have been produced. Deviations that you detect early on in the process are easier and cheaper to correct than those found at the end of the process. The major checkpoints of the training process are:

- needs analysis and evaluation
- pilot courses (within course development)
- trainer certification
- finalize budget
- finalize training plan
- course preparation
- validate training
- evaluation.

The most important checkpoint is evaluating the needs. If we identify the needs incorrectly, all else that follows is built on sand.

Responsibility

The training manager should also identify, by name, the people responsible for carrying out each task or step in the process. Attaching a person's name to a responsibility is a sure way of flushing out conflicting responsibilities, gaps and potential overloading.

If more than one person is involved in a process step, one of them should be given the prime responsibility so that nobody can ever say: 'I thought that was somebody else's responsibility to make sure that the task was completed'.

Additional responsibility matrices should be drawn up if there is more than one training organization in the company. The additional matrices should clearly show which courses or types of course are covered by the responsibilities.

Continuous improvement of the process

We should always be looking for ways of continually improving the training process. There are two main ways of improving a process: reducing errors and reducing cycle time (the time it takes to go from the beginning to the end of a process).

To do this you should have a close look at your process by documenting what actually happens at every step. When you design a new process it is very likely that you will have designed an ideal one. It will not show gaps, duplication, dead ends, confusing responsibilities or activities that add no value to the end product.

You can now compare your actual process with the ideal and make sure that gaps are plugged, duplication and dead ends eliminated, and responsibilities clarified.

The long-term view

The training process is a cycle and the cycle time is short term – usually no longer than a year. Managing the training process is essentially operational or tactical but if we always manage training at this level we are in danger of being reactive rather than proactive and may fail to deliver what the business really needs.

We therefore need to have a clear idea of how we are going to deliver training over a longer period and the training strategy provides the long-term orientation.

To put a training strategy together you should have a 'vision' of what training in your organization should look like in, say, five years. You should then map out the years and the key milestones along the way. When you are putting a training strategy together you should ask yourself the following questions:

- How much training will you need to do each year?
- What type of courses will you need to provide?
- What types of people will you put on what type of course?
- What resources will you need in terms of space and trainers?
- Who will you use to do your training?
- Will you use full-time, part-time or consultant trainers?
- What delivery methods will you use?
- How will changes in technology affect delivery methods?
- What business, social and environmental changes are likely to take place?

Every time you cycle through the training process you should re-examine your training strategy to see if it still holds up in the light of new training requirements and corporate policies. This is an example of 'double loop learning'. Try to make your strategy as robust as possible, and only change strategies when there are significant business, social and environmental changes. If your strategy is really robust you will find that you can respond to many changes by adjusting your tactics rather than throwing away your strategy.

It is difficult but essential to find the right balance between constantly chopping and changing strategies, and sticking with a useless and outmoded strategy.

Conclusion

What I have tried to emphasize here is that for effective training to take place it must be wedded to the business. Managers who are trying to implement training strategies need to understand what business objectives training is trying to support and then work out the best ways to deliver them.

Only once the training department has agreed its own basics can it apply itself to the training process. The steps I have outlined here are, of necessity, very brief but if training managers ensure that they are followed then they can have confidence that their training will be serving both individual and business needs.

Further reading

Argyris, C. and Schon, D. A. (1978), *Organizational Learning*, Wokingham: Addison-Wesley.

Barrington, H. and Reid, M. (1997), *Training Interventions: Managing Employee Development*, Institute of Personnel and Development.

Bartram, S. and Gibson, B. (1997), *Training Needs Analysis*, 2nd edn, Aldershot: Gower.

Bentley, T. (1990), *The Business of Training*, Maidenhead: McGraw-Hill.

Boydell, T. H. and Leary, M. (1996), *The Identification of Training Needs*, BACIE.

Bramley, P. (1996), *Evaluating Training Effectiveness*, Maidenhead: McGraw-Hill.

Goldstein, I. (1992), *Training in Organizations: Needs Assessment, Development and Evaluation*, 3rd edn, New York: Brooks-Cole.

Imai, Masaaki (1989), *Kaizen*, Maidenhead: McGraw-Hill.

Newby, A. C. (1994), *Training Evaluation Handbook*, Aldershot: Gower.

Pedler, M., Burgoyne, J. and Boydell, T. (1991), *Learning Company. A Strategy for Sustainable Development*, Maidenhead: McGraw-Hill.

Pedlar, M., Boydell, T. and Burgoyne, J. (1988), *Learning Company Project Report*, Sheffield: Training, Enterprise and Education Directorate of the Employment Department.

Rae, L. (1997), *How to Measure Training Effectiveness*, 3rd edn, Aldershot: Gower.

Rae, L. (1997), *Planning and Designing Training Programmes*, Aldershot: Gower.

Senge, P. M. (1990), *The Fifth Discipline: The Art and Practice of the Learning Organization*, New York: Doubleday.

Thurbin, P. J. (1994), *Implementing The Learning Organisation*, London: Pitman Publishing.

Wills, M. (1998), *Managing the Training Process: Putting the Principles into Practice*, 2nd edn, Aldershot: Gower.

Chapter 10

Identifying training needs

Sharon Bartram and Brenda Gibson

Are organizations today getting a complete makeover? Are they changing from places where we go to every day expecting a job for life to becoming instead dispersed communities of remote workers?

In this chapter we set out to describe the new order of organizations and take a critical look at the process of identifying training needs, putting it into context for trainers and managers alike. We will also consider how to put the process into practice and see how it can work for different types of organizations. After each section you will be asked to consider a number of questions so that you can make use of these ideas in your own organization.

The business context

Commentators on businesses today are painting a picture of great change. Even the language they use is new; Senge (1990) describes business as the 'learning organization', Handy, the 'virtuality dimension' (see Pugh, 1997) and so on. It is true that there is a tendency towards a different type of organization, one with a flatter structure where, in theory at least, people are more able to take control of what they do. If you read Senge's *The Fifth Discipline* (1990) then you will quickly see that the organization is becoming the new religion; turning up for work is not enough anymore, giving your heart and soul to the organization and feeling good about this level of involvement is the current message.

So where does that leave processes such as identifying training needs? Is there still room for them in today's businesses? We think so, because not all organizations are embracing the new order and even if they are they need to be able to direct resources to develop people in appropriate ways to meet their business objectives.

There is also a range of organizations out there. At one end of the spectrum there are the 'next generation' organizations – the knowledge organizations where it has been recognized that the core of the business is based inside the heads of all of the employees. These organizations promote creativity and innovation and at the same time look for ways to guarantee loyalty among their workers. At the other end of the spectrum one might place the more traditional businesses following more of a Taylorist/scientific approach to management. The characteristics of Taylorist businesses are in a strict hierarchical structure with managers deciding how the work should be done and workers doing as they are told (see Table 10.1).

Table 10.1 *Characteristics of different types of organization*

Knowledge organization	Scientific management organization
• More about learning needs than training needs.	• Measuring people against a specific standard.
• Freer, open ended, creative methods.	• Closed approach.
• More about developing learning skills.	• Prescriptive.
• Non-prescriptive.	• Telling people their training needs.
• Letting people find their own way.	• Organizational, job focus.
• Collaborative.	
• Individual focus.	

Where an organization finds itself in this range does not seem to be wholly influenced by the type of industry it is involved in. Next generation organizations are not automatically linked to next generation industries. For example, the call centre is a growing area with high-tech methods and yet the people working in call centres are given clear standards of what to do and how to do it and are monitored from a central point.

Furthermore, wherever organizations are in this range they need people who are capable in what they do. The differences in approach might be marked but the requirement to identify the training needs is still essential to all.

Think about your organization: where is it on the range between these two ends of a spectrum? What approaches do you have for identifying training needs? Are these compatible with your type of organization?

The process of identifying training needs in context

Learning is often taken for granted in organizations. New ways of working, new equipment and technology are frequently introduced without planning either for the learning or the training needs of workers; typically there is an assumption that people will 'pick it up' as they go along. And of course this does happen. The informal learning that Reid and Barrington (1997) talk about in *Training Interventions* is a daily, ongoing occurrence. It can happen by:

- *Trial and error* – the person does something, which may or may not work and eventually the person works out a way that seems to get the job done.
- *Reinforcement* – the person gets feedback from their boss when they do something that either shows them that this was appropriate or not. They will learn to do the same again or avoid the things that cause reprimand.
- *Experience* – the person carries out a task and afterwards thinks about what they have done, perhaps realizing they could do it differently or better. They work out a plan to try out the next time.

Whatever the method, we see the potential outcomes to this informal learning as:

- People take a long time to learn what to do in order to perform their jobs to an acceptable level.
- People may not learn the right things.
- People may get inappropriate feedback that encourages them to do their jobs in ways the organization does not intend.
- People often cannot find ways of doing things differently.
- People are often unaware of this informal process and are unable to explain how or what they have changed in their job.

So, how does identifying training needs help with making learning more effective? Kolb (1984) explains that people learn best when they reflect on their actions, thus internalizing what they do and improving the likelihood of transferring this learning to everyday actions and behaviours. Identifying training needs is a means of making all of this explicit. The process is about planning for the future rather than waiting for the future to happen. It creates a picture of:

By comparing these two states you can determine the learning and training needs for the organization and the individual. You are also in a better position to select appropriate methods to make change happen and to monitor progress towards your goals.

The key to winning support for this process is to show that the business will get a return on any investment it makes in developing its people. The notion that learning will become less haphazard may not be the decider, although it makes sound sense. We think you have to show how identifying training needs contributes to the achievement of business goals and is an integral part of business planning. Demonstrating your business awareness and talking the same business language as other managers will go a long way towards this. You can influence how you are perceived professionally by thinking about learning as a commodity and treating it in the same way as other managers would treat the purchase of new equipment. Take this as an example: if the organization were considering the purchase of new equipment there would be some trigger to say this was necessary, in order to:

- Meet an increased demand in the product.
- Produce the product more efficiently.
- Keep up with competitors.
- Get ahead of competitors.
- Win new customers.

There would be an investigation into the options available, the costs and the pros and cons of different courses of action. By weighing up these factors a decision could be made.

Learning can be treated in the same way. First, there will be a trigger to say that something needs to change. The trigger could be from within the organization or it could be an external influence. You may find you are dealing with a combination of triggers. Some examples (taken from *Training Needs Analysis*, Bartram and Gibson, 1997) are shown in Table 10.2.

Table 10.2   *Learning triggers*

Positive triggers	Negative triggers	External triggers
● Taking on new people.	● Customer complaints.	● New legislation.
● New products.	● Accident records.	● Changes to legislation.
● New customers.	● High turnover of new	● Customer requirements.
● New equipment.	recruits.	● Competitor activity.
● Requests from managers.	● Loss of customers.	● Supplier activity.
● Appraisal interviews.	● Decreases in productivity.	● Professional body
		regulations.

Your next steps are to work with others to determine the changes required and then to investigate and compare the current situation to the future position. By analysing this information you and others will be able to decide what actions to take to achieve the desired changes. You can cost these and compare them either against the benefits to be achieved or the likely impact of not taking actions.

Think about your organization: is learning considered an integral part of business development? Do you show how learning can be achieved efficiently and cost effectively? How do you demonstrate your business awareness?

Identifying training needs in practice

You can give your identification of training needs a flying start by knowing what you are looking for and involving the right people. Start from the triggers and:

1   Create a clear picture of the likely changes
   ● do these imply
      – new systems or procedures?
      – new or revised job responsibilities?
      – new or revised knowledge and skills?
      – a demand for more people?
   ● decide on the method for gathering information.

2.   Investigate the differences between the current and future situation
   ● decide on the method for gathering information
   ● see what gaps you can identify.

3.   Analyse the findings to determine training plans
   ● decide which methods of training will best bring about learning
   ● consider what the training will cost
   ● consider how the organization and the individual will benefit
   ● dvaluate the cost of taking no action.

To illustrate how this three-step approach works let us place ourselves in a small manufacturing company. Let us say that the trigger for identifying training needs is the imminent introduction of a new product. Our business plan is to sell this new product to our existing customer base to gauge the impact. If this goes well we will expand our customer base, winning new customers from our competitors.

   We will take each of the three steps we have described in turn and consider the possibility of our manufacturing company being either a knowledge organization or one run on scientific management principles. We will then suggest different strategies and methods to meet the needs of both types of organization and compare them by considering the pros and cons of each method.

1. Create a clear picture of the likely changes

You want to get a general idea of what the likely changes will be so that you can direct your investigation in the right direction. Tables 10.3 and 10.4 describe how this might work in practice in our two types of organization.

Table 10.3   *Strategy considerations*

Knowledge organization	Scientific management organization
Managers have strategic role, providing information for others. Managers act as coaches and facilitators.	Managers make decisions. Managers act as organizers, controllers.
Strategy Organization-wide involvement of people from all levels to identify the likely changes the introduction of a new product will make. For example, need for more staff, the need for people to do their job differently, the need to change timescales and so on.	Strategy Work with managers, helping them to analyse what the likely changes for people will be as a result of introducing a new product. For example, need for more staff, the need for people to do their job differently, the need to change timescales and so on.

Table 10.4   *Research methods: pros and cons (Continued)*

Methods		Methods	
Research by project teams		*Questionnaire to managers*	
Bring together a variety of people from different areas of the organization.		Produce a set of questions to send to managers	
Pros	Cons	Pros	Cons
• Encourages the sharing of ideas. • Devolves reponsibility. • Developmental in itself for project team members. • Increase potential for acceptance. • Efficient use of time. • More like to be innovative.	• Not all views heard. • Time needed to develop the team. • Depends on getting the right mix in the team.	• Saves time on gathering information, particularly if managers are situated at different sites. • Can be completed when it is convenient for the managers.	• Might not ask the right questions. • No feedback process for checking understanding. • Time taken to analyse responses. • Response limited by questions. • Impersonal. • Potential poor response rate • Functional emphasis.

Table 10.4   *Research methods: pros and cons (Concluded)*

Research by manager with own team		Interviews with managers	
Bring together managers and teams for discussions.		Arrange interviews with individual managers.	
Pros	Cons	Pros	Cons
• Continues the development of relationships. • Uses existing relationships to save time.	• Insular. • Falls back on previously held assumptions.	• Opportunity to check understanding. • Opportunity for in-depth discussion. • Convenient for managers. • High response. • Rich source of information. • All views heard.	• Time consuming. • Relies on trainer's understanding of new product. • Functional emphasis.

Research by individuals		Group discussions	
Give guidance to individuals to quantify changes.		Bring groups of managers together, from within functions or across functions.	
Pros	Cons	Pros	Cons
• Leads to commitment to learning. • Develops learning skills as part of process.	• Time consuming. • Large amount of data to be assimilated.	• Synergy from shared ideas. • Speedier ways of gathering information. • More of a strategic view.	• Getting people together. • Dominant views take over. • Relies on trainer's facilitation skills.

By the end of this step you and others will have explored the likely changes and will have a shared understanding of who to involve in the next step.

2. Investigate the differences between the current and future situation

Finding the right way of gathering information is important; this is the data that the process of identifying training needs hinges upon. Any method you use will have good points and drawbacks. Table 10.5 shows some methods that we have tried, together with their advantages and failings.

Table 10.5 *Methods of information gathering*

Method	Advantages	Failings
Questionnaire	• Quick way to gather information. • Having a structure to questions helps with the analysis of data. • Can be used with high numbers of people.	• Depends on quality of question. • No opportunity to check understanding. • Impersonal approach. • Respondent may look for the 'right answer'. • Poor response rate.
Card sort	• Gets peple thinking. • Gives people a starting point. • Can be developmental in itself. • Cards can be devised for people or they can create their own. • Works with a range of topics. • Something different.	• Some people may see it as a game and not take it seriously. • People may look for the 'right way' to respond. • Can take up a lot of time. • Breaks into working routine.
Interview/discussion with individuals and groups	• Opportunity to share ideas. • Opportunity to check for understanding.	• Can be difficult to get people together. • Can be time consuming. • Breaks into working routine. • Amount of information to analyse.
Direct workplace observation	• Can be done as part of work routine. • See how people do jobs in reality. • Opportunity to ask questions to test knowledge.	• The way people do their jobs may be affected by the knowledge that someone is watching them. • Requires skills in giving feedback in a constructive way.
Keeping a diary or log	• Developmental in itself. • Enables the person to reflect on what they do.	• Can be time consuming. • Dependent on quality of information recorded.

Once we have a clear picture of the changes required when introducing the new product, we can go ahead and find out more specific information. If our company were a knowledge organization, then the methods for this would need to be creative and involve the individual as much as possible. We would probably choose from card sorts, questionnaires and keeping a diary or log. The way we would use these methods to identify training needs would be:

● *Card sort* Have ready a whole range of statements written on separate cards for the individual to decide if this is something they need to do in their job once the new product is launched. Example cards might be: tell customers about the new product; train staff on the new product; make the new product and so on. The individual could add cards too. When they have sorted out what they need to do, ask them to organize their chosen statements into priority based on what they will be doing that is totally new to them (high priority), what they do already but want to do differently/better (medium to low priority).

- *Questionnaire* Instead of statements on cards, have ready a series of open-ended statements for the individual to complete. Example statements might be: To tell customers about the new product I will need to know...; to train other people about the product I will need to...and so on. Send the statements out to people by internal post or e-mail and attach guidance notes for completing the statements and the date for return.

- *Keeping a diary or log* This method would be useful if the introduction of the new product meant additional work for people. Brief people on how to maintain a diary or log and provide a pro-forma for doing this. Encourage them to record what they do, how they do it, whom they communicate with and so on. Then ask them to think about how they will need to adapt their routines to fit in their additional responsibilities.

If our organization were run on scientific management lines, we would choose methods that would help the managers define the training needs of their staff more specifically. We might choose questionnaires, interviews or discussions. Also we might opt for direct observation in the workplace. The way we would use these methods to identify training needs would be:

- *Questionnaire* Prepare a set of questions that ask for specific information. Examples might be: describe any new tasks the person will be involved in; do they have the knowledge and skills to carry out these tasks; describe the new knowledge and skills they require and so on. Send the questionnaires to the relevant managers, setting a time for completion and return.

- *Interviews/discussions* Instead of sending out the questions, use these as a basis to find out information in meetings with individual or groups of managers.

- *Direct observation* Use this to support one of the other methods to get first hand information on how people do their jobs and how changes to knowledge and skill requirements will affect their everyday practice.

By the end of this step you will have a lot of information about specific changes to job content, knowledge and skill requirements for you and others to analyse to draw out the training needs and make training plans.

3. Analyse the findings to determine training plans

You want a straightforward way of handling all of the information you gather so that you and others can easily draw conclusions and make decisions. The different methods you use in step two will require different approaches for analysis. We have found that applying content analysis can be helpful where the method for identifying training needs has been open-ended such as with questionnaires, interviews and discussions. Transfer the responses from individuals onto a matrix to highlight emerging themes and patterns. Where the method is less open-ended such as card sorts, direct observation and keeping a diary then we have tended to use numerical analysis, such as frequency counts, calculating averages and making comparisons to identify trends. Sometimes the information generated needs a combination of analysis techniques. Keeping a diary or log can fall into this category in that there might be aspects of the data that can be analysed numerically alongside data that needs to be analysed for its content.

Back to the example for the last time. In our knowledge organization we would use numerical analysis with the card sort to determine how many times certain cards were selected and how high a priority they had. From the open-ended statements we would create a matrix and record the themes and patterns emerging from people's responses to show the training needs. With the diary or log we would create a matrix from the comments about how new jobs would be fitted into routines. Also we would add up the amount of time people spent on certain jobs, the number of contacts they had and so determine the feasibility of giving them additional work. We would then consider options, for example finding others who could take on new tasks instead and the training needed to make this happen.

In our scientifically managed organization we would create matrices to show the themes from the questionnaires and the interviews/discussions. With the direct observation we would list the tasks completed and the number of times these were undertaken or how long these took to complete. We would list the skills observed and add up the number of times these were used throughout the work. From this we would draw conclusions about the priority, knowledge and skill needed to do the job currently and compare this to the new knowledge and skills that would be required.

By carrying out analysis in this way you can decide what type of training method will best achieve results in meeting training needs as well as identifying the costs and benefits. You can then compare: on-the-job instruction or coaching; self-teach technologies; off-the-job strategies and in-house training versus external provision.

Think about your organization: how close does your practice of identifying training needs match this three-step approach? What opportunities do you have to try out the three steps? How will you match our ideas to fit your organization more specifically?

Summary

The way businesses are managed falls somewhere between the points of the next generation knowledge organization and the more traditional scientifically managed organization. Whatever direction organizations move in, however, there will always be a need to enable the people who work there to make the best contribution.

A systematic approach to identifying training needs ensures that people are offered opportunities to learn which are efficient and effective.

Perhaps it is time to give training and development a makeover. It would be a pity if the relevance of processes such as identifying training needs were lost through outdated language and perceptions about how these can contribute to individual growth and business success.

Further reading

Bartram, S. and Gibson, B. (1997), *Training Needs Analysis*, 2nd edn, Aldershot: Gower.

Kolb, D. A. (1984), *Experiential Learning: Experience as the Source of Learning and Development*, Englewood Cliffs: Prentice-Hall.

Newby, A. C. (1992), *Training Evaluation Handbook*, Aldershot: Gower.

Pugh, D. (1997), *Organization Theory: Selected Readings*, 4th edn, Harmondsworth: Penguin Books.

Reid, M. and Barrington, H. (1997), *Training Interventions*, 5th edn, Institute of Personnel and Development.

Senge, P. (1990), *The Fifth Discipline, The Art and Practice of the Learning Organization*, New York: Doubleday.

Chapter 11

Designing effective training

Diane Bailey

Training and the business

Learning is a key element of an organization's competitiveness and this challenges training and human resource professionals to design and deliver appropriate training, which makes a quantifiable and demonstrable contribution to the skills that individuals need.

This chapter will focus on the issue of design within the context of the training process. This includes strategy and planning through to validation and evaluation. Specific attention will be paid to the range of training methods and media available. Key people issues will also be highlighted, such as who is involved in the design, when to use external assistance and how to meet the needs of the audience.

The context of the organization

In order to deliver real business benefits, training must be designed to be relevant to the organization's performance needs. The model in Figure 11.1 shows one way in which training and its effects can be linked to high-level business objectives in order to add value and ensure appropriate performance.

Where performance at any level within the model falls short of that required, a performance improvement is needed. Where required levels of skill and ability are not present, improvement is also needed and training designed for groups, teams or individuals will be necessary to rectify the performance or skill deficit. The effectiveness of training will ultimately be evaluated in terms of the organization's success in achieving its goals and objectives (evaluation of training will be discussed briefly in this chapter and in greater detail in later chapters).

Required performance   Judging performance

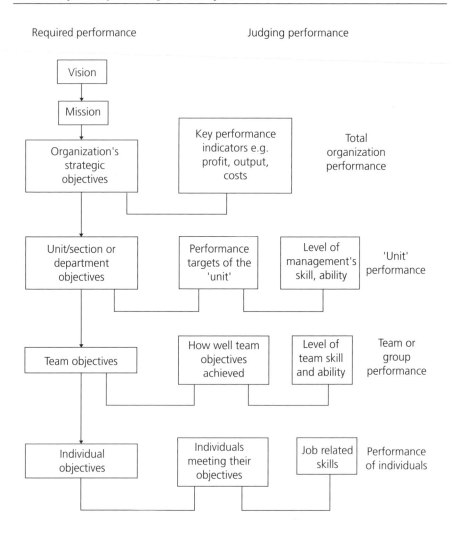

Figure 11.1   Linking training to business objectives

Training policy and strategy

Ideally, all training should be designed as part of a training policy and strategy. The training policy forms the backdrop for all decisions about training. The training strategy is an essential reference for the annual training plan and sets all training activity squarely in the context of strategic goals and organizational needs.

The training policy and strategy must meet the expectations of the senior management team. The training function or training manager must know and understand these expectations and develop a training strategy that meets them. Otherwise it is unlikely that senior management support for, or belief in, training will be sustained.

The training function needs to help the organization develop a strong training culture, which positions training and development as an important resource to the organization. Effort will be needed to:

- raise awareness of training and development and their benefits
- create interest in training as a way of addressing and meeting business problems and needs such as competitiveness
- convince managers and the workforce that training and development are valuable to them and the organization
- encourage individuals to value the learning opportunities presented by training
- develop a culture of continuous learning and development.

Planning training

Training should only be carried out when there is an identified performance need. This need can be identified in a number of ways such as training needs analyses, requests for help by managers, planned change, e.g. introduction of new computer systems or identified performance shortfall. Alternatively it might be identified through problems being experienced in the business such as high levels of staff turnover or be prescribed through continuous personal development programmes or mandatory professional training requirements.

Training outcomes should be specified at the outset and planned in terms of:

- specific aims and plans with which the training is to be linked (development plans)
- the training purpose, i.e. what will be different or better in performance if the training is successful (development objectives)
- the learning to be achieved, i.e. what individuals should know or be able to do as a result of undergoing the training (learning objectives)
- how effects and results will be measured (evaluation objectives).

As a precursor to any design work, these issues about what the training will achieve and what it will contribute need to be clarified and agreed. Only when they have been agreed with all stakeholders involved should the training function carry on with the necessary design work.

Who to involve in designing training

The role of the training function is to design, or have designed, and put into place, training which meets the performance needs of the organization. Its role is also to use its own competence and expertise to help all stakeholders contribute effectively to the training design. The training function will be involved in determining which performance needs are to be addressed, what training is required, what the training should achieve and how the training is to be delivered.

Likely stakeholders in training design and their probable expectations are indicated in Figure 11.2.

Who should design the training?

The appropriate design work can be carried out by members of the organization's HR or training team or by an outside training provider or consultant. The choice of who carries out the design work will depend on the type of training required, the target audience, the resources available and the timescales.

To design effective training, the organization also needs to ensure that it has the relevant subject matter expertise and also needs to ensure that it has the necessary skills. These include training analysis skills, being able to determine the most effective training solution/approach, training design skills and knowing how to evaluate training results and outcomes.

Before taking a decision about whether to carry out the necessary training design in-house or with outside assistance the training function will need to be clear about the main requirements of effective training design and the key activities and tasks involved. These include:

- clarifying the business need
- analysing training needs
- evaluating and choosing alternative materials, methods and media
- specifying the aims of training provision
- specifying training objectives in behavioural, observable terms
- identifying skills to be developed and cognitive input to be delivered
- designing exercises, activities, ice breakers, etc.
- designing and developing appropriate tutor/trainer materials – notes, handouts, activity briefs, OHP slides, etc.
- designing and specifying evaluation strategy and instrument(s)
- piloting and validating training materials or events before roll-out for general use
- training trainers or tutors in the use of the material

- designing an internal marketing campaign
- working with line managers to ensure training provision
- arranging or carrying out an appropriate evaluation exercise.

In order to design effective training solutions those involved require some key skills and competencies. These include, not in priority order, the following:

- understanding the organization and its operation
- defining performance shortfalls or new requirements
- research skills
- working with subject matter experts to obtain technical, specialist or subject information
- defining training aims and objectives
- project management skills
- negotiation and persuasion skills
- detailed knowledge of training methods and media available – their uses and limitations
- matching methods and/or media to training need(s), the organization, and the circumstances of use
- high levels of interpersonal skills
- specifying evaluation criteria and evaluation instruments
- advising on or carrying through internal marketing of the chosen training solution.

When to involve external assistance

There are a number of reasons why an organization may need to involve external assistance. For example, there might be a shortage in in-house resources or a gap in in-house knowledge, skills or subject matter expertise. Alternatively, there might be requirement for a fresh perspective. There is little doubt that by using high profile external providers training can sometimes be given an added sense of value and authority. Indeed external providers can also provide access to informed ideas re: best practice approaches.

Another valid reason for bringing in external expertise and help is that, over time, organizations can become stuck in their ways. Working with external providers who are not restricted by in-house 'baggage' can help to develop individuals in the training function, update existing in-house knowledge and skills, broaden in-house experience, raise awareness of over-familiar training problems and issues and further clarify the business need for the training being designed.

Stakeholders	Stakeholder expectation
Senior management	<ul><li>sustained or improved competitiveness</li><li>improvement in specific performance need</li><li>an approach which is congruent with the organization's strategy</li><li>careful use of resources – financial and human</li><li>training which will reflect best practice and meet any legislative requirements</li><li>proposals for cost-effective evaluation.</li></ul>
Line managers (as recipients of training)	<ul><li>training appropriate to their needs</li><li>assurance that the training is designed specifically for them</li><li>clearly defined business and learning objectives</li><li>minimal disruption</li><li>clear benefits for selves and for the organization</li><li>improved skills, abilities and knowledge.</li></ul>
Line managers (as managers of staff receiving training from others)	<ul><li>to be consulted</li><li>involvement at an early design stage</li><li>minimal disruption to their work and that of their department</li><li>clearly defined objectives and benefits</li><li>choice of method which suits their staff and their circumstances</li><li>training which will reflect best practice</li><li>demonstrable contribution to effectiveness.</li></ul>
Line managers who have to offer/deliver the training themselves	<ul><li>to be equipped to deliver the training solution effectively</li><li>complete support in terms of material, training design, evaluation criteria and methods</li><li>to be protected from embarrassment and/or failure</li><li>appropriate/feasible delivery methods</li><li>clarity about monitoring and reporting on progress and problems.</li></ul>
Personnel function	<ul><li>to be consulted/involved</li><li>that training designed will meet:<ul><li>– identified organization needs</li><li>– any legislative requirements e.g. health and safety</li><li>– any budgetary constraints.</li></ul></li><li>to be informed at agreed/appropriate stages.</li></ul>
Workforce in general	<ul><li>assurance that trainers understand their role/work</li><li>training which is relevant to them and their needs</li><li>clear explanation and positioning of training suggested/offered</li><li>some personal benefit e.g. greater knowledge, transferable skills, better working methods</li><li>honest feedback on how they do.</li></ul>
Customers – internal or external	<ul><li>a competent workforce</li><li>a workforce which understands customer needs and is willing to meet them</li><li>working methods which enhance customer service.</li></ul>

Figure 11.2   Stakeholders in training design

Delivery considerations

Training design can only be successfully undertaken after the factors in Figure 11.3 have been considered.

Training need	• Is this concerned with knowledge acquisition, skill development or attitude change?
	• Is it about personal development or team/organization development?
	• Does it require group learning, or can it be learned individually?
	• What is the subject matter and how much expertise do in-house trainers have of this area?
	• What methods work well with this particular topic?
	• What experience is available in-house in the design of training using these approaches?
	• Will the most suitable training approach work well in our circumstances?
Target audience	• How much do they already know?
	• How receptive are they likely to be to the training?
	• What level or pitch should the training be set?
	• What are the group's learning preferences?
	• What pressures/demands on the audience may affect them?
	• Are there any special needs?
	• What will add credibility to the proposed training?
Resources available	• How much time and money can be committed to the training need?
	• Will expert/specialist inputs be required from others?
	• What facilities and materials are available?
	• How much time is available for development?
	• How is the training to be evaluated?

Figure 11.3   Delivery considerations

Having made some decisions based on how best to ensure learning takes place for the precise target audience the ideal design solution can be matched with the resources available. This approach means that the likely problems resulting from a less than 'ideal' solution can be identified and their potential adverse effects guarded against, as far as possible.

Choosing appropriate training methods and media

There are three dimensions which inform the choice and identification of appropriate training approaches and strategies, these are:

1. The range of delivery mechanisms/strategies available.
2. Different styles and types of training/learning activity.
3. Different training media available.

The space available in this chapter does not allow these ideas to be developed fully. However, it is possible to say that delivery mechanisms/strategies available include group training/group learning, coached development and self-study. A range of possible training approaches also exists within each as shown in Figure 11.4.

Mechanism/strategy	Possible approaches
Group training/group learning	<ul><li>lecture/presentations</li><li>courses/workshops/seminars</li><li>peer-study groups</li><li>action learning sets</li><li>focus groups</li><li>discussion groups</li><li>guided practical activities and exercises in teams/groups</li><li>project planning and management, in teams.</li></ul>
Coached development on-the-job	<ul><li>programme of coaching interventions by manager</li><li>'sitting next to Nelly'</li><li>support from a formally appointed sponsor or mentor</li><li>supervised practice</li><li>properly briefed delegation</li><li>one-to-one instruction</li><li>workplace practice and experimentation</li><li>tasks and projects</li><li>use of personal development plans with feedback from manager.</li></ul>
Self-study	<ul><li>formal distance learning courses</li><li>self-study material e.g. CD-ROMS</li><li>planned reading/research – with self-assessment or feedback from manager or trainer.</li><li>individual written activities and exercises</li><li>video watching (with question brief)</li><li>intranet or Internet training</li><li>practical experience linked to learning logs.</li></ul>

Figure 11.4   Possible training approaches

In addition to the approaches and methods listed above a wide range of activities exist which can be presented as part of the training approach. These include discussions (in plenary or syndicate groups) – observations of, or involvement, in role play; simulations; self-discovery based, for example, on guided practice and the use of learning logs; exploration; experimentation; challenges; giving and receiving feedback; briefing and debriefing; listening to audio cassettes; watching linear video or trigger video and discussion of the contents; games; individual action planning.

The trainer needs to weigh the pros and cons of each type of activity, choose it to fulfil a specific purpose and balance its use with a number of other activities to ensure the chosen training design has pace and variety and that as many learning styles as possible are addressed.

The third dimension is that of the training media available for the transmission of knowledge and ideas and the development of skills. The chart in Figure 11.5 highlights how various key training media can be effectively used.

Good training design attempts to use as many senses as possible and to meet as many learning styles and preferences as possible. A carefully selected range of methods and media will enliven training. Too much variety will, on the other hand, confuse learners and make training delivery unnecessarily complex.

The needs of the audience

In order for training design and delivery to be effective the requirements of the target audience need to be considered in terms of the message, the audience, the vehicle/method, and barriers to communication.

These four elements are inextricably interlinked. For example, if the training needs to put across messages about customer service, then these should be appropriate/relevant to the level of audience participating. It is no good telling senior managers how to deal with customer complaints – it would be better to cover, for example, the value of complaints as customer feedback and the strategic impact and benefits of improved customer service. The message needs to be meaningful otherwise the audience will switch off and devalue the training effort.

The vehicle/method also needs to be appropriate to the audience. For example, giving junior people a problem and asking them to solve it in discussion groups may not work, because they may not have the intellectual capacity or experience to deal with the problem. They may need more guidance than this. Demonstrations or illustrations might work better.

Part of the training design should be to consider the need for pre-training preparation. This could involve reading or pre-course work to ensure that everyone who attends a course or event has achieved at least a minimum

Medium	Effective use	Not effective for
Text based material	• widespread promulgation of information, facts and knowledge issues • getting a basic message to a geographically dispersed audience.	• developing skills • engendering group values • complex ideas • audiences who do not read well or where English is a second language.
Linear video	• modelling required behaviours • adding 'clout' to a message • enthusing the audience • dealing with emotive issues and values.	• use unless trainer familiar with video • detailed knowledge input • use without clear briefing • complex facts or ideas.
Trigger video	• provoking thought and discussion in group or in self-study use • guiding discussion on best practice.	• passing on facts and figures • when a supporting brief has not been prepared.
Audio cassettes	• modelling issues such as approaches to customers, questioning techniques • developing listening skills • getting 'news' issues to a wide audience quickly • some self-study situations.	• complex ideas • where interaction and feedback to learner is needed • where diagrammatic or visual input is necessary.
Computer-assisted learning	• one-off training needs which are likely to be repeated • dispersed target audience.	• where large numbers need to be trained quickly unless PCs are widespread • developing skills.
OHP and foils	• group work • to draw attention to key points.	• very large presentations • when reproducing speaker's whole script.
Models, diagrams, pictures	• when the visual aspect is important to learning • finding a way round a keyboard.	• to illustrate theories and concepts unless supported by careful explanation.

Figure 11.5   Training media – uses

Medium	Effective use	Not effective for
Handouts	• as exercise briefings • to give clear precise instructions • provide record of verbal instructions or diagrams • summarize key points • provide guidance for transfer of learning to workplace.	• when they are poorly produced • where they appear 'heavy' or complex.
Self-study packages	• regular training needs for small numbers • geographically dispersed audience • part-time staff • knowledge-based training • when properly briefed and debriefed • when a variety of media used • some form of feedback is possible to the learner.	• as a stand-alone supported approach • interpersonal skills training.

Figure 11.5   Concluded

understanding of the topic before they get there. This helps to ensure a reasonably even playing field in terms of what everyone knows. Pre-training knowledge tests and skill checks are also valuable from the evaluation point of view. To prove that the training has made a difference, the trainer needs to know where learners are starting from.

In terms of training design the trainer needs to be alert to the demands made by:

• learning
• behaviour
• results required.

For best effects it is important to consider what a particular piece of training will deliver in terms of new knowledge, skills, ideas and abilities and also what the individual will do with that learning in their job. The trainer will need to develop a design which includes or specifies how the learner is to transfer what they have learned to their workplace and integrate it into day-to-day standards and behaviours. The final issue to be considered is how the required results can be measured and be seen to have resulted from the training provided. The training designer's role is summarized in Figure 11.6.

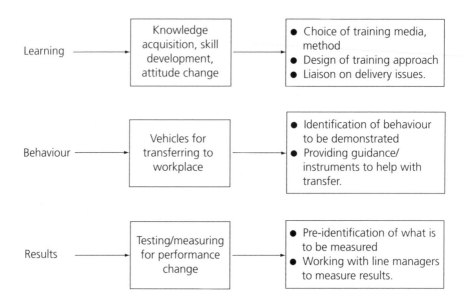

Figure 11.6   The training designer's role

Planning in evaluation

Later chapters of this handbook deal in detail with the evaluation of training but this chapter will touch briefly on how evaluation issues need to be considered at the training design stage.

As everyone in training today knows only too well, resources are limited and all training design and activity needs to be justified in terms of what it adds to the organization. Training designers have to be aware of the need to:

- justify the investment in training
- ensure that training really has made a difference to the organization and to individuals
- be able to identify areas in which further training may be required in order to achieve the results desired
- evaluate the training investment in terms of costs vs bottom line benefits.

Evaluation aims to make a direct link between the resource allocated to training and the practical business 'deliverables' which these achieve. The model in Figure 11.7 presents an overview of how and where this evaluation activity fits in with other activities in the overall training process.

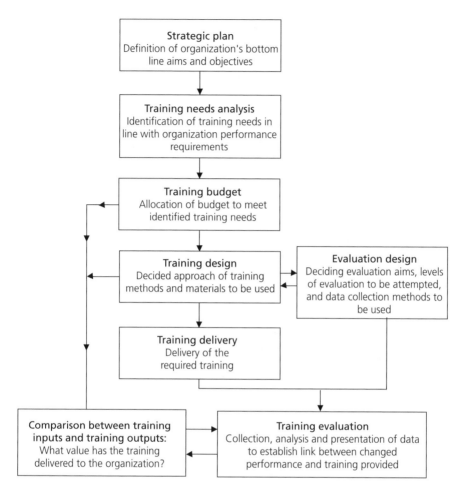

Figure 11.7   Evaluation and the training process

Evaluation should begin during training design, but the bulk of evaluation activity actually takes place after the training has been delivered. At the design stage, the focus is on planning the evaluation effort, and this involves:

- deciding which level of evaluation is to be attempted
- deciding what aspects of training need to be evaluated
- choosing the evaluation methods to be used
- identifying what trainers will evaluate and what others in the organization will evaluate
- costing the evaluation effort as part of the overall training spend.

Evaluation and validation

It is important for anyone involved in designing training to be clear about the difference between evaluation and validation of training. Both concepts are valuable in their own right, but they are also quite different in terms of what they measure.

Validation answers the question, 'Will our expenditure on training result in well designed training?' Evaluation answers the question, 'Has our expenditure on training delivered a significant value to the organization?'

Validation is concerned with testing training materials, methods and approaches for their suitability, appropriateness and effectiveness. Its focus is limited to evaluating the *design* of the training. It is concerned with:

- how satisfactorily the training materials, methods and approaches work
- the extent to which the training content covers all the relevant issues
- the timing and sequencing of activities
- the relative pros and cons of different methods and approaches
- the acceptability of the proposed design to the target audiences.

Planning evaluation during training design

The impact or results of training can be evaluated at a number of different levels. One of the first steps in planning an evaluation strategy is to decide what levels are appropriate. The level of evaluation will determine when the evaluation needs to be carried out and the likely sources of data for evaluation.

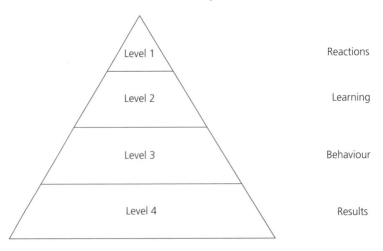

Figure 11.8   The Kirkpatrick model of evaluation

One evaluation model of value to those involved in designing training is the Kirkpatrick model, shown in Figure 11.8. This model identifies four levels. For those involved in designing training a further level, a level 5 could be added. This would incorporate the need to evaluate the training investment in terms of training costs vs bottom line benefits (see Figure 11.9).

Evaluation level	Possible training design issues
Level 1: Reactions This level measures participants' attitudes to the training provided. It will give an indication of initial reactions and feedback on how participants felt about the training accommodation, materials and methods, used, etc. *It does not measure how much participants have actually learned.*	● Design of questions to gauge reactions. ● Facility to ask questions at identified intervals or points. ● Design of 'happy sheets' or immediate post-event questionnaires. ● Later follow-up.
Level 2: Learning This level measures the learning achieved as a result of the training. It measures participants' ability to demonstrate the knowledge and skills which were the focus of the training. *It does not measure the long-term retention or impact of learning.*	● Design of questionnaires, quizzes, self-assessment activities for use at specified points or post-training. ● Designing in practical activities such as role-plays, team tasks etc., to assess learning as part of the event. ● Involving line managers in pre-and post-training observation. ● Debriefing and/or testing of learners once back at work. ● Testing long-term retention by follow-up approaches after training is complete. ● Link with level 3 below.
Level 3: Behaviour This level measures the impact of training on an individual's performance at work. It tests the extent to which learning achieved during training has been translated into new workplace behaviours and practice. *Repeat evaluations over a period of time can help to measure learning retention.*	● Pre- and post-training 'testing'. ● Use of workplace observation at specified intervals. ● Gaining involvement and support of line managers. ● Post-training projects and assignments. ● Repeat evaluations.

Figure 11.9   Design issues for training evaluation (continued)

Evaluation level	Possible training design issues
Level 4: Results This level focuses on measuring the correlation between training and business results. This can be very difficult to prove. There are, however, a number of bottom line benefits which can be achieved through and linked directly back to training. These may include: reductions in staff turnover, reduce costs/overheads, improved quality, increased customer satisfaction, increased sales, fewer grievances and complaints, improved cost: turnover ratio.	• Working with line managers to identify what is to be measured. • Remembering and addressing requirements of IiP, if appropriate. • Possible use of 360 degree feedback. • Comparison of pre- and post-training performance against statistical data. • Planning to evaluate at this level once per year. • Limiting evaluation at this level to really significant training initiatives e.g. organization-wide induction. • Management development. • Customer service. • Quality/TQM. • Culture change.
Level 5: This extra level attempts to relate investment in training directly to bottom line results.	• Agreeing with senior management how this will be done. • Identify which training initiatives should be evaluated at this level.

Figure 11.9   Design issues for training evaluation (concluded)

The framework in Figure 11.10 highlights both the validation and evaluation issues which you may need to factor in at various stages in your training design.

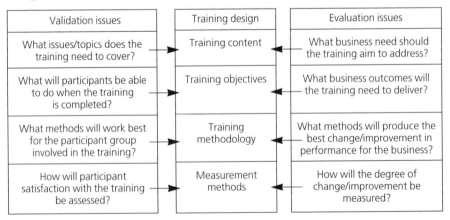

Figure 11.10   Validation and evaluation issues in training design

Conclusion

As this chapter indicates, the design of effective training can be a complex issue and needs to be approached with care. However, provided those involved in the analysis and design elements have the appropriate skills and the time available, a systematic approach will result in effective training which will be of value both to the individuals concerned and the organization.

Key reminders for those involved in the process include:

- What are the organization or individual performance requirements that need to be addressed?
- What will change after the training is complete, for example, attitudes, skills, performance, behaviours?
- What needs to be learned and by whom?
- What training approach is likely to be most effective?
- What training approach can be managed within available resources and circumstances?
- Which methods and media should be /can be used?
- What is to be evaluated and how?
- Who is to design the training?

Further reading

Bailey, D. (1998), *The Training Handbook*, London: Gee Publishing.

Darling, P. (1993), *Training for a Profit – A Guide to the Integration of Training in an Organization's Success*, Maidenhead: McGraw-Hill.

Honey, P. and Mumford, A. (1996), *The Manual of Learning Styles*, Maidenhead: Peter Honey Publications.

Knowles, M. (1996), *The Adult Learner*, 3rd edn, Houston TX: Gulf Publishing Company.

Mumford, A. (1997), *How to Choose the Right Development Method*, Maidenhead: Peter Honey Publications.

Rae, L. (1996), *Planning and Designing Training Programmes*, Aldershot: Gower.

Rae, L. (1992), *Guide to In-Company Training Methods*, Aldershot: Gower.

Sloman, M. A. (1994), *Handbook of Training Strategy*, Aldershot: Gower.

Chapter 12

Going forward with competencies

Binna Kandola

Competencies are seen as the glue that binds an organization together and are now firmly established as the basis of a strategic approach to human resources. A combination of factors has contributed to their popularity and their increased use in assessment, selection and development programmes. These include:

1. The fact that competencies seek to identify those factors which differentiate high performers from weak performers. Consequently, they are seen as a way of increasing productivity, and in the private sector, profits.
2. The foundation and structure they provide for all key processes particularly selection, appraisal and promotion.
3. The anti-discrimination legislation which requires organizations to be objective in the way decisions are made about people. Competencies provide the basis for sound processes.
4. The way that they enable employees to focus on effective behaviour at work i.e. those that will make a difference to performance.

This enthusiasm has fuelled a lucrative market for publishers, academics, conference organizers and consultants, all keen to explain and provide tailor-made competency frameworks. While the industry can seem a jungle of jargon and definitions, plagued by arguments as to the merits of one method over another, the overwhelming message is that competencies are 'a good thing'.

However, no approach can be a panacea and within the HR profession there have been calls for less reliance on required competencies and an approach that does not stifle other skills. The worry is that while companies need to be flexible and adapt to new circumstances, competency frameworks could become inflexible and restrict the workforce's potential. So playing devil's advocate for a moment let us see where the potential problems lie.

First, there is the matter of time and cost. It is difficult to change the competencies a company requires from its workforce at the same rate that the marketplace demands those changes. A framework which promotes a limited number of required competencies immediately inhibits the flexibility a company needs to survive. Frameworks that not only specify which competencies are desirable, but describe how those competencies should be demonstrated, go even further to discourage new ways of working.

A wider problem with competencies is that they are rarely focused on the future. Research carried out by *Competency* magazine (1995) found the typical framework included planning, organizing, decision making and innovation, but did not reflect the need for individuals to transform themselves, acquire new skills or adapt to circumstances. Given these concerns, it becomes valid to ask how well competencies are serving modern day organizations.

Different approaches to competencies

The diverse approaches to competency identification, interpretation and implementation complicate even the basic issue of defining what is meant by a 'competency'. The industry itself embraces different philosophies, inputs and, more critically, outputs. This is probably best exemplified by approaches at opposite ends of the spectrum. At one extreme the Management Charter Initiative (MCI), the UK's lead body for the field of management, focuses on tasks and outcomes. At the other extreme there are purely behavioural competencies, as developed by McClelland and Boyatzis, which concentrate on the characteristics of successful performers.

The MCI method (*Management Standards Directory*, 1992, The National Forum for Management and Education and Development) indicates the areas of competence and fields of knowledge that a person has to be able to demonstrate effectively. Performance is broken down into outputs that must be achieved if they are to be considered competent in that particular area. It is a form of hierarchical task analysis applied to management. (A study carried out in 1994 estimated that the MCI framework had been used in the data gathering process by 60 per cent of organizations that had developed competencies.)

Boyatzis (1982), however, defines competency as 'an underlying characteristic of a person in that it may be a motive, trait, skill, aspect of one's own self-image or social role, or a body of knowledge which he or she uses'. Furthermore this underlying characteristic is causally related to effective or superior performance in a job.

This approach is based on the view that there are differentiating competencies that distinguish superior from average performers. While popular, this methodology has its difficulties. It assumes that all differences between good and effective performers are appropriate discriminants. It is the horn and halo effect writ large. Furthermore, it completely disregards the context in which a person operates, and yet this has a bearing on the way they perform. Being able to communicate in a small group does not automatically mean that the individual will be able to cope with the larger group setting.

In the end it comes down to a choice between task-oriented vs worker-oriented approaches. Each camp has its supporters and critics and its pros and cons. However, the split is in many respects a false one. The key is knowing when to use one rather than another and how to combine them to produce the approach that works best.

Organizational vs individual competency

Much of the debate about the usefulness of competencies, particularly in fast moving business environments, stems from the conflict between individual and organizational competencies. Individual competencies – the focus of many projects in the UK – look at the features required of people. Organizational competence on the other hand aims to identify those areas in which the organization excels, and which give it competitive advantage. Once identified, these enable individual competencies to be developed.

Supporters of organizational competence point to the dramatic changes facing organizations. People are now carrying out a variety of tasks and are expected to be more flexible in the workplace. To accommodate this shift large organizations are, in a sense, seeking to acquire characteristics associated with smaller companies – to be responsive, flexible, close to their customers. However, to define the type of people needed to achieve specific goals and visions, organizations must first identify their core competence. Without an overarching strategy, and a clear definition of organizational values, concentrating on individual competencies is ultimately wasteful.

The most positive way forward is to focus on the needs of the business first. This is by no means easy and demands a new clarity of vision and understanding. Organizations must not only discover that which differentiates them from competitors but that which also provides a sound basis for future growth – their core competence.

Focus on the future

Unprecedented rates of change in business place a premium on forward looking competencies. Yet many of the frameworks in use today are based on the past. Furthermore, they can easily become bureaucratic mechanisms for controlling people's behaviour, restricting potential rather than releasing it.

The competency approach is generally favoured by larger organizations.

Research has shown that competencies are regarded as being of less use to smaller businesses and those working in highly competitive or rapidly changing markets. Ironically, the methodology chosen to replicate the qualities of smaller, more effective organizations is one they themselves would not use. It is easy to see how competencies can become part of a bureaucracy. The effort and expense involved in developing new competencies make it difficult to transform competencies as quickly as the organization itself needs to change.

There is also a risk that competency approaches will inhibit rather than encourage the effective use of people at work. The trend towards generating detailed descriptions of behaviour is setting tight boundaries around the ways people perform. Here competency is in contention with the notion of diversity and the need to manage people in a flexible way. The increasing use of competency-related pay can only make matters worse and reduce diversity. It is also being compromised by the practice of 'cloning' – identifying competencies solely on the basis of existing successful performers.

Pushed to its logical extreme the competency approach wants more people to behave in the same way as those who are currently successful within this organization. A key requirement is, therefore, to be clear about the context within which people will be working, what will be expected of them and to set this against the wider cultural constraints which prevent people from performing rather than assuming that developing people against a pre-ordained list of competencies will provide a solution.

Implementation issues

While these issues clearly need to be taken into account, adopting the following approach will enable organizations to go forward with competencies.

Think strategically

Rather than placing too much emphasis on the detailed descriptions of ways of working, it is important to clarify organizational values and ensure that each person's objectives allow them to work within those parameters.

A strategic approach requires individual and organizational competence approaches to be married together. If individual competencies are to be meaningful, they have to be placed clearly within the overall mission and strategy of the organization. Thought must be given to where a business is going, its core strength and how people will be expected to operate.

Understand the options

Competencies run the gamut from almost totally worker focused approaches like Hay-McBer (consultancy) to MCI's task-focused methods. Organizations should be aware of the range of options open to them and the way they can be constructed. They must ask themselves what they want to use the competencies for in order to identify the best approach to take.

Relate competencies to jobs and tasks

By ignoring the jobs and roles that people carry out, we risk developing competencies based on what people say is required for the job without examining their relevance to the tasks they perform. The Disability Discrimination Act has made it even more important to relate the two. Organizations must now adapt their wholly people-centred competencies back into an organizational and work setting in order to identify what reasonable adjustments they need to make to accommodate someone with a particular disability.

Incorporate values

We have already discussed the drawbacks of selecting employees based on the nature, motives, traits and values of the people who are already successful in an organization. A more appropriate approach is for the organization to define the way it wants to operate and identify the type of behaviour which reflects its values. The next step is to see if the people selected share those values and whether those who are employed live up to them.

This is becoming more important as the need for ethical conduct in all walks of life increases. Competency frameworks that persist in looking only at the individual will neglect to take into account the growing wider economic, social and political contexts in which organizations operate.

Competency of competency builders

Another issue which can impact the effectiveness and fairness of any competency-based approach is the capability of those who design and develop the frameworks. It is not uncommon to come across frameworks which are deeply flawed. Small sample sizes of only 25 or fewer interviewees are not sound bases for constructing what should be integrated competency frameworks. Descriptions and performance levels are often inconsistent in their approach and poorly written; some are simply discriminatory in an unjustifiable way. And there seems no logic to the widely varying numbers of competencies in employers' frameworks.

Training and development

Competencies are best used as a tool kept in the background until they are needed. They can be of particular benefit in structuring the training and development of people. This will obviously need to flow from the performance management system.

Performance management systems need two critical ingredients: objective setting and review and development and planning. It is in the development and planning area that competencies can be particularly effective. It can be used to identify skills or other qualities that the person may need to develop in order to do their job more effectively, or perhaps to progress to a different role. Having identified these needs with the person, in conjunction with the line manager or maybe even via a 360 degree feedback approach, specific training and development actions can be taken. To assist in this process organizations can produce development directories. These are lists of ideas (e.g. training courses, books, videos, open learning material, activities that can be incorporated into everyday work) that can be used by individuals to create their development plan. In effect it is a database containing ways in which people can be developed on any particular competency.

Using competency-based processes for assessment and development also has its own training and development implications. Access to skilled assessors can be a key factor in how you run an assessment centre. For example, internal staff may need special training depending on the particular assessment methods being used. Where psychometric tests and personality questionnaires are involved, at least one assessor must be trained and certified for their interpretation. However, this does not necessarily mean they will have sufficient knowledge to assess on the centre as a whole. But for other types of assessment exercise, a rigorous and thorough assessor training may be enough.

What differentiates a good assessor from a poor one is the ability to concentrate on getting evidence. Less competent assessors have difficulty extracting evidence in interviews because they fail to call for concrete examples of behaviour. They also find it hard to recognize evidence when it comes along, as in group exercises and presentations.

Assessors should also be able to give accurate oral and written feedback to assessment and development centre participants and to role-play consistently and objectively in interactive exercises like one-to-one simulations.

Organizations have their own role to play here by adopting a process which includes internal accreditation of assessors – to develop, monitor and maintain standards among its assessors. Too often compromises are made at the first stage. Assessor training is little more than a briefing on the timetable and exercises. To be effective, assessors must be able to demonstrate competent use of the basic skills of assessing and they also need a thorough knowledge of the exercises, competencies and the programme timetable. To reduce the amount of time required for formal, i.e. classroom type training, introductions to the basic skills can be done through distance learning and familiarity with exercises can be achieved by shadowing experienced assessors or attending a 'pilot or dummy' assessment centre.

Evaluating competencies

Usually a lot of effort goes into ensuring that people in parts of the organization are comfortable with the competencies that have been produced. Typically, this will involve ensuring that as many people as possible participate in the process either in the data gathering or the reviewing of the draft competencies. This process of involvement and asking for feedback and refining the competencies as a result, will increase the likelihood that they are not only accepted but also used.

It is essential that competencies are reviewed regularly, say every two years, to ensure they remain aligned with the direction of the business. Validation studies, however, are carried out far less frequently. A validation study will seek to establish whether the organization has a solid foundation for its HR management practices and that competencies can be used with confidence in a range of ways. A process that identifies the link between specific behaviours and performance outcomes will also enable the HR department to promote the behaviours that are important to the organization, as well as setting a benchmark against which future progress can be measured.

Comparing the performance of certain roles with competency requirements has additional benefits. Not only will the organization be better able to prioritize training and development on the areas which give it greatest return on investment but staff will also be able to increase their effectiveness in their roles.

Summary and conclusion

The crucial question to ask before starting down the competencies path is 'what do we want to use the competencies for?' Whether required as a framework to support future strategies or to underpin a management development programme, the answer will help to decide the best approach.

Competencies are an aid to managing and developing people and as such should only come into the foreground for management and development purposes. When companies look to competencies for the answer to every-thing, or treat them as an end in themselves and do not consider the pitfalls, problems with flexibility emerge.

Equally, selecting people on the basis of the nature, motives and traits of successful people already in the organization may do little to prepare for the future. Encouraging effective behaviour through competence-related pay could well stifle diversity in the workplace. An organization should begin by defining the way it wants to operate, identify the type of behaviour which sup-ports this and only then assess whether the people selected share those values or whether those already employed live up to them.

It is only through promoting education and awareness that competencies will continue to be used effectively in organizations. Companies must under-stand precisely what competencies are and develop a definition which is meaningful to them. There also needs to be a greater understanding of the diverse competence approaches – not so that we can debate which approach is best – but so that we can decide which approach will have the greatest impact on the bottom line for individual organizations.

Case study 1: using competencies constructively

At the end of 1995 Lloyds Bank and TSB Group merged to become the UK's biggest financial services retailer. It was a time of great change in business practice and direction, and in order to prepare for the challenges that lay ahead it was agreed that a new competency framework should be created to help staff develop as they met these challenges. This would draw upon the best features of previous approaches but become a more strategic tool.

Matt Hudson, who works in Lloyds TSB Strategy and Policy Department, explains: 'We wanted a competency framework which would underpin strat-egies for the future, support brand and corporate values and act as a common language'. This was no mean feat given that the framework needed to cover a wide range of business units and working environments – including over 2600 branches – and needed to be easily understood by 80 000 employees.

The new framework identified six role types in operation throughout the company. Every job was allocated one or two of these roles – strategy role, people management role, specialist role, and so on – together with six key competencies. For each competence, core behaviours – standards expected regardless of role – and role-specific behaviours were identified. However, rather than imposing levels of competency by which these behaviours would be measured, it was given to the job holder and line manager to decide how the behaviours would be demonstrated at a local level.

Having created the framework, a series of pilots were conducted to ensure the model could be used in all areas of personnel work – from structuring management development programmes, designing assessment and development centres through to succession management and planning.

Benefits of the approach

A high level of face validity existed, but through discussion groups and questionnaires it was possible to firmly establish the relationship between specific behaviours and effective performance. Questionnaires given to job holders and their corresponding managers across the six roles revealed strong links between behaviours identified in the framework and effective performance. While further proving the validity of the framework, it was also found that links between specific behaviours and performance outcomes could be identified. This meant the HR department could promote those behaviours which made a difference to the organization and had most impact on the bottom line.

Another important benefit of this approach was that employees were involved in identifying what constituted effective behaviour and how their role fitted into the changing priorities of the company. However, the key to the success of the framework was the way in which it combined both an individual and organizational competence approach. The former describes the behaviour required by an individual in their particular job. The latter focuses on the areas the organization is good at and which give the company its competitive advantage.

The Lloyds TSB framework started with the competencies which were important to the new company, and clearly defined the core behaviours expected from employees. It then made clear which competence was relevant to which role and how that behaviour should manifest itself. Finally it enabled each individual to decide how best to pursue this behaviour in their own place of work. The individual can therefore see how the competence promotes effective performance in their own role while also contributing to the overall direction of the organization.

Case study 2: underpinning management development

The London Borough Council of Ealing uses a competency framework to underpin its management programme. First introduced in 1995, the programme aims to develop managers on an individual level and help them contribute to the objectives of the council. This is done through a process of needs assessment and corresponding learning opportunities.

Kwame Akuffo, Ealing's Chief Organizational Development and Strategy

Officer explains the framework: 'Ealing produced a set of competencies covering four key areas of management: managing people; managing the service; managing information; and managing self. Each of the four headings is then broken down into a relevant group of specific competencies'. The competencies describe the skills and standards required for effective performance in each job, so every manager has a clear indication of what is expected of them and how they measure up.

Development centres provide the focal point for assessment and the identification of learning goals. As part of this, Pearn Kandola occupational psychologists, analyse each individual's performance through two group exercises, a one-to-one interview and 360 degree appraisal. The latter technique combines questionnaires from three colleagues and between three and five direct reports.

Pearn Kandola relate this evidence to the competency framework, and help the council's managers realize their strengths and weaknesses and so identify the competency-specific development they require. According to Kwame Akuffo 360 degree feedback is also useful in that it establishes a dialogue for clarifying people's roles within the council. Cost-benefit evaluation has shown the approach has had a positive effect and there have been perceptible improvements in the performance of the majority of participants.

Further reading

Boyatzis, R. (1982), *The Competent Manager: A Model for Effective Performance*, Chichester: John Wiley.

Byham, W. and Thornton, G. (1982), *Assessment Centres and Managerial Performance*, London: Academic Press.

Byham, W. and Krauzer, S. (1996), *The Selection Solution*, Pittsburgh: DDI Press.

Competency (1995), 'Trends and Developments in the Use of Competency Frameworks', **2**, 4, Industrial Relations Service (IRS).

Walker, J. (1992), *Human Resources Strategy*, Maidenhead: McGraw-Hill.

Woodruffe, C. (1990), *Assessment Centres*, London: IPD.

Chapter 13

Developing your business through Investors in People

Norrie Gilliland

Repeat after me. '*Investors in People is a business development process – not a training initiative . . .*'

It is vital to set Investors in People firmly in the context of business development, because otherwise you could miss out on one of the most powerful business development models yet devised. There are many approaches to developing organizations, and the thread running through all of these approaches is people.

Investors in People is not a scheme or a programme, it is a flexible framework that helps you develop your business by building on strengths. But you have to adapt it to meet the needs of your organization if you want to get the best from it.

Approaching it sensibly

Over the past few years, I have worked with around 200 organizations of all types and sizes, using Investors in People as a framework for developing their people in line with their business objectives. I will let you into a secret. Sometimes the organizations I work with do not even know they are 'doing' Investors in People until we are many months into the process. For example, I was doing some HRD consultancy work in a small foundry and one day the MD asked me if I knew about a thing called Investors in People. I asked what he already knew and what his feelings were about it, and he said he thought it was probably just one of those management fads. He was surprised, to say the least, when I told him he had been 'doing' Investors in People for nearly nine months.

There is nothing new about Investors in People. What makes it unique is the way it pulls business development and people development together, into a nationally-recognized framework. Organizations thinking about introducing quality initiatives such as ISO 9000 series, or the European Model for Business Excellence (the so-called EFQM model) or customer care programmes will find it an ideal way of supporting them.

Objections to Investors in People

For readers with a healthy scepticism of Investors in People and other 'quality initiatives', let me first deal with the downside and some of the pitfalls that might be encountered by going about it the wrong way, or for the wrong reasons.

I have seen plenty to convince me of the potential for real business benefits from Investors in People. I have also seen the dangers of approaching it superficially – just 'for the badge'. That is pretty much a waste of time and could rebound on your organization, because people would spot it a mile away.

Investors in People is not an award. It is public recognition of the good practice adopted by your organization in:

- planning and reviewing the business;
- planning and resourcing the development of your people to achieve the goals and targets set out in the business plan;
- taking effective action to meet training and development needs;
- evaluating the results;
- setting the 'culture' that will get the best results from people.

Some of the objections I have heard about Investors in People are illustrated in Table 13.1 along with my responses to them.

The big issue here is that business people must not reject the Investors in People concept as irrelevant when they have not looked closely at it. Do not short change yourself, but find out more before you decide.

What is in it for me?

Organizations become successful by developing new markets, products or services, or getting smarter at what they already do. Sustainable progress can only come from people. It does not matter how fast the microprocessor runs if your operations are constrained by people. People are the only means of sustained business development, and the only means of making your systems work better.

If this is blindingly obvious, ask yourself how good your organization is at making that kind of investment and at adding *real* value to the business? Investment in training and development is often laughably low given the

Table 13.1   *Scotching some myths about Investors in People*

'Investors in People is bureaucratic.'	Definitely not. It will only become bureaucratic if you let it. You only need to have a written plan for your business, which includes a plan for training and developing your people in line with your goals and targets. Any other systems you might devise will be for your benefit – not for Investors in People. If you have paperwork in place for ISO 9000 etc., it will almost certainly dovetail with the requirements of Investors in People.
'Investors in People is a training initiative.'	Big mistake. If this is what you think, you are really missing the point. Of course Investors in People deals with training and development, but it is about much more than that. It is about changing cultures, improving communications, and getting your people really motivated.
'People will all be running off on training courses. Who will be there to keep the business running?'	Improbable. Would you really send one of your employees on a training course they do not need? Anyway, there are many ways of developing people. Training is just one of them.
'Apart from another badge on our letterhead there will be no real benefits.'	Not true. There are lots of examples of companies that can testify to the business benefits of working through the Investors in People process. You really should find out more (read the rest of this chapter for a start).
'I know an organization that is a recognized Investor in People and goodness knows how they got it.'	IiP is good practice, not best practice. It does not ask for perfection. Maybe if you mention to the organization in question that they are not living up to the standard, they could do something to improve.

value it might add. That might be the reason why some managers do not give much thought to training – because, compared with the major capital programmes they are responsible for, the sums of money involved in training and development seem hardly worth bothering about. However, the investment could be repaid many times over, and much more quickly than other investments.

The benefits claimed by organizations that have adopted the Investors in People approach are many and varied. Here are a few examples from companies I have worked with over the last few years.

● A small company in accounting software increased its sales by 30 per cent without increasing the number of staff, by sending three people on a carefully chosen sales training course.
● A large manufacturing company regained a lost contract with a highly valued customer after re-skilling people on the shop floor.

- A small company that supplies and services photocopiers reduced service call times by 50 per cent on average by investing in some basic on-the-job training, so that administrative staff could talk customers through faults on the phone.
- The same company discovered that one of their existing staff was a home computer buff and was able to move into computer sales, with some basic training.
- A nursing home managed to maintain bed occupancy consistently at 95 per cent in the face of local authority budget cuts, when competitors were struggling at around 80 per cent.

If you are not convinced by this anecdotal evidence, look at Table 13.2. It shows figures taken from research carried out for the Royal Society of Arts in December 1994 which compared 300 recognized Investors in People with the national average, on three key financial measures: return on capital employed, pre-tax profits, and sales per employee.

Table 13.2   *Comparison of Investors in People companies with the national average*

Measure	National average	IiP recognized companies average	Percentage difference
Return on capital employed	9.38 per cent	18.93 per cent	+101.8
Pre-tax return profit margin	3.03 per cent	4.67 per cent	+54
Sales per employee	£77.447	£112.108	+44.71

Comparison of recognized Investors in People with the national average. Source: 'RSA Inquiry – Tomorrow's Company'. Published 1994. Reported in *Management Today*, August 1995, and *Director* magazine, December 1994.

I think these figures speak for themselves. Wouldn't you like to increase sales per employee in your company by 44 per cent?

Of course, no one is claiming that these results were achieved solely through adopting the Investors in People framework; but it is interesting that these 300 companies beat national average figures by such a significant margin.

What is in it for my employees?

I believe it is in the *cultural* aspects of Investors in People that individual employees have most to gain. Of course, we should expect them to get the training they need to meet the organization's goals and targets. However, going beyond that, there are major motivational benefits to be gained by involving people in open communication, letting them see that you value their contribution, keeping them informed about their progress and getting their ideas.

Blind ignorance and blind faith

I often visit companies where managers have a low regard for training. I call this 'blind ignorance'. It is one of the key areas that Investors in People deals with. The flip side is the 'blind faith' syndrome, which is usually expressed as 'training? oh yes, I believe in it totally. Anyone who wants to go on a course gets it'. This makes me cringe.

I visited a company recently where the MD was supposed to be very pro-training. His concept of training was sending managers to business school or sending the engineer on a hydraulics course, if they wanted it. But no attempt had been made to establish the business benefits. It was done because training was seen as 'a good thing'. Meanwhile, there was no budget for training people on the production line and customer complaints were going through the roof.

Awareness, assessment, advice and action

There is a real need to:

- *Raise awareness* of Investors in People, what it really means, its true potential for business development, and how successful organizations have used it for their benefit.
- *Help people to assess* where their organizations stand in relation to the standard, and how they can improve.
- *Give advice* on how to do it.
- *Enable organizations to take specific actions* to move closer to the standard.

The national standard

Let us look briefly at what the Investors in People national standard says.

Investors in People is based on four principles, supported by 23 indicators that provide the 'meat' of the standard.

The standard requires you to:

- Make a public commitment from the top to develop all employees to achieve your business objectives. So, everyone in the company needs to know about your vision, goals and targets, and how they as individuals can help to achieve them. They need to know that the commitment comes from the top of the organization, and that it is supported and actioned right down the line.

- Regularly review the training and development needs of all your employees. Everyone in the company needs to understand the arrangements for reviewing training and development needs in line with what the company is trying to achieve. Managers in particular need to know where they fit into this. They will probably need to be trained or briefed on how to review the needs of their people and to agree objectives for training and development activities – you cannot just expect them to know how to do it.

- Take action to train and develop individuals on recruitment and throughout their employment. Effective action is a key aspect of the Investors in People framework. It is not about people running off to courses all over the place. It is about making sure that the training they need takes place at the right time and that it is effective.

- Evaluate your investment in training and development. How will you know it has worked? Has the individual learned what you wanted them to learn? Can they apply it to the job? Has it helped to improve individual and team performance? Has it helped you to achieve your business goals and targets?

I like to consider the four principles as forming a loop, around a central core of satisfied customers, committed employees and financial returns, which all organizations are trying to achieve in one way or another. This is illustrated in Figure 13.1 on page 146.

The 23 indicators state in detail the standard that prospective Investors in People must reach in order to be publicly recognized, and which they must retain thereafter. It is against these indicators that your organization would be assessed. I will not reproduce them in detail here for lack of space, and also because their meaning is not always clear without explanation and discussion. If you want to, read the official literature that spells out the standard in detail. You can obtain a copy through your local Training and Enterprise Council in England or Wales, the local Enterprise Company in Scotland, or the Training and Enterprise Agency in Northern Ireland.

The five key themes

A very practical way to consider the standard is to think of it as consisting of five key themes for running a successful organization. These are:

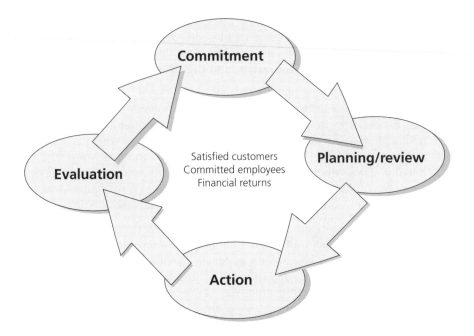

Figure 13.1   The four principles of Investors in People

- planning
- communications
- performance review
- management effectiveness
- training and development processes.

Let me describe these a little more fully, using my own words, rather than those of the standard.

Planning

The keystone of the Investors in People approach is the planning of your business and planning the development of your people within that context. This is done by creating and maintaining a flexible written plan for the business, together with a plan that sets out the organization's training and development needs, and says how they will be met. Clear goals, targets or objectives should be specified to ensure these plans are put into practice.

Communications

Communications is a recurring theme throughout the standard. This includes making sure all your staff know the broad aims or vision of the organization, how you expect them to contribute to its success, developments in the business and progress against targets, what opportunities they can expect for training and development, and who is responsible for making sure it happens.

Performance review

The standard requires you to review regularly the performance of the organization against the goals and targets set out in the business plan, and the performance of teams and individuals in contributing to their achievement. This in turn might highlight training and development needs, or other things you might need to do such as improving systems.

Management effectiveness

Effective managers are crucial to the success of any organization, and to the achievement of the Investors in People standard. You will need to consider the effectiveness of your managers in supporting individuals in their development, helping them to identify their training and development needs, agreeing objectives for training and development actions, and evaluating what effect these actions have had on knowledge, skills, attitudes and performance.

Training and development processes

You will need to ensure that effective training and development processes are in place to meet the needs of the business and individuals. This starts with effective induction and initial training for new people and for staff taking on new jobs or responsibilities within the organization. A very important aspect is the evaluation of the impact of training and development on individuals and teams, and on business performance.

The standard considers these processes in much greater detail, but I hope I have given a flavour of the main areas it covers. They are nothing more than common sense. But are they common practice in your organization?

Who is covered by the standard?

All employees should be covered by the organization's commitment, and its training and development activities. People often ask how literally this should be taken. I usually ask 'how much damage could that person do to your business?'

If a part-time secretary fails to pass on an important communication and you lose an order, was that because you did not give that person sufficient information and support? If you brought in some temporary production workers to cope with an order, would you need to explain to them how to do the job according to your quality standards? Could you afford not to?

Also, if you run a branch network, you need to make sure that the furthest flung site is not neglected in terms of effective communications and training. If you frequently sub-contract with people who are important to the delivery of your core business, you need to take appropriate steps to include them in your communications and briefings. And do not forget people in that often-neglected twilight zone, the night shift.

Commitment from management

Commitment must come right from the top of the organization. That means the chief executive, managing director or equivalent. Another important consideration is the role of the line manager. In my experience, this is one of the most neglected areas. Managers and supervisors are often the weakest link in the chain, and it is usually not their fault. Investing in your people simply will not work without the active involvement of managers at all levels. But you have to support them in doing it. Do not think that managers will somehow just manage it.

Training and development options

Investors in People is about *training* and *development*. I often feel there might be a case for outlawing the word training, because everybody thinks they know what it means, but few really do.

We are talking about how to engage the talents and brains of your workforce. Training is only part of the equation, because there are many ways of developing people, like getting their best ideas, giving them additional responsibility, involving them in solving problems and making decisions, or putting them in front of key customers to find out what their real needs are. There are literally dozens of ways to help people develop, for their own good and for the good of the business.

Continuing commitment

Top management must be able to demonstrate an understanding of the costs and benefits of training and development. They must also show continuing commitment to developing people. That means training and development must be high on the management agenda. Management must embrace it – and visibly.

The 'virtuous circle' of T & D

You are no doubt familiar with the 'virtuous circle of training and development'. The flip side is where people are not involved in the business, get little or no training, frequently make mistakes, and managers spend most of their time putting out fires. You will recognize this as the 'vicious circle', one with which so many organizations fight a daily battle. In fact, it is more invidious than that. It is a downward spiral from which many organizations are unable to escape.

Developing our earlier theme of the four Investors in People principles as a loop around the achievement of satisfied customers, committed employees, and financial returns, the virtuous circle is illustrated in Figure 13.2.

It can be seen that Investors in People offers a common sense approach to developing the business by ensuring that everyone knows where they fit in, that they are trained and developed to achieve the organization's goals, and that the results are properly evaluated.

Looking for a return on investment

You need to evaluate the effectiveness of your training and development actions. This is the area that tends to cause organizations most angst. I almost always find that they are doing some kind of evaluation, but do not realize it.

If you employed sales staff would you measure their sales performance on a daily, weekly or monthly basis? Probably all three. That sort of evaluation would give you a feel for whether the money you spent sending them on a sales training course last month was well spent. It would also reflect your hopes for the business and help you determine which of the staff have improved their performance as a result and which might need further help or development. Of course, it is not always as easy as that to evaluate the impact of training and development on the individual or the organization, but there are more possibilities than you might think. They just need to be brought to the surface.

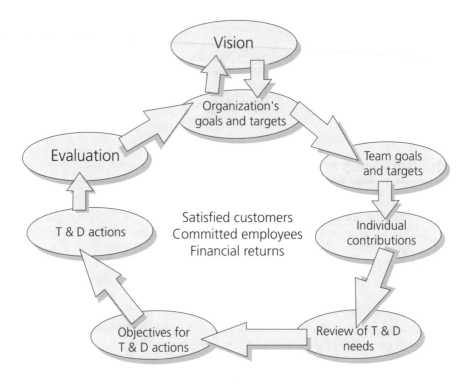

Figure 13.2   The 'virtuous circle' of training and development

What should you do now?

First, you could try completing the following simple checklist. Then go out and ask your people whether they agree with your scoring. Once you have done that, put a call in to your nearest TEC or LEC to find out what help they can offer.

Consider the following:

- Do you know where you want your organization to be three to five years from now?
- Are your senior colleagues clear on this? If they are not, how can you expect your workforce to be?
- Have your objectives been translated into a written plan that drives the business and is reviewed in the light of market forces?
- Have you let your employees at all levels know exactly what your objectives are?

- Do you regularly review the skills your employees – including your managers – need to meet your goals and targets?
- Do you set aside resources to meet the training and development needs of your employees, in line with your business plan? Do you make sure you get value from this investment?
- Have you introduced induction programmes for your new recruits?
- Have most of your employees been given some form of *necessary* training to meet your business goals and targets within the last 12 months? If not, was this a management decision, or simply default?
- Do you ask questions to find out whether the actions taken were the best way of developing people? Have they worked? How do you know it helped the business?
- Do you ask your people what they think about the way the organization is run? And do you really care about what they tell you?
- Do you ask your people for their ideas to improve the business? Do you act on them?

Nobody starts from zero. You must be able to respond positively to some of these questions. If you cannot, how on earth have you managed to stay in business? If you have, you are already on the way to becoming an Investor in People, and improving your business. The absolute essential is to integrate Investors in People into the business, not to look on it as something additional. It is about how you do business. This is a message that many business owners and managers have yet to grasp.

Further reading

'RSA Inquiry – Tomorrow's Company' (1994), London: Royal Society of Arts.

Gilliland, N. (1996), *Developing Your Business Through Investors in People*, Aldershot: Gower.

Gilliland, N. (1998), *Train Your People and Whack the Competition*, Aldershot: Gower.

'Investors in People' and related literature is also available through Training and Enterprise Councils in England and Wales, Local Enterprise Companies in Scotland, and the Training and Enterprise Agency in Northern Ireland. This literature may be published from time to time under different business themes relevant to Investors in People. The above organizations will be able to advise what is current.

Chapter 14

Open learning

Vaughan Waller

Open learning (OL) as a methodology is difficult to define because it now encompasses techniques from many other forms of learning. For instance, OL can often be combined with distance learning and, therefore, is likely to be self-paced. So, let us assume for the purposes of this chapter that OL is where the student is not restricted in any of the ways that he or she undertakes learning. The media used can be almost anything, the location can be anywhere, the choice of subject types unbounded and the learning pace almost entirely left up to the student.

It is because of this versatility that OL has now been adopted in so many companies that are intent on making learning generally available to their workforce. This is not only in order to improve the performance of individual employees (and hence the company's bottom line) but to enable them to enhance their skills and be better at their jobs or, in current parlance 'work smarter not harder'.

OL in a company normally centres around an OL centre which is frequently renamed the Flexible Learning Centre, the Personal Learning Centre, the Learning Resource Centre and, sometimes, with tongue-in-cheek, the Early Learning Centre. Basically, all these 'centres' are the same thing – a collection of various media, equipment to run them if required and personnel to support the students or users.

Some companies spend a small fortune on making their centres both pleasant and functional to use; they make all the latest technology available and buy just about every course that anyone will ever need. Often, however, they find that the centre is little used and, so, produces a poor return on their investment. Other companies buy one personal computer and a selection of core programmes and find that there are not enough hours in the day to meet the demand. Clearly, therefore, there are ways of making OL work in a company – and just as many stratagems that will fail. This chapter illustrates the main building blocks for the successful implementation of OL.

The case for OL

If jobs never changed and no one ever made a mistake, learning in the workplace might be unnecessary. However, this has never been true and conventional wisdom now dictates that it is our mistakes that give us the best opportunities for learning. Add to this the factor of organizations reorganizing, rationalizing and downsizing and it becomes clear just how much of a priority learning has become.

Nonetheless, getting people to learn new skills and improve their personal performance through any medium can be difficult to achieve. It is not that people *cannot* learn the new skills that will enhance their performance, rather, it is sometimes that they do not *want* to learn. It might be that employees do not want to admit that they need training in a particular subject, an issue common to other chapters in this book but particularly relevant to OL. In the main, an OL facility is used voluntarily. By various means a subject is chosen for study and the student with his or her manager decides how, when and where to study it. If employees are forced to learn, the result is usually counterproductive. So, if a company wants to enhance the skills of its workforce, it has to establish a process which will create the required atmosphere: in other words, the process must establish that:

- Learning is a good thing.
- Your company wants you to learn but is not going to force you.
- The learning experience is free to the learner.
- While there is not actually a pot of gold at the end of it, there is a worthwhile end product.

In other words the process offers something for everyone.

Once the student, manager and other interested parties decide that training is required, a company then has to make a choice between conventional tutor-led means or an open and/or distance learning approach. The former method is as valid today as ever, but is not the only way. It suffers from several disadvantages:

1. It is costly both in terms of tutor, venue, travel and other associated costs and also in the cost of the student being away from his or her workplace.
2. Peer pressure often results in a student who works slowly being left behind by quicker colleagues in a class and vice versa.
3. The course, once finished, cannot be revisited easily except by reference to course notes or doing it all again.
4. The quality of the course is at least partly dependent on the performance of the tutor.
5. The tutor has to contend with students who are joining the course at different knowledge levels.

6. In many cases the students have little opportunity to interact with the subject material.
7. Unless there is an examination or test of some kind at the end of the course it can be difficult to ascertain if the training message has been assimilated.

OL can address all of these problems but it is safer and more proper to say that a combination of both OL and tutor-led courses, is optimum.

OL and training needs analysis

One way of identifying the training needs of the workforce is to carry out a training needs analysis (TNA). However, the important decision to be made is to determine which training needs can be effectively addressed by OL; which needs can only be tackled with conventional training, and which will need a bit of both. It should also be borne in mind that, while a TNA will identify performance gaps, the process – by its very nature – will miss those subjects which employees want to study but probably would not think to ask about.

One of the big advantages of OL and, in particular, multimedia based training is that, for a relatively small outlay, an employee can be 'converted' to the idea of personal development. Too many companies believe that all training must be work-related and directly or indirectly have a beneficial effect on that company. For example, what would the reaction be if employees asked their training managers if they could use the OL centre to brush up on their French before they went on holiday? The likely response from many organizations would be to reject the request on the basis that such learning had little or nothing to do with the employee's work. However, it only takes a little consideration to realize that in allowing employees to enrol on a basic French course managers would be encouraging learning, demonstrating that the OL centre is a useful place to go and opening the doors to a range of other subjects on offer. Furthermore, if employees are willing to do the French course in their own time, what does the company have to lose?

Of course a TNA should also be linked with an appraisal process. When appraisals are carried out effectively then the two-way process identifies both what the employee thinks they need and what their manager thinks they need. The process also needs to be subject to regular review and when conducted with a positive and developmental agenda it becomes self-perpetuating and enjoyable, rather than something dreaded by manager and employee alike. One other important aspect to point out here is learning styles. OL is more flexible to the individual student's approach than a tutor can be – for obvious reasons. The student controls his or her own pace and method of learning and, although pre-written courseware is seldom available in different styles, the same course will fit many styles if the course design is good.

Planning the OL centre

Spending time on planning an OL centre will ensure more than anything else that it is successful. It is easy to buy a few multimedia computers and a shelf of generic courses, stick them in a room somewhere and wait for the queues of would-be students to form. Sadly, this will never happen. There are many books available on how to set up an OL centre and this chapter can only mention some of the main planning points.

One of the most important points is to establish – before any purchasing or recommendations are made – whether staff will be *allowed to use* the centre. This single factor is, by far, the main reason for OL centre failure.

Line managers are under all sorts of pressure and they expect nothing less than full commitment from their team. If a team member decides or wants to take several hours away from his or her desk to complete a course, often the answer is: 'Do it when you have finished what you are doing now' or, in other words: 'Maybe, one day'. While this is understandable, it is a hurdle that needs to be overcome before a centre is opened. In most cases, the solution to this is to get the whole of the management team on your side, from the chairman or chief executive downwards. Their endorsement and support of the OL centre is of incalculable worth to the centre's future success.

At one company an employee sent two questionnaires to separate levels of management. To line managers the question: 'Do you encourage your team to use the OL centre?' was answered positively by 80 per cent of respondents. The rest of the team members were asked: 'Do your line managers encourage you to use the OL centre?' and was answered positively by only 20 per cent. This result is by no means unusual and the issue to which it relates must be addressed early on.

Another prevalent attitude is that being seen to be using the OL centre is, in some way, ignominious; it is an admission that the students are not as good at their jobs as they say they are. Again, there is a view among some employees that OL centre based training is not 'proper' training compared with going away to an expensive management college for a week and networking with peers in the bar. Those who think in these terms often try to denigrate the OL centre by referring to it as the 'Early Learning Centre'. Unfortunately, these people think too conventionally, probably have a hidden agenda where training is concerned and may never be convinced of the value of OL.

To overcome such obstacles needs both a good internal PR engine and also a person who will champion the facility come what may. This person must be almost obsessed with the success of the project and must spread the word that OL is here to stay with missionary zeal. He or she also needs to be helped by a sponsor from senior management, who will add weight to the message and will silence the doubters.

Assuming that these hurdles are overcome, it is possible to proceed with the fun part – putting the centre together and stocking the shelves.

Many companies properly regard their OL facilities as something to be given a high profile. This means siting it in a highly visible place both for the staff who will pass the centre every day and for the visitors who will be impressed by what it says about the company. Visibility to everyone is crucial for an OL centre's success.

By the same token, it has to be accepted that this is a place for serious study and, if it can be managed, it should be both private and welcoming, and as comfortable as possible. Booths created, perhaps, with acoustic screens are a must. If possible, some area should be made available for students merely to read and write. A separate area in an ante-room should act as an information centre where courses can be discussed with an administrator. Shelves can be filled with the packaging of the courses so that students can examine the course content in advance.

The concentration level required for multimedia based training is much higher than for the equivalent tutor-led course. A well designed course will require thoughtful interaction from the student. For this reason sessions should be of no more than two hours with a break after the first hour. Of course, OL is not just computer based training. Audio tapes and videos, as well as other learning materials including all forms of computer based material, should be considered for an OL centre.

When it comes to buying courseware the choice is either generic or bespoke. Creating your own multimedia based training is no longer the prohibitively expensive and complex enterprise that it used to be. It is, however, something that is best left to the experts if budget permits.

If you decide to use multimedia based training, take the advice of those companies which specialize in providing such things rather than the in-house IT department, which will almost certainly never have come across that sort of technology before. Try to avoid your OL centre's computers being integrated into the company network since this will slow the PCs down and/or will cause problems when buying multiple licences from multimedia training vendors. Remember that your main aim is to facilitate training so that, when students come away from the centre, they are thinking only of the training and not of the medium used. Ensure, therefore, that both the courses and the computers are fully technically supported.

Another group of people to get on your side is the training department itself. There can be a lot of resistance from training staff who may regard the advent of OL as a threat and not, as it should be, an opportunity. Wherever possible, OL should be integrated into the existing training provision and this can only be done successfully with the wholehearted participation of the existing tutors. Existing training staff will be invaluable allies if you can get them on your side but deadly enemies if you do not – and working in isolation will be fatal.

Marketing and running the centre

If marketing in the sales sense is the creation of a sales opportunity, then marketing in the OL sense is the creation of training opportunities. Needs have to be identified, solutions found, objections countered and training delivered.

It is important to make sure that everyone in the company knows of the centre and what it has to offer. Some administrators believe that providing 'give-aways' is the key to success but experience shows that this is not so. The administrator or training manager must publicize the OL centre as much as possible and one way of doing this is to ensure that there is something different going on at the centre every week. This could involve, for example, organizing 'language days', where a native speaker comes in to encourage conversation in their particular tongue. New courseware must be broadcast by whatever means available, for example, via internal e-mail shots and/or posters.

It is also essential to have the OL centre manned for all its opening hours and the person given the job of OL centre administrator must not be told to do the job as part of other duties, because this will give the wrong impression to potential students. If this person is otherwise too busy to do the job successfully then usage will suffer accordingly. This post should be recruited like any other – either internally or externally. One of the main selection criteria should be that the successful candidate wants to do the job.

Encouraging usage

One of the most effective ways of generating OL centre usage is the mosquito technique. This is where the administrator is persistent in chasing managers and staff alike to use the centre and berates them when their particular personal or department usage figures drop below the average. The publication of usage statistics or the use of an open register is a good way of forcing – or even shaming people – into using or endorsing the centre. This is not to say 'bums on seats' at any price but, if the planning has been effective, there should be something at the centre for everyone.

Those keen on seeing a return on investment will require usage data in terms of the number of hours of student time – per head or by department and every other permutation.

There are two ways of collecting usage data. On each computer a front-end menu can store who, from which department, did what and for how long. But this can miss non-computer based study. Some companies use a simple paper based logging system which makes the simple but obvious assumption that if the student was doing presentation skills from 3pm until 4pm, then he or she did one hour's training and you need no more proof than that. Those who require more proof can put other methods in place to check that the student did actually do the course.

Integrating OL with existing training

Multimedia based training, when used in an OL centre, has one major advantage over other forms of training. Regardless of the situation, the training will always be of the same quality. This makes it particularly appropriate as the core of a course or a pre- or post-course module. Most importantly the multimedia element can bring all those using it to a standard level. For example, training on how to use Powerpoint is difficult if some members of the class do not know how to use a mouse. Perhaps those who want to do a course on Powerpoint 97 should first be directed to use an OL course on how to use a computer and on Windows 95. Such a strategy would save tutor time and make the whole class more productive.

A good example of integration is the Royal Marsden NHS Trust under the guidance of the Training and Development Advisor, Lorraine Stanley. This group of hospitals needed to run assertiveness training for a large number of its staff but found that a full day's course was difficult to arrange. Additionally, some staff already knew something about the subject whereas others were completely new to it. So it was decided to put everyone through a generic multimedia based package on the subject, which would take about two hours. This was done whenever the staff could fit it in – sometimes in the middle of the night. Then a half-day seminar was organized where the tutor organized the material around the multimedia based course. This produced the best of all worlds. The approach not only worked out cheaper than a classroom based course but was also enjoyed by the majority of participants. Follow up enquiries several months later showed that retention had improved too. Comparisons with tutor only and multimedia only training will be carried out next, but the combination of tutor-led and multimedia based training is expected to be the most effective.

Evaluating OL

Remember that, when evaluating multimedia courses, it is not the quantity of mouse clicks that determines how interactive the course is, but the quality of the required interaction. Repeated 'click to continue' is not interaction: you might just as well read a book. Without a tutor, self-paced OL can only tackle facts and concepts. Practical skills need practice and virtually all management or soft skills require some human intervention. The classic example of this is presentation skills where knowing all the techniques in the world will not replace the value of practising in front of an audience.

Similarly, some method has to be adopted to ensure that the training messages contained in OL courses have been absorbed. Collecting usage statistics is one way of showing that staff are receiving training but it is just as important to develop procedures to ensure that the training is achieving its goals. If OL is integrated into conventional training, students can take tests devised by the tutor. It may be intended that the training programme will lead to a qualification of some sort in which case a suitable examination or means of assessment will already exist. However, in most cases there is no need to establish whether a manager completing a course on business meetings, for instance, has reached an NVQ level or similar. It is merely necessary to establish that the student has assimilated the training messages.

The most effective way of doing this is as part of the appraisal process. Appraisals should concentrate on an individual's performance over time and training should be applied accordingly. The whole process should be a progressive cycle of determining the training need, enabling that training to take place, evaluating the performance improvement and, once again, applying the appropriate training. A more rigid examination procedure would probably not encourage learning. Again, this reflects an attitude issue. For many people learning is something they last had to do at school and they may have hoped never to do again. But, if learning in the workplace is shown as something that can be enjoyed with attainable goals it has a much better chance of success.

What the future holds for OL

A great deal has been spoken and written about the need to create learning organizations and lifetime learning opportunities. However, employees will have to be convinced that it is to their benefit if such initiatives are to succeed. OL is bound to play a major role in this provision and, with the advent of delivering learning via the Internet or intranets, overall costs will certainly be driven lower. Just-in-time training or training-on-demand is now becoming much easier to deliver but negative, entrenched attitudes to learning will have to be dispelled first. Since many companies seem reluctant to allow employees away from their desks to improve their performance, undertaking training at the desktop is an affordable and valuable alternative. This can now be achieved by delivering training materials using the company's network, via the Internet or its internal company equivalent, an intranet.

If employees, sitting at their desks, decide to undertake a training course then their concentration may be marred by the common distractions of the average office. It seems to be the accepted right of a manager to interrupt whatever a person is doing at their desk – and a training course is no exception. Therefore the best place for learning is an OL centre. That is not to say, however, that OL cannot take place at the desktop. In many circumstances an employee needs quick, just-in-time access to certain topics which will aid his or her performance. This is now possible and easy to achieve via an intranet. However, this is performance support and not OL *per se*. Many people have suggested that the former will replace the latter. Instead, one complements the other and is a further extension of the possibilities of OL.

Conclusion

OL has already proved its value but companies that want to get the best value from their OL centres need to establish best practice in their set-up, running and marketing practices. With learning taking such a priority in business it becomes imperative that managers utilize every opportunity to encourage their staff. In this respect OL is, and will continue to be, one of the most accessible forms of learning in the workplace.

Further reading

Howard, R. (1996), *The Learning Imperative*, Cambridge, Mass: Harvard Business School Press.

Malone, S. (1997), *How to Set up and Manage a Corporate Learning Centre*, Aldershot: Gower.

Scott, A. (1997), *Learning Centres*, London: Kogan Page.

Chapter 15

Development through Self-Managed Learning

Ian Cunningham

This chapter makes the case for the use of Self-Managed Learning (SML) as a basis for the development of any staff at any level in the organization. It covers some of the main background ideas before elaborating on the structures used in Self-Managed Learning.

The first problem to tackle, however, is that of language. When we came up with the term Self-Managed Learning in 1978 we were the only people using the term (the 'we' referred to here is a group of us at that time working in higher education). As time wore on, however, others started to apply the concept to their work and according to an Industrial Society study (1998), 38 per cent of organizations now use the term.

So what is 'Self-Managed Learning'? A simple distinction to make here is between 'weak' self-managed learning and 'strong' Self-Managed Learning. The capitalized version is the version described here and relates to a very precise structured approach to learning. The weak (lower case) version describes any kind of approach which gives responsibility to learners. One reviewer of the Industrial Society report rightly raised the issue of what these 38 per cent of organizations were actually doing. The reviewer was critical of organizations that appeared to be abdicating responsibilities to their people by saying 'it's over to you – we aren't going to support your learning – you have to be self-managed'.

This way of thinking is linked to other aberrations such as the use of 'empowerment' to justify letting people sink or swim (and letting the non-swimmers drown). The best advocates of empowerment do not do this, of course. They recognize that moving away from so-called 'command and control' methods requires new ways of working and new structures to replace the old. It is not simply a matter of removing all the glue that holds the organization together and then wondering why the place falls apart.

One problem with the weak version of self-managed learning is that it is used as a concept to cover any vague self-development type activity. This might be giving people distance learning packages, offering a learning resource centre or having a discussion about learning at an appraisal interview and then sending the person off to 'self-manage' their learning. In other cases people are put through a so-called 'development centre' or through 360 degree feedback, helped to write a personal development plan and then left to self-manage it.

These weak version approaches tend to be characterized by laissez faire approaches with poor support over time for the learner. Our research has shown that the pay-off from such approaches is low and individuals can be quite critical of this sloppy approach to development. The strong version Self-Managed Learning is about providing appropriate support so that people can really take charge of their own development. It is a poor parent that throws a non-swimming child in to the deep end without support – and it is a poor organization that does the equivalent to its people regarding their own learning. Furthermore, a good parent would not criticize their child if they needed rescuing when they did not have sufficient support. So managers who criticize their people for not delivering on personal development plans, for which their organization has provided inadequate support, are behaving both inappropriately and unfairly.

Why Self-Managed Learning?

In a world where there is growing pressure for increased results from fewer people, organizations have no option but to invest heavily in learning and development. The problem is that there is not always a correlation between expenditure on training and development and pay-off for individuals and organizations. Also individual learning may not integrate with organizational needs. Yet it is essential that individuals should be 'helped to take on greater responsibility for their own development and growth' (to quote the Institute of Personnel and Development, 1995).

The key requirement, then, seems to be to create a situation where learning:

- is owned by the individual,
- is properly supported, and at the same time,
- is closely integrated with organizational needs.

This is what SML aims to do.

What is Self-Managed Learning?

SML is about individuals managing their own learning. This includes people taking responsibility for decisions about:

- what they learn
- how they learn
- when they learn
- where they learn, and most fundamentally
- why they learn.

All of this is carried out in the context of live organizational needs. But organizational needs cannot be met without individuals feeling a personal sense of commitment to what is required by the organization. You can compel someone to sit in a classroom – but you cannot guarantee what he or she will learn.

Although everyone manages their own learning to some extent, it is clear that just telling people to take charge of their own learning can be very inefficient. Research indicates that people who are effective at. for example, leading major organizations, have managed their own learning very well throughout their careers. This does not mean, though, that they have been on more courses than others. Managing their own learning has meant the person using a wide range of opportunities for learning. These include:

- learning from others around them
- travel
- reading
- secondments
- projects
- being coached/mentored.

The examples quoted are only a few of the many experiences we can use for learning. Self-managing learners use a range to suit themselves. The problem is that unstructured, unplanned learning is very inefficient. Our research on successful top managers and leaders shows that they set clear goals for themselves in relation to their learning. It is not purely random.

Self-Managed Learning principles

SML is a structured approach to learning that not only makes the process work more efficiently but also helps people learn things they would not otherwise learn. Some of its key characteristics can be summarized under the following 'Seven Ss'. Each of these is now discussed.

1. Strategic

SML demands that people take a strategic stance in relation to their own learning. Strategy here means thinking long-term and with 'the big picture' in mind. Too often learning is driven by short-term tactical demands – an exam to pass, a new computer system to learn about. There is nothing wrong with such tactical learning – it is just that on its own it is too limited for the complexities and challenges we face in modern organizational life.

Too often people focus on just learning those skills related to narrow job requirements. These need to be balanced with attention to longer term needs such as preparing oneself for unknown futures. Many of the people made redundant in the 1980s had learned quite well how to do their current job. But when new technology or new organization structures hit them they were ill prepared for the changes.

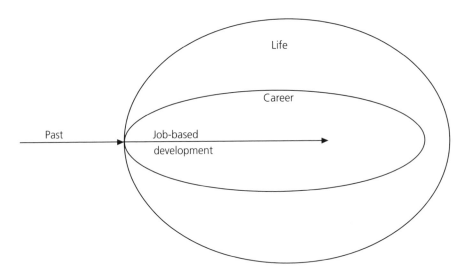

Figure 15.1   A strategic approach to learning

Figure 15.1 shows one way of mapping this issue. People may need to get a sense of their current abilities, qualities, values and interests to prepare for future career and life opportunities. Often it needs a context in which the person can clarify these for them to become more strategic. For instance a person may say that they have problems with time management. However, it may be that an underlying issue is the lack of balance between home and work. So one might end up addressing this bigger life issue alongside the specific job-related needs. Figure 15.1 does not imply an either/or choice. It is necessary to work on the problem at both levels. In the process the person can become more effective in work and have a more balanced lifestyle.

2. Syllabus-free

There is no required curriculum or syllabus in SML – the learning is driven by the real needs of individuals and their organizations. Learners may need assistance to help them to make their choices of what to learn, but such help avoids authoritarian control.

As will be apparent in the example of time management mentioned above, the key is understanding the needs of the learner before being able to respond. The average parent knows that when they were raising their baby, they first had to learn from the baby before the baby could learn from them. The baby makes noises and movements which the parent must understand in order to help the baby to learn. And when the baby starts to develop language the parent must listen to the baby and encourage it. The problem is that this process is reversed at about the age of five as the child goes to school and gradually is inducted into a system that goes from teacher to learner, not the other way round.

In the above I am not assuming a totally passive role from the person assisting the learner. The best managers assume a coaching role with people who report to them, and such coaching is based more around questioning and support than around direction and control (see Cunningham and Dawes, 1998).

3. Self-managed

People have to take responsibility for their own learning, but this is not a selfish activity. Self-managing includes the necessary interactions with others.

A simple model suggests that there may be four approaches to learning, and that people often go through these approaches in stages. I will take each approach in turn.

- *Dependent*   In this mode learners may be highly passive, expecting others to teach them everything without them needing to take initiative. Learners may also absorb uncritically what others tell them. This mode can be characterized by laziness and procrastination. It is clearly seen by some as a product of experiences in education.

- *Counterdependent*   This mode is associated with rebelliousness, a rejection of new ideas, anti-authority behaviours and high levels of criticism of anyone in a teaching role. Counterdependence is also associated with learners playing down the need to learn, not listening to others and often a tendency to passive–aggressive behavioural patterns. A simple way of characterizing it is to compare it with the teenager who says 'I'm not influenced by my parents; I just do the opposite of what they say!'

I would guess that many trainers and developers would recognize both patterns of behaviour. Often individuals can flip between these so that they oscillate between dependence and counterdependence. One reason for this is that neither pattern is showing autonomy or independence in learning. They are both reacting to authority and can be seen as patterns that a person in the organization has not grown out of.

- *Independent*   In this mode learners are prepared to learn for themselves. They take initiatives, actively seek learning experiences, enjoy the pressure to perform well and welcome feedback on their work. This mode is one that organizations say they increasingly need and it is associated with a more entrepreneurial and empowered style of working. The danger is that an overemphasis on independence can lead to a selfish self-centredness. Therefore this mode needs balancing with the next one.

- *Interdependence*   Interdependent learners are keen to learn from others, to support others in their learning, to share their own learning and to collaborate in teams. They listen to others, question others to find out new ideas and information and they enjoy engaging in dialogue with a wide range of people. They characterize the best of a learning organization approach.

In reality the last two modes are also a balanced pair like the first two (see Figure 15.2). Independence and interdependence at best go together. The person who can stand on their own feet and look after themselves is also going to find it easier to be open and sharing with others (since they do not see others as a threat or challenge) so the distinctions are ultimately not showing two separate personalities. Organizations need people who can balance independence and interdependence.

This now leads back to the role of Self-Managed Learning. SML programmes ideally encourage the balanced approach described here. By challenging people to come up with their own learning needs SML promotes independence. But the person has to negotiate their learning requirements with others and engage in processes to support other people's learning, hence providing the interdependent balance.

This approach is not always smooth and easy. People can flip back into dependent and counterdependent modes. Hence SML programmes need careful design and a support structure that can address these issues.

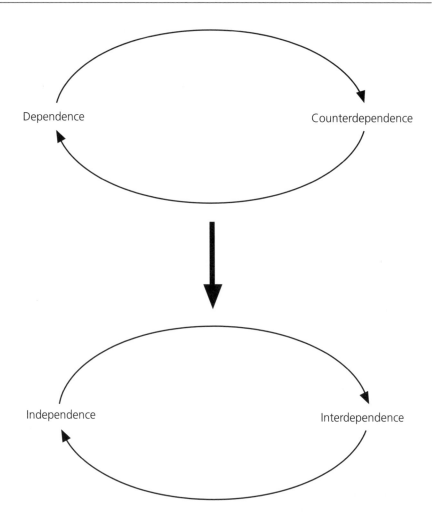

Figure 15.2   Becoming self-managing: four approaches to learning

4. Shared

The learning is located in a context. SML requires learners to connect with others and especially to integrate their learning with organizational needs. This, in part, comes via one specific SML structure, namely the use of a *learning contract* as a means for people to specify what they want to learn – and to share this with others.

A learning contract is more than just a fancy name for a 'personal development plan' or an 'action plan'. Such plans often stay as interesting wish-lists (the equivalent of New Year resolutions). A learning contract is different because:

- It is a serious written document that is negotiated between the individual and relevant interested parties.
- It is a living document that individuals refer to regularly.
- It covers long- and short-term development needs and spells out a programme to meet these.
- It has measures of achievement built in so that pay-off to the individual and the organization can be monitored.

The way we achieve the above is to get people to answer five questions – and to write down their answers to these. The questions are taken in order and move the person from the past to the present and to the future.

- *Where have I been?* (How has my career progressed? What have I learned from past experiences?)

  This question helps the person make sense of their past experiences. The reason for starting with this question is that we are a product of our past. Either we were born this way (the genes) or we had accidents that changed us or we learned to be this way. Whatever the reason it is 100 per cent due to the past. So in order to move on we need to explore where our current capabilities, values and beliefs came from. We may need to modify some of our ingrained habits if we are to move on.

- *Where am I now?* (What kind of person am I? What are my strengths and weaknesses? What are my guiding values and beliefs?)

  This question locates the person's current situation. The person may have evidence from a range of sources to help them address this (see Figure 15.3). Sometimes people want to leap straight in to the next question (on goal setting) but we have found that getting a secure sense of the present is essential as a baseline for considering the future.

- *Where do I want to get to?* (What kind of person would I like to be? What strengths can I develop? What weaknesses do I want to address? What are my short- and long-term goals?)

  This question focuses now on the future – and Figure 15.1 can help people see the need to balance goals at different levels.

- *How will I get there?* (What action is needed for me to progress from where I am to where I would like to be? What learning do I need to undertake – and how will I do it?)

  The answer to this question in essence provides the person's own plan of action and is equivalent to a curriculum (in a traditional educational programme). The learner may draw on a whole range of methods to

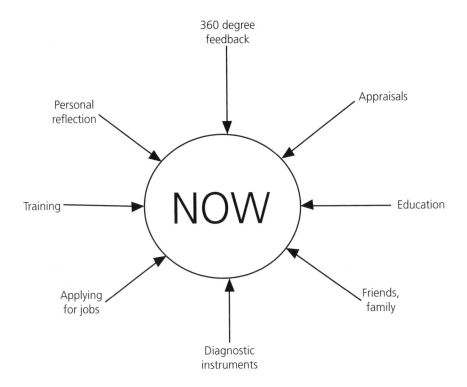

Figure 15.3   **Sources of information that address the question 'where am I now?'**

achieve their goals including the standard training offerings (e.g. work-shops, courses, seminars and conferences) as well as coaching and men-toring assistance, learning packages, secondments, projects and so on. There is nothing that needs to be excluded except on the grounds of cost or organizational policy. At one level when the person is pursuing their learning contract it can look like any other development process. The big difference though, is that the learner will be working to a carefully crafted plan as created in the learning contract. They will not be ran-domly going off on courses or haphazardly ploughing through learning materials. They will have clearly identified strategic goals and they will be aware that they will need to show progress to those with whom they have entered into the contract.

- *How will I know if I have arrived?* (How will I demonstrate the achieve-ment of my goals? What will be my measures of achievement? What evidence will I be able to show?)
  This last question is vitally important. The learner is contracted to

learn against specified goals and they need to show that this has happened (after a period of time – typically six months to a year). This question adds considerable bite to the SML process and is one example of a difference between learning contracts in SML and less rigorous programmes that might use the label 'self-managed learning'.

5. Supported

Learners are supported in meeting the goals they set themselves in their learning contract. One support structure is the *learning set*.

The learning set is one mechanism that ensures some of the benefits mentioned above. In SML programmes individuals are grouped in 'sets' of about five or six persons. The set is the primary place where each person negotiates their learning contract and reports progress on it. The set typically meets every four to six weeks and provides an arena for both support and challenge. Participants comment that the set provides a unique, cost-effective forum to push individuals to learn in depth and to solve real business problems at the same time.

Attending a set is not like going off on a course: set meetings only work on practical issues that have a bearing on the business and the needs of individuals in the set. Indeed, when I worked in Shell we were asked to ensure that the pay-off from the programme, in money terms, was measurably greater than the cost (which we did). However, organizations with whom we work are clear that the major benefits come over time: individuals really do learn to take charge of their own development.

This not only enhances their performance but can reduce training costs. (It is not that training ceases with SML, but rather that it becomes better targeted. In businesses such as the international drinks company, Allied Domecq – which uses SML extensively – training events were only put on if enough people had the need for them specified in their learning contracts.)

One crucial support factor is the role of the set adviser. This person is present in the set to assist it to function effectively. The role may be played by someone in HR or training but can be effectively carried out by a good line manager or team leader. The reason for this is that the role is not one of teaching or training but of providing support for the set. Such support may at times be in the form of challenges to people to address tough learning needs, so it is not just a cosy facilitative role (see Cunningham, 1998, for a more detailed discussion of the role).

6. *Structured*

SML provides a rigorous structure in order to help learning – but the structure is content-free. That is, learners decide for themselves how to use the structure. SML is not a 'free for all'; it operates within the real constraints of organizational life and requires self-managing learners to work within resource and policy limits.

Some of the specific learning structures used have been described above, but they are not exhaustive of all the possibilities. SML programmes need to be carefully designed to suit the organization, its culture and its strategic direction.

7. *Stretching*

SML is not an easy option. Some people think that managing your own learning via SML must be a laid back way to learn. It is not. The requirement to set goals and meet them is a tough-minded approach to learning – and having to meet regularly with colleagues to discuss progress means that learners have to keep to their agreed plans (or consciously change them).

Conclusion

The above provides an outline of some factors in SML. However, our experience is that each programme has to be designed to suit each organization. Also organizations have used SML in different ways. Cable and Wireless used it to foster development in a variety of regions of the world including Europe, North America and the Middle East. They also found that the approach was especially valued by technical staff, secretaries and administrators as well as by managers (see Webster, 1995).

PPP healthcare in the UK similarly found that having launched SML with senior managers, their front line customer service staff valued having the same opportunities for development. On the other hand Arun District Council in Sussex, UK started SML with middle managers and then extended the process to all senior managers and directors (including the chief executive). Sainsbury's used SML as a basis for a major shift in the role of personnel and all their 600+ personnel professionals went through a nine month programme.

However, all the SML programmes in the organizations mentioned had in common a carefully thought through design that then had to be well managed. This highlights that SML needs to be part of a strategic approach to development and it needs the focused commitment of senior people in order to make it happen effectively.

Further reading

Cunningham, I. (1998), *The Wisdom of Strategic Learning: The Self-Managed Learning Solution*, 2nd edn, Aldershot: Gower. This book goes into much more detail about SML and its underpinnings. Research evidence is quoted and there are many examples of SML in practice.

Cunningham, I. and Dawes, G.D. (1998), *Exercises for Developing Coaching Capability*, London: Institute of Personnel and Development. This is a pack of 32 exercises plus supporting documentation and a commentary on the exercises. It takes an SML stance on coaching and elaborates on ways of making it happen.

Industrial Society (1998), *Managing Best Practice No. 40, Self Managed Learning*. This report shows the problems of the confusion about terminology. It covers mainly what I have called 'weak version' self-managed learning.

People Make the Difference (1995), London: Institute of Personnel and Development.

Webster, J. (1995), 'Self Managed Learning in Cable and Wireless', *Croner's A–Z Guide for HRM Professionals*, Issue 6 (21 November 1995), pp. 6–8. This short article outlines work carried out in the company over a period of years. The article is based on an internal evaluation report on SML.

Chapter 16

Personal development

Michael Waters

What is personal development?

Personal development can be described as the process of experiencing or bringing about personally meaningful change at some level of our being. That change is likely to be perceived as taking us 'forward' as a person, and at its most profound is generative or even transformational in its effects.

A snappier definition might be: change *of* self, *by* self, *for* self. 'Of' implies that development is truly personal only if it is actually *about* me – if it makes a difference not just *to* me but to the me I am. 'By' suggests that personal development is fundamentally a self-initiated, self-directed process. Significant life experiences and other people can conspire to create the conditions in which my development occurs, but I am primarily responsible for any changes I seek to bring about. 'For' implies that I am the immediate beneficiary of a purposeful process.

A distinguishing feature of personal development is respect for the development process itself. The very experience of going through a personal development programme (or its experiential equivalent) may be as, or more, important than any specific practical benefits resulting from it. The journey really can mean as much as the destination, whereas job-specific training is mainly outcomes-focused. Besides, the outcomes of personal development are by definition less determinable, more varied and self-referential. *I* decide what counts as personal development for me and virtually anything can count. Because personal development can only be metabolized in and owned by the individual it concerns, he or she seldom needs to be convinced of its value.

Personal development processes

There are many ways to characterize the primary processes of personal development. One key process term is *recognition*. This draws attention to personal development as a process of self-discovery, revelation and increasing self-awareness. For example, we may come to recognize in ourselves recurring patterns of thought and behaviour and to see how they have channelled or inhibited our growth. Recognition may be stage one in a multi-stage process of change.

Another key process word is *(re-)connection*. From this perspective, personal development is construed largely as a matter of contacting and integrating the various 'parts' or aspects of ourselves. For example, it may involve bringing our heart and mind into closer alignment, one benefit of which might be more confident decision making. Or it may involve the recovery of a 'lost' part of ourself, such as the carefree child within.

A third key process term is *realization*. This suggests that personal development is about bringing into being latent, or only partly exploited, talents and inner resources. An example would be learning how to make greater use of our potential brain power. Becoming all that we are capable of becoming is also called *self-actualization*.

A fourth term, and one which presupposes even more strongly our incompleteness as beings, is *acquisition*. This implies the familiar view of development as a process of adding to what we already know, can do or are. For example, we can gain new skills, acquire more empowering beliefs and add to our stock of knowledge, and thereby experience personal expansion. Acquisition can be construed as complementary to realization: new tools and information help us to make better use of innate resources. It can also reflect a deficit model: we need new tools and information to make up for some lack within us.

These process terms should be of more than theoretical interest to HRD professionals. Although they may not map simply onto the provision of courses, materials and services in the real world, there is no doubt that some providers lean towards a 'putting in' or acquisition view of personal development and others towards a 'pulling out' view, emphasizing recognition and realization. Some blend the two, while others work from an holistic healing perspective with an emphasis on 'putting together' or reconnection.

Generally speaking, 'putting in' approaches tend to come closest to conventional forms of training and sometimes imply a deficit model of its functions and value. 'Pulling out' approaches tend to be predicated on positive assumptions about people and development (we are already resource-full, we do not have to be sick to get better) and to use methodologies peculiarly appropriate to *personal* development. These include guided self-discovery, education in its literal 'drawing out' sense as opposed to training, and key processes in such helping relationships as counselling and coaching.

Personal and professional

Within a training and development context, personal development is best understood in terms of how it relates to/differs from *professional* development.

Professional development is primarily about occupational role development. It is about enhancing knowledge and technical skills, and assisting employees to acquire the wherewithal to fulfil current and future job requirements. Personal development is much more about the development of the ('whole') person. It is the development that occurs when individual employees are construed, or construe themselves, first and foremost as people, and is predicated on the premise that people are always much more than the roles they play. So, for example, accountants are people who happen currently to be engaged in the activities of accountancy, and almost certainly in many other activities besides.

In reality, personal and professional development are not so easily distinguished. This has something to do with our variability as human beings: the relationship between the role and the whole differs from person to person. But it is also because the label 'personal development', denotes a spectrum of provision as follows:

- At one end of the spectrum (the 'professional' end) are in-house or bespoke training activities which may be *called* 'personal development' but which substantially reflect the company's own development priorities. If the label is appropriate at all, then it is because these courses and materials tend to concentrate on 'soft' (people) skills as opposed to hard (technical) ones, sometimes with the implication that personal development is a form of remedial development for designated cohorts of staff: 'They're good IS managers, but they've got a lot to learn about handling people'.

- Further along the spectrum, and what most frequently purports to be personal development, is what might more accurately be called *customized professional development*. Such training addresses or purports to address the needs and interests of the individuals concerned and may be training activities they have selected for themselves, because they 'like the sound of them', perhaps, or think they might be beneficial for career enhancement. Alternatively, they may issue from personal assessment, appraisal, performance review or personal development planning. But choosing an IT course because it looks useful or attending a seminar on negotiation skills in order to become a better manager are still essentially *professional* development experiences. Whatever their personal spin-offs, and there may be many, they are focused more on the role than the whole. Customized professional development is *for* me, but it does not need to be *about* me in any significant sense.

- The middle section of the spectrum would be occupied by on-the-job and employer-facilitated opportunities for personal development. Comparatively formal (i.e. planned and explicit) versions would include learning interviews, participation in action learning sets, job shadowing, outdoor management training and some forms of coaching, with the emphasis on professional skills. Secondments also offer opportunities for personal expansion. For example, there is much evidence that teachers seconded through the Teacher Placement Service, or 'twinned' with managers from industry (e.g. as part of the National Westminster Bank's Face 2 Face scheme), benefit personally as well as professionally. Informal activities might include personal development through teamwork, skills modelling at the initiative of the individual and the maintenance of a reflective journal.

  The quantity and quality of opportunities for *in situ* development depend upon the organizational culture. Is it a development culture generally, one which places a premium on learning, innovation and creativity? Is the climate trusting, open and supportive? Is there an emphasis on learning teams, project work, exploratory action and learning from mistakes and failure? Are there ample possibilities for quality feedback and genuine dialogue? Are managers and internal consultants empowered to facilitate the learning of individuals by teasing out personal insights and growth points that emerge from a work or training activity? Is there a lot of 'talking up' – of people and the organization as a whole?

- Towards the other end of the provision continuum (the 'personal' end) are the opportunities employees may have for genuine personal development. Those funded and/or supported by companies tend to fall into two broad categories: programmes linked explicitly to the development of professional capabilities and those intended to promote self-improvement more generally.

Propersonal development

Some companies need to be persuaded that personal development is a sound investment rather than a cost with risky pay-backs. That is, they need to feel confident that there will be determinable and desirable outcomes in the work situation. One solution is to make explicit how the personal development programme is designed to impact directly upon the participants' skills and activities. We do not yet have a term to describe personal development programmes designed to address professional development needs, but a suitable term might be *propersonal* development.

'Propersonal' development would include the development that individuals might need to experience before being able fully to discharge such challenging responsibilities as inspiring colleagues. 'Inspiring' is not an isolated skill that managers can simply be taught to perform. It presupposes a great deal about the people who are doing the inspiring, for example, their levels of self-esteem and self-efficacy. In other words, some managers may need to develop as people before they can be 'inspiring' professionals.

'Propersonal' would also cover learning-to-learn skills and other kinds of underpinning and overarching capabilities. An example would be helping staff to manage their thoughts, attitudes and feelings so that they could make the best use of professional training and the skills acquired from it.

One of a number of starting points for propersonal development could be the use of one of the many instruments now available for personal profiling and personality assessment. An example is 'The Management Style Indicator' (Business Minds, St Albans, UK) which identifies the predominant thinking patterns that underpin management competencies.

There is also a link between propersonal development and career development – terms which are frequently coupled together. This is understandable, given that the latter is for many people a mix of personal and professional development. As Pemberton and Herriot (1994) observe, 'career' has come to mean 'the planned development of personal skills over time, rather than the movement of individuals on career ladders or succession plans'. But it is important to recognize that personal development can take place without any intention of career 'advancement', and the latter can occur without genuine personal development – hence the need sometimes for propersonal development. It is one of the main reasons that people 'find themselves' in, or get promoted to, jobs that do not fulfil their most powerful personal needs.

The alternative to personal development linked to specific job requirements is provision in the form of general and usually 'open' programmes, seminars and workshops. These tend to be standardized products suitable for people from a variety of occupational backgrounds. Examples include 'Investment in Excellence' (The Pacific Institute, Seattle) and 'Impact and Effectiveness' (The Institute of Human Development, Tonbridge, UK). Participants are addressed first and foremost as people and only secondarily, if at all, as employees of particular organizations. Each programme has its specific objectives, but the general aims are typically about challenging limited beliefs, developing positive thinking, personal effectiveness and self-confidence and setting and achieving goals.

There are some well-known providers of open programmes (e.g. Mind-store, The Covey Foundation, Dale Carnegie Training, The Pacific Institute) and a host of smaller, less well-known or more specialized training organizations, including NLP organizations. Nowadays, serious self-improvers have no end of opportunities for pursuing their interests either in a private capacity (if they can meet the costs!) or supported by their employers. In addition to short and long courses, seminars, workshops and other 'events', there are video- and audio-based personal development programmes (Robbins, 1993), training materials for self-development (Davies, 1995), CD-ROM, CBT and on-line materials, such as *Plan Your Own Development* (Maxim Training, Brighton, UK, 1997) so that personal development can be pursued in the car or the lounge as well as in the training room or open learning centre. In other words, from a provision and resource point of view, there is ever-increasing choice and flexibility with regard to the options for personal development.

Personal development as strategy

Given that provision for personal development is now a multi-million pound industry, is there a compelling rationale for personal development as a T & D strategy? One point of view is that it cannot be avoided. In a fast-changing, uncertain world where flexibility, adaptability and skills acquisition are the names of the game, individuals have no option but to take a substantial degree of responsibility for their development and employability. Paradoxically, security comes less from having a job than from having the wherewithal to get one. This sense of inner security comes above all from feeling resourceful and self-directed, and having marketable skills.

Companies may also have little option but to support personal development initiatives, though for ethically-challenged organizations, personal development can be the loophole through which they evade training responsibilities and use personal development plans (PDPs) less for nurturing employees than for ensuring that individual development aligns with corporate objectives. However, many companies do now accept that personal development is an entitlement for the staff they may have at some stage either to shed or to adapt to very different work requirements. The reciprocal entitlement is the expectation that individuals will commit to the company for the duration of their employment.

In resource terms, a compelling argument for championing personal development is that it can make job-related training work – 'work' in the sense of underpin, complete and make more sustainable. The argument is that training that focuses upon skills and behaviour is mainly a grafting operation. New material may be introduced, but there is little attempt or time to root it in the deeper soil of an employee's existing beliefs and values or self-image or models of the world.

Organizations that seek to challenge the thinking, attitudes and values of their employees need to do more than engage their professional personas; they need to engage employees personally at all relevant levels. The options here are as follows:

1. Ensure that all training events have a personal development dimension.
2. Run personal development programmes prior to or alongside occupational training.
3. A third option is mentoring and/or one-to-one coaching. The latter is currently in favour, conspicuously among executives with the means to employ external personal development consultants – a burgeoning occupational group particularly rich in people with NLP and sports psychology/coaching backgrounds. Attitudes to mentoring as a means of support for personal development vary from organization to organization. It is embraced, for example, by many companies and most state schools in the UK, in part because it is seen as a means of enhancing the personal development of mentors as well as mentees, but eschewed as old culture by some major commercial organizations, such as Microsoft. DIY forms may be the trend of the future.

Learning organizations and personal development

Other arguments for supporting personal development are equally powerful though perhaps less conspicuous on the company balance sheet. Some come from contemporary theorists in the areas of the learning organization, leadership and systemic thinking, including the view advanced by Joe Jaworski (1996) and others that the way to transform an organization is through personal transformation. Learning organizations need employees committed to learning for renewal and to self-leadership as a prerequisite for leading others.

However, individual development is not necessarily the same thing as organizational learning. An employee can learn things that do not benefit the company. Learning organizations clearly need employees who are not just self-improvers but who are capable of taking risks and learning through exploratory action. They also need systems to capture and mobilize the things learned. Personal development alone will not produce a learning organization, but employees who feel nurtured and supported as individuals are more likely to become naturally entrepreneurial and contribute willingly to organizational development. As Bob Garratt (1995) observes, 'personal development is a crucial energising force which opens up the rest of the development process'.

This 'energising force' can move in subtle ways. It can secure employee goodwill and enhance the feel good factor. Employees frequently express appreciation for development opportunities that are not obviously connected to their actual jobs and often report unexpected consequences that impact in some way on job performance. The conclusion seems to be that companies reap the benefits of employees who have reaped the benefits of personal development. Quality open programmes can be a sound investment for companies with faith. It is not 'just' that they help employees to feel valued and nurtured, nor 'just' that they contribute to a culture in which growth and learning are valued in themselves. It is also that they respect and work with the 'whole' person and so bring about desirable systemic effects. That is, changes experienced in one aspect of an individual yield changes in other aspects, or have spreading effects, so that what might first manifest itself as greater empathy with a partner at home generalizes into greater empathy with colleagues in the workplace.

Advice on personal development

The following are pointers to good practice in personal development provision.

1. Strive for congruence. Organizations that support personal development need to make policy and practice as consonant as possible with the spirit of personal development. In terms of provision, that normally means avoiding both *prescription* ('All middle managers must go through programme X') and *proscription* ('We don't allow sabbaticals, job exchanges etc.'). Both stances imply that the organization knows best what individuals need for their own development.

2. Offer opportunities both for individual (customized) professional development and for broader personal development. The integrity of the organization is at risk if the former is passed off as the latter when clearly it is not. Assessment centres and most appraisal systems are more concerned with the former – and rightly so. Organizations have a legitimate right to develop employees in line with corporate aspirations. This is consistent with the standards of IiP. But it is legitimate also for employees to seek development possibilities in line with their personal aspirations.

   One option is to give staff an entitlement to genuinely personal development activities through the kind of credit system that some companies (e.g. GEC Avionics) use for professional training purposes. An alternative is to offer free training on any subject, and hope both to stimulate levels of development and to increase staff satisfaction – an approach tried with success by London Underground's District Line. In the spirit of personal development, employees should have scope to decide how, when and where to address their personal development needs and interests. Outdoor management training may be right for one person; a weekend retreat might be right for another. They might both be right for the same person at different times.

3. Clarify the ownership of personal development plans and portfolios. As a rule, the organization has a more legitimate stake in plans which emphasize professional development needs and intentions than those which are more truly personal in nature. Accept also that some individuals may seek PDP-related support from peers rather than from line managers. Managers may need to be prepared for this.

4. As a rule, do not link opportunities for attending 'open' personal development programmes too overtly to corporate agendas. An opportunity offered and accepted as a gift ('it's something for me') is less likely to be rejected and more likely to be received positively.

5. Enable anyone with a staff development or management function to develop relevant 'propersonal competence' – i.e. the capacity to appreciate the personal development requirements that underpin professional practice. The question they need to address is: 'How might this individual need to grow personally in order to carry out job tasks more effectively?' Helping individuals to address themselves to this question is the next challenge.

6. Encourage a proactive approach to career and personal development. It needs to be an ongoing concern rather than a reaction to a 'crisis' (restructuring, redundancy etc.), though some organizations seem, perversely, to reserve their best personal development opportunities for the employees they are about to dispense with! It is also the case that organizations in flux can benefit from giving employees opportunities to explore the personal implications of the changes affecting them. For example, Lloyds Bank introduced a 'Personal Development Initiative' for payment services personnel to explore their changing relationship with the bank and the skills they needed.

7. Encourage employees to see themselves as 'self-employed' and the organization as their current best customer. This is generally healthy for all parties and little risk to organizations caring enough to secure the willing commitment of staff. The message to individuals needs to be 'invest in yourself as a company invests in R & D'. Serious self-improvers will expect to invest in themselves and to be invested in. Companies need to be prepared to negotiate development opportunities as part of recruitment packages.

8. Cater for more than self-starters. Bear in mind that with personal development there tends to be an inverse relationship between need and

inclination. Those who thrive in 'contract cultures' and other uncertain environments, such as the self-reliant and the entrepreneurial, tend to make self-development a priority. Some even become self-development junkies (Waters, 1997). Employees who lack self-direction and are low in self-esteem are often reluctant self-developers. Organizations need strategies to nurture proactivity in the diffident and disinclined.

9. The following are some indicators of quality personal development programmes:

    ●   They tend to limit numbers to facilitate full participant interaction (through events on a rally scale can work, especially at emotional and motivational levels).
    ●   They tend to have a generous ratio of coaches to participants so that the latter receive one-to-one guidance when necessary.
    ●   They seek to work on personal development generally as well as on specific course objectives. (One major training company, Hemsley Fraser, explicitly promises to 'develop personal qualities such as self-confidence, motivation, initiative and positive thinking' on every course it runs.)
    ●   They tend to build in time for personal reflection as well as for interaction and exercises.
    ●   They are likely to run over two or more days, and may well consist of 'modules' separated by days or weeks. Personal development processes often need time to ripen, and often ripen best when the programme is not simply linear in structure and when it works on more than one level of consciousness.

10. Stock staff libraries and resource centres with as wide a range as possible of personal development books, tapes, CDs and other materials. Include materials on learning, NLP, popular psychology, self-help, health and healing, success, wealth-creation, life planning and spiritual development as well as materials on 'organizational' favourites such as time management and teams. Personal development opportunities should also figure in intranets and other knowledge management systems.

Further reading

Casey, D. (1993), *Managing Learning in Organisations*, Milton Keynes: Open University Press.

Davies, E. (1995), *Unlocking Your People's Potential* (Training Activities), Cambridge: Fenman Training.

Forrest, A. (1996), *Fifty Ways to Personal Development*, London: The Industrial Society.

Garratt, R. (1995), *Learning to Lead: Developing Your Organisation and Yourself*, London: HarperCollins.

Hodgkinson, L. (1993), *The Personal Growth Handbook*, London: Piatkus.

Holbeche, L. (1997), *The Impact of Flatter Structures on Careers*, Oxford: Butterworth Heinemann.

Jaworksi, J. (1996), *The Inner Path of Leadership*, Berrett-Koehler Publishers.

Jones, S. (1996), *Developing a Learning Culture*, Maidenhead: McGraw-Hill.

Lickson, J. (1996), *The Continuously Improving Self: A Personal Guide to TQM*, Menlo Park, CA: Crisp.

Megginson, D. and Whitaker, V. (1996), *Cultivating Self-Development*, London: IPD.

Pedler, M. and Boydell, T. (1994), *Managing Yourself*, 2nd edn, London: HarperCollins.

Pemberton, C. and Herriot, P. (1994), 'Cutting through the career jungle ...', *Professional Manager*, January, 18–19.

Robbins, A. (1993), *Personal Power*, (audio-cassette programme), Robbins Research International, Inc.

Waters, M. (1996), *The Element Dictionary of Personal Development*, Shaftesbury: Element.

Waters, M. (1997), 'Beyond the Lotus-Eater', *Management Skills and Development*, March, 38–39.

Chapter 17

Personal development plans

George Boak

Personal development plans, or PDPs, as they are commonly called, have become one of the most widely used development approaches in the UK. These action plans for learning and development are usually agreed between line managers and individual members of their teams although some are agreed between individuals and the training department – particularly when the employees in question are identified as potential high-fliers, and the training department has a remit to develop them through (among other means) various kinds of work experience. This chapter will concentrate mainly on the first type of PDP – the kind agreed between line managers and their team members – although much of what makes a good PDP of that type will also apply to PDPs agreed directly with the training department.

Specifically, three practical questions will be addressed:

1. What are the benefits of PDPs?
2. How can we use PDPs most effectively?
3. How can trainers and personnel specialists help line managers and their teams make the most of PDPs?

The benefits of PDPs

Where PDPs are agreed between a line manager and the individual members of his or her team, they have the potential to focus development resources and activities on individual, job-related learning needs.

Over the period of the PDP, individuals can then use a variety of methods and available resources to improve their knowledge and skills. These might include attending training courses, taking on new responsibilities, undertaking short secondments, carrying out research projects or receiving coaching from the line manager or from team colleagues.

Working in this way benefits both the company and the individual, because the PDP targets are agreed with a knowledge of the organization's needs for skilled and knowledgeable performance. In this respect PDPs are one key component of developing learning organizations where, in the words of Barham *et al.* (1988), training and personal development are an integral part of daily activities, and where learning is a continuous process, closely related to actions in the workplace.

As for the potential benefits of PDPs, these can be outlined as follows:

1. They can ensure that learning is relevant, both for the individual and the organization. The goals of the PDP can be matched to the learner's needs and opportunities, so they can develop the right skills for their circumstances.
2. They can be motivational, inspiring the individual to learn.
3. They can help to focus support and resources on an individual's learning needs. They can create pressure for more task rotation, for more opportunity for relevant practice, for more suitable training.
4. They can help people to develop their skills of independent experiential learning, which will enhance their ability to manage changing situations and changing needs in the future.

Of course, these are potential benefits; they are not guaranteed with every PDP. Much depends on how PDPs are used.

Ten reliable guidelines

For PDPs to achieve their potential, they must be used intelligently, with time spent on planning and support. They are not likely to produce good results if line managers and team members hurry through them in one annual meeting. It may take several meetings and several drafts to produce a sensible PDP, and several review meetings throughout the year to support it.

Based on experience of using different kinds of work-based learning plans, and of working with organizations where formal personal development planning systems are in place, here are ten reliable guidelines for producing effective PDPs.

1. Win commitment

The first requirement for an effective PDP is the commitment of the learner. People cannot be made to learn if they do not want to. The best PDPs are types of learning contract that express clear, agreed targets to which both the learner and the line manager are committed (Boak, 1998). If there is some

freedom for the individual to design their PDP, they will be much more motivated to achieve its objectives.

This means that a line manager should, on the one hand, be receptive to
suggestions from their team members about what those team members would
like to learn, and on the other hand be prepared to be patiently persuasive
about what they believe the team member should learn. It should be obvious
(but it sometimes escapes line managers) that a person who does not accept
they have certain learning needs will not spend time trying to address them.

This is one reason why the drafting of a PDP may take more than a single
meeting. It helps if each party has a chance to raise their suggestions, put forward their reasons, and then allow the other party some time to think about
what has been said before engaging in further discussion. Even when two
people work closely together, there can be some surprises for both parties
when PDP proposals are first aired.

2. Make them relevant to the company and the learner

Effective PDPs help both the company and the learner. Both parties want to
develop particular skill areas but sometimes there has to be compromise.
Some objectives are primarily for the company (although the line manager
should be able to make the case that the individual will also benefit from
them) and some may be more for the individual (although the learner should
be able to make the case that the company will also benefit).

The PDP's aims, and the reasons behind them, may also reflect an interesting pattern of different timescales. Relevance does not necessarily mean
obsession with the here and now. The line manager may want the team member to take action to improve on a skill that is causing a current performance
gap, but the team member may be more concerned with skills and knowledge
that will be relevant to a move into a different area of responsibility, which
they hope will happen next year. Of course, the line manager will also be concerned with ensuring the members of the team have the knowledge and skills
to cope with future challenges, but the most immediate pressures on line managers are usually to achieve the task objectives of their section, not to manage
the careers of their staff.

Some structured needs analysis can often help the parties to produce a
more effective PDP. This is particularly true in the case of less obvious learning needs. For example, a person about to undertake a new project may realize that they need to learn about the facts of the project and where it fits into
the company, and about the other people who are also working on the project,
their names and their abilities. But they may be much less aware that, for
example, they need to improve their influencing skills and their teambuilding
skills if they are to be successful on the project.

3. Set clear objectives

Some PDPs are large in scale. They consist of a clutch of disparate goals the individual is expected to achieve over the next 12 months, with little detail about action plans or measures of performance. Others are expressed in the shorthand of inputs, or 'experience', rather than clear learning objectives, i.e. the team member will attend this or that training course; they will get experience of working more closely with these or those specialists. Such PDPs may be better than no personal development plans at all, but they are by no means as effective as they might be.

A more effective approach is to be clear and specific about objectives. Rather than setting out a shopping list of eight or ten loosely-defined aims the effective PDP will pick out four or five clearly focused areas for development. The purpose of a PDP is not to predict what the person will learn and develop in the next 12 months, it is to create action plans that aim at priority areas. Clear objectives, clear action plans and specific review targets also have a positive effect on motivation.

The better PDPs also explicitly target outcomes – the development of the learner's knowledge and skills – rather than inputs such as attending courses and gaining 'experience'. Of course learners and line managers sometimes have difficulty defining skills, and may need assistance and support. Part of this assistance may be in the nature of needs analysis to identify priority areas for development and to provide a language for discussing and recognizing skills.

4. Make them realistic and stretching

The objectives in a PDP should be realistic; that is, they should be achievable in the time period. Ideally, they should contain a degree of stretch, so that learners need to apply themselves in order to be successful. They should not be a summary of what a person is likely to learn anyway. In the normal course of events, these desirable characteristics of effective PDPs are not easy to achieve. It is difficult to predict precisely how much improvement an individual will achieve over the course of a year – the most common duration of a PDP – and the progress of personal development will benefit from intermittent monitoring, review and negotiated revision.

5. Be flexible and adaptable

Some company schemes incorporate a PDP into the performance planning and review system, so that the line manager and their team member will review the task objectives and the personal development objectives agreed for last year, and then agree task objectives and personal development objectives for the year ahead.

Sometimes the company scheme requires the parties to link the PDP closely with the planned task objectives. So line manager and team member devise the PDP solely (or mainly, depending on the scheme) on the basis of next year's task objectives. There is a neatness and simplicity about this, which has obviously appealed to the designers of these schemes, but it unnecessarily restricts the scope of the PDP.

In a similar vein, an increasing number of companies use competency models to support their human resource development activities. Some companies may be tempted to suggest that PDPs should be expressed in the language of these competencies but again this is an unnecessary restriction.

PDPs can work well with competency models, as long as the models are used to inform the PDP, and not to limit the possible scope or objectives. The danger of the rigid use of a model is that it may lead people away from a contemplation of their own performance in the workplace, and therefore away from areas where they really want, or need, to develop.

In the same way, PDPs should give careful consideration to the task priorities of the next 12 months, but should also give scope for development beyond and outside of that.

6. Make good use of resources

Managers and learners need a good awareness of the available resources that can support learning – not only knowing what courses are on offer from the training department, but also understanding about how people can best learn from work activities. Levy (1991) identifies four sources of individual learning about job-related skills:

● education
● training and development
● a challenging work role
● lessons learned from key work relationships.

The action learning approach to development is founded on the basis of the belief that people learn best when they are able to reflect upon their own efforts to tackle difficult problems in the workplace (Revans, 1980).

Attending the right training courses can provide people with a motivational boost to learning, but so can new challenges in the work role, and creating new work relationships. Relatively small changes in job content – by adding new responsibilities and tasks, or new projects – can create new learning challenges. Encouraging team members to coach each other in their particular areas of expertise and responsibility can make excellent use of resources.

7. Encourage learning

Some people can undertake challenging experiences without learning much – or anything – from them. This may be because they have too much of a focus on completing the task, and very little focus at all on learning.

Managers can help people to learn more effectively from experience by:

- making them more conscious of learning as an (important) activity;
- helping them to understand their development needs;
- helping them understand the learning process and develop their learning skills;
- encouraging them to review their progress in developing their skills.

One of the most important tools in helping people to develop their skills and to learn from experience is the Learning Cycle, and the idea of learning styles.

Since its development and promotion by David Kolb (1976) and Peter Honey and Alan Mumford (1982), the cycle has been in widespread use on training and development programmes.

According to Honey and Mumford, people acquire skills by undertaking four different types of activity, represented on the cycle as action, reflection, theorizing and planning.

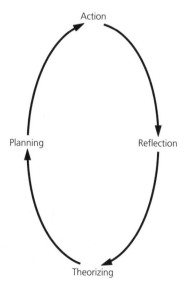

Figure 17.1   The Learning Cycle

Using the cycle to structure a PDP a learner and line manager can:

- Identify specific skill areas for development.
- For each skill area, agree specific actions the learner will undertake.
- Identify a relevant base of supporting knowledge or theory and how it can be acquired – by books, videotapes, or training courses, etc.
- Plan for discussion and reflection on the experience, and for further development planning.

In this way, the line manager and their team member can agree a series of activities that will lead to a genuine development of competence.

The best PDPs encourage a mixture of planning and opportunism. To paraphrase Mumford's description of Type 2 management development (1993), this type of learning:

- occurs within the activities of carrying out the job;
- has the joint aim of completing the task, and also achieving some personal development;
- is planned beforehand and reviewed after the event by the line manager and team member.

The review of a PDP should, naturally, concentrate first on progress against the agreed objectives, but the individual's skills of learning can also be enhanced by encouraging them to reflect on unanticipated learning which might have arisen out of experience.

8. Support and review

The most effective PDPs are discussed and reviewed throughout the course of the year. It is not possible to predict 12 months in advance the effects of changes in job demands on learning needs and opportunities. Neither is it possible to estimate how much progress a team member might make in 12 months in learning a specific skill. Targets can quickly become irrelevant, and should be reviewed when circumstances change.

9. Evaluate

PDPs should be assessed at the end of their term. The original plans should include performance measures, which may have been amended in the course of the year, and the line manager and the team member should evaluate progress, celebrate success and ask whether their planning process could be done better next time.

The prospect, and practice, of assessment is fundamental to PDPs. Clear targets, and the involvement of the line manager in reviewing progress at a specified time, enhances the learner's motivation, and can improve the accuracy of any evaluation. Assessing progress against the agreed targets is also a means of evaluating whether the PDP has been effective or not, and can lead to improved planning in the next cycle.

10. Recognize possibilities

Part of a PDP should look beyond the immediate horizon. PDPs are not just about correcting faults in current ways of working, but about opening the door to new possibilities too. Where a person has successfully developed a relevant skill or a new area of job-related knowledge, ways should be found, where possible, for them to exercise it, whether by stretching the current job or by more project work, or by planning more radical career moves.

The trainer's role

Personal development plans encourage line managers and all other employees to think of learning and training in a broader context than just attendance on the courses provided by the training department. What then is the role of the trainer in relation to effective PDPs? Do trainers need to help the line teams design and carry out PDPs? Very often the answer to this last question is 'Yes'.

In most organizations – particularly when PDPs are first introduced, or if the PDP scheme is in need of improvement – the training department can assist line managers and learners in four important ways.

1. Trainers can help line managers and their staff to understand the potential of using PDPs, and in particular they can help line managers develop the understanding and the skills that will enable them to agree effective PDPs. A good understanding of the processes of learning, learning styles, factors which affect the motivation to learn, and how to negotiate a learning contract, will help line managers enormously. Similarly, a good understanding of learning processes and learning styles will help individuals to think more clearly about how to meet their development needs.

    Trainers will provide a valuable service if they can help both the line manager and the team member to be confident about what they can achieve through learning. People often believe in firm, unchanging lines that separate things they can do from things they are 'no good at'. It is often worth challenging this belief.

2. Trainers can help individuals identify their own learning needs, by providing needs analysis questionnaires and realistic models of good practice to encourage reflection of performance. They can also provide tools to help people seek and evaluate feedback on their own performance.

3. Line managers will still look to trainers to provide courses. In fact, the introduction of a PDP programme will increase the requests for formal training – at least at first, as new needs are identified.

    As well as offering the required training, and making sure it is of the right quality, the training department can raise awareness of the range of programmes that are available, and take some simple steps to make sure the programmes are relevant to the workplace. For example, in one company:

    ● All applications to training courses must include comments from the individual's line manager, stating the reason for the application (as well as a similar statement from the learner).
    ● Short training courses usually end with an action planning session, where each participant sets out what they will aim to do in the workplace with what they have learnt on the course.
    ● Short courses are evaluated not only immediately after they have finished (i.e. at the end of the day) but also three months later, where feedback is sought on the value of the course in improving performance in the workplace.

    These simple measures help to relate short course provision with action on the job. The company training department also runs longer management development programmes, with work based projects and short learning contracts that directly involve the line manager.

4. Sometimes trainers may find themselves taking on parts of the role normally played by a line manager. They may help the learner with needs analysis, through discussion or through suggesting ideas and tools the learner might use. They may discuss possible development activities and resources with the learner, and even work through a draft plan for personal development. This is sometimes an official role the department plays in relation to trainees, but it can be a useful unofficial role, too, particularly for more senior staff, who may not have much daily contact with their line manager. In this latter case, the helping role usually emerges out of a good relationship between a particular trainer and a senior manager.

A manager's guide to introducing PDPs

1. *Win commitment*   Ensure the learner helps to create the PDP, and feels committed to it.
2. *Make PDPs relevant to the company and the learner*   Use both synergy and compromise to relate PDPs to corporate work needs and to individual needs.
3. *Set clear objectives*   Reach a small number of clear, specific objectives of outputs that are priorities for the learner.
4. *Make them realistic and stretching*   The objectives should be realistic and contain a degree of stretch, so that learners need to apply themselves in order to be successful.
5. *Be flexible and adaptable*   Avoid unnecessary restrictions. Allow each line manager and learner the widest possible choice.
6. *Make good use of resources*   Use training courses and the opportunities available in the workplace.
7. *Encourage learning*   Help people to understand learning processes, and keep them aware of what they are learning.
8. *Support and review*   Discuss the PDP throughout the year, not once a year.
9. *Evaluate*   Assess and evaluate the PDP at the end of its term.
10. *Recognize*   Where learning opens the door to new possibilities, help the learner to step through.

Further reading

Barham, K., Fraser, J. and Heath, I. (1988), *Management for the Future*, Hemel Hempstead: Ashridge Foundation for Management Education.

Boak, G. (1998), *A Complete Guide to Learning Contracts*, Aldershot: Gower.

Honey, P. and Mumford, A. (1982), *The Manual of Learning Styles*, Maidenhead: Peter Honey.

Kolb, D. (1976), *The Learning Style Inventory*, Boston, MA: McBer and Co.

Levy, M. (1991), *Work Based Learning – A Good Practice Model*, Blagdon: Further Education Staff College IB 2845.

Mumford, A. (1993), *Management Development: Strategies for Action*, 2nd edn, London: IPM.

Revans, R. (1980), *Action Learning*, London: Blond and Briggs.

Part Three

Advanced techniques in training and development

When people speak about the latest technologies that are available to training professionals they are not only referring to the advances being made in IT. This section of the handbook introduces some of the latest technologies and models that underpin advanced trainer performance.

This is a tremendously exciting section of the handbook for anyone who is interested in how trainers and development managers get the best results. Many of the writers in this section have internationl reputations and are recognized as being at the forefront of their fields. It is of course in the introduction of innovative ideas and techniques that the T & D profession continues to move so fast. This does not imply, however, that these subject areas are untried and untested. Most have been around for many years. T & D professionals who want an insight into advanced techniques can see here what is involved and where such techniques are best applied.

Chapter 18

Transactional analysis at work

Julie Hay

You may associate transactional analysis (TA) with California in the 'sixties! You may, on the other hand, be aware that it is now a recognized psychotherapy within the UK (and many other areas of the world). Or perhaps your exposure to TA has been with someone who is aware of the latest developments and of the need to convert the therapy models before they are applied to organizational settings.

All of these would be accurate perceptions. TA did indeed emerge first in California, many years ago. Current international accreditation in the clinical field of TA entitles the holder to entry in the UK Council for Psychotherapy Register. And there are three more fields of TA application, each with international accreditation in their own right: organizational, educational and counselling.

Between them, these fields have generated a substantial body of theory and practical applications. This chapter can only skim the surface – it takes several years to qualify as a transactional analyst. I have therefore included a brief history and definition of TA, a selection of the best known concepts, and brief mentions of some other TA aspects. I very much hope this will stimulate you to find out more for yourself.

A brief history

The originator of TA was Dr Eric Berne (1910–1970). A Canadian who became a US citizen, Dr Berne trained as a psychiatrist and psychoanalyst. From around 1949 until 1958 Berne developed many of the basic TA theories. From 1958 he ran regular seminars at which others also contributed to the growing body of TA concepts. The first TA conference was held in 1963 and the International Transactional Analysis Association (ITAA) was formed in 1964, albeit it with very few members outside the USA. Ten years later the

European Association for Transactional Analysis (EATA) was created; since then there has been an explosion of interest in TA within Europe so that for some years now there have been more EATA members than the ITAA has in the rest of the world. Although TA was originally developed by therapists, it was quickly adopted by many organizational consultants and educators. As with most new approaches, this led to some problems when people failed to recognize the true depth of the material and taught it as a series of simplistic solutions. Fortunately, other models came along and replaced it as the current fad, so that serious students of TA were left to apply it in competent and potent ways.

There are now four well-established specialisms, each with international examinations for the award of Certified Transactional Analyst (CTA). This involves around four to five years of ongoing competence development, supervision, a dissertation based on a significant piece of work, and an oral examination with a panel of four qualified analysts. Various CTA training programmes in the UK and the rest of Europe have been granted university accreditation at master's level and this process is being extended all the time.

There is also a further level of certification as a Teaching and Supervising Transactional Analyst (TSTA), which usually takes another six or more years. TSTAs and Provisional TSTAs are the ones who provide the training and supervision for those seeking CTA accreditation.

What is TA?

Transactional analysis was originally the term used to refer to the analysis of transactions, or interactions, between people. Such analysis used Berne's original concept of ego states as observable phenomena – hence the notion that your *Parent* ego state may be transacting with someone else's *Child* ego state, or perhaps it is your *Adult* with their *Adult*. However, transactional analysis as a label has now come to mean the whole body of interlocking TA theories and frameworks, plus the underlying philosophical assumptions. When we analyse interactions nowadays, we need to mention that we are doing transactional analysis 'proper'!

TA, then, is both a theory of human personality and a system for the improvement of human relations. Its application to organizations provides a systematic approach to understanding the links between human needs and behaviours and the ways that organizations are effective or ineffective in solving their problems and serving their customers. By observing limiting beliefs and ingrained behaviour patterns, an analyst can offer guidance on ways to create healthy organizational cultures in which individuals can function effectively, creatively and enthusiastically.

TA has a strong philosophical base. The key beliefs are:

- All people are OK as human beings, even though their behaviour may be unacceptable.
- People have an urge to grow and develop themselves, even though they may be repressing this without being aware of it.
- We make decisions and are therefore responsible for our behaviour. We are likely to have made these decisions when we were very young and lacked options and information – a function of TA is to help us understand this and make fresh decisions where our old choices are leading to current problems.

The aim of using transactional analysis is to create more autonomy, which Berne described as claiming yourself, owning yourself, deciding on your own destiny. He suggested three elements to autonomy:

- *Spontaneity*   Being free to chose what to do and having many options.
- *Intimacy*   Able to be open, close and trusting.
- *Awareness*   Knowing what is happening now.

Contracting: the key to TA effectiveness

There is a significant principle that arises from the philosophical assumptions of TA – it is practised as part of a contractual arrangement. Contracts may be written or verbal; the main point is that we discuss and agree why we are interacting when we plan to use TA to help someone grow.

In other words, clients are expected to use the theory to understand themselves better and to take action to increase their own autonomy. The transactional analyst does not analyse the client and make decisions on their behalf. Nor do they do things to the client. Instead, the parties agree desired outcomes and share responsibility for working towards them.

In the case of organizational work, there are at least three parties to such a contract: the trainer or consultant, the participants or clients, and the organization itself. The rights and responsibilities of all parties must be respected and balanced. Contracts operate at different levels and all levels need to be clear to avoid unwitting sabotage.

- *Procedural*   Administrative details, such as when shall we meet, where, how often, who keeps notes, what are the payment routines?
- *Professional*   What am I offering as professional analyst, trainer, consultant, mentor, coach etc., what do you need, how competent am I to meet your needs?
- *Psychological*   What might occur outside our awareness, how might either of us sabotage the process?

This latter point has been extended by Micholt (1992) to describe the dynamics as a function of the psychological distances between the parties. If the trainer gets too closely aligned with the participants, the organization's needs may be neglected. If the trainer is too close to the organization, participants may perceive them as a management spy. Participants and their organization have been known to collude against the trainer when the topic is something that both parties resent spending time on, such as safety training or equal opportunities awareness. Psychological distances within three-cornered contracts can be shown in triangular diagrams: the lengths of the sides are altered to show where potential collusion exists. The aim is, of course, to maintain an equilateral triangle. Note also that contracting is a basic principle in TA – if no contract has been established we are not truly applying TA.

Ego states

If contracting is the key principle, ego states are the basic building blocks of TA. Berne wrote that they were systems of thinking, feeling and behaving. Although we often talk as if there are only three ego states, Parent, Adult and Child, he actually pointed out that there were many, which he grouped into three systems. He also referred to structural and functional ego states. Structural relates to our development and is what is there; functional is how we use what we have. This is rather like saying we have a heart – structural – and it beats – functional. The heart may be structurally deficient or it may be malfunctioning, or both.

When we consider the structural ego states, Parent contains what we have copied from others, Child contains recordings of how we have been, and Adult is the here-and-now, current reality state. Berne also wrote of Integrated Adult, which is what we have as a result of incorporating into the present the useful parts of our Parent and Child ego states.

Our functional ego states are often given more specific names, such as Controlling or Critical Parent, Nurturing Parent, Adapted Child, Natural or Free Child. Adult has tended to be called simply Adult in both models, although I have recently started to use the term Functional Adult in order to distinguish it more clearly from the structural version.

Berne identified four aspects to the diagnosis of ego states: what behaviour are we noticing; how are other people reacting; is there an historical antecedent; and how does the person experience themselves? Outside the therapy context, we tend to use only the first two aspects – you are unlikely to get a constructive response if you interrupt an angry person to ask if they think they are in their Parent ego state, or if they realize they are acting just like their real parent did! Even using the reactions of others can be risky – for instance, a senior manager stuck in Parent will perceive everyone else as being in Child. A lot of confusion has arisen because writers have solved this problem by using only the behavioural diagnosis to describe ego states. They have then linked this to Berne's structural model and suggested that only logical, problem-solving behaviour is Adult. However, this same behaviour may actually be a repeat of the behaviour of someone they knew in the past. It may even be a repeat of them if they were a serious child! Moreover, emphasizing it means that people feel that any emotions, including friendliness, fun and creativity, are negative – a major loss for them and the organization.

One way of resolving this is to use a new set of diagrams (Hay, 1982), developed after several years' organizational experience, that make a differentiation between Behavioural ego states, which are what we can observe, and Internal ego states, which we can only speculate about as the possible source of the behaviour. In many cases, analysis of the behaviour will be enough to enable us to select our own ego state in order to interact effectively; in more complex situations we will need to 'guess' what is happening internally so we can respond to that.

TA 'proper'

Transactional analysis 'proper' is the analysis of interactions between people, or more correctly between their ego states. A transaction is an exchange of attention, or a stimulus and response. Berne identified three types of transactions and three corresponding *rules of communication*:

- *Complementary transaction*   Rule: the communication can continue.
- *Crossed transaction*   Rule: the communication will break down and something different is likely to follow.
- *Ulterior transaction*   Rule: the outcome will be determined at the psychological level.

Note that a complementary transaction is not necessarily 'good' and a crossed transaction is not necessarily 'bad'. It merely means that the ego states match or do not match. If someone is haranguing you from their Parent to your Child, it may be very helpful to cross the transaction and shift to an Adult to Adult mode.

Awareness of the ego state model alerts us that we have several options; we can 'choose' our ego state to correspond to the other person in a way that gives us the best chance of a successful interaction. We can also watch out for transference, a phenomenon that occurs when we 'transfer' the characteristics of someone else onto the person we are interacting with. For example, we may relate to our manager as if he or she were one of our former schoolteachers, or to a more junior employee as if they were a child. Countertransference occurs when they respond to us as if they are our old schoolteacher or our child!

Strokes

Stroke is a transactional analysis term for a unit of recognition. Any interaction with others is therefore an exchange of strokes.

Strokes are probably the secret of the universe. We all have a biological need to interact with other human beings. Without such contact, we fail to develop, as happened to the orphans in Romania. Solitary confinement is retained as a severe punishment precisely because we realize how stressful it is to go without human contact. Although we vary in the amount of recognition we need, we must all get at least a minimal amount of attention from others if we are to function as healthy individuals.

We all learn as children that we can stimulate negative strokes more readily than we can positives. Annoy someone and they pay attention to you! Because strokes are a biological necessity, we will then unwittingly settle for negatives rather than being ignored. This is why the same children are constantly in trouble at school. It also explains why some employees are regularly subject to warnings and disciplinary action – they and their managers do not realize that this gets them far more attention than people who perform adequately. How often have you known a manager call someone into the office to speak to them, with appreciation, for continually performing at an acceptable level?

Strokes vary in their level of intensity, they may be positive or negative and we each have our own customary patterns of giving and receiving them. Strokes may also be classified as conditional or unconditional. The traditional view of organizations implies a conditional form of stroking – recognition is something that results from performance of the task. Unconditional strokes add an important dimension; such strokes do not have to be 'earned' through work achievement or appearance. Asking someone about their family or their spare time activities is a powerful form of stroking that involves relating to aspects of them which may otherwise be neglected during worktime.

Strokes have different degrees of value to us. It depends on the nature of the interaction, our feelings about the stroke giver, and our personal preferences for what aspects of our personality or behaviour get stroked. Some of us like our recognition to be about work performance and achievement; others are more comfortable with strokes about our families and personal relationships; yet others get more of a kick when people show a keen interest in our exciting spare time activities.

We also vary in our sources of strokes. Being part of a team means that strokes are available to us from many directions. Working alone yields fewer strokes. Working closely with customers may lead us to rely on the customer instead of our colleagues for our recognition, so that our loyalty to our own organization is weakened. Each change in our circumstances will cause a corresponding deficit in our stroking pattern until we can re-establish a new source of interaction. Of course, if we are dissatisfied with such a relationship we may welcome the opportunity to begin elsewhere.

Why do we have these difficulties? One way of understanding this process is to look at the effect of change on our relationships with other people. In the course of a normal week, we are likely to have contact with colleagues, friends, and family – these interactions add up to a pattern of recognition from others that confirms our sense of identity. Change disrupts this pattern. Even a holiday alters the normal weekly quota, as we rely on our holiday companions to counterbalance the lack of interaction with colleagues and customers.

Consider the impact of a major change, such as moving to another organization. It will take some time to recreate adequate stroking patterns in areas such as new boss, new colleagues, new procedures, new customers, new tasks, new products. The new team may have well-established stroking patterns between themselves and need time to incorporate you. In the meantime, strokes from your former team may have abruptly ceased. Being aware of the nature of stroking patterns allows us to consider alternative stroke sources while we establish new relationships. This will minimize the potential stress associated with the change and give us an easier transition.

Psychological games

Remember that negative strokes are better than no strokes at all! A psychological game is defined as a repetitive sequence of complementary, ulterior transactions leading to a well-defined, negative pay-off for all parties. The key clues that we are playing a game, therefore, are:

- It is repetitive – it 'happens' to us over and over again, often with different partners.
- It is predictable – anyone watching it could predict the sequence and the outcome.
- It has ulterior transactions – we are not saying what is really going on.
- There is a switch – at some point the communication shifts and the ulterior is revealed.
- All involved get negative pay-offs – we feel not OK, either as a loser or as one-up.

It may seem strange that we would engage in psychological games when they lead to such negative results. However, game playing is out of awareness and has a number of 'advantages'. For example, it meets our biological need for strokes; it justifies our view of the world; it often allows us to avoid responsibility in some way; and it gives us something to talk to our friends about. Put another way, games fill up the time, they keep people around us, they reinforce our frame of reference and they remind us that we are alive.

A popular way of analysing games (and therefore being able to stop them) is to use the Drama Triangle devised by Karpman (1968). He pointed out that games are very like dramas on the stage, with three major roles involved: *Persecutor, Rescuer, Victim*. We can use a triangle to show the roles and plot the moves. Thus, in the common organizational game of Uproar, one person acts like a Persecutor and treats another as a Victim. A third person then attempts to Rescue the Victim – but this involves Persecuting the original Persecutor. At that point, the Victim starts to Persecute the would-be Rescuer, who now feels like a Victim. So the original persecutor now Persecutes the original Victim for Persecuting their Rescuer. This pattern can continue indefinitely – and in a lot of meetings, it does!

Remember that it takes at least two people to play a psychological game; we cannot accuse someone else of playing a game with us without at the same time divulging that we played the game with them; and that all of this happens outside our awareness.

Discounting

Games continue because we unknowingly discount. Discounting is an internal mechanism, which occurs outside our awareness and involves us minimizing or ignoring some aspect of ourselves, others and/or the situation. We discount in order to maintain and reinforce our frame of reference. We just do not seem to notice things that would lead us to change our minds or our behaviour.

There are four levels of discounting:

1. We may discount the existence of something, e.g. management do not keep records of absenteeism.
2. We may discount the significance – management do not realize that absence levels are higher than they should be because it is unimportant.
3. We may discount the change possibilities – management do not accept it is possible to do anything about absenteeism.
4. We may discount personal abilities – management cannot get their act together!

Life positions

Berne introduced the concept of life positions as our attitude towards ourselves and others. Thomas Harris (1973) made the topic famous by calling his book *I'm OK, You're OK*. Ernst suggested a grid called the 'OK Corral', containing the four variations of: *I'm OK, You're OK: I'm not OK, You're OK; I'm not OK, You're not OK; I'm OK, You're not OK*. 'OK Corral' is a rather dated term nowadays. The life positions can instead be referred to as our windows on the world (Hay, 1982).

As small children we all attempt to make sense of the world. We want to be able to predict what will happen. We also tend to believe that we cause everything! We therefore draw some conclusions about whether we and others are OK or not on the basis of what does happen. We also lack sufficient experience of the world and therefore tend to rely on what other people tell us (or signal to us at the ulterior level).

For example:

- For *I'm not OK, You're OK* – we have no way of knowing that our clumsiness at dressing ourselves is a normal part of growing up.
- For *I'm not OK, You're not OK* – if someone we love is taken into hospital, we may think we caused them to be ill, and that they have deserted us.
- For *I'm OK, You're not OK* – if we are constantly compared favourably to others, we may come to believe that we really are superior.

When we grow up, most of us will spend plenty of time believing that we and others are OK. However, under stress we are likely to revert to our childhood conclusions. The life positions are the key to many of the apparently negative ways we behave. Psychological games are played so that we finish the game in a way that reinforces our basic life position. Discounting serves to maintain the not OK life position we have adopted.

Positive strokes invite *I'm OK, You're OK*. Negative strokes invite one of the other three *not OK* positions. Our life position also determines the way we accept strokes. Offered a positive stroke, someone in *I'm not OK, You're OK* will think you are just trying to be kind. The *I'm OK, You're not OK* will be condescending and arrogant. The *I'm not OK, You're not OK* will be suspicious and wonder what devious reason you have for pretending to be nice to them when they do not deserve it.

Script

Our script is a personal life plan formed through a series of decisions made early in life in response to our interpretations of events. By the time we are six or seven years old, we have decided who we think we are and how we will live our life. We generally push this decision out of awareness yet continue to behave in line with it.

We devise a script for much the same reason as we choose a life position – we need to make sense of what is going on around us. We therefore interpret what happens to us in the best way we are able. Unfortunately, our lack of experience and knowledge means that we often draw inaccurate conclusions.

We are also heavily influenced by what the grown-ups tell us. If they say we are stupid, or beautiful, or just like a particular relative, we may well accept the labelling and decide how to live it out. Berne wrote of the brothers who were both told by their mother that they would finish up in a mental hospital – one became a patient and the other a doctor!

Berne pointed out that our scripts are often like fairy stories. For example, we may behave like Cinderella, waiting for a prince to come and save us from a life of drudgery, or Robin Hood, robbing the rich to help the poor. Fairy stories have a limited number of themes; although the names of the characters change the same themes occur in a wide variety of cultures. Similar themes also appear in myths and fables.

Working styles

We also have counterscript messages. These were first described by Kahler (1974), who called them drivers to reflect the way in which the behaviours seem to take over and drive us. They start as helpful messages about how to behave in order to meet the social and cultural demands in our environment. However, we then confuse them with our sense of OKness, coming to believe that if we fail to behave in these ways we will be not OK. We may also judge others by their level of driver behaviour.

Hay (1992) calls them working styles and points out that each has positive characteristics when we bring it under conscious control. Most people will recognize positive and negative aspects of each in themselves, but usually with a preponderance of one or two of the styles:

- Hurry Up: works quickly, responds well to deadlines; gets a lot done in a short time; makes mistakes, lacks attention to detail; gets impatient, finishes others' sentences.
- Be Perfect: is accurate, checks carefully; well organized, looks ahead for potential problems; includes too much detail, checks over and over; criticizes over minor details, rarely satisfied.
- Please People: good team member, encourages harmony; intuitive and aware, considers others; anxious for approval of others, will not confront; feels misunderstood, hurt by criticism.
- Try Hard: enthusiastic, energetic with new ideas; thorough at following up all possibilities; loses interest and moves on to new things; tends not to finish, others have to take over.
- Be Strong: is calm under pressure, copes with stress; conscientious, strong sense of duty; will not ask for help or admit weakness; may seem cold and distant, or overly jovial.

What next?

A good way to learn about TA is to attend a 101, the officially recognized introductory course in transactional analysis. It covers a set syllabus, so that wherever in the world you attend a 101, you will learn about the same broad range of TA concepts. (The '101' in the title is based on the educational system in the USA, where it is customary to refer to introductory courses as 101s, more advanced courses as 202s, and so on.)

101 courses are run only by transactional analysts who have attained international accreditation to do so. Great care is taken to maintain standards and provide a high quality learning experience that incorporates accurate and consistent information about TA.

Membership of EATA is via membership in a national association. For the UK, this is the Institute of Transactional Analysis – contact the author on 07000 234683 for details.

Further reading

Berne, E. (1975), *What Do You Say After You Say Hello?*, London: Corgi.
English, F. (1971), 'The Substitution Factor; Rackets and Real Feelings', *Transactional Analysis Journal*, Part I 1971, **1**(4), 225–230, Part II 1972, **2**(1), 23–25.
Harris, T. (1973), *I'm OK, You're OK*, London: Pan.
Hay, J, (1992), *Transactional Analysis for Trainers*, Maidenhead: McGraw-Hill. (Republished 1996 by Sherwood Publishing.)
James, M. and Jongeward, D. (1971), *Born to Win*, Wokingham: Addison-Wesley.
Kahler, T. (1974), 'The Miniscript', *Transactional Analysis Journal*, **4**(1), 26–42.
Karpman, S. (1968), 'Fairy Tales and Script Drama Analysis', *Transactional Analysis Bulletin*, **7**(26), 39–43.
Micholt, N. (1992), 'The Concept of Psychological Distance', *Transactional Analysis Journal*, **22**(4), 228–33.
Stewart, I. and Joines, V. (1988), *TA Today*, Lifespace Publishing.

Chapter 19

NLP at work

Sue Knight

To know your past look at your present condition.
To know your future look at your present actions.

NLP: the territory

Have you ever experienced that state when everything you did was going just right and you felt in harmony with yourself? It might have felt as though you were completely focused, pulling in one direction and achieving exactly the results you have always wanted. Or perhaps you can remember times when you surprised yourself by exceeding your wildest expectations of what you dreamt was possible in your work and in your life.

Conversely, have you ever felt that life and work were just not going your way and that whatever you tried to do you seemed to hit some sort of obstacle? Perhaps you have found yourself in a downward spiral, recognized that you have been in such an emotional state before but still have no conscious means of breaking out of this cycle. Or perhaps you have been in emotional states where you were so stressed that you were unable to draw on the inner resources that you knew you had.

If you have been in these places then you might have wondered what made the difference. Just how did you get yourself into any of these states – good or bad – and how did you either prolong them or break out of them?

The ability to unpack these states in order to have new choices is at the heart of neuro linguistic programming (NLP). Using NLP allows people to achieve a consistency of performance that might otherwise have escaped their grasp. Take the example of watching someone who excels at what they do and wishing that you could have some of their inspiration and skill in a way that would help you to achieve those same results. You might have admired a colleague and wanted to have some of their magic for yourself or, alternatively, wished that you could understand what it was that made them different so that others could learn the same skills.

Typically, however, when people ask those who have a special quality what it is that makes them different they receive a shrug of the shoulders or, at best, a vague description of what that person does – responses which are frequently frustrating for those who want to emulate a special performance.

Yet this is precisely the territory of neuro linguistic programming. NLP is the process of eliciting the 'difference that makes the difference' between the top performers and the rest. It is the means of identifying not only the conscious processes that enable us to achieve top results but especially the unconscious processes – the talents and skills and subtleties in thinking and behaviour which are outside our conscious awareness and which we therefore take for granted.

We each have an excellence within that enables us to achieve exactly the experience that we have in our lives and in our work. We have a structure to our experience, which is evident in the way that we act and in the way that we speak. We have patterns in our behaviour and in our thinking that form the basis of the results we achieve in our work, our relationships, our life.

NLP is the process of modelling these patterns to identify the structure of our own, or others, experience so that we can reproduce those results for ourselves or we can teach them to others.

Elements of NLP

So what are some of the elements of NLP?

Neuro represents the way we use our senses to take in, to hold and to communicate information, ideas and thoughts. It is concerned with the way we use our mind and our physiology to achieve results. For example, we are unique in the way we use our senses; some people may make greater use of their ability to visualize ideas whereas someone else may rely more on how an idea sounds. Then again there are some people who manage largely by gut instinct – a 'feelings' way of processing ideas. Recognizing how you think can provide you with some of the clues as to how you achieve the results that you do. In particular it can help to explain why it is that you get on so well with some people with whom ideas flow and yet with others, even getting the simplest idea across is a struggle.

Linguistic is the part of NLP that is to do with recognizing the patterns in the language we use both internally to ourselves and with others. By identifying the patterns in language we can recognize how we make sense of our experience and whether the sense we make works for, or against, the results we want to achieve. Quite unintentionally we may use language in a way that takes us off track from the results that we want to achieve and we need to be aware of this and make more effective choices, especially when our business depends on the way we communicate.

For example, if we ask someone to do something for us, and they say they cannot, the most usual question that is asked in response is 'Why not?' With the best intention in the world this typically gets exactly the opposite of what we want. When asking 'Why not?' you invite the other person to bring to mind all the reasons why they cannot do as you ask. On the principle that 'what you think is what you get' you have just entrenched them into a position of not being able to carry out the task. Far better to ask 'What can you do?' or 'What would happen if you did do this?' You then begin to open the door to possibilities. To be skilled in the way that you use language is to be skilled in the way you influence yourself and others to achieve what you and they want.

Programming is about the mental and behavioural strategies that we run to achieve results and experience. By understanding how we do what we do, we give ourselves choice to repeat the results that we get, to enhance them, to get more of what we get or to get something else. For example, you will have a structure to the way you build relationships with people, to the way you create a first impression, to the way you gain acceptance of your ideas and the way you achieve the goals that you want. Equally you have a structure to the way you get yourself stressed, to the way you sometimes procrastinate, to the way you sabotage some of your most passionate desires and to the way you repeat experiences in your life. When you understand how you do all of these things you begin to have choice – choice to do more of the same or choice to do it differently.

By influencing the way we think in the way we make meaning of our experience we can influence the way we feel and the way we respond to situations and to people. NLP is at the heart of personal development and by developing ourselves we develop the way we work. Personal growth is directly proportional to business growth. We may introduce all sorts of models and processes to enhance our business but I believe that real growth and change must ultimately come from within.

Above all else NLP is a state of mind – a passionate curiosity to discover the 'difference that makes the difference' in order to learn and grow. This is what is known as 'modelling'.

Applications of NLP

There is a wide range of business applications for NLP, as follows.

Modelling excellence

Each company has its top performers – those people who excel at what they do and who excel in that specific business. One of the most recent projects that I have been involved in was the modelling of top consultant tutors in one of the leading financial consultancies. By watching and listening to these top performers in action it is possible to elicit the conscious, and the unconscious, processes that constitute the 'difference that makes the difference' between those who achieve a consistency in their success and the rest. Once unpacked in this way these skills and thinking processes can be taught back to both the original subjects and to others who aspire to this excellence in their performance.

One-to-one coaching

Modelling can also be used as the basis for high performance coaching. This is especially significant when used with a chief executive or a managing director, as it is typically their thinking and behaviour patterns that ripple out in everything that they do to form the culture of the business. When 'modelled' and fed back to them these senior people have choice – choice to continue to do more of the same in the knowledge that if they do what they always did they get what they always got, or to do it differently. In choosing to do it differently they can decide what sort of role model they wish to be to the rest of the business and in so doing bring alive mission and values statements that might otherwise just remain as ignored pieces of paper on the office walls.

Take the example of when we coached the operations manager for the commercial arm of a leading training organization. This person epitomized the conflict that existed between the commercial and the charitable arms of the business in the way that they thought about the relationship between the two. To be able to manage strategically and inclusively this manager needed first of all to understand this inner conflict before trying to resolve the external issues. By providing feedback and focusing on this thinking pattern, the coaching helped the manager to act differently in a way that led to a 'win' for all parts of the business.

Eliciting strategies for success

The programming part of NLP relates to those strategies of thinking and acting that get us the results that we have in our lives today. In effect, we have programmes that result in feelings and responses both from ourselves and from others. If we are able to think creatively we have a strategy to do this. If we are able to present an idea or a proposal in a way that others readily accept, similarly we have a strategy within ourselves that makes this possible. Equally, if we find ourselves depressed we are running a strategy that maintains this state also. Sometimes we use our strategies in ways that support our ultimate goals and sometimes we use strategies, which although satisfying an unconscious goal, may thwart our desires to achieve something more productive.

One of the organizations with which we have worked wanted to enable their managers to consistently access strategies for creativity so that they could generate new and innovative solutions to everyday business issues. They used NLP processes to do this.

Managing relationships

One of the earliest discoveries made through the modelling processes within NLP was the skill with which some people built and maintained rapport with others around them. The result of this exquisite skill was their ability to relate at a very deep level to those with whom they were working; and this, in turn, resulted in an exceptional ability to influence and be influenced. Managing relationships has entered the vocabulary of most of the businesses that seek to excel in the way that they sell their services or their products. It has also become a part of the culture of those businesses that recognize this, that to succeed they need to attract customers for life. People do business with people who can relate to their needs (spoken and unspoken) and who can, with sensitivity and flexibility, support them in the achievement of their goals. The cornerstone on which all the technical solutions hang is rapport.

There are an infinite number of patterns that make us unique in the way that we think, speak and act. Did you know, for example, that some people initially need to see ideas presented visually in order both to understand and accept them? Whereas there are others who like to have proposals talked through because their primary sense in their ability to understand is auditory. Then again there are those who, because they have a preference for anything kinaesthetic, need to feel what is being presented and will need to experience practically the ideas being put forward. Do you know which of your key clients need to be shown, talked through or walked through your presentations and what sequence they need you to do this in? The more flexibility you have the more influence you have on the results that you can achieve.

Customer satisfaction

Achieving customer satisfaction means meeting the customers' needs and doing so in a way that ensures you meet your own. Effectively, this involves negotiating a win/win in every transaction that you have, whether that is with your internal or your external customers. To do this you need first of all to be able to elicit your customers' needs and, perhaps surprisingly, people are often poorly skilled in expressing either their needs or the conditions that have to exist for these needs to be satisfied. Often needs are communicated unconsciously or only hinted at. To excel in your ability to satisfy these conscious and unconscious needs requires exquisite sensitivity to body language and verbal patterns as well as the flexibility to respond to these signals.

This is where NLP comes into its own. Most fundamental NLP training involves honing your skills so that you can detect subtle changes in both yourself and in others and hence begin to match the patterns detected.

Creating a learning organization

More than ever before we depend on our ability to learn. I recently heard that the skills held by the typical office worker of today will be redundant in two years time. And this is true for more than just office workers. So the challenge then becomes how to help ourselves to learn continuously and how to create a learning culture in the organization of which we are a part? There are many ways to do this and NLP offers an insight into the thinking and the behaviour that either accelerates this culture or hinders it.

At the heart of this learning culture lies the belief 'that there is no failure – only feedback and learning'. If you have an organization in which the employees and especially the leaders operate as if this is true you have the essence of a learning organization.

In a recent project we facilitated the top team of a company to operate out of this belief in the way that they gave and received feedback to each other and, subsequently, with their staff. As they acquired the skills to do this it first of all transformed their board meetings. It then impacted on the performance appraisal process of the company as a whole, allowing them to pick up difficult issues which began to emerge as part of the appraisal discussions. They were then, as a management team, in a position to act or coach others to act in ways that were profitable for the business.

How to implement best practice

If one thing is true about NLP it is that everyone will use it and present it in their own unique way. Below is a checklist of questions that you can use to find an NLP training school, consultancy or practitioner that will suit your business and personal needs.

● Do they practise what they preach i.e. if they are talking about rapport are they in rapport with you? Or have they built rapport with other people whom you know?

- Do you feel comfortable with the way they are and what they present?

- Do they use NLP as a means to an end rather than an end in itself?

- Do they use language that fits your culture and your personal style? NLP can be riddled with jargon which is not necessary to achieve business results.

- Do they have experience and a record of success in what they are offering?

- Do they have any successful examples of previous similar projects?

- Have you seen them in action and do you like what you see and hear? Most of the NLP training schools and consultancies have open days where you can go and meet them and sample the way that they work. Contact them directly for details of these. The Association for NLP holds a conference twice a year at which many of the leading trainers are present. This is an opportunity to experience not only the different trainers but also some of the different applications and styles that are on offer.

- Are they registered and recognized by the Association of NLP?

- What are the principles and beliefs on which they base their work and do these fit with your own?

- Are they biased towards applications in therapy, hypnosis, counselling or business and if so which bias suits you best?

- Do you have references of others with whom they have worked?

- What is their level of qualification in NLP and is it what you want?

Training and development in NLP

There are recognized standards of practice with NLP. The Association of NLP holds details of these standards. Examples of the available qualifications in NLP are:

- *Fundamentals of NLP* This is not usually certified, but nevertheless acts as a foundation training for the subsequent levels of certification. This takes the form of an introduction to NLP in terms of what it is and practice in some of the most recent discoveries through NLP.

- *Practitioner or Business Practitioner* This will have applications to both the individual and to the business in which they work. A business practitioner programme will also concentrate on the applications of NLP to the business world as well as to the individual's growth within that world. This will equip the delegate with all the core skills of NLP.

● *Master Practitioner*   This will enable the delegate to master the process of modelling and most trainings at this level will require the delegate to conduct a modelling project which is assessed as part of the training.

● *Trainer training*   Completion of this will enable the delegate to run their own certified training programmes in NLP that are recognized by the ANLP. The ANLP helpline is 01384 443935.

Further reading

Andreas, S. and Andreas, C. (1987), *Change Your Mind and Keep the Change*, Real People Press.

Andreas, S. and Faulkner, C. (1996), *NLP: the New Technology of Achievement*, London: Nicholas Brealey.

Grindler, J. and Bandler, F. (1976), *The Structure of Magic*, Science & Behaviour Books.

Grindler, J. and Bandler, F. (1979), *Frogs into Princes*, Real People Press.

Knight, S. (1995), *NLP at Work*, London: Nicholas Brealey Publishing.

Knight, S. (1999), *Introducing NLP*, Wimbledon, London: Institute of Personnel Development.

Knight, S. (1999), *NLP Solutions*, London: Nicholas Brealey Publishing.

Knight, S. (1999), *Personal Selling Skills*, The Sue Knight Books & Talks Ltd.

Laborde, G. (1984), *Influencing with Integrity*, Palo Alto, CA: Syntony Publishing.

Seymour, J. and O'Connor, J. (1993), *Introduction to NLP*, London: Aquarian Press.

Chapter 20
Accelerated learning

Lex McKee

Accelerated learning is simply learning at an accelerated pace. This can be on an individual, group, or corporate basis. By 'learning' we embrace the whole learning process including registration, assimilation, integration, application, and recall of the desired attitudes, skills, or knowledge. In future, we can look forward to examples of corporate learning at such a fast rate that the corporations involved may legitimately be called 'accelerated learning organizations'. How does this affect you?

If you are a training professional, this has clear attractions. It will halve your training times, and/or your costs (Rose, 1991). Couple this with the improvements in self-esteem, personal initiative, problem-solving ability, and the overall performance improvement associated with accelerated learning programmes, and you have many good reasons for experimenting with the approach. However, perhaps the chief reason for advocating accelerated learning methods is that they tend to rekindle enthusiasm for learning amongst participants.

Outline of the methodology

This chapter proposes a practical template to help you either reform an existing training programme or which you can use as a framework for designing a new programme. The template covers all the major phases necessary to make learning 'accelerated'. We will acknowledge the key sources for each phase as we progress, since accelerated learning is a synthesis of many disciplines.

The template itself uses two of the key tools employed by accelerated learning: mind mapping and mnemonics. The Mind Map® shown in Figure 20.1 gives you the big picture overview of the approach. The phases of the model correspond to the key word acronym 'M.E.S.S.A.G.E.' since the model

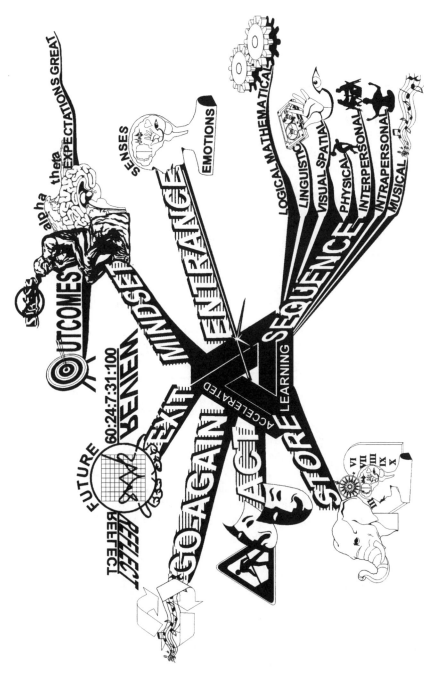

Figure 20.1 The Mind Map

217

works equally effectively in any communications scenario where we wish to get our *message* across.

Mindset

Our 'M' is for 'mindset' – the starting branch connected at 1 o'clock. Mindset is the foundational phase of any accelerated learning event, since our neuropsychology has the power to veto any learning if our emotions are not positively engaged. Through his research on hypnosis and memory, Ernest Rossi has concluded that all memory is dependent upon our state-of-mind. Since learning is vitally linked to memory, we may safely say that all learning is state-dependent. Helping learners access an optimal state-of-mind for learning is our first priority. There are three major ways we can do this:

1.   Encourage the learners to set realistic outcomes for the learning, so that they arrive in an appropriately expectant state-of-mind.
2.   Orchestrate a low-stress, high-energy environment that invigorates the senses, and stimulates the imagination and curiosity.
3.   Increase the likelihood of brain-wave 'entrainment' (see below).

On the first point, I would like to commend our old friend, the joining instructions, as an underutilized resource. Joining instructions offer a superb first contact opportunity to set the tone for the learning. The appropriate use of images, colour, believably enthusiastic style, testimonials, and mixture of broad canvas approach backed up by suitable details – all these can engender a sense of positive expectation in each delegate's mind.

Second, music, flowers, big peripheral posters, non-hierarchical seating, natural light, scents, space, fruit, water, and variable temperature controls can all help shift paradigms for the learners. Most of these components are present during nursery education. However, as we mature through the school system, our learning environment tends to suffer from progressive sensory deprivation. While communication of concepts becomes increasingly abstract with complexity, we tend to forget that the only way into our minds is via our senses. Any learning environment that makes it easy to grasp new concepts directly through the senses will help accelerate the integration process.

Third, I mentioned 'entrainment'. Entrainment is the phenomenon of a following response. In certain situations biological systems and cycles can become synchronous. An example would be where individual women living in close, restricted proximity will notice their menstrual cycles becoming synchronous. While we are not sure how this happens, the following response is also exhibited in group dynamics. Certain leading individuals tend to influence the group mood and behaviour. Clearly, it is best that the trainer asserts a positive influence over the group at the point of first contact. There is much we can do as trainers to ensure this happens, and, I commend an investigation of neuro linguistic programming (see Chapter 19) since it highlights many of the mechanisms of influence.

The final word on entrainment is to do with the emergence of sound and light technology. The brain is rather good at this following response. Due to the involvement of the Olivary nucleus, the brain is able to entrain itself into a dominantly alpha or theta-wave state (the two key brain waves associated with assimilation and integration of learning). The mechanism is relatively simple. If a co-ordinated sound and light signal is sent to the right ear and eye, and an alternative signal is sent to the left ear and eye in isolation, the Olivary nucleus will identify the difference. If this difference is the equivalent of an alpha or theta frequency, a receptive brain will demonstrate a 'frequency following response', generating more of the equivalent brain waves. This means that any learner comfortable with the technology can switch their brains to the most appropriate frequency, before, during, or after learning, depending on the result they want.

One of the most dominant uses of this technology likely to become common practice in future will be to provide quiet time after learning. Fascinating research into the usefulness of flotation tanks has shown how beneficial time-out can be for the recall of information. If there is no interference with learning directly after acquisition, the brain can have a real chance to integrate its new discoveries. Conversely, leaping out of the seminar room to pick up your messages is one of the best ways to ensure maximum interference and minimum recall.

What happens if we do not access a positive mindset? The limbic system, a group of organs in the middle of the brain, is associated with long-term memory and our emotional state. If we feel threatened or bored our limbic system either switches down to our lower reptilian brain where we have our fight-flight-freeze instinctive reaction to perceived threat, or up to our right hemisphere where we can go off day-dreaming instead of wasting time being bored. Most of us have experienced both these options during training – especially our mind 'blanking' when we are under stress. This is why a low-stress, high-energy environment is so important.

Entrance

Our first 'E' is for 'entrance' – the second branch on the Mind Map® connected at two o'clock. Entrance is the information gathering phase of any accelerated learning event. At a raw sensory level, every learner displays a different range of preferences for visual, auditory, or physical information processing. Stereotypically, a dominantly visual learner really does need to see the big picture in order for the information to make sense. For dominantly auditory learners, the information has to be on their wavelength. This includes the way the information sounds. For example, using a poor quality music system will distress a dominantly auditory person, regardless of the style of music played. Physical learners are literally information handlers. The best way for them to take in the information is to manipulate some kind of physical representation of it or to have scope to move around, changing their body posture while they 'get to grips' with the concepts.

On the Mind Map®, I have also mentioned emotions. The mindset phase runs continuously throughout the model. We must continue to positively engage the learner's emotions. During this phase, it is important that the learner perceives the information as being useful, meaningful, or pleasurable. Since we are soliciting the involvement of the logical brain as well, we will want to present the benefits of the information. Practically, this is often portrayed as an exercise about the world's favourite radio station – WIIFM ('What's In It For Me?'). What has the information got to do for the learner in order for them to want to be fully committed to mastering it? Conveniently then, this phase may be summarized by two radio themes: WIIFM as the station, and VHF (Visual Hearing Feeling) as the bandwidth that ensures a very high frequency of assimilation of the new material. Colin Rose (1992) puts it this way, 'The more ways you teach, the more people you reach'.

As you build your template, you will want to brainstorm as many sensory rich ways as possible to broadcast your initial exposure of the information to be learned. This goes for self-study too. How can you visually and colourfully portray the information? How can you make it sound most attractive? And, how can you make it easy to get a handle on it?

Finally, we could do a great deal more with physiological learning. While not all subjects lend themselves to physical learning, all learning can benefit from physiological shifts. It is particularly important to enforce regular breaks – ideally every 40 minutes. These do not have to be long breaks – two minutes is sufficient – but they should involve a shift in posture. The body's lymphatic system is vital for the removal of toxins. Unfortunately, it is only flushed by muscular activity. This means that if we remain stationary for too long, toxins build up in our system, and pain, plus poor attention, can result. During some of your breaks, try exercises that cross the body's central vertical line of symmetry. Since the left half of the body is controlled by the right side of the brain, and vice versa, crossing the central line by touching your left knee with your right hand, and then your right knee with your left hand, will ensure that both sides of your brain are being stimulated. You may be pleasantly surprised at the flashes of insight your learners get through just taking time-out to switch on their whole brain.

What are the consequences of not broadcasting to all the senses? Understanding something does not guarantee memory. The more sensory channels you use to broadcast the information, the easier it will be for the learners to tune back in to that information when they want to find it again – it is on a broader bandwidth. If you choose to ignore one wavelength, you automatically exclude ease of learning for all those who have that channel as their favourite wavelength.

Sequence

Our first 'S' is for 'sequence through the seven intelligences' – the branch at four o'clock. It is not enough to gather information or new skills. This new data must become personal to the learner, and processed in such a way that it becomes deep learning. This is where accelerated learning has drawn heavily on the work of Professor Howard Gardner of Harvard University. Gardner's work on a model of seven intelligences has 'right adjusted' our appreciation of our full complement of intelligences. The world of commerce rightly prizes the first two intelligences: mathematical/logical intelligence and linguistic intelligence. However, many learners demonstrate high levels of the other intelligences: visual/spatial (high in architects); interpersonal (high in HRD professionals); intrapersonal (high in reflective professionals); physical (e.g., surgeons, technicians), and musical (often high in advertising functions and well as in the performing arts).

We have suggested sequencing through these seven intelligences so that:

1. we can keep most of the people happy most of the time, and
2. we can help learners develop their full complement of intelligences.

While there is huge overlap between the entrance and sequence phases (especially when in comes to visual input and visual/spatial intelligence, or physical input and intelligence), the emphasis during sequencing is on *processing what has already been gathered*. In an ideal accelerated scenario, learners would spend up to 70 per cent of the training event integrating their learning by using their seven intelligences to deep process what they have learned. This leads to much higher levels of action on the learning back in the workplace. Since the learners have owned their learning, they are far more likely to change their behaviour as a result. There will also be much higher levels of recall.

How would you go about switching on the seven intelligences? Mathematical/logical intelligence thrives on sorting information and making logical connections. Pin-board activities, or any tools that help delegates re-arrange materials into new logical sequences will help develop this intelligence and so integrate the learning. Linguistic intelligence has strong links to our subconscious acceptance of the sound of our own voice or thoughts. Putting new learning into our own words is a powerful way to increase acceptance of the information. If this can be combined with drama in the tonality, a sense of fun can be engaged thus getting the limbic system on our side. With the limbic co-operating, long-term memory is guaranteed.

Pin-boarding will also encourage the application of visual/spatial intelligence. Mind mapping, Ishikawa diagrams, force-field analysis, and flow-charting are all grist to the visual/spatial mill. Interpersonal intelligence comes into play in any form of group activity, especially when active listening is used to hear the message behind the message, and key questioning skills are employed to test assumptions. Intrapersonal intelligence thrives when delegates are given quiet time to find their own associative links between the new information and their previous experiences. Intrapersonal intelligence activities answer the question, 'What does this mean for me?' or 'How can I use this?' Physical intelligence is activated when participants are left to explore how pieces of a particular puzzle work together.

Another application is encouraging groups to demonstrate any continuum physically instead of just visually. You might suggest that opposite corners of the room represent extremes of the continuum. Participants can then distribute themselves through different locations, and even heights, to show their perception of the data. This can be a fascinating way for trainers to gather informal feedback on how the training is going for the participants. Any delegate at the 'this is not working for me yet' end of the spectrum can then be asked, 'What would it take to get you from here (points) to here (stands at the desired position)?'

I have left musical intelligence till last since it is probably the most under-utilized of the intelligences. Advertising professionals have known and used the power of music for decades. Few other things evoke such an immediate emotional following response. Few other things can code information faster. Many delegates with a 'terrible memory' have no trouble recalling words from their favourite songs. Of course, the fact that they repeat the words over and over helps, but there is nothing to stop the enterprising trainer harnessing this useful habit.

Karaoke technology has allowed us to provide backing to well-known songs. It is then a simple matter for a group of delegates to rewrite the words using the key learning points, or their chosen action points. Even the shy members can become involved in the process, and then clap along while the extroverts take to showbiz.

Rap music is particularly effective at coding and recalling information. This is due to the combination of strong rhythm and rhyme – thereby using the linguistic left hemisphere and the rhythmic right. It takes a bold group to rap away, but the trainer can again ease the process by providing a rap beat backing track to help the group get in sync.

What if we choose to save time and avoid the sequence phase? Short-cuts at the integration phase will often result in poor retention, poor ownership of the learning, and thus, poor behavioural carry-over to the work environment.

Store

The second 'S' is for 'store'. Mnemonics, flash cards, acronyms, limericks, and mind mapping are all major ways to lock down the key points of the learning process. It is important to emphasize here that we only want to codify the key points. Verbatim learning is a waste of mental capacity. If the learners can edit the information, putting it first into their own words and concepts, they can then go on to establish the hierarchies of thought. Tony and Barry Buzan call this the 'Basic Ordering of Ideas'. On our Mind Map®, the highest order of ideas are the branches attached directly to the central image. As we move progressively towards the periphery we may encounter higher levels of detail, yet lower levels of organization. If the brain wishes to follow the easiest flow of associations, the strong central image and bold first level of ideas will be simple to recall. I see mind mapping as a graphical user interface for the brain. It is 'point-and-click' biotechnology. A strong central image is easy for the brain's biodatabase to find and call up. If you have designed your map well, the next levels of thought should spring to mind. This is very similar to the ideas of groups, folders, and files in computer systems – or filing cabinets. By way of contrast, standard key word bullet points do not present the brain with sufficient distinctiveness to facilitate ease of storage or recall.

If we do not give attention to storage activities, the delegates may leave a session very impressed with the trainer, enthused by the information, but find themselves unable to articulate what exactly it was that they learned.

Act

Our 'A' is for 'act'. This is action within the safe environment of the training event. It is important for learners to notice themselves getting it right. During this phase of the model you might introduce some kind of team challenge. For example, the trainer could become the game show host, or the referee of the contest between teams. A team challenge quiz could take the form of two teams devising questions for each other based on the mastered information. What about competitiveness? Despite some popular psychology that derides competition, we remain a competitive species. Furthermore, competition seems to release a great deal of enthusiasm and energy. It has helped me raise energy tremendously towards the close of the training day – much better than just saying 'thank you' and 'goodbye'.

What if we choose to remove this phase? It is my belief that we would lose an opportunity to boost the learners' confidence in their own ability to learn. After a high energy word quiz, I have often made the comment in passing, 'How did you like your end of term examination?' Most people laugh as they come to the realization that their knowledge has been tested and they have all come out as winners.

Go-again

'G' is for 'go-again' – the part most directly influenced by Georgi Lozanov – founder of what has become accelerated learning. Here we encourage the learners to revisit their own path of learning by orchestrating a review concert. Music (usually Baroque) that uses 60 beats per minute, is used as a delivery mechanism for the key review landmarks along the journey. Encourage your learners to listen to the sound of the music, and to let themselves become absorbed in the music – just like going to the movies. Then let your voice become an instrument in the ensemble. Time your phrases so that they synchronize with the time signature of the music. You thus become an exquisite lyricist, a minstrel, leading your audience along the road they have already travelled.

After a bit of practice you may find yourself able to synchronize with the group to such an extent that your vocals accompany the out breath of the most relaxed individuals. They will have synchronized their breathing (and their brain waves) to the beat of the music. By pacing their breathing rhythm you will be pacing their perception of reality – an experience that many find very refreshing.

This 'suggestopaedia' approach was the first form of accelerated learning. Lozanov's use of baroque music, hypnotic language patterns, and psycho-drama for activating deep learning led to the first statistical evidence of a truly accelerated learning process.

Exit

Finally, our last 'E' is for 'exit' – the opposite book-end to 'entrance'. At the exit point, we want the learners to do three things:

1. to develop a habit of reflecting upon learning;
2. to commit to a systematic review of the material;
3. to visit the most immediate future scenario where they are likely to be able to use the learning.

Many professionals keep a learning journal. Without reflection – a form of attention – our nervous system diminishes the significance of the material. We simply do not notice opportunities to apply it. Whatever gets your attention, gets you. Anything that you pay quality attention to becomes encoded in your bio-recognition mechanisms so that you are mentally set to notice future occurrences.

If we combine this reflection with creative use of our imagination to visit possible future scenarios, we can become hard-wired for action. There will be a cue to use the information in the future – something in each delegate's sensory experience that will flag the opportunity to apply the learning. By helping them visit possible events in their imagination, you can help them identify their own unique triggers to remind them to act.

We are fortunate that every healthy brain on the planet has a similar rhythm for transferring information from the 'insignificant' (short-term memory) category to the 'significant' (long-term memory) category. If you can encourage participants to review their learning and action points within one hour, after one day, one week, one month, and at the 100 day marker, they will be able to recall everything they paid attention to.

A practical example of implementation

The Registry of Accelerated Trainers teaches touch typing in three hours using the M.E.S.S.A.G.E. model.

Mindset is attended to by boosting each individual's confidence in their own memory recall (through mnemonic coding). A visualization of speed typing also sets their minds to expect and recognize success.

Multi-sensory entrance is obtained visually through an attractive storyboard; auditorily through the delegates saying out loud the words of the storyboard while physically rehearsing the correct finger movements. All three senses are thus engaged at the same time.

The seven intelligences are sequenced through by:

- Using shuffled cards containing the storyboard to stimulate mathematical/logical and visual/spatial intelligence (as they are placed in the correct order), and interpersonal intelligence through team work.
- Using the participants own creative writing to switch on linguistic and intrapersonal intelligence.
- Using physical intelligence throughout the finger-drill exercises.
- Using musical intelligence through a mnemonic song, and the rhythmic use of a drum machine to pace the exercises.

The storage phase has been integrated during the exercises, since this is primarily a motor skill. However, to make the review easier at the exit phase, a coloured Mind Map® summarizes the content *and* the approach – making it a transferable model. The act phase is demonstrated through delegates filling out a partially blank keyboard template. The go-again phase is a simple review concert, revisiting the path of learning, and including anything unusual that has happened with each unique group. This pacing of the group's unique experience enhances the personal reality and relevance of the approach. Action planning at the exit phase, coupled with a reminder of the review rhythm, ensures that the new touch typists visit their future scenarios where they will use their new skills.

Conclusion

The strength of accelerated learning is not so much in its new techniques as in its systematic sturdiness. The trainer can have confidence that it is founded on robust research, and that they already have all the resources necessary to begin accelerating their training process. If the trainer is able to start with a 'safe' and sympathetic group, even the most unusual aspect – the review concert – will prove to be easy to deliver.

Further reading

Buzan, T. (1974), *Use Your Head*, London: BBC.

Buzan, T. (1986), *Use Your Memory*, London: BBC.

Buzan, T. (1989), *Speed and Range Reading*, Newton Abbot: David & Charles.

Buzan, T, and Buzan, B. (1993), *The Mind Map Book*, London: BBC.

Dryden, G. and Vos, J. (1994), *The Learning Revolution*, Aylesbury: Accelerated Learning Systems Ltd.

Goleman, D. (1996), *Emotional Intelligence*, London: Bloomsbury.

Hutchison, M. (1994), *Mega Brain Power*, Hyperion.

Prashnig, B. (1996), *Diversity is Our Strength – The Learning Revolution in Action*, Profile Books.

Rose, C. (1983), *Accelerated Learning*, Aylesbury: Accelerated Learning Systems Ltd.

Rose, C. (1991), *Accelerated Learning System 2000 Training and Development Program*, Aylesbury: Accelerated Learning Systems Ltd.

Rose, C. and Goll, L. (1992), *Accelerate Your Learning*, Aylesbury: Accelerated Learning Systems Ltd.

Rossi, E. L. (1993), *The Psychobiology of Mind-Body Healing*, Norton.

Russell, P. (1979), *The Brain Book*, London: Routledge.

Scheele, P. (1993), *The PhotoReading Whole Mind System*, Wayzata, Minnesota: Learning Strategies Corporation.

Training in Accelerated Learning

The Registry of Accelerated Trainers provides training in accelerated learning, numerous applications, and neuro linguistic programming. PO Box 98, Aylesbury, Bucks, HP19 3YX.

Mind Map® is the Registered Trademark of The Buzan Organization, used with permission.

Chapter 21

Action learning

Krystyna Weinstein

Action learning is a 'process' underpinned by a belief in individual potential: a way of learning from our actions, and from what happens to us, and around us, by taking the time to question, understand and reflect, to gain insights, and consider how to act in future.

In this chapter I will be taking a look at what constitutes an Action Learning programme, what it is for, when it is useful and how it can be designed. For trainers, facilitators and developmental managers action learning can be a highly effective way of helping people in organizations learn fruitfully while achieving a practical outcome for their organization. It has many advantages over more traditional methods of 'training'; and its constant emphasis on daily practicality makes it an attractive proposition to organizations seeking relevance in any learning and developmental undertakings.

The main elements of action learning

The six main elements of an action learning programme are:

1. *The set*   The same small group of people – five or six – who meet regularly, ideally once a month for a day, to work together in a supportive yet challenging way, and allocating to each member, at each meeting, time to work on their own project.

   'I was amazed at how the non-experts in a given field can help you by asking intelligent questions ... their lack of familiarity with my issue caused me to explain it from basics, and often made me think more laterally.'

   'It's the diversity in the set which is the richness.'

2. *Work-based, real-time projects or tasks*   Each person (or the set as a

whole) focuses on a work issue/quandary which needs to be resolved or implemented and uses it as the 'learning vehicle'. Projects can focus on something new to be tackled, something that is of concern, or something that needs to be attended to. Ideally, participants should be able to choose projects that are important and need to be resolved, and that will give them a chance to develop their own skills, qualities, or behaviours.

'I learnt what was practical, what was bearable, and what was acceptable ... next time I make proposals I need to consider those on the receiving end much more.'

'Hearing others' projects broadens your horizons, gives you the bigger picture.'

3. *The 'processes' in the set*   An action learning set adopts particular processes as it works. Each person has their own 'airspace' (of up to one hour) in which to work on their project. Meanwhile the set members adopt a helpful questioning approach. They focus on helping the person with air-space to think through what he or she is doing and why, what assumptions they are making or beliefs they hold, what they would like to do and what is stopping them. The set avoids giving advice, or having general discussions. The focus at any one time is on one person. Finally, the set helps each individual create some action plans to work on before the next meeting – when they report back on actions, and on what they are learning.

'As you talk you resolve your own problems – if you're honest about what you say ... as you explain things to the set you hear your own inconsistencies. ...'

'Good questions tease out the real issues. They make you think. Often they're questions you haven't thought of, or ones you wouldn't dream – or want – to ask yourself.'

4. *A set adviser*   At the start of an action learning programme, a set needs to work with a facilitator whose task is to help the set work, keep to the processes, and learn. The set adviser models helpful behaviours, as well as asking the set – when appropriate – to become aware of how it is behaving and working.

'I used the set adviser and his way of 'managing' us as a model for managing.'

5. *The duration of a programme*   Programmes normally last between five and six months though some continue, at the request of participants, for longer. This allows projects to be implemented – an important aspect of action learning.

'Time is crucial. You become like a sponge – gradually saturated – and then you need time before it begins to drip out ...'

'Going round the learning cycle once isn't sufficient. We meet monthly and feel – and can see – that we've matured over time.'

6. *The emphasis on learning*   The focus on both action and on learning is a distinguishing feature of action learning. The learning encompasses a wide variety of elements and will occur while participants work in the set, and while they work on their projects. Participants are encouraged to become 'opportunistic' learners, i.e. realizing that everything that they do, or that happens, offers a learning opportunity. So, the set will be asked to focus on their insights and learning after each 'airspace', and at the end of each set meeting. The focus of the learning is on processes as much as on the 'content' of any project.

'I've learnt that I learn best when challenged by others.'

'It's given me the confidence to disagree.'

'I'm more aware of the effect I have on others.'

Every programme should also have a 'sponsor' – a senior manager who appreciates the value of such a programme, and give it his or her full backing and support.

The rest of this chapter explores – briefly – what makes active learning so effective, lists the benefits, and discusses how it is a step in the direction of a learning company.

A questioning approach

Action learning is a 'questioning' approach. The questions that participants ask of one another as they work in the set – always with a focus on the project or task they are working on – are an invitation to stop and consider, rather than to rush in with answers, solutions or justifications. So, participants learn to ask helpful and thoughtful questions. They also learn to listen – not as easy as it sounds!

Reg Revans, the 'founding father' of action learning, describes learning 'L' as consisting of two elements: programmed or taught learning 'P', coupled with asking questions 'Q'. So, 'P' is what we learn on courses, or from books, or what we have picked up in the past and do unthinkingly. 'P' is also all our beliefs and assumptions that underpin so much of what we do – again, often unthinkingly.

It is the emphasis on the Q that is the more important. By asking others, and ourselves questions, we challenge, and are challenged. In action learning all the various 'Ps' are up for questioning. The purpose of questions posed in action learning is to prompt thought and reflection – from which emerge insights, learning and effective actions.

Reg Revans' fundamental equation is: $L = P + Q$. Others have added to this: $L = P + Q + A + R$, where A = action, and R = reflection.

Much of action learning also focuses on the Kolb learning cycle (see Figure 21.1): moving through the elements of action, followed by recall and reflection, onto consolidation of the insights, and finally onto planning next moves, in the light of what has been learnt. To gain the most from action learning, however, participants need to be encouraged to be aware of an 'inner' cycle (see Figure 21.2 on page 232) where they address their fears and prejudices, and take the 'risk' of being different.

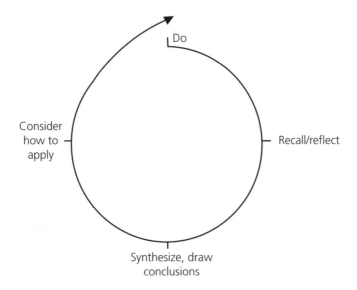

Figure 21.1   Kolb's learning cycle

Tackling problems not puzzles

In action learning, the task or projects that participants work on should be what Reg Revans calls problems, i.e. daily quandaries, uncertainties or issues which have no one way of being resolved and no one solution. He makes a useful distinction between what he calls puzzles and problems. We are dealing with puzzles when there is a known answer to our questioning and probing, only we do not yet know it. Probably another course or some more reading will give us the solution.

Someone who is learning to use a word processor would gain little from attending an action learning programme. But someone given the task of determining whether staff in a given department would benefit by having

Figure 21.2   Inner experiential cycle

individual word processing facilities would find this a useful project to work on in an action learning programme.

An equal focus on action and learning

Everything we do reflects our skills, qualities, beliefs, values and assumptions. It is by becoming aware of how these underpin our actions – and recognizing which are 'positive' and which may be 'negative' factors – that we can begin to take stock of what we need to change, discard, or rethink, if we are to become more effective in our relationships with others.

Because of its emphasis on communication processes and learning, action learning provides an ideal mirror in which we can begin to see ourselves more clearly.

Learning with and from one another

One of the tenets of action learning is that we learn best and most effectively when we learn in the company of others who are also learning. None of us has a monopoly on knowledge or insights. We all have a host of questions, which we voice, or keep silently to ourselves. By working and learning with others, we are able to share knowledge, insights and perceptions, as well as hear each other's doubts and questions.

'Managerial learning is a social exchange in which managers learn with and from each other during the diagnosis and treatment of real problems (and opportunities)' (Revans, 1980).

Returning to work after a set meeting, tackling their project, and then coming back to the set and talking about what they have achieved – or failed to achieve – acts as a rhythm, and doing this several times over a period of some months: for participants this 'rhythm' is essential to anchoring the learning.

It takes time

Action learning takes time. It takes time to learn – and unlearn. It takes time to build up trust among a group as they work and learn together; it takes time for members to feel free to discuss some issues that they may never have discussed with anyone before. It takes time to build up confidence to do things differently; and it then takes time to practise and perfect what we have begun to do differently.

Is anything taught on an action learning programme?

On a classic action learning programme there is no teaching. This is probably one of the most difficult aspects of action learning for new participants to understand. How can you learn without being taught?

It *is* possible, as participants come to realize. Everyone brings so much experience and knowledge, and as people share with one another, they gradually perceive that between them they often have insights and even answers, and do not need experts to come along and tell them. This is not to dismiss experts or expert knowledge. But there is a time and place for them. Action learning programmes are often run after taught courses, to help consolidate the knowledge that participants have acquired – either through lectures, case studies or reading.

The values of action learning

There is one other important aspect to action learning: the values and beliefs that underpin it. Reg Revans is very clear about this. Honesty with one's self and with others; respect for others and their viewpoints, trying to understand, rather than judging them; and accepting responsibility for what one does – these are fundamental to successful action learning. Without them, there is little real achievement (although there may be results), and certainly no learning.

The emphasis in action learning is thus on taking responsibility for one's actions, on helpful questioning, thinking, avoiding the impulse to give advice, passing judgement on anyone, or finding easy solutions to problems. Problems presented initially are often symptoms of other deeper problems. It is those that action learning aims to reach.

Figure 21.3 encapsulates all the elements of action learning. If one of them is missing, the full benefit of action learning will also be missing.

'I can now admit to having made a mistake – to be honest.'

'You realize you're not alone with your worries and concerns, or alone to resolve them.'

Who is it for?

Action learning is for everyone: engineers, shop-floor staff, sales and marketing personnel, trainers and developers, middle managers, clerical assistants,

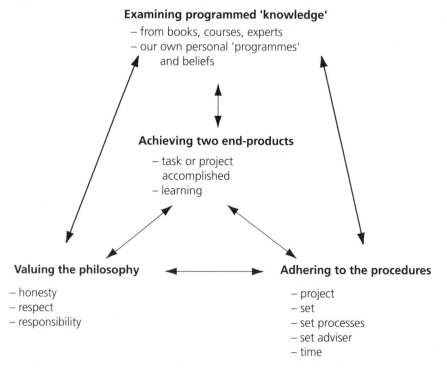

Examining programmed 'knowledge'
- from books, courses, experts
- our own personal 'programmes' and beliefs

Achieving two end-products
- task or project accomplished
- learning

Valuing the philosophy ←——→ **Adhering to the procedures**

- honesty
- respect
- responsibility

- project
- set
- set processes
- set adviser
- time

Figure 21.3   The four Ps of action learning

senior managers and managing directors, hospital administrators, para-medical staff, nurses, social workers, teachers and lecturers, shop retail staff, bankers, bakers, builders, and people in IT.

Programmes have run in every type of organization – education and health service, local government, banks and building societies, manufacturing companies, service companies, the police, charities, and in community projects.

Sets are selected so that people within them are able to help one another, even if they come from different functions – sometimes even different organizations. They are normally made up of people with similar levels of responsibility; in other words, a senior manager and a junior employee are unlikely to work in the same set. However, they may do so very successfully when such a 'vertical slice' set has as its task to resolve, for example, a company-wide assessment scheme.

When is it useful?

An action learning approach can be applied to the following circumstances:

- When we are confronting a new situation we have never been in before.
- When we are working with a new group of people we have never dealt with before.
- When we want to test out new ways of working with people we already know: in teams, or simply managing staff or relating to colleagues.
- When our jobs or work roles change and we are not sure what our responsibilities are, or how to relate to other staff.
- When the organization we work for is facing a major dilemma and needs to move forward.
- When we feel there are untapped human resources around us that we are ignoring, i.e. when involving people in working on resolving issues that affect them in organizations.
- When the organization we work for is faced with challenges in the future and needs to establish strategies and plans.
- When trying to deliver this elusive concept called 'empowerment'.
- When we want to change the way things have been before.
- When we want to change something in our own personal make up, such as the way we do things, the way we react, i.e., personal development.
- When, as part of an NVQ or MCI initiative, we need to attain competence in a given area.

So, to use organizational terminology, action learning is effective for organizational development, team development and personal development. It also has a powerful role to play in any training or development programme:

- As an integral part of 'development' programmes.
- As a follow-up to/or integrated into more traditional courses – to anchor and consolidate the learning.
- As an integral part of distance learning programmes, to offset the 'loneliness of the long-distance learner'.
- On practice-oriented professional programmes, to offer opportunities to share experiences.

Above all:

- It is an opportunity for networking across an organization, helping members to understand the different functions within that organization, and the issues and quandaries that colleagues have to face.
- It is a forum where people can share difficulties and problems, without fear.
- It provides a model of a new way of both communicating and managing.

The processes of action learning encourage helpful and effective ways of communicating. When the emphasis is on 'dialogue' with others, participants learn not only to pose searching questions, but to listen (not as easy as it sounds!), and to help others resolve their own queries and issues by encouraging them to think and reflect. In fact, several participants have likened the set to having a group of mentors.

Benefits of action learning

Practitioners and 'users' have highlighted the following benefits of action learning:

1. To resolve real business problems: 'It's a bridge between analysis and implementation. Its rigour comes from benchmarking and improvement. It's not a fad; it has a long scientific pedigree ... It focuses on improving actual performance, not analysis'.
2. To improve social processes: 'Action learning is itself a social process and organizations are realizing that social processes underpin their success'.
3. To empower people: 'Content is a false trail. Experts don't provide the answers. Someone will always know more! We need to encourage people to say, "Let's try it," and have confidence in their abilities and insights'.
4. To improve leadership qualities: 'Being authentic is the only way to be a true leader ... Learning to manage yourself has to come before managing and leading others. Action learning makes people examine themselves and their actions and motivations'.

5. Learning to cope with change: 'More traditional programmes don't deliver the change and differences looked for back at work... It's the only programme I know where you can actually see people change'.

Why have organizations used action learning?

The reasons for running – or attending – action learning programmes are many and varied:

- Some companies had tried all the 'traditional' courses they could find, but found that little learning was being transferred back into work.
- Several felt that action learning was an important adjunct to taught two- or three-day courses.
- Many were looking for developmental programmes, and felt that action learning, because of its practical, work-focus, would be most pragmatic.
- Many wanted to engage their staff in more hands-on projects.
- A number believed that this was the best way of creating working networks across their organizations.
- Many were attracted by action learning's emphasis on learning, rather than simply achieving 'bottom-line' results.
- The majority felt sure that the best results occur when participants are trying to resolve their own day-to-day problems.

Surrey County Council, just one of many organizations now using action learning, listed the following reasons. It:

- is a good support mechanism for managers;
- provides very useful thinking time;
- provides space for reflection;
- counteracts stress – slows pace of work down;
- highlights experiential learning;
- is very empowering;
- is good for self and manager development, working on real management issues;
- is very powerful for individuals;
- enables the development of counselling skills;
- enables the development of consultancy skills, analytical questioning and problem solving;
- provides space for self-discovery;
- produces ways forward on work issues;
- unlocks and unfreezes;
- helps with the management of change;
- provides cross-departmental and external exchange opportunities.

Not all organizations are ready for action learning

Action learning may not, however, be suitable for all organizations at a given point in their life. They may simply not be ready for it, may not have the culture to contain people who feel empowered and confident, and who think and question – or indeed may not want to create such a culture.

Action learning can be subversive because:

- it values everyone
- it is democratic
- it stresses questioning
- it stresses listening
- it insists on actions
- it gives courage
- it encourages responsibility
- it examines everything.

However, another view might be that action learning could be used to kick-start some radical changes in an organization, provided the idea is bought into by the most senior managers, and they themselves endorse and support such programmes.

Different types of programme

Programmes may be run in-company, i.e. only people from one organization participate; or may be mixed-company ones, where participants are from different companies and organizations. Within these programmes there are four types of projects:

1. In-company programmes where everyone works on projects within their own department or section, i.e. a setting with which they are familiar.
2. In-company programmes where they work on projects in unfamiliar departments or sections.
3. Mixed-company programmes where they work on a project based in their own work area.
4. Mixed-company programmes where the project is not only in a different company, but also in an unfamiliar department or section.

The most common are the first two. The third – mixed-company but participants working on their own projects – are normally for senior people.

An example of the fourth are programmes run in multinationals or organizations containing many separately managed companies. One example of such a programme took place in a ferry company, with operations in many European countries. The participants came from each of these countries, and represented many functions; each set then focused on an issue to be resolved in one particular field of activity – such as finance and freight. Another possibility is a mixed-company set, with participants drawn from separately managed companies within a vast conglomerate.

Designing action learning programmes

To be successful action learning programmes need to be carefully and well designed. Some of the elements that need particular attention are:

- Clarity about the objectives of the programme, and communicating them to all who are concerned and actively involved.
- Being clear and explicit about the nature of action learning, and how it changes people.
- The support of senior managers and participants' managers.
- The design of the programme: being clear whether it will be part of a 'taught' programme, whether it will be a free-standing programme, and whether participants will be given access to resources during the programme.
- Determining how the programme will be evaluated and by whom it will be evaluated – participants themselves, their managers, clients, or even their staff?
- Selecting carefully who will participate, i.e. who will benefit from the design, coupled with the programme's objectives and hoped-for outcomes; and allowing those selected to choose if they wish to participate.

Action learning and the learning organization

A great deal is currently being written about the value of a learning organization – one where learning is a way of life. Yesterday's answers are not necessarily those for tomorrow, and the challenge is to enable the entire organization, i.e. the individuals who make it up, to share their learning – their knowledge, experiences and insights – with others.

As Bob Garratt, author of the book *The Learning Organisation* (Garratt, 1987) has put it: 'Action learning is a process for the reform of organizations and the liberation of human vision within organisations'.

Many other authors refer to action learning processes as underpinning a learning organization. In their book *The Learning Company*, Pedler, Burgoyne and Boydell (1991) say: 'Action in the learning company always has two purposes: to resolve the immediate problem, and to learn from that process'. A recent study on how learning takes place in organizations, carried out by the Institute for Research on Learning in Palo Alto, California, concluded that: 'The most powerful organizational learning and collective knowledge-sharing grows through informal relationships and personal networks – via working conversations in communities of practice'.

Peter Honey, in an article entitled 'Establishing a Learning Regime' (Honey, 1994), postulates ten learning behaviours, which are remarkably similar to the learning that participants claim to gain on action learning programmes.

All these quotes – and there are many other similar ones by authors such as Peter Senge and Gareth Morgan – sound familiar to anyone who has experienced action learning. Gareth Morgan, however, has said that '... You can't create a learning organisation ... but you can enhance people's capacities to learn and align their activities in creative ways'.

One could, in a sense, claim that the basis of a learning company is a network of like-minded people, who enjoy the challenge of working in an action learning way. They form a powerful network which will share and exchange insights and information, provide help and support for each other in their work and personal 'experiments', will ask questions and challenge supportively and give feedback. They will, in other words, learn with and from one another and in the process 'transform' themselves and the organization they work for.

An action learning set may, in fact, be a learning company in microcosm!

Further reading

Beaty, L., Bourner, T. and Frost, P. (1993), 'Reflection on Being a Set Member', *Management Education and Development* (MEAD), **24**, part 4.

Garratt, B. (1987), *The Learning Organization*, London: Fontana.

Honey, P. (1994), 'Establishing a Learning Regime', *Organisations and People*, **1**(1).

McGill, I. and Beaty, L. (1992), *Action Learning*, London: Kogan Page.

Pedler, M., Burgoyne, J. and Boydell, T. (1991), *The Learning Company*, Maidenhead: McGraw-Hill.

Pedler, M. (1997), *Action Learning in Practice*, 3rd edn, Aldershot: Gower.

Revans, R. (1980), *Action Learning: New Techniques for Management*, London: Blond and Briggs.

Weinstein, K. (1998), *Action Learning: A Practical Guide*, 2nd edn, Aldershot: Gower.

Chapter 22

The art of facilitation

Pat Young and Anthony Landale

What is facilitation?

As organizations get to grips with what empowerment really means so the thinking about the skills required to manage is undergoing a significant reassessment. No longer can managers rely on traditional command and control structures for their authority; instead they need to find a different approach, one that will enable them to manage effectively in different situations – in one-to-one settings, in teams and with clients.

These new skills that managers are having to learn can be described as facilitation skills. The dictionary definition of a facilitator is: 'one who makes easier; one who assists the progress of another'. However facilitation should not be seen as some softly, softly approach to working with others. On the contrary it can be, and often is, extremely challenging. But the emphasis of facilitation is on collaboration and co-operation and it is this focus which has attracted the interest of trainers and managers as they look for ways to improve working practices.

This chapter is aimed at all trainers and managers whose objective it is to encourage others to learn and work together. In it we propose to look at the principles of facilitation, what it means to work as a facilitator before going on to consider how facilitation can be applied in practice

The principles of facilitation

Facilitation is the way you lead, guide and follow a group or an individual – be that as a teacher, a trainer, a manager, a consultant or a supervisor. To achieve excellence as a facilitator you need to adapt your facilitation so that it is appropriate to the aims, the needs, the level of experience, the duration and the context of the people you are facilitating.

Put in another way, managing or training is no longer seen to be effective when you are relying solely on telling people what to do and how to do it. The focus of the trainer or manager who uses facilitation is to help people be self-directed. This does not mean, however, that you are giving away your power. Rather it means you need to be ready and able to adapt your style in order to help the person or group achieve its purpose.

As a facilitator you need to be aware of the role you have for the situation you are in (i.e. are you team leader, consultant, teacher?) and then decide which of three modes of authority to use. The three modes that facilitators need to utilize in this respect are:

1. *Hierarchy*   This is where you as the facilitator direct the learning process or the group meeting. You exercise your power over it and do things for the group. You lead from the front by thinking and acting on behalf of the individual and the group. In hierarchical mode, the manager is in absolute control and everybody knows and understands this. Hierarchically managed businesses have a clear (explicit), or unstated (implicit) command and control system; there is commonly one right way of doing things, usually the manager's. The danger of operating solely from this mode is that the manager may not be using the expertise contained within the team, may be unable or unwilling to allow team members to take any responsibility, and will therefore stifle initiative.

2. *Co-operation*   This is where you share your power and manage from your knowledge and experience. You work towards enabling people and teams to become more self-directing by conferring with them. In co-operative mode the manager and the team make decisions together. Essentially they meet to make decisions as peers, everyone has an equal say, and responsibility is shared and owned by all team members.

    Many managers say they manage co-operatively, but when it comes to the crunch they make the decisions themselves. When this happens the manager has moved back into hierarchical mode. There will of course be occasions when this is absolutely necessary, but many of these 'flips' back into hierarchy are driven by the manager's anxiety rather than need. The co-operative mode makes full use of the manager's and the team's expertise.

3. *Autonomy*   This is where you respect the total autonomy of the individual or the group. You do not do things for them or with them; rather you give them freedom to find their own way, exercising their own judgement without any intervention by you.

    In autonomous mode, the manager gives authority and responsibility to the team to make decisions, and agrees to abide by the decisions the team makes. This mode makes full use of the expertise contained within the team, implies a high level of trust, and demands maturity and respon-sibility from both the manager and team.

There is, of course, no right mode. The effective facilitator is able to move between all three modes effortlessly, depending on the needs of the situation. Although there will always be situations which demand hierarchical manage-ment because of the nature of the job or some current crisis, effective busi-nesses are managed hierarchically only when hierarchy is appropriate.

So far so good, but there is another important aspect of facilitation which concerns both the use of these styles and how they are applied in learning sit-uations. The following dimensions of facilitation will help readers to identify their approach when working with others.

The dimensions of facilitation

Planning

This is the goal-oriented aspect of facilitation, the 'what to do' rather than the 'how to do it'. The question that facilitators need to have in mind here is how the individual or group can meet its objectives.

In hierarchical mode the manager may simply impose planning decisions without consultation. In the process they may, or may not, have sought relevant information and conducted research. Equally, facilitators acting in this mode might provide supporting reasons for adopting a particular plan and, again, they might not.

In co-operative mode the facilitator will negotiate the planning process with the individual or the group. In the autonomous mode the facilitator defines with the group the goals and objectives but thereafter all planning is undertaken by group members on their own.

Meaning

This is the knowledge aspect of facilitation and enables individuals and groups to understand what is going on and to make sense of their experience.

Operating from the hierarchical position facilitators may, for example, decide to tell an individual or group why a certain change initiative is happen-ing and what it means. Informing in this way may make sense from the facili-tator's perspective and their interpretation might even have some truth to it but it will be limiting since it is based on just one perspective.

In co-operative mode the facilitator might prompt the individual or group to consider for themselves what change might mean to their working lives and they might help the group to make sense of what is happening by, for example, sharing helpful models or personal experiences.

In autonomous mode the facilitator leaves the individual or group to arrive at their own conclusions but this also has its dangers especially when an individual or group does not feel it has enough information to make sense of what is happening. In such cases the manager may find people feeling abandoned and demoralized rather than empowered.

Confronting

This is where the facilitator challenges the individual or the group and it is here we see that facilitation is far from being an approach that relies on being nice to others. Confronting others is all about tackling resistance to change, about raising awareness of blind spots and helping individuals and groups to face things that they have been avoiding. Hierarchically the facilitator might challenge someone head on about their behaviour by highlighting it directly or perhaps by asking confronting questions.

The process of feedback is often used as the mechanism through which co-operation is used. The individual or group agrees to the feedback given by the facilitator, they look at the reality of the challenge together and use it as a basis for learning or development.

In autonomous mode the facilitator will typically be working with a high trust group or perhaps as a mentor/coach with an individual. It is in these contexts, where the individual or group feels safe and supported, that people will start to challenge themselves.

Feeling

Organizations often have taboos around expressing feelings and it is in this dimension that the facilitative manager/trainer has to be aware of their own emotional responses and those of the people they are working with. This is the area which concerns sensing and managing the mood of the group.

Hierarchically, you can see trainers acting in the feeling dimension when they use energizing games and techniques to try and alter the feeling state of the group. In beginner groups, facilitators have to be especially sensitive to those times when members are suppressing feeling. In such cases it is important to guide people to identify, own and accept their own feelings.

Co-operatively this can be done by facilitators prompting individuals or groups to share what they are feeling and by sharing their own views about the importance of feelings. Meanwhile the autonomous group or individual will spontaneously express and celebrate in their own way at their own chosen time.

Structuring

This is the formal aspect of facilitation that deals with achievement of aims and objectives. It involves methods of learning and the ways of working and how they are to be structured.

The modes of authority that a facilitator can adopt for this dimension are similar to that of planning. The facilitator may decide hierarchically what they as a group will do, and when they will do it, without reference to anyone else. Alternatively they may work co-operatively with the individual or group, drawing from them their ideas and preferences or, in autonomous mode, encourage the individual or group to set up their own self-directed experience.

Valuing

Here we are talking about the integrity aspect of facilitation – the ability of the facilitator to build trust and to create a supportive climate which honours and respects the individuals he or she is working with. The aim here is to build a climate in which people can be genuine, in which they feel free and willing to disclose their reality, and which keeps them in touch with their true needs and interests.

The facilitator who works out of hierarchy here can achieve much by setting clear ground rules and by expressing positive feelings. Such expression has to be authentic, however, and it requires that the facilitator is in touch with his or her own genuine thoughts and feelings. However, the whole issue of valuing implies sharing responsibility with others – so for the climate to be maintained the facilitator will also have to work co-operatively. Working in co-operative mode the facilitator will honour the choice that others make and by prompting others to adopt nurturing, validative and supportive behaviour will help build a valuing climate.

It may well be the facilitator's aim that after some time working with either the individual or the group he or she is able to work in autonomous mode. This is where the individuals concerned have beliefs and attitudes which affirm and respect others and themselves.

These then are the six dimensions and facilitative trainers and managers will be conscious of when each of these dimensions pertain and the choice they have about how to exercise the appropriate authority in order to be effective. We will now go on to some of the underpinning qualities of facilitation.

Building awareness and skill

Managers and trainers who want to become adept facilitators need to start by working with themselves. The principle at stake here is that you can only facilitate others in areas in which you yourself have explored.

To know oneself is, of course, an ongoing endeavour and it requires us to commit to ongoing development on all levels – mental, emotional, physical and spiritual. It is important to note, however, that this does not mean we are aspiring to be perfect in any of these areas but rather that we are comfortable with who we are. To borrow the transactional analysis (TA) model it is not about 'You're OK and I'm not OK' but rather working towards 'I'm OK and you're OK' or, if you like, working towards a genuine acceptance of yourself.

Some of the questions potential facilitators might ask themselves here might focus on how comfortable they feel with their body, with their thoughts, with their feelings and with their beliefs? The issue is not to feel as if you have everything under control but rather to know yourself well enough to know where you feel solid and where you feel less sure of yourself. Everyone has their strengths and weaknesses, their peculiar quirks and their private thoughts. The effective facilitator, however, will have explored more about themselves and understood how this affects their behaviour.

Developing this level of self-awareness is important for facilitation because it enables us to feel comfortable with other people. If, for example, there are aspects of ourselves that we do not like then we will find it hard to accept other people who display the same traits?

This aspect of learning to accept ourselves so that we can be more available to others is often both new and refreshing to people who come to facilitation. In challenging ourselves to be more 'who we really are' we start to liberate ourselves from our prejudices and genuinely open ourselves up to others. Such an attitude is essential to facilitating others.

Another key underpinning quality that facilitators need to develop is the art of attentive listening: 'Listening is much more than hearing. Hearing is the auditory information. Listening is an intellectual and emotional process that decodes physical, intellectual and emotional input in a search for meaning and understanding. Effective listening occurs when the listener correctly understands the sender's meaning' (see Mulligan, *et al.*, 1988).

What we learn here is that the ability to listen is a crucial component of interpersonal relationships. For example, how do you feel when you are not listened to, when you are misunderstood, or when what you say is forgotten?

As a facilitator listening well and attentively is a powerful way of 'being' with another person. It honours more than just the words of the speaker but rather helps people to feel as though they have really been seen and valued.

The trick is to listen to someone as though they are the most important person in the world, which, at the time they are speaking to you is, of course, true. If you want to develop into an effective listener then you might begin with this checklist:

1. Have a reason for listening.
2. Demonstrate skill in giving attention.
3. Use silences and infrequent questions.
4. Encourage the other person to talk.
5. Try not to interrupt the other person.
6. Suspend judgement.
7. Allow yourself time to think and wait before responding.
8. Be able to repeat what the speaker says.
9. Be able to rephrase in your own words what was said.
10. Check that you have understood.

The other primary skill which a facilitator needs to develop is that of facilitative speaking. Making skilful interventions arises from first having listened attentively. For the skilled facilitator there are then a range of possibilities. These include:

- The appropriate use of questions which encourage further examination of a particular issue or which challenge an individual or group about its behaviour or attitudes.
- Suggestions which might, for example, help an individual to look at an issue from a different angle.
- Reflections which throw light on the content of what has been said.
- Observations which might notice what is going on inside you the facilitator, might focus on what is happening in the group or highlight events happening outside of the room.
- Imaginal input such as the use of storytelling which has the impact of engaging the imagination or putting a different framework on what has been said.
- Attributive interpretations where some psychological meaning is attributed to a piece of behaviour in terms of motives, desires, emotions or thoughts.
- Feedback which provides the learner with the opportunity to check reality and also invites reflection.

It is important to note that these skills of building awareness, listening and speaking sound desperately simple but require great attention. Facilitation cannot be learned overnight, it requires commitment and needs to be practised and honed over time.

Facilitation in action

Facilitation is a useful skill for trainers and managers to learn whatever the situation in which they find themselves. In times of change it is more and more important that people find the flexibility of attitude and behaviour that allows them to respond to new and emerging conditions. However, there are a number of workplace processes and occasions where facilitation is an especially appropriate management response:

- *Mentoring*   A useful definition of mentoring is that provided by David Clutterbuck (see Chapter 24) when he talks of it being 'off-line help by one person to another in making significant transitions in knowledge, work or thinking'. The mentor has a role in this respect of helping the mentoree grasp the significance of what is happening in their work and their life.

    The potential of mentoring has been recognized by many organizations but often there is little formal training given to mentors in how to be effective in the role. The use of facilitation skills which emphasize how to support, challenge and enable the development of others can provide a model for prospective mentors.

- *Coaching*   Akin to mentoring, coaching is, according to the *Oxford Dictionary,* the way to 'tutor, train, give hints to, prime with facts'. However, the power of coaching again lies within the relationship of coach and coachee. In this respect it is a partnership of trust with the emphasis on endeavour and learning.

    The coach who is flexible in the mode of authority he or she uses and who truly believes in the potential of the coachee will achieve the greatest success.

- *Training and development*   In the area of people skills there is less and less emphasis on presentation-led training. Instead the focus is on encouraging people to develop themselves. Facilitation encourages people who want to learn to examine their own self-limiting beliefs and explore their own greatness. Such an approach is especially useful when the event is relying on high participation and involvement from delegates.

- *Consultancy*   So much of a consultant's skill depends on their listening ability and their ability to make telling interventions. The old adage of consultants borrowing your watch to tell you the time is only true of those consultants who have one method or idea to sell. In needing to pay close attention to what people say and by working co-operatively with clients, consultancy provides many opportunities to show how a facilitative approach can add real value.

- *Personal performance*   Individuals who want to build on their own performance can use facilitation both to see where they are blocked and to gain support from others as they seek to change their attitudes or behaviour. The facilitative approach challenges people to face up to what is not working, stand behind their true intent and develop the skills and competence that they have been lacking.

- *Team leading*   Much of this chapter has provided a focus for how managers can work with others in groups and teams. In an empowered or a delayering culture facilitation is imperative. Managers simply have to find new ways of working with others and they can only be effective by enabling others around them to fulfil some of their potential. Facilitator as a title may not have quite the same kudos as manager or director but it is a far more appropriate method of managing people for the times we are in.

A final note on process

People who come into contact with facilitation will find that one of the first concepts that they come across is that of 'process'. This is about how something gets done rather than the task itself. To use the analogy of the iceberg the content part of the task is the ice that sticks up above the water. The momentum of the iceberg and its bulk underneath the water is the process and this includes our feelings, our values, our relationships, our personal history and the organizational culture. Managers and trainers who develop facilitation skills quickly come to realize that employees need to be addressed at both levels.

One useful model for people who are working with group process is that of inclusion, control and openness.

Inclusion is essentially about belonging or not belonging to a group. It is about being, or feeling, included or excluded. It is also about including or excluding others. The anxieties which arise around inclusion focus on meeting others and being accepted by them. These anxieties may lead us to reject or to feel rejected by others. Inclusion issues are also about our feelings of significance or insignificance and can be highlighted by the question; 'Am I in this group or not?'

Control is about influence and power. The questions which highlight control as an issue are: 'Am I competent and able in this group?' and 'How much, if any, authority do I have here?' Facilitators can highlight control as an issue by asking employees to reflect on whether they give or take from the team, whether they feel willing and able to negotiate and whether they feel powerful or powerless.

Openness involves meeting others and making contact with them at a basic human level. It is about being willing and able to accept yourself as you are, and accepting others as they are. The anxieties which prevent openness revolve around acceptance and proximity. 'Am I acceptable and therefore near to the centre of this group, or am I unacceptable and therefore on the periphery?' Openness issues include the need to be seen and be heard as a human being and to be treated with basic respect.

At any given time people working in a business or a team will have inclusion, control or openness issues. Individual team members will also have their own inclusion, control and openness issues, and these will manifest in some of the behaviours mentioned above. Effective management is impossible if such issues are ignored. This is not to say that everything must be perfect, unfortunately the world is not always like that. What it does mean is that managers and teams must find ways to address the relationship issues which will inevitably arise, hopefully in such a way as to 'facilitate win/win' outcomes. Developing an awareness of inclusion, control and openness issues is a great place to begin.

Conclusion

The potential benefits of developing facilitation skills are many but the real magic of the approach is that it brings into the open opportunities for learning and development which can then be translated into performance improvements.

Whether you are working as a facilitator in one-to-one or in one-to-many situations by using this approach you are operating from a principle that believes in the potential of yourself and others – a principle that sits squarely in line with the realities of business today.

Further reading

Heron, J. (1989), *The Facilitators' Handbook*, London: Kogan Page.

Heron, J. (1990), *Helping the Client,* London: Sage Publications.

Heron, J. (1993), *Group Facilitation*, London: Kogan Page.

Hunter, D., Bailey, A. and Taylor, B. (1996), *The Facilitation of Groups*, Aldershot: Gower.

Hunter, D., Bailey, A. and Taylor, B. (1998), *Co-operacy*, Aldershot: Gower.

Kolb, D. (1984), *Experiential learning: Experience as the Source of Learning and Development*, Englewood Cliffs: Prentice-Hall .

Mulligan, J., Eales, M. *et al.* (1988), *The Personal Management Handbook*, H.P.R.G. Sphere.

Schon, D. (1983), *The Reflective Practitioner: How Professionals Think in Action*, Arena.

Senge, P. *et al*. (1994), *The Fifth Discipline Fieldbook*, London: Nicholas Brealey.

Yalom, I. (1985), *The Theory and Practice of Group Psychotherapy*, 3rd edn, BasicBooks Inc.

Chapter 23

Performance coaching

Sir John Whitmore

When coaching first entered the business arena it was considered an additional management skill that principally applied to staff and career development. Today, however, it has become widely accepted as a management style relevant to the people related functions of all managers and has been described as the essential management style of the future.

This chapter will consider the principles that underpin coaching and will look at the behaviours and attitudes that coaches need. It will also set out a simple map of coaching and highlight those areas where coaching is appropriate in the workplace. Finally, the chapter suggests that coaching is a natural behaviour and an invaluable life skill for us all.

The principles of coaching

From early this century behavioural and cognitive psychology reinforced militaristic management models of power and control. In a very simple analogy, behaviourism sees humans as empty vessels into which information or conditioning has to be poured by parents, school teachers, trainers and managers. Once our cup is filled we perpetuate the process by pouring our contents on others. It is, in my view, a cynical, pessimistic view of human nature and a fundamentally flawed one.

In the 1950s and 1960s, however, a new wave of psychology began to take hold, fathered by luminaries such as Huxley, Maslow and Rogers. Instead of just studying pathology and behaviour, these explorers looked more deeply into the human psyche to understand the motivation, the meaning and the potential, which is also part of the human condition. This humanistic psychology viewed people more like an acorn or a sapling possessing all the potential to become a magnificent oak tree.

Coaching draws from these humanistic traditions. It highlights that our potential to learn, to perform and to enjoy is dependent upon increasing the *awareness* and the *responsibility* of the individuals concerned.

Some people, of course, are eager to realize their potential but are unsure of how to do it. Others, the damaged saplings, require a 'gently. gently' approach which will gradually raise awareness of their condition and of the benefits of moving on until they can begin to make conscious choices and take responsibility for their own progress. Let us now take a closer look at these key principles.

Awareness is defined as 'self accessed, high quality, relevant input' which means that a person's awareness is gained through the mind, the senses, and the emotions. Awareness may be of self, in the case of personal development, of others in the case of people management or customer care, or of objective material things or circumstances.

A simple helpful analogy is driving a car. A good driver will be highly aware of all the constantly changing conditions and circumstances that affect his or her progress. A poor driver will be less observant of road conditions and other road users, less aware of his or her own tiredness or other limitations, and less sensitive to the car's movement.

Responsibility in people is their true sense of total ownership of what they do and even of what happens to them. Taking full responsibility is inseparable from having choices or recognizing the choices that we all have. Some people are genuine victims of circumstance, but far more live in a 'victim consciousness' unwilling to take responsibility for the circumstances which they have created for themselves. Full responsibility cannot be imposed, it must be chosen if the performance benefits of it are to be reaped.

To return to our driving analogy, when a driver is highly aware, he or she will know that it is not the road conditions, the other road users, or the inadequacies of the vehicle that create most of our problems, but the way we react to them. This recognition empowers us to be much better drivers.

Methodology of coaching

Awareness must be self-generated or responsibility is absent. Telling you to be aware, or what to be aware of, does not make you more aware. Only you can choose to be more aware. A coach evokes awareness in you from you. This can be done either by challenge or by asking you a question which, if you are to answer at all, causes you to pay attention to something. As to what the coach should get you to pay attention to, it usually starts with the very things you are already paying attention to, because they are the things that you feel are wrong, uncomfortable, give you problems and need improvement or they are the things that you most want or believe to be the way forward.

If the coach encourages you to pay attention to something else he or she is going to take responsibility away from you and follow his or her own agenda. Of course, as a manager you may well have your own agenda, and rightly so, but the person you are coaching may be more available and amenable to your concerns if you have paid attention to his or her issue first. In this respect a fundamental principle of the coaching manager is to be seen as a support, not a threat. Your purpose as a coach is therefore to bring to the coachee a higher quality of awareness than normal, or than previously existed, to the relevant area, and this requires both skill and, in some cases, persistence. It will involve an exploration of the goal, the way towards it and the obstacles that will need to be overcome on the way. It can be seen that this would apply whether the goal is an aspect of personal development, the successful completion of a task, or the learning of a new skill.

As awareness increases, especially when it is self-generated, so the responsibility also increases. Also, as the goal and the path become clearer and the blocks are negotiated so the coachee more readily sees success on the horizon and may well become eager to take responsibility as well as the credit and the self-esteem that go with it. Their success on this occasion gives them more confidence to resolve the next issue themselves with less need for coaching. They are building self-reliance now. This process constitutes continuous staff development on the job.

Attitudes and behaviours

The attitude of the ideal coach might be described as optimistic about human nature and potential. It is people-orientated, supportive, non-judgemental, non-manipulative, objective, non-controlling and requires possession of a balanced ego. These words are not often the first we associate with business managers and they indicate why it is hard for some managers to make the grade.

The behaviour we most readily associate with traditional management is tell, instruct, criticize and command. However this type of behaviour not only removes responsibility but also reduces awareness because awareness stems from people thinking or experiencing for themselves. If I tell you something, it saves you from having to think about it or experience it yourself. Facilitative questioning is the predominant behaviour of good coaches.

To illustrate the purpose and skill of asking questions I am going to turn away from business for a moment and focus instead on tennis. The most used and least useful command given in all ball sports is, 'Keep your eye on the ball'. Make no mistake 'keeping your eye on the ball' is probably the single most valuable focus in tennis but I assert that the command to do so will not cause you to keep your eye on the ball; asking the appropriate questions will.

- If I ask you to tell me which way the ball is spinning each time it comes towards you, you will not be able to give me answers unless you focus on the ball.
- If I ask you where the ball manufacturer's name is each time as your racket makes contact with the ball, you will be obliged to watch the ball right onto the racket.
- If I ask you which way or how fast the ball spins after it bounces, it will also ensure your focus follows the ball.
- If I ask you how high over the net the ball passes, after it leaves your racket, you will get accurate feedback on the results of your action.
- If I ask you how close the ball is to your opponent's racket when you first recognize the direction of spin (from the ball, not the stroke), you will see the ball just as it leaves your opponent, and get earlier directional input.
- If I ask you where the approaching ball is in relation to the net at the moment you are going to hit it you will learn something about your tactics as well as keeping your eye on the ball. In fact, by merely noticing this you may find your decision making will be delayed, making it harder for your opponent to read your intentions.

You cannot avoid watching the ball if you are to respond out loud to any of these questions. In other words they compel you to watch the ball in a way that 'Keep your eye on the ball' does not. But these questions do far more than that, they cause you to focus to a higher degree than normal. This in turn provides you with better than normal input regarding the precise direction, speed and trajectory of the ball which your mind/body system automatically processes and to which it can thereby respond. The questions keep the responsibility for the answers where it needs to be, with the performer. The answers provide the coach with feedback that he can compare with his own observations to determine the quality of the performer's attention.

Effective questions

From the example above, it can be seen that the coaching interventions were all questions. However, not all questions are effective. The criteria for effective questions are as follows:

- They must be *open questions*.
- They must *compel* the performer to pay *attention*.
- They must demand a *higher* degree of focus, detail and *precision* than normal.
- They must provide *a feedback loop* to the coach.

It can be seen that all the previous tennis ball watching questions meet three or all of these criteria. They are open, they compel attention, they call for detail, and in most cases the coach can compare what he sees with what the player reports. It can also be seen that 'Keep your eye on the ball' meets *none* of these criteria which is probably why it does *not* work!

Through the very simple analogy of watching a tennis ball, I hope I have been able to convey the behavioural criteria that pertain to coaching interventions on any issue from sport to work, from task completion to personal development, from a complete coaching session to brief management exchanges, and from individuals to teams.

A simple map of coaching

Key principles: Awareness and responsibility.
Key skill: Asking effective questions.
A sequence: Goal setting   What do you/we want?
 Reality   What is happening now?
 Options   What could you/we do?
 Will   What will you/we do? And when?

This GROW sequence would only be used in the case of a complete coaching session on a new task or development issue. There is nothing particularly special or unusual about this sequence; it is simply a logical structure for addressing anything from an individual problem to a team meeting. On the majority of occasions, however, brief coaching interventions might fall into just one or two of these categories.

The fears and pitfalls associated with the use of coaching generally concern the time people imagine it takes to coach compared to telling, and the non-acceptance by the culture or the recipients of coaching. Neither of these concerns is fully justified. As you get more skilled at conducting a coaching session, the time taken is considerably reduced. And it takes no more time to use brief coaching principle interventions than it does to tell. After a little early suspicion of any change of management style, most coachees, as we call them, far prefer to be coached than to be told. The internal pitfall of being unable to break old prescriptive habits is the one that gets most of those who fail.

It should have become clear by now that the role of the coach is to raise the coachees' awareness and responsibility, which has far more effect than telling people what to do or how to do it. If I am going to tell you how to do something, by implication I have to know more about it than you do. This is not so with coaching. Successful coaching is not dependent on the coaches' superior knowledge. This is becoming increasingly important for managers who, in this time of specialization and fast technological progress, will frequently have less knowledge than their subordinates. However, managers with a coaching style can manage effectively and with confidence even in areas of which they have little knowledge or experience.

The business applications of coaching

Let us now examine the many ways we can apply these principles and practices at work. This is by no means an exhaustive list of applications, but it does illustrate the wide variety of applications and the particular benefits of using coaching in these situations.

- For staff development coaching may be used in conjunction with, or even in place of, appraisals and personal performance indicators. However some of the more judgemental appraisal systems fly in the face of the best coaching and performance improvement practice and need radical revision. Development coaching normally takes the form of a coaching session which may last up to an hour or more in which the coach will use effective questions to help the coachee identify his or her own development needs and formulate the appropriate action steps. This may be followed up at intervals with further coaching sessions to check on progress and adjust the plans.

- Development coaching is sometimes performed by independent professional coaches and a growing number of people are making use of personal coaches outside the workplace altogether. In the United States the profession of independent personal and professional coaches is expanding fast and several national professional associations of coaches have recently been formed. In the UK coaching has not developed in this direction to the same degree.

- In all areas of training, and in particular for the delivery of standard company training courses, coaching is very relevant. Training is usually seen as being fairly prescriptive and companies in which a coaching programme is in place soon find themselves having to alter their training practices to be consistent with the coaching culture. Experienced trainers normally take quite easily to coaching skills.

- Line managers with a long history of telling may find a coaching style much harder initially, but extremely rewarding and productive later as their skills develop. Productivity improvements show up fastest in situations where the coaching manager has a high degree of autonomy, such as in the smaller retail shop chains. It is worth noting that, in general, female managers and younger managers find the coaching principles more in line with their natural style than older males.

- In the training of new recruits coaching is particularly useful. This is because previous work or life experience is often negated and under-valued by a prescriptive style of management but welcomed, valued and built upon with coaching.

- In the learning of new skills coaching also adds value. This is because it follows the learning style and sequence of the learner rather than the teacher thereby making learning easier. It also caters for individual differences and preferences in the performance of tasks to produce better results and improved confidence and self-esteem.

- Motivation and, in particular, self-motivation is greatly enhanced by coaching for it offers choice and ownership, and satisfies the higher needs on the Maslow hierarchy for self-esteem and self-actualization which are the aspiration of many employees today. If these needs are not met by a change in management style, these people will seek to meet them elsewhere and their discretionary efforts, if not their total presence, will be lost forever.

- Problems can also be solved very effectively with the use of coaching. So often we find that business problems remain a problem because either the goal is not established with sufficient clarity, or the reality has not been recognized in its fullness. Once G and R are clarified in the GROW context, it is surprising how frequently the solution emerges.

- For the delegation of tasks there is no better way than coaching because it ensures that both parties clearly understand what is to be done and what has been understood. All gaps in knowledge or understanding can be filled in and even the unexpected pre-empted.

- Team leadership by any other method than coaching is, by its nature, autocratic and therefore may well not achieve mutual team responsibility. Internal conflict can only be properly and permanently resolved by a coaching approach. Team ground rules must also be formed by coaching rather than by imposition if they are to be maintained willingly.

- The executive role and role model should be one of coaching if coaching is to be the management style of the organization. Too many executives freely use terms like support, facilitate, coach, and empower but their behaviour is quite the opposite. When this happens disillusion and cynicism will result. To coach well should be an executive imperative.

- Every management communication, however small, would be improved by being based on the all important twin principles of awareness and responsibility. In the application examples mentioned above I have used the term coaching but this does not necessarily entail a full coaching session. In fact the majority of interventions based on the coaching principles will consist of no more than a well chosen question which obliges the other person to think for themselves, to be more aware and to take more responsibility. Management by coaching may initially be marginally more time consuming than telling, but in the medium term much time is gained as those being managed become more self-reliant.

Conclusion

In reality, the coaching principles are quite straightforward and they remain constant for a very wide variety of applications. However, intellectual understanding alone of these principles does not make one a coach. The effectiveness of coaching grows with practice and refinement and this in turn demands commitment, the willingness to change and the willingness to fail on occasion. A two-day coaching skills course may enable managers and prospective coaches to understand the principles and start practising. Thereafter follow-up programmes and a buddy support system are highly recommended. Once this is in place it is surprising how quickly committed coaches begin to get great results as well as enjoying hugely improved working relationships.

I will end with a challenging assertion: *Coaching is a natural behaviour. Telling is actually a learned bad habit.*

Here is my reasoning ... when your child brings home homework you have a number of options. At one end of the spectrum you could do it for them or tell them exactly how to do it. This action offers the obvious benefit of taking the minimum time and of your child getting high grades. At the other end of the spectrum there are parents who do nothing to help their child in the belief that it will make them become more self-reliant. In fact most parents do neither of these. What they do, even if they have never even heard of coaching, is to sit with their child and ask questions which help their child find his or her own answers. They coach them, and this is not just because, or only when, they know the subject.

Why is it then that these caring parents go to work and treat those they manage in a highly prescriptive way? Why do they treat their child so differently? Is it because at work short-term solutions are more important than quality work or staff development, or is it because they simply do not care enough about those they manage? I believe that once we begin to care more for one another we will begin to coach naturally.

Further reading

Cartwright, S. and Cooper, C. (1988), *No Hassle*, Harmondsworth: Penguin.
Chomsky, N. (1985), *Turning the Tide*, London: Pluto.

Chopra, D. (1996), *The Seven Spiritual Laws*, London: Bantam.

Cockburn, L. (1988), *Out of Control*, London: Bloomsbury.

Covey, S. (1995), *First Things First*, New York: Fireside.

Eales-White, R, (1995), *Building Your Team*, London: Kogan Page.

Frankl, V. (1973), *The Doctor and the Soul*, New York: Vintage Books.

Gallway, T. (1975), *The Inner Game of Tennis*, London: Cape.

Goleman, D. (1995), *Emotional Intelligence*, London: Bantam.

Handy, C. (1995), *Beyond Certainty*, London: Hutchinson.

Hemery, D. (1991), *Sporting Excellence*, London: Collins Willow.

Kinsman, F. (1990), *Millennium*, Harmondsworth: Penguin.

Kriegal, R. (1996), *Sacred Cows*, New York: Warner.

Maslow, A. (1971), *The Farther Reaches of Human Nature*, Harmondsworth: Penguin.

Peck, S. (1978), *The Road Less Travelled*, New York: Touchstone.

Russell, R. (1982), *The Awakening Earth*, London: Routledge

Semler, R. (1993), *Maverick*, London: Century.

Whitmore, D. (1991), *Psychosynthesis Counselling*, London: Sage.

Whitmore, J. (1996), *Coaching for Performance*, London: Nicholas Brealey.

Wilber, K. (1995), *Sex, Ecology, Spirituality*, Boston: Shambhala.

Chapter 24

Mentoring: developing two for the price of one

David Clutterbuck

The rapid rise of planned mentoring schemes, both within companies and between business and the community, has been one of the success stories of the late twentieth century. In part, this is because mentoring is a 'natural' skill – until recent decades, the vast majority of learning was passed on from one generation to another orally as a fundamental survival strategy for the species. In part, also, it is because effective mentoring typically results in learning by both people involved – indeed, some schemes have been introduced primarily to provide opportunities for the mentors to learn. Hence the title of this chapter.

Yet for every really successful mentoring scheme, there is at least one that fails to deliver significant benefits, for either party. The reasons are numerous, but typically relate either to inadequate or ill-informed planning, or to people's inability to use their innate mentoring skills effectively. Like any in-built skill, from drawing to listening, mentoring needs to be developed to be useful. Unlike most other such skills, however, poor mentoring can be harmful to those at whom it is directed.

The origins of mentoring lie in Greek mythology, where Mentor acted as an adviser, counsellor, guardian and stimulator to the young Prince Telemachus, while his father was abroad fighting the Trojans. In more modern times, mentoring has evolved through apprenticeship to become a widely applicable means of transferring wisdom in almost any area of endeavour.

The official definition of mentoring by The European Mentoring Centre is 'Off-line help by one person to another in making significant transitions in knowledge, work or thinking'. Taking the elements of this definition in turn:

- Off-line: because the mentor normally has to be outside the chain of command or discipline, in order to establish a relationship of openness and trust, and to offer an unbiased perspective on the issues raised by the mentee.

- Help: because the mentor responds to a variety of needs, both emotional and intellectual, hands-on and hands-off.
- By one person to another: because, although the mentor would typically be older and more senior than the mentee, this is not always so. What counts is the depth and breadth of relevant, transferable experience.
- Significant transitions: because without some clear developmental purpose, the relationship is unlikely to deliver meaningful results.
- Knowledge, work or thinking: because the transition may be in any of these areas.

Other definitions of mentoring abound, but they all seem to fall into either the European model, which emphasizes development, empowering the learner, and self-reliance; or the US traditional model, which emphasizes career-sponsorship, the power and influence of the mentor and having things done on the learner's behalf. Traditional US mentoring tends to use the term protégé to describe the learner; European developmental mentoring prefers to refer to mentees.

The chart in Figure 24.1 offers some broad guidelines to what mentoring typically does and does not involve:

Always . . .	Sometimes . . .	Never . . .
Listening with empathy	Using coaching behaviours	Discipline
Sharing experience and Learning (usually mutually)	Using counselling behaviours	Appraisal (as line manager)
Professional friendship	Challenging assumptions/ being a critical friend	Assessment for a third party
Developing insight through reflection	Opening doors	Supervision
Being a sounding board	Being a role model	
Encouraging		

Figure 24.1   What mentoring involves

The dynamics of mentoring

All mentoring and 'helping to learn' relationships derive from a set of largely complementary roles.

Recent work by the European Mentoring Centre on mentor competencies has identified two dimensions that shape all one-on-one development relationships in business. These are the 'influence' dimension and the 'need' dimension.

The influence dimension is about power in the relationship. At one extreme, the mentor dominates the relationship, telling the mentee what to do, why and how, and pulling strings to further the mentee's career. This usually is not very rewarding from a self-respect or emotional point of view, but can be a swift route to the top – if you do as you are told.

At the other extreme on the influence dimension, the relationship is about emancipation or empowerment – enabling someone to take responsibility for his or her own development. This, in theory at least, is now a common part of most large companies' training and development strategies.

On the need dimension, one extreme concerns the mentee's intellectual needs. The other concerns his or her emotional needs. This dimension is sometimes expressed as the challenging–nurturing spectrum.

Where a relationship sits on these dimensions depends upon its goals. If sponsorship is a primary goal (most UK companies do not see this as a particularly desirable objective, for obvious reasons of avoiding favouritism) then it requires a fairly high degree of directive behaviour on the part of the mentor. The corresponding goal at the other end of the influence dimension is empowerment. The goal on the intellectual needs dimension is 'assisting with learning' on the emotional dimension, it is support (Figure 24.2).

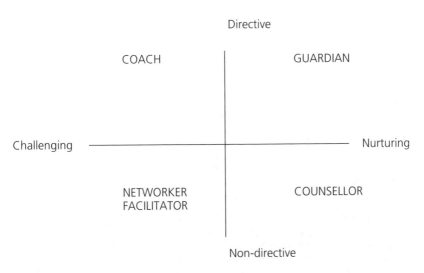

Figure 24.2   The different dimensions of mentoring

Four 'helping to learn' roles fit very easily into this matrix. Coaching fits easily into the directive/challenging box because it is the coach who sets the agenda and the pace of learning, albeit usually with the agreement of the learner. While modern concepts of coaching emphasize ownership of the *issues* by the learner, feedback comes mostly from the coach and the learner does not own the *process*.

In the opposite corner, counselling is a non-directive, learner-centred means of supporting someone. Counselling behaviours are important to help the learner gain the confidence and motivation to seek self-reliance and self-managed learning.

The guardian role ranges from adviser through to outright sponsor. Guardians support the learner by alerting them to opportunities to gain experience or advance their careers. The networker/facilitator opens his or her network to the learner and helps them find new sources of learning. This is a very hands-off role compared to that of guardian (see also Figure 24.3).

Responsibilities of the four core roles

Coach
- Help mentee set viable personal goals.
- Explain why you think something needs to be challenged.
- Probe with questions to challenge thinking.
- Help mentee accept and think through challenge.
- Offer help in dealing with it.

Guardian
- Assess barriers and ways around them.
- Open doors.
- Know your strengths and weaknesses as a role model,
- Understand and explain the politics behind operational problems.

Networker
- Understand what a mentee needs networking for:
  - getting things done
  - expand their knowledge.
- Recognize who and what you/your mentee know.
- Gather the information to make the best recommendation.
- Discuss the best approach.

Counsellor
- Actively listen and make sure you understand their side.
- Keep it upbeat by refocusing on positive outcomes.
- Use your experience to help the mentee to come to own conclusions.
- Explain and justify your comments.

Figure 24.3   Responsibilities of the core roles of mentoring

Mentoring vs other methods of knowledge transfer

The differences between mentoring and other cognitive approaches, such as coaching or teaching can be obscured when people misuse the terms. At its simplest, the differences can be expressed as follows:

- Teaching passes on *concrete knowledge*. It does not normally involve close relationships. The teacher tends to be an authority figure and there is relatively little opportunity to develop one's own views about the subject matter.
- Tutoring transfers *wider, contextual knowledge*. The relationship encourages a degree of discussion and development of original thought and can become closer personally than teaching. The tutor still tends to maintain the power of greater knowledge, however.
- Coaching transfers *skills*, in the main. It breaks down tasks into steps, which the learner can practise. The coach observes and gives feedback. He or she may or may not be more expert than the learner – so the relationship is much more equal.
- Mentoring, on the other hand, develops the learner's capabilities by providing reflective space. It transfers *wisdom and tacit knowledge*. Within the relationship mentor and mentee are equals, even if one party is hierarchically superior, and – where it works well – both parties acquire learning.

Why the sudden popularity of mentoring?

The reasons for this sudden rise in popularity and interest are several. Among them:

- Increased disillusionment with classroom training as the primary means of learning in organizations. Learning is more intense when people have an opportunity to reflect upon what they have learned, or to think through for themselves the issues they need to deal with. Mentoring is a very efficient method of providing such reflective space.

- The rapid spread of Investors in People has focused attention on one-to-one methods of employee development. Similarly, quality standards, such as the European Quality Award, led companies to review just how to ensure employees have the competence they need for the job. The management standards promoted by the Management Charter Initiative cannot all be acquired by reading books or attending workshops; they have to be acquired on the job, drawing on the skill and experience of other people.

- The Henley/IoD report on competencies for directors has focused attention on the need for some form of personal help for top managers to think through and manage how they acquire the level of competence required.

- Recognition that appraisals often do not lead to any real changes in the competence of the appraisee, and that proactive help over time is often needed to help people think through how they are going to improve.

- Increasing emphasis on self-development – i.e. on making people take greater responsibility for their own development, rather than expecting 'the company' to manage their learning.

- Increasing complexity of career paths. Very few people now have linear career paths where it is possible to see what steps lie ahead. The reality for most people is that they need to both maximize the potential for learning in the job they have now, and constantly be alert to opportunities to move by degrees into new roles. Managing both the major and the minor transitions becomes a lot easier when you have a dispassionate but well-disposed coach or mentor, who can take a broader perspective and help you think through the options and implications of each opportunity.

- New organization structures. The movement of most large organizations from narrow, multi-layered hierarchies to much flatter structures has meant that many managers have found themselves with much larger jobs to cope with, and hence, often, with much larger transitions to make. In these circumstances, it is invaluable to draw on the experience of someone who has been there, seen it and done it before.

- Some organizations have gone even further in recreating their structures. Project-based organizations may no longer have permanent managers for permanent teams. Rather, an employee may report to several project team leaders on a variety of projects over the course of a year – or even at the same time. These organizations have often found that it makes sense to use the project leaders as temporary coaches, focusing on current needs for skills and knowledge and to have a permanent 'home manager' as a mentor, focusing on longer term development issues.

Types of application

In recent years there has been an explosion of mentoring programmes, for all sorts of people, with all sorts of development needs. In each case, the mentee benefits from the mentor's greater experience. For example:

- Graduate recruits have been helped to learn the ropes more quickly, more effectively with a mentor to help them. Indeed, whether a company has a

mentoring programme is one of the criteria graduates apply when selecting a potential employer. Evidence from research by companies with
long-established graduate mentoring schemes suggests that mentees
contribute more quickly and stay longer with the firm than people who do
not have this kind of support.

- Returning mothers often need support to help them re-establish the networks they relied upon before they took maternity leave. The more senior
  the employee, the more useful this help is.

- Managerial employees moving to a new job may need help coping with
  the transition. For example, staff at the Inland Revenue, who have been
  big fish in small provincial ponds, frequently find transfer to Somerset
  House in London (where they are an insignificant fish in a big pond) a
  frightening culture shock. Someone who has been through the same
  transition can help them understand that this is nothing unusual and that
  they will adjust.

- Schoolchildren and students, who are at risk of dropping out of their
  studies, or at the other end of the spectrum, who are highly talented, can
  equally benefit from having a mentor. So can the long-term unemployed,
  or young people on probation.

- Top managers, including chief executives, can also find value in having
  someone with whom to discuss their fears, concerns and ambitions. The
  Oxford Regional Health Authority encouraged all new executive directors of health trusts to find a mentor to help them put together personal
  development plans.

Other examples of the use of mentoring include developing euromanagers
(through matching mentees with mentors in other countries); helping professionals such as head teachers, personnel managers, or young lawyers cope
with the demands of new jobs; and underpinning company-wide competency
programmes.

Formal vs informal

Why is there a need for a formal intervention to promote mentoring? After all,
people often seem to find a mentor without any third party intervention.

The problems with informal approaches are several. First, not everyone has
the skills to mentor effectively. Certainly, even 'naturals' find it helpful to
hone their skills by understanding the processes and practising techniques.
Second, informal mentoring tends to promote favouritism – people gravitate
naturally towards helping relationships with those for whom they have greatest empathy; in other words, people like themselves. So informal coaching

and mentoring may preserve and reinforce discrimination within the workplace. Third, close, helping relationships across the genders easily become the butt of gossip and innuendo, if they are informal.

Formalizing coaching and mentoring schemes:

- helps make sure that it actually happens,
- raises the quality of coaching and mentoring, both formal and informal,
- is inclusive of minorities,
- legitimizes helping relationships across the gender boundaries.

What makes an effective mentoring scheme?

Studies by the European Mentoring Centre show that mentoring schemes work best when they:

- Begin with a clear rationale and purpose. It has to be evident to both the organizers, the participants and to other people, who will observe the scheme, why it is needed, what benefits will be expected and how success will be measured.

- Understand the development climate within the organization. How do managers feel about spending time on this kind of activity? What incentives and education may be needed to persuade them to give 'developing talent' a higher priority?

- Establish a formal structure to administer the scheme. At the minimum this should include a top management champion – preferably the chief executive – and a scheme co-ordinator. Best practice will also include some form of continuing support for mentors/coaches and a planned programme of review.

- Select and match mentors and mentees carefully. Simply putting people together and hoping they will get on is not enough. Yet an over-scientific approach can be equally disastrous. Key principles for selection include:
  - balancing ability to establish rapport against potential for learning
  - allowing the mentee at least some opportunity to select from a pool of trained mentors
  - making all relationships probationary for the first few meetings and building in an automatic review.

- Provide training for both mentors and mentees. At the very least, this helps mentees/learners take on mentoring/coaching roles in their turn towards others. Training for coaching and mentoring works best when it is interactive, practical and has a solid base in current theory. An important principle of both coach and mentor training is that it cannot be achieved effectively through a 'sheep-dip' approach. Initial training provides the understanding of the skills and approaches, but the development of competence as a mentor or coach requires both practice and the opportunity for continued peer discussion and review. Best practice may also involve training the line manager in more advanced coaching techniques, to share the development burden.

● The purpose of the helping relationship has to be clear. In coaching, the coach and learner have to have a clear agreement on the learning goal and how they will recognize when it has been achieved. In mentoring, the goals may have much wider scope, but it is evident that relationships which have a clear sense of purpose achieve more than those that do not. The goal may evolve or circumstances may change but the more consciously that process is managed, the more effective and enjoyable the relationship will be.

● Measurement and review are important to identify problems with the scheme and with individual relationships, and to demonstrate that the scheme is delivering results. The processes for handling measurement and review will vary from organization to organization, but most will be able to adapt *The Mentoring Diagnostic* (European Mentoring Centre, 1998) which provides a set of checklists and questionnaires to help manage each of the stages in a mentoring programme or relationship.

Evolution of the mentoring relationship

All successful relationships go through several phases. At first, the pair needs to establish rapport, which may take a few meetings, or simply happen, depending on how naturally fitting they are. Then they begin to set clear goals and direction. Before long, they have moved into the most productive phase, where learning flows both ways and the mentee experiments with the ideas and advice gained from dialogue with the mentor. Finally, as the pace of learning begins to flag, the two have to consider how to wind it down.

The beginning and the end are the most sensitive phases. If there is no rapport, the relationship will never get off the ground. If, as it runs its natural course, too great a dependency occurs on one side or both, then the ending may be difficult. The mentee, for example, may feel abandoned or trapped. Getting the balance and timing right in letting go is an important skill for the mentor.

The skills of mentoring

In large part, the skills of mentoring consist of knowing when and how to move between one role and the next, in response to the mentee's needs. However, there are several core skills or capabilities, which all mentors need. These include:

● Good communication skills, especially listening and questioning (effective mentors spend 80 per cent or more of the time listening).
● A sense of humour.
● Good rapport building.
● An interest in developing others (and preferably a track record in doing so).
● An interest in continuing to develop themselves.

These skills and capabilities will be reflected in what mentors actually do. The box in Figure 24.4 compares the perceptions of a sample of 100 mentors and 100 mentees, at senior management level, as to the most important behaviours mentors exhibit.

	Mentee responses (per cent)	
Sounding board	80	
Listener	73	
Critical friend	67	

Mentor responses	Importance (per cent)	Most time (per cent)
Listener	89	61
Giver of encouragement	83	22
Sounding board	83	56
Critical friend	78	67
Counselling	72	28
Confidant	72	22
Coach	39	28

Figure 24.4   Most important behaviours of a mentor

To avoid usurping the line manager's role, the mentor needs to remain constantly aware of the boundaries of the relationship. The two charts below help put these boundaries into context.

A final word

Although mentoring is a very powerful developmental tool, the organization wishing to use it widely should consider first:

Line manager	Shared	Mentor
Performance appraisal	Encouragement, motivation to learn	Help learner develop insights into causes of poor performance
Agreed developmental goals within learner's current job	Shape goals beyond current job	Help learner manage the integration of job, career and personal goals
Help learner build relationships within the team	Help learner build relationships outside team	Help learner build relationships with line manager
Find opportunities to stretch learner's performance	Find opportunities to stretch learner's thinking	Challenge learner's thinking and assumptions
Give constructive feedback through observation	Help learner develop skills of intrinsic observation	Help learner accept and manage feedback constructively
Role model for task fulfilment and growth	Role model of general behaviour	Role model for personal achievement and growth

Figure 24.5   **Development roles of line manager and mentor**

● Peers
Support each other

● Line manager
Focus on task
Focus on improving current performance

● Individual
Take responsibility for own development

● Mentor
Focus on capability
Focus on long-term development/potential
Support

● HR
Balancing short- and long-term development

Figure 24.6   **Responsibilities in the developmental net**

- What benefits it particularly wants to bring about through mentoring.
- Who the target group will be; or whether to introduce an 'all-comers' scheme.
- How it will measure progress and outcomes.
- How it will find and train sufficient capable mentors.
- How to support mentors thereafter.

Sources of advice and help

The European Mentoring Centre, c/o Association for Management Education and Development, 14 Belgrave Square, London, SW1X 8PS.

Further reading

Carter, S. (1994), *An Essential Guide to Mentoring*, London: Institute of Management.

Caruso, R. (1990), An examination of Organisational Mentoring: The case of Motorola, Dissertation, London School of Economics.

Clutterbuck, D. (1985), 'Everyone Needs a Mentor', *IPD*.

Clutterbuck, D. *et al.* (1998), *The Mentoring Diagnostic*, Burnham, Bucks: European Mentoring Centre.

Clutterbuck, D. (1998), 'The Learning Alliance', *IPD*, October

Hay, J. (1995), *Transformational Mentoring*, Maidenhead: McGraw-Hill.

Megginson, D. and Clutterbuck, D. (1996), *Mentoring in Action*, London: Kogan Page.

Megginson, D. and Clutterbuck, D. (1998), *Mentoring Executives and Directors*, Oxford: Butterworth.

Chapter 25

Drama-based training

Roger Hancock and Geoff Davies

As everyone knows, drama is a powerful method of communication, but it does more than just impart information in an interesting way. What makes it so relevant for training and development is that it touches people's feelings and challenges their attitudes, and in so doing provides significant learning opportunities.

The ways in which such training can be applied are numerous – some organizations use it to communicate their latest company-wide management strategy, others to raise awareness of sensitive policies, while individual managers can benefit from drama-based training in learning essential inter-personal skills.

In this chapter we will be taking a brief look at how drama is used, how it is different from role-play, before focusing on the four different drama-based training approaches. At the end of this chapter we have outlined what a typical drama-based training day might include and provided some sample activities which trainers might use.

The current context

Drama is a fundamental human activity. We all understand it because we have been involved in it from early childhood. Put simply, it is people imagining they are someone else, somewhere else, in another time. Every society in every age has had its own form of drama and it has for centuries been used to put over social, moral and political messages because it is such a powerful form of communication. It is engaging, entertaining and provides a means of making sense of the world.

Drama has many contexts and many forms. It may take place in a theatre, in films or on television. Those people who wonder what relevance drama has, need only be reminded how people get wrapped up in their favourite 'soaps' to get an indication of the potential it has for training and development.

We may know that drama represents a pretend world but it is one with which we identify strongly. The reasons for this are clear. We do not just watch drama, we become emotionally involved in it. We get angry, upset, irritated, afraid. We laugh and cry. It brings us close to real experiences but at the same time drama provides safety because it is happening to somebody else. More than this, drama can invoke real change. Many people will remember the story in the soap 'Brookside' about an abused woman who killed her husband. It caused an outcry at the time and directed people's attention to real cases that might have been neglected. Such drama enhances our awareness of aspects of life that we may have ignored. Information is soaked up and we take it in. We remember the characters and their situation and as a consequence the learning stays with us. It is this quality that makes it such an effective method of training.

Beyond role-play

The ideas behind the use of drama in management training flow from the development of the concepts of Drama in Education (DIE) and Theatre in Education (TIE) in the 1960s and 1970s in schools. Although there is considerable overlap, DIE differs from TIE in that TIE was mainly the work of theatre groups and DIE the practice of individual teachers in the classroom. Both approaches emphasized the use of drama as a learning medium, providing an effective way of involving the children in the examination of difficult issues and helping with the development of language and cognitive skills. It is only in recent years, however, that these ideas have started to be utilized for the education of adults in management and interpersonal training, as trainers recognize the limitations of other techniques, in particular the use of role-play.

Role-play is a powerful aspect of drama and can help people who want to practise new behaviours that they have learned, but this approach has its problems. Though many people enjoy role-play and even look forward to it, there is increasing evidence that many others dislike it, feel uncomfortable, and become tense and nervous when asked to participate in this way. When this occurs the role-play begins to get in the way of the learning rather than being an effective learning tool. Drama-based trainers take this into account and use role-play as one of a range of techniques that can help within a learning context. We will expand on the range of options in the next section.

In essence, drama-based training utilizes all the ingredients that already exist in an organization and that form the basis of any good play or film. These include passion, despair, jealousy, ambition and conflicting interests. The drama involves people from all social classes and organizational levels, and can spotlight personal, group and organizational needs.

Those who know how to work with this medium can target virtually any learning outcome considered relevant or important. It can be about any situation where people meet and include any group of people inside or outside the organization. Topics, to name but a few, can include team-building, appraisal, discipline, motivation, time-management, stress, attitudes to safety, customer care or sales.

Approaches

Drama is always about people, communication and relationships – the main attributes of a successful company. And what drama-based training does is highlight or explore how people cope with, or solve, the problems they face on an everyday basis. In this sense it brings something new to training; it looks at people not just as employees but in their widest social context and provides a dynamic way of seeing how their working relationships can be improved.

There are four main forms of drama-based training.

1.   Live theatrical performance

This involves a piece of theatre, usually on a stage, based on a business issue of interest and relevance to the audience. Typically used for conferences and large events, it is especially valuable when organizations are launching a new product or strategic initiative, supporting a current or future training programme or looking to change the corporate culture. Such performance is like going to watch a play. Indeed, sometimes well-known plays are used to explore the diverse challenges faced by managers. More often though, the play presents a clear, believable world based on the organization that is easily recognizable. In this respect the drama is based on research and the script has been written to make certain important points or to raise crucial issues.

Drama in this form carries great weight, involving concrete stories and well-developed characters. This gives it an important advantage over a talk or a video and helps to grab and hold people's attention.

Furthermore, a well-performed piece of theatre allows the audience to pick up important concepts placed in a realistic context, and the behaviour of the characters can be studied and analysed almost as if in a laboratory. The story-line of drama is also important here. It reminds people of the key messages and helps them to absorb new ideas and information, consider solutions to common problems, and be encouraged to recognize their own behaviour.

The main limitation of this approach is the time it takes to prepare the script and the need for good actors and competent direction. To be effective, considerable time needs to be allocated because it must be carefully planned and scripted and a team of actors or a theatre group has to rehearse and perfect the piece. Furthermore, a stage or large area for the performance has to be found and the auditorium may need to be tiered to ensure that every one in the audience can see.

2. Interactive drama

This second form of drama is where the course members do not just watch the action as if it were a play but take part in a range of drama processes to enable them to step into the fiction and make contact with the characters and the situation.

In this form of drama there is always a specific problem within the action and the audience are asked to help. Very soon, members of the audience realize that this fictional problem is actually their own, a clear reflection of their workplace. The characters are 'hot seated' and speak directly to the audience who can ask questions and make comments, and in so doing, reveal their thoughts and feelings. The driving force for the audience is being engaged in the process and being drawn in by the dramatic tension created. They recognize the dilemma and identify and empathize with both the situation and the people. Because it seems real this approach has great appeal. The audience may be observers but they are engaged in the action and are asked for their opinions of the actors' behaviour. From their safe seats they can pretend that they know all and can do all; they can explore all the possible avenues and try out different solutions. They can take big risks because they do not have to live with the consequences.

This freedom gives people the opportunity to find out what they know and what they need to know. At times they are saying 'That is me or could be me'. So often, after a drama-based training session, members of a group will say, 'I saw myself', or, 'I didn't know that I did that and I didn't appreciate the full effects of it. Now I see the real problem and I can begin to face up to my situation back at the workplace and perhaps solve it'. Sometimes a process of self-realization can be painful but, because in this case they are looking away from themselves, it gives them the opportunity to see clearly the real issue.

It is also important to point out that there is no need, as in a simulation, to show or replicate the actual events themselves. For example, in the case of suspected sexual harassment, it is the victim's interpretation of the events that is important. How do they see what happened? Moreover, there is the effect this has on the non-participants that the trainer works with. What is the view of the other workers? What will be the effect of a disciplinary decision? Is it too lenient or too severe? Is it fair?

How the topic is introduced is, of course, especially important. For this you need a frame, an approach, and a reason for further investigation. Usually this is achieved through a short intriguing scene that contains all the elements of the problem. It could be a letter of complaint, a blistering row, a demand for change from management or an outside authority. It could be an image of some future state, a dream of improvement. Through such devices the audience is lured in. By being addressed as the experts they become the experts. Their role therefore, even if they are complete novices, is as advisers, and their status is raised accordingly.

So often training courses are designed as if the course participants know absolutely nothing about the topic even though they may have been in the business for years. When this occurs the result can be counter-productive. However, when they are presented with a drama situation that is relevant to their lives and are asked for their comments and opinions, they respond as adults, becoming involved and engaged. In effect they are being recognized as people with expertise and responsibility. By grappling with a concrete experience they are given the opportunity to learn and remember.

Interactive drama is most effective for groups of around 15 to 20 people where you can achieve maximum involvement and it typically takes between one and three hours. In this respect it can be used as the basis of a complete course, as an introduction to a course, or to provide a way of testing learning already covered in a course. It can also be used for smaller conferences.

It usually requires a facilitator and two or three actor/trainers and achieves a high level of engagement from the audience. Our feedback generally tells us that people who have been on an interactive drama course remember the characters and the situation and then apply the learning to their own situation. Managers have also told us of people who have changed their whole attitude and behaviour after attending such a course.

3. Drama conventions

The third use of drama in training is the use of a range of drama techniques now available to individual trainers to facilitate their training group without them ever having to 'act' or role-play. They are based on the many conventions available to the playwright or director. 'Empty Chair', 'Role on the Wall', 'Thought Bubbles', 'Conscience Alley' and 'Corporate Brain' are all examples of simple techniques that enable course participants to step into a fiction, influence the action and thereby facilitate greater understanding of a situation. These techniques are very familiar to drama teachers and can be of great value to management trainers. Their main use will be to examine a particular people issue or problem.

● 'Role on the Wall' is a way of thinking about or creating a major character in the scenario, using an outline drawing that becomes surrounded by a series of statements about that person. This is placed on the wall so that it represents a permanent presence to be referred to and used during the ensuing training session.

- 'Conscience Alley' is a very simple technique which is used when a person has to make a difficult decision. One member of the group, or the trainer, walks slowly between two lines of people. While he or she walks, ideas and arguments are spoken out by other members of the group as if they were his or her thoughts. One side could be for and the other against. When the character reaches the end, the decision might be made or not. It is a very dramatic technique which works because it concentrates on all factors of decision-making, including the irrational and the emotional.

- 'Empty Chair' and 'Corporate Brain' are similar in that a whole group becomes the brain of another person. 'Empty Chair' is a very simple technique which at first seems odd. An empty chair is placed in the centre of a circle. Nobody actually sits in that chair, but everyone is asked to accept that a person is there. It could be someone created by the group or a particular character at the centre of the situation. It works like this. Everyone is that person and therefore can answer for that person. Also, at the same time. anyone can ask a question, i.e. everyone can ask and answer. A question is asked by one person and then answered by another. No one person bears the full responsibility of taking on the role. The group creates and explores together. This technique is quite demanding but very effective.

- 'Corporate Brain' is very useful when the situation mainly concerns the relationship between two people. Two chairs are placed opposite each other. Half of the group sits behind each of these chairs. They represent the brain of the person in that chair. One of the group sits on chair A, another on chair B and then the interaction starts. However, the person on the chair can only say what their brain tells them. When A speaks, B then turns round to their group brain and asks how he or she should reply. The corporate brain gets into a huddle and has to work out and then agree its response. B says the words and then has to wait for A and its brain to decide what is the most appropriate response, and so it goes on. Each side can see the result of their decision immediately. In 'Corporate Brain' everyone is involved but not up front and at risk. Ideas can be filtered privately through A or B by even the most inhibited of people. This technique is very effective for very low-key, private interactions between two people at work, e.g. two colleagues who are not getting on well, or a manager and employee or a sales assistant with a customer, as well as public negotiations between leaders such as management and trade unions, or a conflict between two interest groups, e.g. production and maintenance.

These techniques, which are only examples of what is available, are basically simple to organize and easy to use by the individual trainer.

4. Theatrical training techniques

The fourth form of drama-based training is the use of the training techniques that are used to train actors at drama schools. These have been found to be very useful in helping individuals and whole groups discover their creativity, energy and power, to enhance their personal impact, and improve their communication, presentation and behavioural skills. As a corporate, creative, artistic, activity they are also very effective as teambuilding exercises. Drama-based games and exercises get everyone involved very quickly. The subject or content is not important. Some are games that raise the energy levels or encourage concentration or contemplation. Others are about social interaction and co-operation. Many are about the development of particular personal skills such as the use of the voice and self-presentation, or the development of creativity or artistic skills.

A course made up of these types of activities could lead to some form of corporate artistic activity – a play, a pantomime or a show. One has only to consider the range of skills that are involved in a production to realize how useful such an activity could be to a group who work together. The quality of the performance is both the end product and the means, and many organizations are discovering that the only way they can distinguish themselves from their competitors is by exploiting the many artistic and creative skills and abilities of their workforce. Drama activities are about expression, confidence and self-esteem, the very qualities that successful organizations need.

Conclusion

As a trainer or consultant, in deciding what form of drama you wish to use, the crucial requirement is to understand very clearly what learning you want to achieve. If this is for a particular company, in-depth research and discussion is essential to enable you to decide which particular form of drama is most appropriate.

If you decide on forms one or two, you then have to find people to play the parts who are able to act and remain consistently in role. To be 'hot seated' by a well-informed audience requires considerable skill and knowledge, as well as the flexibility to be able to respond to the ideas and directions of the group. It is not easy and so the best people are those who combine some knowledge and interest in drama or acting with experience of the real world, and particularly the workplace.

There is no doubt that drama has tremendous potential as a learning medium in training and there are a small but growing number of training companies who are experimenting with different aspects of this approach. Some are concentrating on actor-enhanced role-plays but others are looking for opportunities to use the many other drama techniques which could make a huge contribution to effective training. The strength of drama lies in those vital areas of training concerned with building successful working relationships with colleagues or customers, which is perhaps the most difficult area.

If training managers are looking for a novel approach that could have a big impact and make a difference to the way people behave, they could do much worse than give drama a try. As Richard Clark, Senior Safety Manager for BP says, 'From the learning point of view drama is both fun and effective'. What more can you ask?

A drama-based training day

1. Many people start with icebreakers. This is not always necessary but you need some form of introductory activity such as a game or exercise, of which there are hundreds to choose from. The success of the day might depend on what you do in the first half-hour, so do not underestimate the importance of this time. What you do depends, of course, on the needs of the group. People might need warming-up by having an icebreaker but equally they might need energizing or relaxing or to be encouraged to concentrate. Often the main need of a group is simply to get to know each other. Even a group from one organization may not know each other sufficiently for the purpose of the day, since they could be from different offices or departments or levels. A mixer activity such as Chinese Years (see page 282) is often worthwhile.

2. The next stage is to introduce the concept of drama and help people realize that they can actually do it. It is a good principle to start with activities that ask the participants to work as a whole group with everyone involved and nobody watching. 'Cross This Space' is fun and allows everyone to let their hair down (see page 283); 'Liar' (page 283) and 'Excuse Me' (page 282) are rounds. Each individual does some simple activity, within a context, in turn.

    In effect, everybody creates or starts their own play with their neighbour, lasting no more than a few seconds. These three activities, while being fun in themselves, have eased the group into drama and proved to them that it is for them. It is not just for those who are 'artistic' or 'theatrical'.

3.   Having achieved this, you then move on to deciding what you are going to do. If the course has a clear topic or focus, e.g. appraisal, safety, discipline, then all the activities can be designed to explore and investigate this area. However, if the aim of the course is concerned with personal or team development, the subject becomes immaterial and can be anything that arises from stages one and two.

One well-known way of helping people to decide on the particular focus or topic for the drama is the process of storytelling. In a round, people try a 'one word story', followed by a 'one sentence story', and then a group storytelling exercise to get them into creating stories. Everyone can do it because the basis of all drama is a story. This can be followed by the whole group, or smaller groups, spending time creating their own full story that will later be their drama. 'Pass It On' (see page 283) could be how you create the character for this story. Another approach is for the group to brainstorm their ideas. The title word for the brainstorm could be a place, for example, a sales office. This could be followed by people thinking of the characters they might find there and the sort of comment such characters might make, e.g. sales manager, 'If the product isn't right, we can't sell', or office worker, 'The administration still has to be done'.

4.   The next stage is to decide how they are to present their story.

The presentation can take many forms according to the skill and talents of the group, but you have to give people the opportunity to demonstrate what they can do. If the earlier processes have been effective, this will be very easy and people will reveal aspects of themselves which will sometimes be a complete surprise to even their closest colleagues. It is amazing how in every group of people there are talents that can be used.

An artistic presentation requires a tremendous range of skills and abilities. Some will find their strength in the writing of the script or the production. Some will want to act, dance or sing, but others may wish to be involved with props, costumes and the setting. Others will favour publicity and advertising. There will be something for everyone to contribute as part of the team.

After the performance, there will exist a group of people who have worked creatively and closely together to achieve a specific end. They will have developed as a team and as individuals, and revealed their creativity. It is a process that is fun in itself but the qualities developed are also directly relevant to the activities in the workplace.

Games and exercises

Chinese Years

Give everyone in the group a sheet with all the animals and the appropriate Chinese years. Tell them to find out what they are and sit according to the correct sequence. They then introduce themselves as 'George the Snake' or 'Susan the Dragon' etc. This works as a mixer and usually causes a few laughs.

Excuse Me

In a round, and in turn, each person starts a simple conversation with the words 'Excuse me'. The first time this can be on any subject, e.g. 'Excuse me, could you direct me to the post office (or railway station)?' Later you can limit the interactions to a particular place, e.g. the office, the pub, the store.

Pass the Clap

Again, this is a round where everyone stands in a circle. Each person claps twice, passing the clap onto the person on the left and so on round the circle. When they can cope with that you introduce a complication such as a stamp. For example, this time each person stamps on the floor twice with the right leg and passes on the stamp to the person on their right and so on. When you think they can do that, you then try both together – the clap going left and the stamp going right. It sounds simple but it is amazing how difficult many groups find it. It demands concentration and yet is fun for all.

One Word Story

You all sit in a circle. Each person says one word only. You start the story and then in turn they follow with a word which must make sense, be consistent, and be grammatical. They are creating a group story. They have to listen very carefully and then add to what they have heard. Everybody is involved but not too much is asked of each individual. This can then lead to a 'one sentence story' or story-making where anyone can add an idea at any time.

Liar

The group is in a circle and the game starts with one person performing a simple mime, e.g. brushing their teeth. The person on their right asks them what they are doing but is lied to, e.g. person one might suggest they are digging a hole. Person two then has to mime digging a hole and the person on their right then asks them what they are doing; they also lie, and so on. Each person therefore has to do a simple mime and suggest a different one for the person on their right.

Cross this Space

This is another way of leading people into drama. The group is in a circle. Count around in threes or fours. Tell them that all they have to do is cross from side to side as if it is a different place. Then say, 'Number ones, cross this space which is now covered in sticky toffee'. Always start with whatever number you yourself are, and give an example. Quickly change to 'Twos, this space is covered in ice' then threes or fours, with the space being for example, hot coals. Change often and quickly and when they have got the hang of it, introduce the idea that they could cross this space as different people or even animals. Give some examples, such as monkeys, models on a catwalk or riding a motorbike. When you are sure, give them the opportunity to suggest ways of crossing the space.

Pass It On

This is a very simple introductory activity.

Make the group sit in a circle with everyone holding a piece of paper and a felt-tip pen. The idea is that at each stage, each person draws something on the paper and then it is passed on. Some people have said it is a bit like 'Consequences' but the difference, which is crucial. is that in this, at each point, you are supposed to look at the paper and add something that is appropriate and consistent.

This technique can be used to create a group of people who may be the characters in the drama that follows. For example, '1. Draw a large egg shape on your piece of paper. Now pass it on. 2. Now we are going to create a group of people, starting with their faces. In the middle of the piece of paper, draw a nose. Pass it on. 3. And now, two eyes. Pass it on. 4. And now, a mouth and so on.' When everyone has in front of them a picture of a person they give that person a name and then think about that person's life. Finally they introduce their person to the group and the group then asks further questions about the character of the person. In this way the group gets to create and know all the people who will be in their drama.

Further reading

Boal, A. (1992), *Games for Actors and Non Actors,* London: Routledge.
Boal, A. (1979), *Theatre of the Oppressed,* London: Pluto Press.
Brandes, D. and Phillips, H. (1978), *Gamester Handbook,* London: Access Publishing.
Davies, G. (1983), *Practical Primary Drama,* London: Heinemann.
Heathcote, D. and Wagner, P. J. (1979), *Drama as a Learning Medium,* London: Hutchinson.

Chapter 26

Role-play

Morry van Ments

Role-play is one of the most powerful tools that a trainer can use because it has a big emotional impact, and is the nearest thing to practising a situation in real life. As such it is likely to remain in the participant's memory for months or even years. But, because it is such a powerful tool, it needs to be used with care and unfortunately many role-plays are badly run, and result in bad experiences for both the trainer and trainee. This chapter will look at the principles of role-play, the guidelines that a trainer needs to follow and a systematic approach.

What is role-play?

A working definition of role-play is:

> Asking someone to imagine that they are either themselves or another person in a particular situation. The situation may be defined in space and time, and by information, resources, constraints, and the social, industrial or political environment. They are asked to perform tasks in that situation and to deal with circumstances which arise. Whilst doing this, they will be assisted or constrained by the personal and professional characteristics of the role which they are undertaking.

There is nothing unusual about taking roles. In everyday life a man may be a husband, father, accountant, footballer, special constable, gardener, scout, churchgoer and motorist. Our behaviour, speech patterns, and responses will depend on which role we see ourselves in at any particular time. Socially functional people have no difficulty at all in switching from one role to another.

In role-play the participant is asked to behave as they would do in a certain situation and in a certain role. There may be observers who will join in the debriefing and learn from their observation, but the strongest learning is likely to come from the actual experience of role-playing.

Role-play is therefore not theatre. In essence, acting consists of bringing to life a dramatist's ideas (or your own ideas) in order to influence and entertain an audience; the reaction of the audience is the important thing. By contrast, role-play is the experiencing of a problem by the role-player under a particular set of circumstances so that their own ideas emerge and they develop understanding or skills. It is not done to entertain or stimulate the imagination of others who are separate from the action. Nor can it, nor should it, be assessed in respect of the effect that the exercise has on outsiders. The validity of the role-play lies in the changes that take place within the role-player.

Uses of role-play

There are different types of role-play. The activity may be used to:

1. Describe, illustrate, or demonstrate a method or skill.
2. Practise a procedure or skill.
3. Learn about how people behave in a situation, particularly in conditions of change.
4. Develop a sensitivity to human emotions and feelings.
5. Provide a stimulant to creativity.

The trainer will usually be concerned with a mixture of 1, 2, and 3, and sometimes 4 or 5. The first of these is similar to the techniques normally used in teaching practical skills; this chapter concentrates on uses 2 and 3 where the student learns how people behave and practises the necessary skills to interact with others.

Strengths and weaknesses

The strengths of role-play are as follows:

- It is motivational and effective because it involves activity.
- It closes the gap between training and real life situations.
- It is more likely to change attitudes than didactic teaching.
- It gives practice in various types of behaviour.
- It enables students to empathize with others and understand their motivations.
- It provides rapid feedback for both student and tutor.
- It permits training in the control of feelings and emotions.

- It is student-centred and addresses itself to the needs and concerns of the trainee who can control content and pace of learning.
- It portrays generalized work problems and the dynamics of group interaction, both formal and informal.

Some of the problems of role-play are that:

- The tutor may lose control over what is learnt and the order in which it is learnt.
- Simplifications can mislead.
- It uses a large amount of time if done properly.
- The effectiveness depends on the quality of the tutor and student.
- Its impact may trigger off withdrawal or defence symptoms.
- It may be seen as too entertaining or frivolous.
- The learning may depend on what students already know. They may introduce unintentionally misleading information.

Preparation

The initial stages of using role-play are the same as preparing for any other teaching task but the stages are more critical than in the normal classroom situation because the whole direction of the session will be set by the preparation undertaken beforehand. Once the session has been set in train it is difficult to substantially change it.

The first step is to decide on the teaching objectives. Does the trainer want to teach facts, awareness, concepts, skills or techniques? Is the purpose of the session tightly defined, or is there a general wish to highlight a range of problems?

The next step is to clarify the position of the role-play in the overall training programme. Is it to be used as an introduction to a subject, as a central feature, as a break or interlude, as a follow-on, as summing up or as revision?

The trainer also has to bear in mind constraints. Is there enough space and is the room suitable? Is there enough time to run and debrief properly? Does the role-play require assistance from other trainers; will external experts be brought in for the debriefing? How much paperwork is required, and can it be prepared in time? What is the fallback position if the session under or over-runs?

Lastly, will the trainer use an off-the-shelf package or design and write the role-play themselves? It is usually desirable to write your own role-plays because they can be designed specifically for the local situation, but sometimes one can use or adapt ready-made ones. The next section, on writing role-plays, covers the steps necessary to produce your own exercises for your own trainees. It is not difficult, and can produce the best results.

Writing the role-play

The first stage is the preparation of a general scenario. It helps at this stage to consider the key actions you expect participants to undertake and the results to be achieved; these actions and results will arise directly from the learning objectives previously set. For example, will the participants have to argue their case, search out or evaluate information, demonstrate that they can follow certain procedures, or assess a situation quickly?

Many role-plays are written in a fairly conventional way and there is a monotonous similarity in many of the ready-made role-plays which are published in book form. Trainers should realize that one of the powerful aspects of role-play is the freedom to experiment with the basic characteristics of the exercise.

Characteristics to consider are:

● Characters: who are the key characters in the scenario? What are the subsidiary roles? Is it possible to arrange spare roles (which can easily be dispensed with)?
● Time: is it in the past, present, or future?
● Reality: how closely does the role-play have to correspond to real facts. Is it possible to fantasize about the situation?
● Personalization: are the characters real, known people or symbolic i.e. known by their function in the organization?
● Size: numbers and grouping of roles.
● Length: does time go slower or faster during the role-play?
● Information: how will information be presented to participants during the role-play?
● Role-allocation: by chance or design? If by design, then how are you going to handle sex, age, background and status differences? Are you going to build in neutral roles, design roles to fit students (dangerous) or change the angle of view and redesign the role-play?

At this point it is advisable to consider rooms, furniture, and any 'props' that may be required. It is important to determine the external constraints so that one does not go too far down a particular path before taking them into account. For example, will there be sufficient time, enough people and the necessary equipment?

This is also the time at which the trainer should consider observations needed in order to have a record of the content (what happened), and process (how/why did it happen) of the role-play. The next step is to consider the role descriptions for the role-players. These are written in the second person using realistic terminology. The following list gives an indication of the features which should be taken into consideration, although not every feature need be commented upon.

Key features of individual roles include:

- Physical attributes (age, sex, health).
- Personality traits (where relevant to the role-play).
- Surrounding circumstances, status, authority, constraints, function authority, power.
- Their skills or abilities.
- How much they know.
- What they believe, social expectations.
- Their objectives, motives, targets .
- Where they get their information/beliefs from.
- What decisions they must make.

Note that attitudes, feelings and emotions must come as a result of the above, not written into the script. It is not a good idea to write 'you are a male chauvinist, and look down on women'. It is better to write 'There are a number of women who work in your department; they are attractive, but too emotional to make some of the hard decisions which need to be made'. Or again, write 'your boss clearly doesn't appreciate the effort you make to pay attention to detail', rather than 'you feel your boss doesn't understand you'. It is not that these statements are necessarily true from an objective viewpoint but they are true in terms of how the person in that role would believe the situation to be.

The next thing is to decide whom they should meet, under what circumstances, to do what, and for how long. The instructions may read 'Your boss has asked you to come and see him, but hasn't said why. Perhaps it relates to some work that you stayed on late to do last week. Luckily, he has asked you to come mid-morning and has said that it may take only about 15 minutes. You go to his office and knock on the door ...'

It is best to keep detail to a minimum at this stage. Extra information may be fed in via the simulation later if necessary using a medium such as memos, news broadcasts, messengers, or telephone calls.

Running the role-play

Introducing the activity

Having prepared the paper work and framework for the role-play, the trainer will introduce the exercise to the participants. If they have never taken part in a role-play before it will be necessary to explain the idea to them. This is best done avoiding the use of the term role-play itself; it is better to use 'exercise', 'activity', 'procedure' because the word 'role-play' tends to summon up the image of play-acting.

You can start by talking about the learning objectives (possibly making this a group decision). You can then lead into the idea of people interacting. Ask 'What do you feel they might say?' and 'Who else might be involved?' Use the answers to these questions to lead into role-play by suggesting that the students who have made these suggestions should try and actually say these things to each other. Hence they are beginning to get into a role-play before the word 'role-play' is mentioned. From there on the situation can be developed, and the trainer can explain the usefulness of role-play in exploring human interactions and their consequences.

Techniques

Many trainers think that there is only one standard way to run a role-play. This is not so; there are a number of ways in which role-plays can be organized. Here are some of them:

●	Fishbowl	– in the middle with observers around
●	Multiple	– twos and threes simultaneously
●	Role-rotation	– give another person a chance to play the role
●	Role-reversal	– switch roles between two players
●	Supporter	– a volunteer from the observers speaks for the role-player
●	Alter ego/doubling	– an extra player reveals the possible feelings of the role-player
●	Consultant group	– caucus or home groups who give advice
●	Mirroring	– re-enact in front of original players
●	Replay	– with modified format or content
●	Soliloquy	– the role-player speaks to themselves aloud. This helps to clarify their minds
●	Chair	– soliloquy using an object to speak to
●	Silent auxiliary	– soliloquy, but speaking to another person
●	Positioning	– re-arrange furniture/players.

Clearly these techniques can be used in combination or sequence if desired.

Starting the role-play

Before the role-play can be started, the roles must be allocated and the participants briefed. Roles may be allocated at random or in some other suitable way, and care must be taken not to build in any false bias or assumptions. The background to the situation must be explained, either verbally or in a written document, and the individual role sheets handed out. Students must be given time to absorb the information and work out the implications for themselves.

If there are any observers, they should be briefed. It is best to brief the observers together with the role-players to avoid any feeling the latter may have of being spied upon or criticized. Indeed, there is often no reason why the role-players themselves should not brief the observers on what points they think will be the most important to focus on. They may, for example, ask the observers to note whether they are using good questioning techniques.

The role-play is started by giving a clear direction: 'You come through the door', 'You meet in the street', and allowing the players to take over.

Problems during role-play

- Player departs from role. Sometimes a participant will start to ask the trainer questions or make comments as a student rather than in role. In cases like these it is best to stop the role-play and explain the purpose of the exercise again, emphasize the fact that they are exploring real human communication problems, discuss the way a role-play works, and then start again. The trainer need not worry about stopping and starting the role-play; people are much more adept at slipping in and out of roles than they are given credit for.

- Poor performances. Drying up. If a participant finds it difficult to carry on, the structure of the role-play might be changed so that they get some support from a volunteer (supporter) who comes from the rest of the class. This person steps forward and stands behind the player and speaks for them until they have gained sufficient confidence to carry on themselves. Alternatively the trainer may call a break in which the player consults with other members of the class (consultant group).

- Lack of insight/empathy. This can often be resolved by reversing the roles so that the player understands the other person's point of view.

- Emotional escalation. The trainer has little or no control over the direction in which the role-play goes. It is sometimes possible for a situation to develop which mirrors too closely an emotional or personal problem for one of the players. The best way to deal with this is to call 'time out' and allow the atmosphere to cool by discussing the key purpose of the role-play. Roles may be rotated between a number of players.

- Not taking the role-play seriously. Clearly one way to deal with this is to point out the usefulness of 'doing' instead of listening to lectures. It is also useful to encourage the player to act as they genuinely feel they want to act, not as they think someone else would; the more involved they can feel, the less likely it is that they will refuse to participate fully.

● Repetition, boredom. It is possible to use different techniques to combat this, but on the whole it is wise to take note of the signs and call a halt to the role-play. There is no reason why role-plays should not be cut short at any point, and the results up to that point discussed.

The tutor's role

Apart from the usual administrative functions, the tutor must also act as adjudicator, control the time, engender energy and correct any problems. It is not the tutor's role to act as a therapist, and to that end you should avoid getting drawn into personal or emotional matters. One of the problems that the tutor must deal with is that of avoiding unwanted learning. There are always hidden agendas in any interaction, and trainers should avoid writing in stereotypes and keep to objective descriptions and facts. It can also be useful to use deliberate non-conventional descriptions e.g the female judge or general, the cleaner with the university degree. Although the role-play is not a game, there may be winners and losers implied by the way the situation can develop. It is therefore important to ensure that reward systems encourage desirable behaviour. Finally, it is possible for a role-player during the role-play to feed in incorrect information out of ignorance without realizing it. These items of misinformation must be challenged and questioned during the debriefing session.

The logic of debriefing

A great deal of learning and crystallization of thinking takes place during debriefing. It follows that a role-play without a systematic, logical, well-conducted debriefing session is only using part of its potential for learning. A simple three-phase scheme can be used with advantage.

Phase 1. Clearing up the role-play

The purpose of this phase is to bring the players out of role and dissipate any tension or anxiety by bringing out assumptions, feelings, and changes which occurred during the run, and by finding out how the players saw themselves and others. It is also an opportunity to correct mistakes, establish the facts, and clear up misunderstandings.

In order to do this, the trainer has first of all to allow the role-players to talk about what happened from within the viewpoint of their role, then to clarify any misunderstandings and find out what the observers saw. The best sequence to use is:

1. Ask the main players for their version of what happened, their impressions and reactions.
2. Ask the subsidiary players for their version of what happened, their impressions and reactions.
3. Ask the observers for their observations.
4. Agree on what happened and the final decision made or situation arrived at.

In order to focus on the role-play viewed from within the role-play itself it is helpful to have in mind a number of stratagems:

● Use open-ended questions, How? Why? What?
● Concentrate on individual players.
● Explore alternative actions.
● Reflect back feelings.
● Insist on descriptive, not evaluative comments.
● Feedback in terms of the observer's own experience rather than someone else's.
● Do not evaluate the quality of performance.
● Do not argue about misunderstood instructions.
● Do not assign motives or make judgements about underlying attitudes.
● Emphasize what was done, rather than what could have been done.
● Use role-titles in discussion, not the role-player's name.
● Interpret actions in terms of the role-play assumptions.

Phase 2. Drawing conclusions

At this point we move from the role-players being 'in role' to the normal classroom situation of trainer and trainees. The purpose is to relate the outcome to the original aims and analyse the way interactions occurred and why things happened that way. Hence we can establish sequences, causes, and effects. It is also an opportunity for players to develop self-observation and observational skills.

The aim of the trainer should be to:

● Draw generalized conclusions.
● Draw conclusions about the way in which people behave.
● Analyse the causes of behaviour.
● Decide on what could be done to improve the situation.
● Extrapolate to the real world.

The stratagems to carry this out include:

- Asking for reasons. Why? How? Who?
- Probing answers. Why not? What if?
- Seeking alternative theories. Is there another possibility?
- Collecting other examples. Where else has this happened?
- Testing conclusions against alternatives. Which makes more sense?
- Giving the views of outside experts.

Phase 3. Develop an action plan

In order to avoid the role-play being seen as an isolated entertainment or break from the 'real' teaching and learning, it is important to arrange for ways of continuing the process within the overall training plan. Thus the trainer may wish to draw out new points for consideration, deduce ways of improving behaviour, or suggest other ways of acting. This is the point at which it should be possible to show how the experience applies to other situations and links with previous learning.

In order to do this, the trainer can:

- Follow up with a repeat of the role-play with variations.
- Follow up with further instruction or practice.
- Organize students into action groups.
- Give students a chance to try out their new ideas.
- Get the students to commit themselves to actions and write up plans on wall posters.
- Agree criteria for success.
- Put a timescale on actions.
- Provide a plan for future learning.

The key to good debriefing is to allow sufficient time, to ensure that each person has opportunities to speak, and to check that you have understood their feelings. The ideal outcome is an agreement on the way forward to explore the ideas and new understandings that have been generated by the role-play.

Conclusion

Role-play is a powerful tool for the trainer to use. The difference between the best and worst run role-plays can be considerable. At worst trainees will be bored, embarrassed and even angry; they may have achieved little, and even acquired erroneous learning. They may be left with a feeling of inadequacy and not knowing what it was all about. But run properly and thoughtfully, the exercise will be seen as a relevant, essential part of learning. It will be an enjoyable and exciting experience, and trainees will be left with greater understanding and a clear idea of how to develop their skills further.

Although role-play is used very widely in training, there are few opportunities for trainers to get the useful practical experience. There are conferences run by SAGSET (see Further reading below) which normally include practical sessions, but there are few training courses. In the end it comes down to being self-aware and constantly analysing what happened in your training sessions and how they could be improved. Perhaps the best thing is to observe sessions conducted by other trainers, or to invite an experienced practitioner to sit in on your sessions.

The rewards of a well run role-play are very great, and both trainer and trainee should find the experience enjoyable, effective, and memorable.

Further reading

Bishop, S. (1995), *25 Role Plays for Assertiveness Training*, Aldershot: Gower.

Collier, K. (1998), 'Once more with feeling – identification, representation and the affective aspects of role-play in experienced-based education', in J. Rolfe, D. Saunders and T. Powell (eds), *Simulation and Gaming Research Handbook Vol. 6 – Simulations and Games for Emergency and Crisis Management*, London: Kogan Page.

Davis, M. and Long, T. (1989), *Active Replay*, London: Blackwell Education.

Ellis, R. and Whittington, D. (1983), *A Guide to Social Skills Training*, London: Croom Helm.

Holsbrink-Engels, G. A. (1994), 'Visions of Dutch corporate trainers on role-playing', in R. Armstrong, F. Percival and D. Saunders (eds), S*imulation and Gaming Yearbook Vol. 2 – Interactive Learning*, London: Kogan Page.

Jones, K. (1987), *Simulations: A Handbook for Teachers and Trainers*, London: Kogan Page.

Jones, K. (1988), *Interactive Learning Events: A Guide for Facilitators*, London: Kogan Page.

Ladousse, G. P. (1987), *Role Play*, Oxford: OUP.

Milroy, E. (1982), *Role-Play: A Practical Guide*, Aberdeen: Aberdeen University Press (Pergamon).

Van Ments, M. (1999), *The Effective Use of Role Play: Practical Techniques for Improving Learning*, London: Kogan Page.

Van Ments, M. (1990), *Active Talk: The Effective Use of Discussion in Learning*, London: Kogan Page.

Yardley-Matwiejczuk, K. M. (1997), *Role Play: Theory and Practice*, London: Sage.

Note: The main source of information and support for Simulation and Gaming in the UK and mainland Europe is SAGSET (The Society for the Advancement of Gaming and Simulation in Education and Training) c/o Peter Walsh, SAGSET, 11 Lloyd Street, Ryton, Tyne and Wear, NE40 4DJ, UK. Web page: http://graph.ms.ic.ac.uk/sagset/home.htm e-mail: *Pwalsh9540@aol.com*

Chapter 27

Applying the skills of counselling

John Nixon

If training and development in the workplace is to concern itself with counselling, it is critically important that all involved know the difference between counselling and counselling skills. In addition, trainers and managers must respect counselling and counsellors for the immense contribution on offer. To combat ever-present cynicism, they must be conversant with its role, its benefits and its risks. They also need to champion the cause of superior quality training, because it will deliver the goods, while the opposite will give yet more ammunition to the cynics.

This chapter aims to clarify the key issues, identify what is involved in counselling and counselling skills, highlight the value to trainers and managers, identify the roles they can take and provide guidance for how they can apply their practice. For ease of reading, use of gender is generic and 'client' refers to the person being helped.

A brief outline on counselling

Mention counselling in a room full of managers, as I did recently, and the reaction you will probably get is one of surreptitious withdrawal. That is hardly surprising given the most commonly understood roles for it have been in bereavement, marriage guidance and helping victims of disasters – unwelcome scenarios which most of us never want to face and with which counselling is inextricably linked.

While much has changed in the 1990s, the perception of its role is still one with negative connotations. If you need counselling or are recommended to go for it, there is something 'weak' about you. Others will at best pity you and at worst, be scornful. Sound familiar? So, to handle the negative reactions in approaching this subject we must be crystal clear on what counselling is and why using counselling skills does not make you a counsellor.

Being clear is not easy because, while definitions of counselling are available (BAC, 1994), authors seldom agree. Some see it as a distinct activity of trained professionals, others see it as a commonplace 'helping' occurrence (Nixon, 1997). Resolving this confusion matters because organizations nowadays want the benefits that counselling delivers. They recognize that counselling is effective in helping people solve problems and solving problems is part of organizational life. But equipping trainers and managers with skills and expecting them to act as counsellors to others is not achievable because ethical counselling at work can only take place when three conditions are met.

1. Both parties to the discussion openly state that person A (the helper) is being a counsellor for person B (the client) (BAC, 1996).
2. The helper is independent, i.e. has no vested interest in the decisions of the client.
3. The helper is publicly acknowledged as a being a counsellor and sees themselves as one. (This almost certainly means they are qualified.)

The implications are clear. Most people in an organization cannot engage in counselling because they have another professional relationship with the client e.g. boss/subordinate. They also have job-related objectives which take priority over helping the client. Furthermore the published role of 'counsellor' requires professional counselling training. Put simply. counselling is a professional activity which can only be done by a person wishing to be a counsellor and who can meet the core conditions of confidentiality, independence and impartiality. Counselling is a vocational activity, with a specific role and a relevance for people 'in trouble'. Counselling skills on the other hand has a major contribution to make in many everyday situations and hence this will be my focus here.

Counselling skills: the nature of the beast

It is a fascinating thing that although there can be quite a degree of mystique surrounding counselling, its skills will be no surprise to most readers. You have probably given or received training in many of them. What is mysterious is that in my experience, course delegates find they are easy enough to understand and willingly agree to their usefulness, but few actually go on to use them. And when managers have attended counselling courses and then fail to apply what they have learned or apply it poorly, the whole subject can become devalued.

> 'My supervisor still doesn't listen. He keeps telling me what he would do in my shoes...' or even worse: 'I explained everything to her, but all she did was keep asking me: "how did I feel"!'

So let us look at the core skills a typical course would include:

- *Listening*   Ideally, the course will identify the difference between hearing, listening passively and listening actively. If I had to choose one skills area to teach, this would be it. Amazingly, it seems to be the hardest to put into practice, yet once mastered, it forms the bedrock for all the other skills. The payback is so great that people who learn how to do it fluently surprise themselves at the improvement in their ability to communicate.

- *Attending*   How to be in the presence of another person in such a way as to allow them to be natural and at ease. This area focuses on intangible things like attitude, mindset and creating rapport and on the tangible, like the ever popular body language and making the environment conducive.

- *Self-awareness*   There are two key aspects of this which could be called cause and effect. The first is being aware of what is 'going on' for yourself in terms of thoughts, emotions and behaviours because these affect your interactions. Being aware gives you choice in what you say or do, whether or not you are being 'congruent'. The second is sensitivity and responding to your effect on the other person.

- *Verbal interventions*   This overlaps with active listening. Common to both are reflecting back, summarizing, paraphrasing and key word repetition. Additions are questioning, scene setting, challenging and self-disclosure.

- *Empathy*   I am often amazed at how difficult it can be to connect with what the other person is feeling. In my experience, women find it easier. Perhaps it has much to do with the competitive nature of work today. Suffice to say, that getting close to experiencing what the other person is feeling is essential.

- *Problem solving*   Techniques which help people solve problems. This is a practical aspect of using counselling skills.

- *Confidentiality*   This is a core condition for the ethical use of counselling skills, simply because 'clients' are likely to 'open-up' and reveal something which they would not normally do. Agreeing the conditions for confidentiality can cause discomfort, so it is vital that trainers address this in depth.

Many of the exercises employed on counselling skills courses work at the cognitive level and represent no threat to participants. Others, especially around empathy and feelings, work at the affective (emotional) level and can easily bring sensitive, personal issues to the surface. Learners may find these exercises almost unbearably intrusive. A member of a senior executive team told me his lasting impression of a course two years ago, was of the tension it created between participants because their working relationships unexpectedly became a central issue. So be aware that unpleasant things can happen on counselling skills courses and trainers must be ruthlessly strict with themselves in assessing their ability to handle the group's emotions and their own. Practising these skills in a 'safe' environment is key. Typical 'corporate' courses are two days in duration, during which time pair and group practice will feature. In my experience this is too short a time to become confident enough to use the skills when back at work.

Alternatives, often public courses, are evening study over a term of several weeks at a local education centre. These are likely to focus on non-work situations and thus have less relevance. Courses over several weekends are also an option, but these are often unattractive to employees. Courses for those who wish to become counsellors are much longer still. They are usually spread over two years of part-time study and result in a certificate after one year and a diploma after two.

There does not seem to be much in-between. This is a pity because becoming proficient with these skills takes determination, a lot of thought and above all, feedback. One way to achieve proficiency is to support learners after a course, perhaps through peer group sessions or one-to-one coaching by a counsellor, for at least a year. Taking such a long-term view has obvious implications on cost. However, in my experience, investing in a two-day course is wasted without follow-up in place.

The first port of call for courses in counselling skills is the British Association for Counselling which publishes both a directory of resources and journals that carry advertisements. The Association for Counselling at Work is a division of BAC and is also a source for counsellors, including those fully versed in supporting counselling in the workplace and who can provide follow-up supervisory support.

Counselling skills: for better, for worse, for whom?

Still on the trail of clarity in counselling, one way is to see its contribution as falling into two camps. The first aligns with the popular perceptions of counselling as discussed earlier and concerns problems and difficulties. I call this the 'crisis and coping' camp. The second is 'to enhance the performance of (the user's) functional role' (BAC, 1996). I call this the 'fitness and function' camp.

The following are the kind of 'crisis and coping' situations that counselling skills will enable a person to manage much better than if they rely on instinct and experience alone.

'Crisis and Coping'

1. Personal or home-related problems which often affect the person at work e.g. bereavement, marriage difficulties, parenting issues, debt, alcohol dependency.
2. Workplace-related problems e.g. redundancy, relocation, bullying, retirement, stress, accidents, conflict.

Here, the most valuable gain is that users learn how to prepare for handling the emotions which are bound-up in these situations. The joy of it is, having learned how to help people cope in crisis, the helper is equipped for sudden, unexpected situations. Here is an example. Jim, untrained in counselling skills is a manager with administrative staff. Unexpectedly, due to global market crises, the company announces it wants volunteers for redundancy, and quickly. Bill, chief archivist, comes to see Jim to ask where he stands. When Jim explains that no jobs are safe, Bill suddenly breaks down. Shocked at seeing a grown man cry, Jim attempts to relieve his own embarrassment with a well-meaning: 'I know how you feel'. To Bill this is crass. Jim's job is safe and therefore he cannot 'know how I feel'. Bill leaves the room even more convinced no one knows or cares how seriously the threat of job loss is affecting him.

Not only would counselling skills enable Jim to support Bill effectively, they would enable him to explore sensitively what is going on for Bill that is making him so upset. It is worth addressing just how far Jim should support Bill and we will do this later.

It is all much more uplifting to look at how counselling skills add 'positive' value. The context here is developmental. Counselling skills enable a helper to empower another to make self-directed progress (Summerfield and van Oudtshoorn, 1995). This is quite different from skills that give advice or prescribe solutions – both normal processes for managers and trainers. Provided the training places counselling skills in this positive context, the user can expect to be more effective in these areas.

'Fitness and function'

1. Personal improvements enabling us to be 'fitter in some way, e.g. confidence, peace of mind, motivation, morale, work/life balance, managing relationships.

2. Function-related improvements enabling us to be more effective in what we do both from a 'doing it better' and 'doing it humanely' perspectives, e.g. communicating, teambuilding, goal setting, group discussions and meeting management, career management, managing change,

recruitment interviewing, appraisal interviewing, coaching and mentoring, discipline and dismissal, selling and servicing customers.

Here, the most valuable gain is learning how to ensure the choice of action and the responsibility for outcome stays with the person being helped, not with the helper. I am not suggesting that this is always appropriate. Clearly, there are occasions when being prescriptive is necessary. But where self-management is the order of the day, counselling skills provide the depth of communication to connect with the motivations of others.

There are many organizational roles which would benefit from these skills in a 'fitness and function' context – roles such as supervisor, team leader, internal consultant, manager, trainer, salesperson, chairman, service engineer, coach, and mentor. All these have the need to function better and to help others function better. I accept the 'crisis and coping' context may seem more applicable to managing than say selling and servicing, but it is a moot point.

It is down to the trainers

'There are times, however, when the boundary between counselling and counselling skills becomes blurred' (Bull, 1996).

This means that the situation can get out of hand when say, a manager uses counselling skills. Take our example of Jim and Bill earlier. Imagine being Jim with a clear directive to halve your departmental budget. Bill has been with the company as man and boy. He is expensive. You have an alternative in the form of a recent graduate recruit. Only this time you use your new empathy and sensitive probing skills. You quietly wait until Bill recovers his composure and intervene: 'This redundancy thing seems much more worrying for you than you expected, Bill?' Bill blurts out how his special needs son requires a lot of financial support and, with his wife now not working, he cannot afford even to contemplate early retirement. At his age, what chance has he got of another job?

As Jim, what are you going to be thinking about? You are caught between a rock and a hard place. You did not know about his son. Your wife earns. Your first thought is 'thank heavens I don't have to face that!' Immediately your sense of justice and compassion is in conflict with your imperative to cut costs. How can you possibly proceed ethically?

But, say you explore this further with Bill. All the time his trust in you will build, thanks to your ability to 'connect' with him. Inside, you are pretty sure that in the end he will have to go. The further you go down the track with Bill, the more he will trust you not to harm him. However, it will be more upsetting to both of you if, in the end, losing Bill is the only way. Both of you will feel betrayed.

This example illustrates the potential for manipulation in its pejorative sense, but there are times when being placed in a position of 'privileged knowledge' thanks to the skill of going beneath the surface, will bring the opposite positive opportunity. For example, your assistant opens up to you about the victimization she feels from another person in the department. Now that you know, you have the power to act. You might decide not to resolve the bullying issue, but instead manipulate the rota to reduce her exposure. Both examples illustrate the risks. In both, the helper has a vested interest. The correct course is to refer the person to a source of professional counselling support. Ultimately, Bill has to cope and the assistant has to resolve the bullying. Both issues are firmly the remit of professional counselling.

So how do we manage this paradox? On the one hand counselling skills enable users to get to the root of issues, positive or negative. On the other, when they do, they are in danger of unethical behaviour. The answer lies in the training.

Make no mistake about this. Many skills courses are promoted by the suppliers as having the answer to managing people for performance and profit. But it is unavoidably down to the purchaser and the trainer to ensure a great deal of attention is given to the moral use of these powerful, emotion-churning tools. It has been stated that they are useful for managers because they are practical and not theoretical, take the following example. 'The NLP model enables us to learn how ... to develop deep levels of communication and trust ... it is about activity and experience rather than theory' (Sanders, 1990). My dispute with this is that ethics are part and parcel of theory. If skills like 'precision questions', 'vocal tone' and 'body language observation' are taught without exploring the underlying principles, it is irresponsible.

There are many more approaches and models which will shape the training within counselling skills courses such as Rogerian, transactional analysis and solution-focused to name three. All of these will endow the training and hence the learners with a particular perspective. Yes, it is reasonable to want the ability, but it is also reasonable for the person on the other end to expect to be treated properly, not duped, investigated or manipulated through misplaced trust.

The training must tackle the issue head-on of 'Why do you want to learn these skills?'. It must focus the learner (and subsequent user) on addressing their motives honestly. 'Why am I helping this person? Is it to move towards my agenda, the organization's agenda or do I genuinely want to help and, while interested in the outcome, am I "invested" in it in any way?' The point at which the user is honest with themselves is the point where the responsibility not to mislead, manipulate, deceive or be 'voyeuristic' must be the most important. To achieve this awareness, training must focus on self-honesty and principles and, in my opinion, trainers in these skills must do a lot of work on their own self-awareness and principles of conduct. In fact, only qualified counsellors with at least two years' experience of vocational practice should train in skills which are being marketed under the banner of 'counselling'.

Counselling skills = communication skills = interpersonal skills

By now, the reader will have connected many of the benefits offered by counselling skills with those of communication skills and interpersonal skills courses, and the reader is right: there is a huge degree of overlap, in fact so much so that they are effectively indistinguishable. 'If you are familiar with "communication skills" or "inter-personal relationship skills", which are taught widely in business, you could think of a counsellor as using a very advanced form of these skills' (BAC, 1990).

An advanced level course in either communication or interpersonal skills will address the same subjects including empathy, attending, verbal and vocal skills. As one manager put it to me, 'Ah, but there's no cachet in interpersonal skills and communication skills, all our people have been on those. Counselling skills sounds a bit different!'

The point was made to me by an experienced counsellor, that the influential author and practitioner, Gerard Egan, trained counsellors by teaching them counselling skills before putting them in a group and asking them to work on their relationship issues. In this respect we can see that skills are skills and learning how to use them takes you towards being a counsellor. This is why the fluent user of these almost 'generic' communication and relationship skills is highly likely to be perceived as a counsellor by the person on the other end, even though the helper may not want to be one in a vocational sense.

So, do we have another paradox? Yes, unfortunately. Train a person in advanced communication skills and they run the risk of being perceived as a counsellor and perhaps behaving unethically. Don't train them, and they will not be as good at helping people resolve problems or to perform better. There is no resolution to this; it is incumbent on those who train in all these areas to spend quality time with their learners in exploration of the effects of skilful, penetrating communication, and the responsibility that goes with creating an atmosphere of trust.

Guidelines for managers and trainers

So let us look at what guidelines there are for trainers and managers who are considering counselling skills. In the first instance, you have to identify your objective.

- If you want home-grown, vocational counsellors the route is clear. They must take on longer term study and practice under qualified supervision.
- If your objective is to help managers cope with emotional situations, then training under the umbrella of counselling makes sense.
- If it is to enhance a person's functional or job ability so that they are better able to help their people perform, then good communications or interpersonal skills courses will match the context better.

Gaining the benefits and minimizing the risks is about being honest from the start. Training in any of the above demands that the user is aware of the importance of behaving ethically. For this reason, teaching the skills must come after working on self-awareness and self-honesty, so that before every helping intervention the user learns to question their own real motive and have a sense of how much probing is useful and appropriate. It takes courage and honesty; precisely the qualities that create trusting and useful relationships.

Conclusion

Training people in counselling skills is like freeing mink from captivity. They may be beautiful but unless constrained, they can cause all sorts of damage to the environment. Purchasers should go on the course first and trainers need to understand the ethical dimension to be confident that they are addressing the difference between counselling and the use of skills. Copies of the BAC *Code of Ethics and Practice for Counselling Skills* must be studied and distributed within the training sessions. Furthermore, a system must be in place for users to be able to refer people for further help and qualified supervision should be available as a support for users. Remember, putting the skills to use takes you closer to being like a counsellor.

Finally, it may pay to choose a course which describes itself as taking an 'integrative' approach. This means that the positioning of the teaching will promote a balanced view across a number of different counselling and skills approaches. This counteracts the potential problem of it degenerating into the 'fad of the moment' and 'quick fix' category, which can affect any new training initiative.

Further reading

British Association for Counselling (1990), *Personal Problems at Work*, Rugby: BAC.
British Association for Counselling (1996), *Code of Ethics and Practice for Counselling Skills*, Rugby: BAC.

Bull A. (1996), *Counselling Skills and Counselling at Work*, Rugby: Association for Counselling at Work.

Carroll, M. and Walton, M. (eds) (1997), *Handbook of Counselling in Organisations*, London: Sage.

Culley, S. (1991), *Integrative Counselling Skills in Action*, London: Sage.

International Teaching Seminars (1998), *Products Catalogue 1998*, London: ITS.

Nixon, J. (1997), 'Line management and counselling', *Handbook of Counselling in Organisations*, London: Sage.

Sanders, G. (1990), 'Counselling models in the workplace – taking NLP into counselling', Employee Counselling Today, **2** (2), pp. 25–28.

Summerfield, J. and van Oudtshoorn, L. (1995), *Counselling in the Workplace*, London: IPD.

Chapter 28

Creating collaborative gatherings using large group interventions

Martin Leith

The newspapers tell us we are living in the 'information age'. But the newspapers have not got the whole picture. We are not just witnessing an explosion of information. What we are seeing is the proliferation of just about everything including lifestyles, fashions, demographic groups, music categories, brands, spiritual practices, TV channels and competitors. It is becoming increasingly difficult to find a way through all of this proliferation, diversity and complexity using the inflexible, machine-like model of organization that we know so well. We badly need a more responsive model.

This chapter considers the approach of collaborative gatherings and how they can help organizations faced with complexity, diversity and change. The issue for trainers and developers concerns not only the set-up of such gatherings but the facilitation skills required for running large groups. Based on this, the chapter is structured to help T & D professionals consider when to use collaborative gatherings, to appreciate the methods on offer, the principles required for design and facilitation and the questions they might typically be asked by those involved.

Application and timing

In a world of great change collaborative gatherings offer the opportunity for people to work together in ways that engender high levels of ownership and commitment. Broadly speaking, collaborative gatherings are convened to:

- plan and implement organization-wide change;
- solve complex problems;
- facilitate breakthrough thinking and innovation;
- enable organizational learning;
- revitalize the organization and create community.

The question of when to convene a collaborative gathering can provide an essential first step when the issue confronting you is complex and uncertain. Other occasions when colloborative gatherings are called for are when the issue is muddled and lacks clarity and the way forward is unclear; when there is a requirement to involve diverse groups with different agendas; or when there is a need to produce breakthrough results quickly.

Perhaps most importantly, however, collaborative gatherings complement a collaborative form of governance. If your organization is not ready for this, all plans involving collaborative gatherings should be abandoned.

Large group interventions: the methods

A wide range of methods exist for creating collaborative gatherings. These are sometimes referred to as large group intervention (LGI) methods, although this is a misleading term because the group does not have to be large – it simply needs to be composed of the right people. Although there are more than 20 different LGI methods, this chapter will focus on the five most widely used methods, namely Future Search, Open Space Technology, Participative Design, Real Time Strategic Change and Simu-Real.

Future Search

Primary purpose: creating an agreed vision and strategy.
Developers: Marvin Weisbord and Sandra Janoff.
Length: two to three days (including two nights).
Group size: ideally 64 people.

The central concept of Future Search is 'getting the whole system in the room' to find new ways forward by working through the five stages:

1.   Review the past from several different perspectives.
2.   Map the present.
3.   Create a range of future scenarios.
4.   Identify the common ground.
5.   Develop action plans.

A Future Search conference is planned by a steering committee of volunteers and managed by two facilitators. Work is done at round tables in mixed groups of eight. Extensive use is made of large sheets of paper taped to the wall. The past is reviewed through three 'timeline' charts – one for personal milestones, another for important organizational or community developments, and a third for global events. Participants then create one large mind map of current reality, and say what they are proud and sorry about regarding the current situation. Each small group generates a vision of the future, which it presents in a creative way to the other groups. Common ground is then identified. The action planning that completes the Future Search is normally done in functional or self-selecting groups. Post-event implementation work is self-managed.

Real Time Strategic Change

Primary purpose: designing and implementing sustainable organization-wide change.
Developers: Kathie Dannemiller and Robert Jacobs.
Length: two to three days.
Group size: limited only by capacity of venue.

Real Time Strategic Change (RTSC) is more than an LGI method: it is a principle-based approach to transforming the whole organization.

RTSC begins with contracting and scoping. This is followed by a leadership alignment event which enables the formal and informal leaders of the organization to understand the RTSC philosophy, agree purpose and outcomes for the change effort and make a commitment to moving forward together.

Next there is an organizational alignment event in which the whole organization, or a substantial part of it, takes part. The design team, composed of members of the different subsystems that will be participating in the event, defines the purpose and outcomes, and develops a sequence of activities that will enable participants to realize them. There is no fixed conceptual framework governing the sequence of activities, although Richard Beckhard's change formula, $D \times V \times F > R$, is sometimes used. This states that the product of D (dissatisfaction with current state of affairs), V (a vision of how things could be) and F (first steps towards realizing that vision) must be greater than R (resistance to change).

The participants sit at round tables in 'max mix' groups of eight. Table work is self-managed and there are just two facilitators for the whole event, supported by a small logistics team. A set of actions normally emerges from the organizational alignment event and the design team will have put in place whatever is considered necessary for taking these forward: infrastructures, internal communication programmes, resource allocation procedures and so on.

The change effort should not be viewed as a big event and a few follow-up activities, but as a continuous cycle of planning, implementing and monitoring. Some of this work will be done in collaborative gatherings, and some will be done off-line. Events have their place, but RTSC is much more than events, it is a wholly different way of doing business.

Participative Design

Primary purpose: quickly redesigning an organization into self-managing workteams.
Developers: Fred Emery and Merrelyn Emery.
Length: one and a half to two days.
Group size: around 24 people.

Participative Design was developed as a faster and more acceptable alternative to the Socio-Technical Systems approach, where a multi-functional task force redesigns the organization, usually taking a whole year to do so. A design created in such a way tends to be flawed, because it is based on an incomplete assessment of reality. Also, workers do not have ownership of the design, and this generates resistance to change. Perhaps most significantly, the organization's underlying power structure remains intact.

Whereas STS is based on what the Emerys call the 'bureaucratic design principle', Participative Design reflects the 'democratic design principle'. This means that those who have to do the work are in the best position to design the way in which it is structured; effectiveness is greatly improved when teams take responsibility for controlling their own work and the organization increases its flexibility and responsiveness when people are capable of performing multiple functions and tasks.

The Emerys have also identified six basic conditions that need to be met if people's work is to be productive and satisfying. There must be:

- elbow room for decision making;
- opportunities for continuous on-the-job learning;
- sufficient variety;
- mutual support and respect;
- meaningfulness;
- a desirable future, not a dead end.

The Participative Design process, which often follows on from a Search Conference, consists of three stages.

1. Pre-workshop activities, which include gaining the commitment of senior management and determining the minimum critical specifications and any necessary constraints for the new organizational design; also educating the organization about the value of the Participative Design approach.

2. The Participative Design workshop. Here participants work in groups of six to proceed through the three parts of the workshop:
    - Analysis, where participants assess how their work is currently structured and notice to what extent the six work conditions are being met,
    - Design, where participants create a work flow design and organizational structure based on the democratic design principle and the six conditions,
    - Implementation planning, where participants agree measurable goals (negotiated later with management); determine training needs; agree procedures for work co-ordination and other key activities; and identify the resources that will be needed.

3. Post-workshop implementation.

The design that emerges from a Participative Design effort will only succeed if any existing command and control culture is replaced with a collaborative one where people control their own work. If the senior managers are not fully committed to making this fundamental change the effort will fail, no matter how good the design.

Open Space Technology

Primary purpose: creating a forum where issues and opportunities are surfaced, discussed and translated into action.
Developer: Harrison Owen.
Length: one, two or three days.
Group size: limited only by size of venue.

Open Space Technology is a method for organizing a self-managed gathering where participants create their own programme of work sessions linked to an explicit theme. In these simultaneous sessions people discuss their heartfelt concerns, explore issues and opportunities and find new ways forward. An Open Space gathering brings people together – often in large numbers and usually representing enormous diversity – to contribute their views, share their ideas and develop plans for creative and collaborative action.

The Open Space approach is particularly effective when there are high levels of complexity, diversity and conflict, and when urgent action is required. A prerequisite is that the focal issue or theme must be of genuine concern to all involved. The group can be of any size, from 10 people to 1,000 or more. All relevant stakeholders are invited, but participation is generally voluntary.

Open Space is based on four principles and one law:

1. Whoever comes are the right people. (Participation is voluntary and more participants do not necessarily make it better.)
2. Whenever it starts is the right time. (Be relaxed about time.)
3. Whatever happens is the only thing that could happen. (Let go of expectations.)
4. When it's over, it's over. (If there's no more to say, move on.)
5. If you find yourself in a situation where you are neither learning nor contributing, it is your responsibility to use The Law of Two Feet to go elsewhere.

The following outline illustrates what happens at an Open Space event:

- Participants gather for the opening plenary. They sit in a circle to indicate that everyone is a leader.

- The facilitator states the theme of the event, describes the Open Space principles and explains what is going to happen.

- Anyone who feels so inspired can offer one or more sessions (such as a presentation, workshop, discussion group or task force) by creating a simple poster showing the title of the session and his or her name, making a brief announcement to the whole group and choosing a time and a space for the session to take place.

- The posters are fixed to the wall and participants sign up for the sessions that they wish to attend. Much negotiating usually occurs at this point: conveners offering sessions on similar topics may decide to join forces and people may ask certain conveners to re-time their sessions to make participation possible.

- Participants then self-organize and pursue what interests them.

- The large group reconvenes at certain points and at the end of the event to share what has transpired. There is often an additional plenary session for prioritizing issues and developing action plans in project teams.

- At the end of the event everyone receives a set of reports from all of the sessions, which usually include action points.

Simu-Real

Primary purpose: providing an opportunity for the organization to learn about itself, make changes to its way of working and accomplish a major task.
Developer: Donald Klein.
Length: one day.
Group size: limited only by size of venue.

Simu-Real enables members of an organization to work together on a real organizational task so that they can see the whole organization in all its complexity, become aware of, and skilled in, dealing with organizational dynamics, and determine what, if anything, needs to be changed. The method is used to help organizations explore differences, solve complex problems, redesign work processes, agree goals and develop plans for realizing them.

The Simu-Real event takes place in a large room which, when the participants arrive, becomes a microcosm of the organization in action. The departments or other organizational units are located in different parts of the room according to their place in the actual organization. This is the 'Simu' part of Simu-Real. The 'Real' part is the task or project that the organization will undertake. The task is conceived by a planning committee, whose members are drawn from the organizational units. The committee prepares all aspects of the Simu-Real event including the room layout and the decision-making process.

The Simu-Real process consists of three action periods, each around one hour in length. During these periods the participants address the task exactly as they would if they were at work. Each action period is followed by an analysis session, lasting around 45 minutes, in which the small groups reflect on what worked during the action period and what did not work so well, and decide what they will do differently during the next action period. The findings of the small groups are shared in the large group. After the third and final analysis session the management team, or other decision-making group, meets in the centre of the room, fishbowl-style, to decide what changes need to be made in the light of the day's events. The planning committee will have already agreed the form of the decision-making process with participants prior to the event.

Principles for creating collaborative gatherings

A principle is 'a general truth forming a basis for reasoning or action' (*Concise English Dictionary*, 1984). By mastering the principles that are common to all LGI methods, you will be able to create your own methods that address the unique needs of each particular situation.

The following are principles for collaborative working:

- *The whole has greater wisdom than the sum of the parts*   Include everyone – external as well as internal stakeholders – who can contribute information, ideas and different perspectives, everyone whose support is vital to the success of the project and everyone who has the power to make things happen.

- *Everything derives from purpose and outcomes*   Plans cannot be made until purpose and outcomes are clear, so first spend time agreeing the reason for your collective existence and then decide what you want to achieve together.

- *Principles determine behaviour*   Agree your guiding principles for working together, such as being open and honest with each other, treating one another with respect and honouring commitments.

- *Be honest*   An honest assessment of current reality is a solid foundation on which to build the future. People must be completely honest, even if this means raising painful or taboo subjects. The completed picture of current reality is likely to be messy and complex.

- *Ownership and commitment emerge from an egalitarian approach*   Collaboration will only be effective if parent–child relationships are abandoned in favour of adult–adult ones.

- *People need to feel they are part of a community*   What really matters to most people is not money – it is feeling part of something bigger than themselves, something they can believe in that brings meaning to their lives.

Principles for designing collaborative gatherings

- *The most effective design is one created by a design team*   The design of collaborative gatherings is not achieved by an elite group or delegated to one or two people, but by a design team composed of people from the different stakeholder groups that will be present at the gathering.

- *Collaboration is a continuing process, not an event*   Treat the gathering as one small part of a continuing process. Put in place a temporary infra-structure to co-ordinate the efforts of any project teams that form during the gathering and ensure that these teams get support and resources from the formal organization. Think about how to involve those who will not be present at the gathering, and consider how to use internal communication and other tools to keep everything moving forward.

- *The people attending the gathering are active participants, not a passive audience*   Do everything possible to minimize dependence and passiv-ity, maximize active participation and mobilize individual and collective power. Ensure that chairs are arranged in one or more circles and small groups are self-facilitated. Exclude games, training modules and speeches.

- *People need time to connect and reflect*   Give participants time to con-nect with themselves, their fellow participants and the task, and include time for reflection.

- *Wisdom comes from an appreciation of the whole system* Invent activities that enable participants to experience the whole system in action and understand the context in which it operates.

- *Make decisions in real time, not off-line, and begin implementation immediately* Do not allow leaders to use collaborative gatherings to gather data for later behind-closed-doors decision making.

- *Engagement means engaging the whole person* Make sure that activities engage the whole person – mind, body, emotions and spirit, and involve all of the senses – sight, sound, taste, smell, touch and movement.

- *Effective gatherings require healthy conditions* Choose a venue where the main meeting rooms have plenty of daylight and ventilation, the seating is comfortable and good food is served quickly. Let participants help themselves to tea, coffee, soft drinks and fruit throughout the day.

Principles for facilitating collaborative gatherings

- *The facilitator is there to hold the space* Create a safe space where participants feel free to express themselves openly and take risks. Hold the vision and encourage the group to stay open to new possibilities and creative breakthroughs, even in the midst of chaos, conflict and breakdown.

- *Facilitation requires a participant focus* Work with what is happening rather than what you think should be happening, and be highly responsive to the needs of the whole, making any necessary adjustments to the programme right there on the spot. Assume that the group knows best what it needs at any given moment.

- *Less is more* Take a minimalist approach. Never do anything yourself that could be done by participants. Ensure that power remains with the group and do not do rescue work. Only make an intervention when absolutely necessary, preferably at the invitation of the participants.

- *There is strength in diversity* Embrace all opinions and viewpoints as part of current reality. Assume that behind all behaviour there is a positive intention. Ensure that those who express opposite points of view or behave unconventionally are not marginalized by the group.

Questions frequently asked

Training and development professionals will typically be fully involved in creating and designing collaborative gatherings. They will also have the advantage in knowing what to expect of such events. However, for managers and employees for whom such gatherings are a new experience, there will be many questions. Here are some of the most commonly posed questions and the guideline answers.

Q: Do we need to train people in things like communication skills prior to taking part in a collaborative gathering?
A: No. Collaborative gatherings give people a chance to exercise skills they already have, and learn new ones 'on the job' through experimentation and role modelling.
Q: I'm concerned about the participants' ability to self-facilitate. Is it OK to bring in a team of facilitators to lead the small groups?
A: There is often a strong temptation to do this, but unless it is firmly resisted, the result will be dependence and little will change.
Q: How can we ensure that members of the leadership team walk their talk?
A: Internal or external consultants can coach the team members before, during and after the collaborative gatherings.
Q: Can we use collaborative gatherings to train large numbers of people in the use of a strategic tool such as TQM?
A: Collaborative gatherings are a legitimate alternative to the slow and sub-optimal cascade method. But tread carefully. People can get resentful when they feel something is being done to them, and you are unlikely to generate the necessary levels of long-term ownership and commitment through any form of manipulation or indoctrination, no matter how subtle.
Q: We have an urgent need to conduct a company-wide training needs analysis and are considering the use of collaborative gatherings. Is this a good idea?
A: Yes. Collaborative gatherings usually whet people's appetite for training and development, and people will probably welcome an opportunity to create their own development plan. Training and development programmes then become strategic instruments as they are driven by immediate business needs identified by participants during the gatherings.
Q: Who else uses these sort of LGI approaches?
A: Here are just a few of the organizations that have used LGI methods to create collaborative gatherings: 3M, Boeing, Boots the Chemists, Dutch Railways, Ford Motor Company, Guinness, KPMG, Local Government Staff Commission for Northern Ireland, Marriott Hotels, Microsoft, Prudential Assurance, Severn NHS Trust, Shell, SmithKline Beecham and United Distillers and Vintners.

Further reading

Alban, B. and Bunker, B. (1997), *Large Group Interventions*, New York: Jossey-Bass.

Rehm, R. (1994) *Participative Design*, self-published booklet.

Senge, P. *et al.* (1994), *The Fifth Discipline Fieldbook*, London: Nicholas Brealey.

Part Four

IT related learning

This section of the handbook is the one that is most likely to expand in future editions. Not only is technology becoming more sophisticated and more user friendly but the latest generation of trainers and employees is one for whom computers have been an ever-present reality. Such employees have no resistance to the use of technology and will surely be intolerant of organizations and/or training functions that do not utilize the latest resource to support learning. So what are the issues of applying technology today to deliver learning in the workplace? In the following four chapters you will find, clearly outlined, what the state of the market currently is, as well as how it is likely to continue to change.

As you would expect there is an underlying enthusiasm in all the contributions for organizations and trainers to harness technology. Perspectives on training and development are changing fast and these authors give us an insight into the issues and opportunities that the profession has to face.

Chapter 29

Web-based training

Colin Steed

Organizations everywhere are looking for a business edge and many have come to recognize that the only competitiveness left is in the service they provide.

That service depends on having people who are continuously upgrading their skills. Knowing how to do today's job is not enough. In today's rapidly changing, global service-oriented business environment, continuous training will become mandatory for organizations that plan to remain competitive, successful and in business. Such continuous training and retraining is needed to support new products and job skills, to develop technical and non-technical education, to build management skills and to enhance customer service. But how do you provide such training cost effectively?

This chapter will highlight the opportunities that Web-based training offers. It will start by providing a brief overview of the Internet and the World Wide Web before looking at the case for Internet training. The chapter will then move onto the issue of whether businesses are ready to use Web-based training and what the specific benefits and drawbacks are for those who adopt this approach.

The Internet and the World Wide Web

The Internet and the World Wide Web have captured the interest and imagination of educators around the world. The phenomenal popularity of the Internet and the rapid adoption of Internet technologies to implement corporate intranets and extranets has created a tremendous opportunity to provide learning materials and services in a convenient, easy-to-use and engaging manner. But before we proceed further let us be clear as to exactly what the Internet and the World Wide Web are.

The Internet is neither a company, a software system, nor a service. It is not owned by anyone. It is simply a generic name given to a global network of computer networks and it enables information to be passed around even when one network or group of networks is out of action. While the majority of users use the Internet for e-mail, its popularity really exploded with the introduction of the World Wide Web. The Web represents an unstructured network of millions of computer sites and uses a facility called hypertext which allows the reader to click their mouse on a highlighted phrase or reference which then takes them to another Web site with information on that subject – a kind of online referencing system. The beauty of the system is that the user does not need to know either where the site is located or what the file is called.

To access the Web, you need a client computer. It must be connected to the Internet and have loaded on the desktop computer a piece of software called a Web browser. This is a standard piece of software – available for all computer platforms – which can display the documents and perform the hypertext links. The most popular Web browsers today are Netscape Navigator and Microsoft Internet Explorer. This software can be downloaded from the Internet and is generally available free.

To deliver content on the Web you need a server computer, where the actual text, graphics, audio, and video is stored. It has requirements similar to those of the client computer: it must be connected to the Internet and must be able to run a Web server program. Note that you can also set up your own server to run a Web site over your local area network without connecting to the Internet. This is what we call an intranet – more on this later.

Why use the Internet for training?

When you use the Internet as a new addition to your training delivery options, one of the first questions that you will probably ask yourself is: 'Is it worth it?' Thomas FoxMcManus, from the University of Texas at Austin, suggests that the Internet has two overriding advantages over all of the other media:

1. The Internet combines advantages of other media so that it conveys video and sound better than a book, is more interactive than an audio or videotape and, unlike CD-ROM, it can link people from around the world more cost-effectively.

2. The Internet is also a vast resource of information. It is, arguably, the largest and most diverse source of information in the world today. It is possible to incorporate the wealth of information available on the Internet in courses. For instance, if you are designing a course on Renaissance art history, you can include links to the Vatican Library and the Louvre, as well as to the Art History exhibit at the Australian National University, and so on.

But to make the real case for using the Internet/Web in education, we should begin by assessing its present impact and potential contribution. In this respect we need to ask three questions:

1. Does it make learning more accessible?
2. Does it promote improved learning?
3. Does it accomplish both of the above points while containing, if not reducing, the cost of training?

Let us look at these in turn.

Making learning more accessible

Each of us probably has a different interpretation of what 'access to learning' means, although most will agree that it means making education more attainable by more people – providing learning opportunities in the workplace, home, college or school. The Web is made for education. Its accessibility is one of its main assets.

Some of the world's best universities and higher education colleges are providing opportunities to students who are unable to attend campus. Until recently, they relied on correspondence, traditional print instruction materials and perhaps audio or video tapes. That is all starting to change now as educators capitalize on using Web-based technology.

The Open University, based in Milton Keynes in the UK, is a prime example of a dedicated distance education institution that uses the Web to support its mission of providing accessible education. In 1994 it experimented with offering an advanced psychology course using the Web. The course was so successful that the following year it offered two computer science courses via the Web, and they now intend to continue to expand their list of offerings. City University, in Bellevue, Washington, USA, is another dedicated distance learning institution. It operates with the mission of 'making education available to all who desire it without interrupting commitments to work and home'. Recently, it established its Education Resource and Online Academic Degree System to take advantage of Web-based technology. At present it provides online an MBA degree programme and a Bachelor of Science in Computer Systems. Through the university's Web site, students around the world apply to the university, register for courses, and complete course work electronically. They can also send questions and assignments to their tutors and participate in specialized live forums.

An example of traditional institutions using the Web as the backbone of their distance learning efforts is the University of Massachusetts Dartmouth Division of Computing Education in the USA. Its Web-based CyberEd full-credit undergraduate and graduate courses make full use of the Web complete with images, sound and video, to present material, test, communicate among students and faculty, and submit assignments. Its goal is to 'create a distance learning environment that rivals the traditional classroom environment in the quality and content of the learning experience ... to encourage a new educational paradigm in which the instructor is no longer regarded as the sole source of all knowledge'. Reports by participants and visitors posted at its Web site suggest CyberEd is well on its way to achieving its goal.

As the list of accredited colleges and universities extending their access to their programmes to students with the Web grows, a new kind of institution – the virtual university – is emerging to challenge the established ones by providing universal access to online degree courses. While not accredited, these 'virtual' institutions are blazing the trail in what will no doubt become the common way to study in the near future.

Promoting improved learning

As we have seen, there is plenty of evidence that the Web is a valuable means to increase accessibility to learning. Evidence on how it can promote improved learning, however, is not so forthcoming. According to Ron Owston's research paper on the subject (*The Teaching Web: A Guide to the World Wide Web for all Teachers*) there is an ongoing debate in the instructional design literature about whether there are any unique attributes of any media that can promote improved learning. This debate stems from the observation that, after more than 50 years of research on instructional media, no consistent significant effects from any medium on learning have been demonstrated. Some researchers argue that no effect can possibly be demonstrated because any improvement in learning that may accrue will come from the instructional design, not the medium that delivers the instruction.

So we cannot simply ask 'Do students learn better with the Web as compared to traditional classroom instruction?' Owston argues that we have to realize that no medium is likely to improve learning in a significant way when it is used to deliver instruction. But he argues that there are at least three distinct learning advantages to Web use.

1. *The Web appeals to students' learning mode* Today's students do not know a world without the computer. It is an integral part of their world and they tend to be more visual learners than previous generations because their world is rich in visual stimuli. Try this simple experiment. Explain in simple terms what the Internet is to your child. Then test them on their comprehension of the concept. Next, show them a simple diagram or video on the subject. You should find that their comprehension following the second method is much better. Now add interactivity into the equation

– and you will find that this is by far the most interesting method for them – they simply enjoy visualizing and interacting, and therefore will find learning much more enjoyable and hence will learn better.

2. *The Web provides for flexible learning*   We saw previously that accessibility provided by the Web is an effective vehicle to help students gain an education without being on campus. A growing number of institutions now want to provide their regular, full-time students with greater flexibility in accessing their courses as well. When you browse through courses listed today, you will discover many courses where faculties have dramatically reduced the amount of face-to-face contact between instructor and student. Instead, they provide Web-based study projects and online activities that students can access at their own convenience.

    Interaction where participants contribute to forums at different times, is called asynchronous communication. The Web provides facilities to permit synchronous communication that allows participants to carry out live conversations and discussions. Additionally, live video can be used to create a learning environment that simulates a live classroom because students can both see and hear each other. This virtual classroom allows students to take part in the class from any Internet connection in the world. The technology to do this is still in its infancy but rapid progress is currently being made in its development.

3. *The Web enables new kinds of learning*   Business leaders are now calling upon our schools, colleges and universities to graduate a different kind of student than a generation ago. Among the skills called for are critical thinking, problem solving, written communication, and the ability to work collaboratively. Owston stresses that, in the hands of able teachers, the Web can play a prominent role in fostering the development of the skills required. Teachers can encourage students to explore the Web with the goal of having them weigh evidence, judge authenticity of data, compare different viewpoints on issues, analyse and synthesize diverse sources of information, and construct their own understanding of the topic or issue at hand. By so doing, they will be well on their way to helping students develop critical thinking and problem-solving skills.

    Students can also develop written communication skills using the Web. The theory is that when students have a real audience to write to – with a real purpose in writing to them – they will become more conscious of their vocabulary, syntax and grammar. Online work provides this authenticity. E-mail, electronic reply forms and Internet newsgroup readers are part of most Web browsing tools, so students do not have to leave the Web to carry out online writing. Teachers who design projects or assignments that incorporate this feature of the Web provide their students with an ideal opportunity to develop their writing skills.

Finally, teachers can also foster development of collaborative skills on the Web. Structuring group projects where group members are in different geographical locations, yet have a common goal to reach or problem to solve, typically does this.

Containing the costs of education

Now that we have seen that the Web can promote greater access to education and improved learning we need to consider the cost of doing it. Research has revealed that the Web can actually lead to decreased per capita costs for training.

The McDonald's Corporation in the US is one organization that has cut its training costs by almost a fifth and expects this to be reduced further once the company's intranet infrastructure is established allowing training to be made available to more people.

Meanwhile in the education sector, the UK Government's initiative to help the UK's 32 000 schools access the Internet for little cost provides another example of what the future holds in store.

So a strong case for using the Web in education and training exists in all of the three main areas discussed. Now let us look at our businesses. Are they ready to use the Internet and the Web for staff training and development?

Corporate intranets

Business has been quick to pick up on the opportunities afforded by the Internet and most are now using its various facilities. There is a similar interest and growth in intranet use. An intranet is a restricted and secure Internet, where companies can use technology popularized by the Internet – such as e-mail, Web pages, browsers and servers – to create internal closed networks accessible only to the company's employees. In effect, an intranet is an internal Internet. It may be defined as 'An internal Web site which the company employs to disseminate information and services throughout the enterprise'.

These services can include e-mail messaging, staff training, staff notices, corporate information, telephone directories, ordering supplies, personnel information, staff records, health and safety messages, company procedures, staff announcements ... and so on. The costs are offset on printing and paper expenses and by the company not having to buy and keep up-to-date many different versions of applications to suit different computer platforms.

Many intranet users suggest that some of the drawbacks associated with using the Internet do not apply to an intranet. Issues such as speed, reliability and security may be issues of concern on the Internet but not with an intranet. Furthermore the applications development on an intranet should be easier than in traditional programming environments because Web applications currently rely on two relatively simple standards – Web browsers and Hypertext Markup Language (HTML). Being based on platform-independent standards, Web sites should be relatively easy to maintain.

It is this rapid take-up of corporate intranets which will facilitate the expected explosion in Web-based training in the near future. Corporate intranets, extranets and the Internet form a rich infrastructure for the realization of a comprehensive learning environment, where individuals have access to:

- interactive self-paced instruction
- skills assessment
- instructor-led training information and registration
- reference materials
- online communication with subject matter experts, instructors and colleagues
- individualized learning management systems.

With such an online learning environment, individuals can develop customized learning plans and navigate through available learning resources without worrying about where and how those resources are provided. Learners can also access their training plans and learning resources at any time and anywhere. As learning resources are updated and added to, they become immediately available to all authorized learners.

Benefits and drawbacks of Web-based training

There is no doubt that the best environment to learn anything is in the classroom. But the reality is that the classroom environment is expensive both in terms of money and time, and tutors inevitably find it difficult to teach at a pace that suits every individual on the course. Self-paced, self-study materials are an alternative but the down-side of using such materials is that they rely on the individual being highly motivated, with the required self-discipline to complete the task.

Proponents of Web-based training (WBT) suggest that this new medium combines the best of the classroom with the best of the self-paced self-study methods.

Let us then look at some of the main benefits and some obvious drawbacks of Web-based training. The majority of them are, of course, applicable to any self-study training – although some are applicable to WBT programmes only. We shall look at the various benefits and drawbacks from two different viewpoints: as a user and manager of WBT, and as a company or department providing WBT to its users.

Benefits for the WBT user/manager

1. *Reduced training costs per head*   The cost of using an interactive WBT programme is significantly less than traditional classroom training. While it is expensive to develop interactive programmes, delivery cost per course is significantly lower per trainee – typically by 20–25 per cent. Additionally, travel, accommodation or subsistence costs can be eliminated.

2. *Learning gains*   Studies have shown that interactive versions of training programmes increase the learner's understanding of the course material by as much as 56 per cent over classroom versions. WBT combines the best of self-paced, self-study training with the best of classroom training in that a course tutor is available and interaction with other course participants is encouraged.

3. *Consistency of presentation*   Course material is presented in exactly the same way to the same standard every time. The training manager can ensure that everyone in the company uses the same material – something which is virtually impossible with CD-ROMs or CBT.

4. *Constantly up-to-date material*   Because course material can be instantly updated on the Web server with any curricula changes (no matter how large or small) the most up-to-date courseware can be used. The new material will also be available to market much quicker.

5. *Timeliness of information delivery*   Take the case where a test is taken in the classroom. Students typically receive the results back in the next class. Using WBT, test results can be delivered back to the student within seconds of completion, providing instant feedback. This scenario can also be used for pre- and post-course assessments to measure the student's readiness for the course or its effectiveness.

6. *Faster completion of training*   One of the primary benefits of self-paced learning is that it allows the learner to control their learning experience. They can work at a pace that suits them best, as well as bypassing training that is not relevant. Because the programmes are self-paced, they are likely to be completed earlier than a single-paced classroom course. Studies have shown savings of between 30–70 per cent in training time.

7. *Content retention*   Because of the interactive nature of the presentation, combining multimedia (text, graphics, audio, and video) in an interactive environment enables the development of courses that simulate real-life scenarios and provide immediate feedback. Learners retain more of the course material than with classroom versions of courses – studies have shown a 25–50 per cent higher retention factor.

8. *Better utilization of instructors*   If you are like most organizations, your best instructors are used most often to conduct the training. With WBT those people can be used for what they are best at – training in the classroom.

9. *Affordable technology*   Unlike most new technological innovations, WBT will not require any new significant expenditure on new hardware or software. Most people have access to a desktop (or laptop) computer, a modem, and access to a telephone line. All that would be needed is Web browser software (generally free over the Internet) and a dial-up account with an Internet Service Provider like UUNET Pipex, Planet Online, U-Net, CompuServe, or AOL. Additionally, different computer platforms can access the same course materials.

10. *Control over course management*   You may limit or extend training opportunities to any small or large groups of students. Security codes and passwords allow absolute control by the training manager over who takes what course. Additionally, billing ID, number of course accesses, and test results can be monitored and controlled by the training manager. The course tutor can also track students' progress, determining how fast/slow the student is progressing through the material or whether the student is having problems with a particular segment.

11. *Training more accessible*   The Internet has opened up a whole new field of training opportunities for anyone who wants to learn. No longer do they have to wait for an available course place. Now they can take a course whenever, and wherever, it suits them.

Drawbacks for the WBT user/manager

1. *New software and procedures*   Students will need to become familiar with Web browser software and using the Internet.

2. *Bandwidth/browser limitations*   Limitations in bandwidth (how much data can be squeezed down the line) may restrict instructional methodologies as slower performance for sound, animated graphics and video play back can sometimes be painfully slow.

Benefits for the WBT provider

1. *Training development costs reduced*   The Internet has introduced a common set of industry standards for developing applications. These include course authoring tools like IBTAuthor, Asymetrix Toolbook, IconAuthor Net Edition, Java and Hypertext Markup Language (HTML) to build the training course on, knowing that it will run on any computer and on any platform (Windows, Macintosh, Unix). With traditional CBT, it is necessary to develop a different version of a course for every computer platform being targeted.

2. *Easy and affordable distribution*   Courses are installed on one computer (the Web server) which students around the world can access through their Web browser. This provides instant distribution to an unlimited number of students – with the advantage of absolutely no packaging, duplication or distribution costs to be incurred by the course producer.

3. *Up-to-date content*   With the course residing on one central Web server, courses can be updated instantly and so provide students with a completely up-to-date course.

4. *No run-time licences*   Courses published can be delivered without cumbersome run-time licences.

Drawbacks for the WBT provider

1. *Bandwidth/browser limitations*   Limitations in bandwidth may restrict instructional methodologies as slower performance for sound, animated graphics and video play back can be slow.

Hardware/software requirements

In order to access Web-based training, you will need certain hardware, software and network connections.

First, you will need a Pentium (or 486) or Macintosh computer with a minimum of 16Mb RAM. It will probably need a soundcard and a good graphics card. Any computer platform is suitable. You will also need a fast modem (at least 28.8 bps but preferably 56.6 bps) and a good printer, capable of printing graphics.

Second, you will need an Internet connection through an Internet Service Provider (like UUNET Pipex, U-Net, Planet Online, AOL, CompuServe).

Your computer will also need certain software loaded and configured, much of which is available free of charge from the Internet. The software supplied by your Internet Service Provider connects you to the Internet. This includes your connection software, plus programs for e-mail, Telnet and FTP.

Finally, you will need a Web browser program. There are literally dozens of Web browsers available for every platform and operating system. The two most popular Web browsers by far are Netscape Navigator and Microsoft Internet Explorer. Web browser programs are basically configured to display text files and images but you will need to download 'extensions' for each browser that you have loaded if you want to display audio and video files.

Conclusion

As with all new technology innovations, WBT offers great promise, but comes complete with its own set of challenges. With major advances in the field occurring monthly, it will not be long before it begins to make a major impact in the distribution of training and education. There is no doubt that network-delivered training, whether it is transmitted over the local area network (LAN), wide area network (WAN), Internet or corporate intranet, is a solution that many companies are going to adopt with increasing frequency. With the abundance of free Web browsers available we now have a platform-independent delivery system which just adds to the lure of the Web for training and development. In the US, the independent Web-based Training Information Center carried out a survey of attitudes of WBT in corporate America which revealed that although less than 20 per cent of companies in the US currently use WBT, more than 70 per cent plan to incorporate it during the next 12 months. Businesses in the UK are sure to follow.

Further reading

The AST IT Barometer Survey 1997, Published by AST Computer. *www.ast.co.uk*
The Durlacher Quarterly Internet Report, Published by Durlacher. *www.durlacher.com*
The Intranet Question: Lifeline or Lead Weight? Spikes Cavell & Co. *www.spikes-cavell.com*
Web Based Training Information Center. www.webbasedtraining.com
Becker, S. *Distance Learning: The Instructional Strategy for the 90s*, Washington. *www.cdc.gov/phtn/primer.htm*
Chute, A., Thompson, P. and Starin, H. *It's time to change the way we train.* *www.lucent.com/cedl/faculty .html*

McManus, T. *Delivering Instruction on the World Wide Web*. University of Texas. *ccwf.cc.utexas.edu/~mcmanus/wbi.html*

Owston, R. *The Teaching Web: A Guide to the World Wide Web for all Teachers*. York University, California. *www.edu.yorku.ca/~rowston/home.html*

Townsend, M. *Internet Directions NETg. www.netg.com*

Chapter 30

Multimedia and CBT

Bob Little

People have always wanted to communicate. Cave paintings, cuneiform, hieroglyphs, papyrus, parchment, paper, the printing press, telegraph, telephone, wireless, television, computers and, now, the Internet are all means to that end.

However, while we now have more information available to us than ever before, the pressures of work today mean that there is less time to assimilate, assess and act on that information. This, in turn, puts pressure on technology to communicate that information more quickly, more efficiently and, hopefully, at lower cost.

It is against this background that business communicators have turned to computer based training (CBT) in all its forms (including multimedia based training) to answer these needs – especially in the field of education and training. The last few years have seen the inventive combination of audio, video, text, animation and graphics in an attempt to motivate learners and make the resulting multimedia programs' training messages more interesting and memorable.

However, there is no benefit in using CBT as a communications medium simply 'because it is there'. Business, and training management in particular, is attracted to multimedia technology to help it communicate for two main reasons:

1. To present a standard message to a widely dispersed audience relatively cheaply.
2. To preserve a unique or rare piece of information or skill (for example, where the people possessing that information or skill could not devote their whole lives to running training sessions).

Development of CBT

The development of CBT was ushered in alongside desktop computers towards the end of the 1970s. The early applications for desktop computers may have typically focused on holding and manipulating large amounts of information but it soon became apparent that they could also be used to interact with people to enhance learning. When this was recognized CBT was born.

Not surprisingly the earliest attempts at CBT, although well intentioned, tended to be dull and were little more than electronic books. Furthermore they were a lot less portable and cost a great deal more than their printed counterparts. Consequently, CBT was not popular. However, as technology improved so CBT developers became more creative and daring, adding graphics and even a few animations to their programs and eventually, in the early 1990s, the technology existed to play text, graphics, animations, audio and video combined in one program.

Programs which contained these elements became known as multimedia programs. Initially, this material was accessed through exceptionally large hard drives (and, often, additional hard drives linked to the computer) but, soon, developers put their programs onto CD-ROMs. In the quest to be more readily practical and attractive to the business community, CBT is constantly evolving. Currently, the main strands of CBT are:

- CBT on mainframe: typically text-heavy on a 'green screen'. This was the first manifestation of the genre and made its first appearance some 20 years ago. This approach was later refined to include context-sensitive 'help' for the terminal operator. Although many people prefer to 'buy the book' (read hard copy in the traditional manner) rather than read text on a screen, many large companies around the world – notably in the finance sector – still use this type of CBT.

- CBT on floppy disk (for use on stand-alone or networked PCs). Although this has an 'electronic book' image, there are a number of courses that use graphics to entertain the user and enhance the learning experience.

- Multimedia based courseware: typically on CD-ROM.

- Interactive video: contained on laser disk and requiring a laser disk player as well as a PC in order to run the course. This approach has largely been superseded by CD-ROM based materials.

- CD-I (compact disk interactive): beloved by a few – notably some NHS Trusts – but not a 'mainstream' technology.

- Networked courseware: either via a local area network (LAN), wide area network (WAN), via a server or, increasingly these days, via the Internet or corporate intranet. Here there are problems with 'bandwidth' – basically because audio and video files are very large and take a relatively long time to download.

● Virtual reality: seen by some as the 'anoraks' approach to CBT. The two main types of virtual reality (VR) are immersive (use of headsets) and desktop. Where CBT is concerned, desktop VR is the predominant approach. It is especially useful in training people in 'disaster scenarios' where, for example, you can simulate an oil refinery explosion or fire without the risks or the costs attached.

Issues for users and buyers

There are, of course, no problem-free solutions and there are a number of potential issues that training managers and users of CBT need to consider.

Platform

Most CBT developers produce material for the PC rather than the Apple Macintosh computer because more people use PCs than use Macs – especially for training and education purposes. However, even within the PC-based technology world, there are a number of delivery platforms available – for example, stand-alone (with material produced on floppy disk or CD-ROM for example), mainframe and some sort of network (including the Internet and corporate intranets).

If you are considering buying a generic program for a large audience, conventionally the main reason for developing CBT programs in the first place, do you want a program which can be played, for example, on a 386 PC or a Pentium 166? Should the machine have a two-speed or a 32-speed CD-ROM? Or should you develop a program for DVD – the 'super CD-ROM' which can contain a lot more information?

If you opt for the lower specification product, you widen your potential audience, but you drastically reduce the speed at which your program will run (and so risk boring the users). It also means that you may have a product which is not as creative as those that run on higher specification machines.

Price

Multimedia programs on CD-ROM which are aimed at the 'home' market sell for, typically, £30 to £50. Those programs aimed at the corporate market sell for around £800 to £1200 although prices have been falling rapidly. Bespoke multimedia programs, typically, cost even more (in a range starting from, say, £20 000). Organizations can only justify spending that sort of money if they have a relatively large number of learners/trainees needing to undertake the program.

Bandwidth

Basically, however fast they are, computers find it hard to deal with the large amount of information contained in audio and video files. Consequently, multimedia programs can take quite a time to download and play – especially if they are being delivered via the Internet. This can be frustrating and is particularly unhelpful if you want the program to inspire and motivate the users.

To overcome this problem, CBT developers have taken to splitting up their courses into 'chunks' or separate, smaller courses; 'streaming' data, and/or reducing the audio/video content of courses.

Alternatively, they opt for 'hybrid delivery', where large files – such as those containing audio and video – and information which will not change is sent to the learners on CD-ROM. The learners load these files onto their PC from the CD-ROM and augment and update this information with further data (in small file sizes) accessed relatively quickly from the Internet. Unlike file-based technology, 'streaming' does not mean that the software program and files must be downloaded every time the application is accessed. By design, all course data is stored on the server, not on the client computer (the student's PC), thus reducing download time and drag on the network. Also, while file-based applications store information on the client computer – thereby depriving central administrators of the ability to successfully manage access to the most current version(s) of the course – streaming provides no such problems.

Computer literacy of users

Training managers and multimedia program buyers probably do not need to be reminded that there are still a great many people in the working population who are not highly computer literate. Stories of people believing that their CD drives are coffee cup holders are not unheard of. The advice here if you want a successful take-up of your latest purchase is, therefore, to ensure that the product comes with the simplest possible instruction and requires little IT knowledge from users.

Compatibility

Not all multimedia programs will run on a given PC without that PC having to be re-configured. This is time consuming and may prove to be beyond the skills of many users – or even open learning centre administrators. It is as well to take impartial advice about the programs before buying them, if at all possible.

When should you use CBT?

Organizations will typically opt for CBT when they face conditions in which 'traditional' types of training are either too expensive or too lengthy or both. It is important to remember that the technology serves the training need.

CBT often has advantages over traditional classroom-based training in the following contexts:

● When you need to train a large number of people.

● When you need to train a widely dispersed workforce.

● When you need to promote a standard message (human trainers will, inevitably, put their own 'spin' on any training course and impose their own personality on the training messages of the course. By contrast, a piece of courseware gives the same message to each user).

● To reduce the costs of training a large number of people. CBT may be expensive to buy but, for example, a CD-ROM costs very little to produce and very little to distribute. Compare this with the travel and subsistence costs involved in bringing large numbers of people to regional locations for meetings or training sessions and you can see why it can look like an attractive proposition.

● To benefit employers and employees. CBT programs can be used out of working hours (to the benefit of employers) and do not have to involve trips away from home (to the benefit of the employees).

CBT can also be used to complement traditional classroom based training. One typical example might be when a large number of geographically dispersed people need to have a certain amount/level of knowledge (for example, product knowledge or behavioural/management theory) before going on to practise related skills (for example, sales techniques or recruitment and selection skills). Here, the CBT can be used to good effect as pre-course study material and, in certain circumstances, can also be used for post-course testing leaving the practical skills – to be taught in classroom/role play sessions. It can also be used extremely effectively in providing people with a 'taster' for a course or event. This marketing application is especially useful when managers want to attract reticent learners onto courses.

How do you find the right CBT courseware?

There are two basic types of CBT: generic (often costly) and bespoke (even more costly). There are also hybrid options. For example, a number of producers such as Xebec and Easy-i will 'customize' their generic products for the customer (for example, adding company-specific sections/logos to generic courseware).

It can be difficult to find objective advice on what courseware is available and whether it is right for your organization's needs. In the UK you can get help from preview centres/re-sellers, such as Flex Training, or from 'multimedia systems integrators', such as CC Information Systems and MultiMedia Training Ltd, the multimedia arm of the MarCom Group.

Can you make your own CBT?

Although this is possible, it is not as easy as some people make it sound. To produce courseware you will need to become proficient in at least one of the main CBT authoring tools: Macromedia's Authorware and Director; Asymetrix's Toolbook and IconAuthor; Pathlore Software's Phoenix family of products; Allen's Quest and Designer's Edge or, alternatively C, C++, Visual Basic and even the ageing TenCORE.

To produce a worthwhile courseware needs the skills of a top class trainer (to structure the program and decide on the teaching points), combined with a top class designer (to make the screens attractive and motivating to the user) and a top class programmer (to make the courseware work). However, it is unlikely that any one person will possess all these skills and only the largest and wealthiest companies will have employees with this combination of skills.

With rapid technological changes can you safeguard your investment in CBT?

Some companies have invested heavily in CBT in the past only to find that their investment has been left behind by the advances of technology. Understandably these companies will be reluctant to invest in CBT again unless someone can give them a guarantee that their investment will be future-proofed.

Consequently, some CBT companies are developing 'migrating tools' and architectures which allow any piece of CBT, written in any authoring language, to be played on any technology – from mainframe to corporate intranet. For example, Pathlore Software's Distance Learning Environment (DLE), based around the Phoenix authoring tool and Macromedia's Pathware 3 – Attain Enterprise Learning System, allows CBT to be 'migrated' to different delivery technologies and helps safeguard companies' investment in CBT.

As this becomes widespread organizations should have nothing to fear from investing in CBT.

Promoting CBT usage

Many organizations seem to fight shy of using multimedia despite the benefits it offers. To address this the company, and the training department in particular, has to tackle some of the fears and doubts people have about the technology. These include the following issues:

- The introduction of CBT will not mean the end of in-house 'stand up' trainers. Trainers might, however, need to have explained to them how the technology can complement the service they provide.
- Users need to be shown and must understand that self-paced learning is effective; that is, managers must persuade users that what they can learn via CBT is just as applicable to the workplace as any classroom-based learning.
- The same issue applies to managers who have to believe in the value of CBT for their teams – not just in terms of its applicability but also as a more convenient and cost-effective method to train employees.
- Those who are purchasing the programs have to have confidence in the technology and be prepared to invest in machines that have multimedia capabilities and in the courseware that will meet staff development needs.
- If staff are not computer literate then managers will need to run introductory programs to help users gain basic skills and explore how multimedia works. In this way they will also be fostering a learning culture.

CBT on the Web

As the Internet and the World Wide Web (the Internet's collection of hypertext linked documents, accessed via a browser) has grown in power, capability and importance, CBT developers have turned their attention to producing courseware which can run via the Internet and corporate intranets. CBT producers, such as Maxim Training, Xebec Multi Media and Pathlore Software have now launched programs designed specifically to run on the Internet and corporate intranets. These products make use of technology which keeps file sizes small and so helps to overcome 'bandwidth problems'.

Up to now, however, Internet standards, which are based on HTML, currently tend to produce CBT reminiscent of the unfashionable 'electronic page turning' variety. This does not allow for student feedback or analysis of student responses, does not enable administrators to keep track of students' progress, nor does it provide a database on information concerning a student's training history. Furthermore, large courses are difficult to maintain when they are HTML-based. Unlike streaming technology, current HTML standards cannot support computer-managed instruction, security, record keeping, or the course management functions that are integral to CBT authoring and delivery products. However, authoring tool producers, such as Macromedia, are launching products – for example, Macromedia's Dreamweaver Attain and Authorware 5 Attain – which are visual HTML authoring tools developed specifically for authoring Web-based learning.

Nonetheless, training managers and would-be CBT authors may feel that with all these difficulties and challenges the time is not yet right for delivering CBT via the Internet (that is, Web-based training). Yet there are advantages – in cost, administration and ease of use terms – of using this method of training delivery.

Using the Internet to distribute CBT also eliminates the cost of distributing proprietary software and publishing material on CD-ROMs – unless, that is, the producer opts for 'hybrid delivery'.

When delivering training materials via the Internet, the buyer only has to purchase the course once, and carry out each update once, and can be sure that any learner logging on to the course has the latest version of that course to study. Managers cannot be so certain that all learners are using the most up-to-date versions of their courses when these courses are contained on distributed CD-ROMs.

Conclusion

There is no doubt that there are many issues which training and development managers who are buying multimedia need to address. Perhaps the greatest of these, however, is their own concerns about the technology itself. Nonetheless the technology is sound and users have shown that they enjoy learning through multimedia based programs. The generations to come will be increasingly used to and adept with technology and will be expecting organizations to deliver, if not all, then at least a significant portion of their professional development through CBT.

Some explanations and definitions

The Internet

A sprawling collection of computer networks that spans the globe, connecting government, military, educational and commercial institutions, as well as private citizens to a wide range of computer services, resources, and information. A set of network conventions and common tools are employed to give the appearance of a single large network, even though the computers that are linked together use many different hardware and software platforms. The Internet comprises two main strands – the World Wide Web and e-mail.

To date, it is estimated that there are some seven million 'hosts' on the Net. The Net is accessible to anyone who has a computer, a modem, freely available software and a service provider.

An intranet

A contained collection of computers and networks within an organization (it may span the globe), connecting the organization's members and/or employees to a range of computer services, resources, and information. A set of network conventions and common tools are employed to give the appearance of a single large network, even though the computers that are linked together use many different hardware and software platforms.

Before embarking on creating and installing an intranet, it is important to have the answers to several crucial questions. For example, is the intranet for purely internal use? Will it serve multiple sites? Will it be deployed across multiple platforms, such as mainframes, Unix, VAX and NT? Does it need to give access to third parties? All these – and more – points will determine the structure for the particular intranet.

An extranet

An extranet, or extended Internet, is a private business network of several co-operating organizations located outside the corporate firewall. An extranet service uses existing Internet interactive infrastructure, including standard servers, e-mail clients and Web browsers. This makes an extranet far more economical than the creation and maintenance of a proprietary network. It enables trading partners, suppliers and customers with common interests to form a tight business relationship and a strong communication bond. It is worth noting that the extranet concept is at the heart of the effort required to advance a traditional corporation into the state of the 'knowledge factory'.

Where can I find out more about CBT?

UK organizations offering non-product specific advice and guidance:

- The Association for Computer Based Training, c/o Ann Lambert, PO Box 71, Radlett, Herts WD7 8ZH. Tel: 01923 853432.
- Brian Tucker, The Forum for Technology in Training, Orchard Chambers, 4 Rocky Lane, Heswall, Wirral, Merseyside L60 0BY. Tel: 0151 342 8606.
- FI TRAINING, Kernel House, Killingbeck Drive, Killingbeck, Leeds LS14 6UF.

UK organizations offering advice and guidance on hardware and/or courseware:

- Vaughan Waller, CC Information Systems, Broadfields House, Broadfields, Headstone Lane, Harrow HA2 6NZ.
- David Willetts, Flex Training, 9–15 Hitchin Street, Baldock, Herts, SG7 6AL.
- Trudy Hayes, MultiMedia Training Ltd, 1 Heathlands, Heath Gardens, Twickenham, Middx TW1 4BP.

Selected producers of CBT authoring tools:

- Allen Communications, 250 Gunnersbury Avenue, Chiswick, London W4 5QB.
- Asymetrix Learning Systems Inc., 225 Marsh Wall, Docklands, London E14 9FW.
- CBT Systems, 5 Heathrow Boulevard, 2/8 Bath Road, West Drayton, Middx UB7 0DQ.
- Macromedia Europe, Pyramid House, Easthampstead Road, Bracknell, Berks RG12 1NS.
- Pathlore Software, 5 The Waterhouse, Waterhouse Street, Hemel Hempstead, Herts HP1 1ES.

Selected CBT courseware producers:

- Easy-I, 42 The Square, Kenilworth, Warwickshire, CV8 1EB.
- Maxim Training, 42 Bond Street, Brighton, East Sussex BN1 1RD.
- Quick Guides, Willow House, Chestnut Lane, Cainscross, Stroud, Glos GL5 3EW.
- Video Arts/Melrose, Dumbarton House, 68 Oxford Street, London, W1N 6LA.

- Xebec Multimedia Solutions, Wellington House, Bath Road, Woodchester, Stroud, Glos GL5 5EY.

Further reading

Anderson, C. and Velkov, M. (1990), *Creating Interactive Multimedia*, London: Computer Books.

Burger, J. (1992), *The Multimedia Bible*, Wokingham: Addison-Wesley.

Chatterton, P. (1993), *Does Your Company Need Multimedia?* London: Financial Times Pitman.

Crainer, S. (1995), *The Complete Computer Trainer*, Maidenhead: McGraw-Hill.

Feeney, M. and Day, S. (1991), *Multimedia Information*, Oxford: Butterworth.

Tucker, R. (1989), *Interactive Media: The Human Issues*, London: Kogan Page.

Tucker, B. (1997), Handbook of Technology Based Training, Aldershot: Gower.

TACT Tile, the newsletter of TACT.

Chapter 31

Games and simulations: a place where opposites meet

Chris Elgood

This chapter takes a look at the different approaches brought to the arena of management games and simulations. It then focuses specifically on computer based games and simulations considering the issue of reality, the approaches made possible through technological development and the specific learning objectives that managers need to consider when using such simulations.

Defining the territory

This has always been an impossible subject area to define – one reason being that it is used by people from quite different backgrounds to describe quite different materials. The social scientists bring one set of ideas to the party, the numbers men bring something quite different. The result may be innovative and enjoyable, but it can also be confusing. Let us take a brief look at the two different approaches.

Material from the field of social science

The exercise known as 'The Prisoner's Dilemma' or as 'Red-Blue' is common currency in training and development departments. Participants are organized into two groups and each group is invited to choose between the strategies known as RED and BLUE. Nothing is known about these strategies except the score which will result from the decisions. If both groups decide on RED then they will get three points each. If they both decide on BLUE then they will lose three points each. If one decides on RED and the other on BLUE then the one choosing BLUE will gain six points and the one choosing RED will lose six points. The groups must talk to each other about their plans and then, separate from the other group, decide what they will actually do. The 'actual' choice is revealed to a facilitator and through him to the other group. It is usual to play several rounds. The normal outcome is that groups agree with each other to choose RED (three points each) but then at some stage during the exercise either one group or the other (or both) decide to double-cross their partners by promising to play RED and then going for BLUE. This exercise, frequently described as a game, more comfortably belongs in the area of psychology and social science because it is investigating behaviour. It can also be viewed as a serious simulation of the tensions arising between separate groups and of the forces that create co-operation and competition.

Material from the field of business economics

At the other extreme is the computer-controlled business simulation in which participants are given a description of an imaginary company and are asked to make quantitative decisions about specific subjects like 'Price to be charged for the product or service'. Values are set for a number of these 'decision variables' and entered into a computer program. The rules built into the program mean that a 'result' can be calculated and displayed on the screen or printed out. The most common form of output is a profit/loss account, showing how well the imaginary company has done. Devices of this sort tend to be generated by economists, or accountants or computer specialists. The title simulation is often used because they have a very clear intention of offering something that is 'similar' to the operation of real-life commercial management. But since they are often played competitively between teams, the word 'game' is common.

A unifying theme

These activities therefore associate people of several different backgrounds. They also bring people whose objectives are wholly serious into an area where 'game' is a natural term and the words associated with games, such as 'non-serious', 'relaxation' and 'fun', are legitimate. There is, consequently, frequent debate about nomenclature. The terms 'game', and 'simulation' and 'exercise' and 'event' and 'experience' and 'activity' are all heard, and people argue about the merits and demerits of enjoyment, competition and application.

A clear unifying theme is the desire to offer participants the chance to learn by experience rather than by academic precept. All the devices have rules of some sort, and since these rules are prepared by people with learning objectives it follows that something we might call an 'instruction substitute' is built in. The design is such that if somebody participates intelligently and enthusiastically then he will learn something, just as if he had been told it in the classroom. If that is so, then what do games and simulations offer that is different from conventional instruction or additional to it?

1.   It is felt that the dynamic nature of the experience places a heavier emphasis on the decision making and encourages participants to consider the issues more seriously. It makes the outcome matter more. The experience of success or failure in the simulated (and perhaps competitive) environment seems to have more significance than the passing comment of a tutor.

2.   Although the consequence of each decision is influenced (among other things) by a learning design, it 'feels' rather more objective than does tutorial comment. Possibly this is due to awareness that the game rules have been carefully thought through and have been reached through hard work and expertise.

3.   Many games and simulations are run in a sequence of consecutive 'rounds' so that participants can learn from each experience and apply that learning to a subsequent situation. The cyclic design also means that long-term features can be accommodated, such as a poor decision in Round One having consequences that are not apparent, say, till Round Four.

4.   It is common for games and simulations to be undertaken by small teams. This introduces a social element to the learning process which often increases commitment and causes the learning achieved to be evaluated more highly.

5.   Games and simulations frequently cover a broad spread of subject areas, the diversity being such that in standard educational practice they would be taught as separate subjects. Games and simulations often have an integrative purpose, showing participants 'How things fit together'.

Business simulations

The rest of this chapter will specifically focus on computer based games and simulations. The central feature of all these is a set of rules – called a 'model' – which attributes a consequence to every allowed input. The idea can be illustrated at the simplest level by thinking of a 'game' which allows the participant to set the selling price for a product at £10 or £11 or £12 or £13 or £14 and, if any of these prices was entered, tells the participant: 'You have won orders for X units of your product'.

Suppose the rules were that a price of £10 won orders for 1000 units and to raise it to £11 meant losing five sales. An input of £11 would then give 95 as the output. If the loss of sales attributed to each step increased regularly by five then £12 would give 85 sales, £13 would give 70 sales and £14 would give 50 sales. This would constitute the model. Participants might be asked to determine the price at which sales revenue was greatest. After five experiments they would have:

$$
\begin{array}{rcrcr}
100 & \times & £10 & = & £1000 \\
95 & \times & £11 & = & £1045 \\
85 & \times & £12 & = & £1020 \\
70 & \times & £13 & = & £\ 910 \\
50 & \times & £14 & = & £\ 700 \\
\end{array}
$$

Participants would know that if the rules in the model were correct then revenue would maximize at a price of £11. Nobody needs a computer to do that! However, the example is meaningful because in one sense this is all a computer ever does. It performs no operations that are different in nature from those a human being can carry out. It just does them at a fantastic speed and with complete accuracy.

A sophisticated business simulation has extensive rules built into it which attribute major or minor consequences to any decision variable, or any combination of variables, and can make these effects come into play at any moment in time. This capability can be seen very clearly if one considers a planning activity in which various things may or may not take place on time. A human being will soon get into difficulties with problems like: 'Suppose the window frames have not arrived by day 18 but the door frames have. How long will I then be held up, assuming I have got the red paint available but not the blue?' The human mind will not be able to cope unaided and the written records will soon become confusing. The computer, however, will get it right every time. If you have programmed certain rules into it, it will apply those rules correctly and inform you of the consequences. Sometimes the results will make you realize that you have not got the rules right: you will not have envisaged all the situations that might arise nor have provided logical consequences for them.

Realism and complexity

One of the criteria by which business simulations are sometimes assessed is that of 'realism'. To what extent is participation really like running a business? This is a convenient peg for discussion because it has a bearing on the usefulness of simulations in training and development.

There is sometimes a tendency to equate realism with high value, and this can be damaging. The current type of simulation originated in business schools where there were quite precise theories about how markets behaved. When theoretical belief was allied to current expert opinion it was thought possible to build a model that gave 'right' answers. So great attention was paid to accuracy, to including all the relevant variables, and to realism. There were certainly limitations, but often these related to the speed and expense and availability of computer technology.

As the technology developed it then became possible to build more and more complex models and the older models attracted comments like: 'It is not very realistic because it does not include this feature and that feature. It does not, for instance, include realistic inflation levels or allow the student to make discounted cash flow calculations'. This search for reality became quite tyrannical and was aided by the fact that business simulations benefit from the novelty factor. Even today, they are far less used than conventional instructional methods and the student who is told: 'Tomorrow we are going to play a business game' is motivated by the expectation of something new.

Training staff too are likely to welcome new features, and when their use of computers allies them with computer people – always keen to demonstrate new capabilities – the novelty factor is powerful. So there is an abundance of business simulations that are very real (in one sense), very complicated and full of exciting technological features. The end result, however, can be that a participant ends the playing experience in total confusion, having failed to isolate any single, clear, cause-effect relationship because the variables were so many.

Such a person has, of course, learnt little. The truth is that complex simulations are sometimes used without fully answering the question: 'What is our purpose in using this device? What are our learning objectives? Is this device an effective and economic way to pursue them?' It is possible to spend a day working on a complex business simulation and learn no more than can be derived from the old accountants' adage – turnover is vanity, profit is sanity.

It is also worth remembering that when players are asked years later what benefit they gained from such a simulation, the most common answer is: 'I learnt something valuable about the skills of working with others in a team'. The clever economic and business relationships built into the model are less frequently mentioned.

Sensible use of technology is highly beneficial

Despite these caveats however, there is still much to be gained from the massive technical developments that have taken place in business simulations. Many new possibilities now exist for those people who value this approach to learning.

Playing in real time

A computer program can maintain a minute-by-minute profile of a market, and the behaviour of the teams in it. While early simulations worked in discrete time periods and only allowed decisions at the end of each simulated month or year, a real time model can say 'A month in real life is a month in the game and you can log on whenever you like. On the 11th day, for instance, you will see your share of the market on that very day, with up-to-date financial results. You can also change your decisions on that day (11th) and you can change them again on the 12th if you like! When you enter a decision, I shall instantly evaluate it, and if it is a better decision than your last one then I will increase your market share and diminish those of the other teams – until they enter a new decision, of course'.

Visual representation

Facilities like a production line can be visibly shown on a screen, and parts of it moved around with a mouse. If a player believes that production will be more economic if he or she places two machines beside each other rather than in line, then he or she can do it, and the program can instantly credit him or her with the increased efficiency (or the reverse) that the model decrees. The same thing could be done with an advertisement, or the location of different types of merchandise in a supermarket.

Face to face negotiation

By using a videoconferencing link, direct negotiations can be conducted with real game participants (competitors) or with role-players acting as suppliers or trade union officials. Physical distance is no barrier, and if the game postulates a supplier in Taiwan then the organizers can alert a contact there to appear on screen.

Dissimilar playing organizations

Until recently, business simulations were set up so that all playing teams operated identical companies. Their fortunes diverged during the game, of course, but at the start they were imagined as all the same in the nature of their activity and their physical/financial state. There are models today in which the teams operate different types of organization and do not necessarily compete with each other. One may be a supplier to another. One may be a manufacturer, one a transport company, one a retailer and one a financial services company. They compete only in the sense that they all want to prosper and to produce a reasonable return on assets. The model is one of economic activity in general, not of a particular market.

Playing on the Internet

The advantage here is the public nature of the medium, the fact that anybody with an e-mail address can take part. Some of the ideas previously discussed are otherwise only appropriate for a company with a substantial IT network. Given sufficient investment by a sponsor, use of the Internet removes that difficulty.

Virtual reality

No business simulation that employs virtual reality is yet in common use, but there is no technological reason why putting on the helmet should not give entry to a boardroom situation in which arguments are presented, events encountered, decisions taken and results viewed. Such things are coming!

There is, then, a wide range of business simulations. It extends from those so simple that they hardly need a computer to those that are so complex that no player will possibly achieve full understanding of how the model behaves. The question then is whether this variety can be matched with learning objectives.

Learning objectives

There are a number of learning objectives that managers who are looking at business simulations will typically need to consider. These include the following:

Awareness

Sometimes the objective may be to make participants aware of issues without, in the short term, expecting detailed understanding. The message is: 'The real world contains all these features and more. To cope with it at the highest level you are going to have to grapple with them'. Participants are encouraged to evaluate what they need to do and to prepare themselves mentally. It is an 'eye-opening' experience. The awareness issue is also significant in terms of technology. Participants may, through a complex simulation, encounter capabilities of information technology of which they were previously ignorant. Having used them once, they may be more inclined to treat them as valuable tools instead of arcane wizardry. The highly complex modern devices are useful in respect of these objectives. They are also useful in business education at the highest level.

Teambuilding

Complex simulations may also be suitable for teambuilding, but more care has to be taken with the level of participant, for constant failure is demotivating. If a team is asked to tackle a simulation in which they feel totally lost, then it will be a demotivating experience and no teambuilding benefit will result. The same effect will arise, though for different reasons, if they are asked to use a simulation that is too easy. The principle involved is the motivational one of 'optimum challenge': people are not motivated by something that appears to be too easy or too difficult, but by something which induces the response: 'We might just succeed with this thing if we tried hard'.

Understanding particular issues

Sometimes a simulation is chosen because an authority (perhaps the managing director) has said, "I want them to understand the meaning and implications of XYZ'. The letters XYZ might stand for almost anything, but a useful example might be 'cash flow, credit control and investment'. Now a really complex simulation will include any feature that might be mentioned, but there are two reasons not to run one. The first of these is that because such a wide range of features are included it may not be possible to single out a desired feature for special attention. The second is the administrative problem of time. Complex simulations take longer to run and the time may not be justifiable when compared with other solutions.

One good solution is to find a simulation which does cover cash flow, credit control and investment without including too many unwanted features. That is to say, one that is selective almost in the manner that a cartoon fastens upon certain characteristics of the subject, exaggerates them, and leaves out many other details. Such things are definitely not realistic in the sense of portraying the whole subject fairly, but they succeed in facilitating the study of desired features. Suitable material exists, and can be located (Elgood, 1997).

Integration

This is possibly the most common use of simulations – to increase understanding of how different functions within a business interact. This possibly reflects the fact that instruction on the major functional areas – such as production, marketing and finance – is still carried out by functional experts and no teacher is specifically charged with combining them.

Simulations are especially useful when they confront players with disconcerting experiences. One example might be winning a high level of orders and then finding that there are insufficient goods to fill them – production having been fixed at the most economic level, which is significantly lower than the demand won. Another example might be insolvency following swiftly upon a successful expansion because credit control had been weak, customers had not paid their debts, and the company was unable to meet the costs associated with increased purchases and increased stock. A simulation provides an environment in which participants can make mistakes and learn from them without paying a real-world penalty.

Conclusion

An examination of the subject of business simulations leads to the conclusion that choosing the right product and using it in an appropriate way is critical to success. It helps to remember that in this field called 'learning by experience' what is in fact experienced by the participant is not the game or simulation as a stand-alone product but the situation created by whoever decides to use it and the manner in which he or she handles it. Different people can use the same device but create radically different experiences for those taking part.

Management games and simulations will always be 'special events' rather than the dominant method in management education – for the understandable reason that they occupy a great deal of time. As a means of 'transmitting' information the lecture is still the most effective means, because it can be proved that the right words were uttered. This cannot be proved in the same way with games and simulations because the knowledge is embedded in the experience and left to speak for itself rather than explicitly stated. However, those listening to a lecture may not have received and understood what was spoken, and may have failed to take in the knowledge. The users of management games and simulations believe that more internalizing takes place through the use of their material, but it is hard to prove and they admit they take up a lot of time in the endeavour.

The test for those who choose business simulations is for them to be able to explain why they have chosen the method, why they have chosen a particular device, and what benefits they expect to follow.

Further reading

Belbin, M. (1981), *Management Teams, Why They Succeed or Fail*, London: Heinemann.

Elgood, C. (1997), *Handbook of Management Games and Simulations*, Aldershot: Gower.

Fripp, J. W. (1993), *Learning through Simulations*, Maidenhead: McGraw-Hill.

Horn, R. and Cleaves, A. (1980), *The Guide to Simulation Games for Education and Training*, London: Sage.

Kolb, D. (1984), *Experiential Learning*, Englewood Cliffs: Prentice Hall.

Rodwell, J. (1994), *Participative Training Skills*, Aldershot: Gower.

Watson, J. (1981), *Computer Simulations in Business*, Chichester: John Wiley.

Chapter 32

Technology supported learning

David Birchall and Matty Smith

As we move inextricably into what has been described as the 'information age', the role of training and development is increasingly central to organizations. However, alongside the greater demands for training and development there is also the issue of how it can be delivered more cost-effectively and how technology can help in this respect.

In this chapter we will look first at the impact of technology on organization, the pressures for change and the opportunities offered by technology. We will then look in some detail at how learning takes place and how technology can support learning. Our focus will be on why there is the need to build interactivity into the learning experience and how the designers of technology based delivery can achieve this.

Changing times: the challenge of technology

The rapid development and deployment of information and communication technologies (ICT) at a time when the marketplace for goods and services and labour becomes more global is leading to a major rethink within organizations. This rethinking of how best to structure organizations is leading many businesses to radically change their ways of working. Cost pressures are leading some companies to introduce more flexible work patterns and contracts of employment. Others are introducing 'virtualization' as they attempt to deploy their dispersed resources more effectively and get closer to the customer. In addition to this, now that technology can free work from the constraints of time and place, people are questioning the time spent in commuting and business travel which is unproductive for both the individual and the company.

Some of the consequences of such restructuring are apparent in the way organizations are becoming more dependent on partnerships and alliances to meet customer expectations. The pressure is also visible in the current interest in knowledge management as organizations look at how technology can help them capture and make knowledge accessible to those that need it.

As a consequence of this heavy demand for new and updated knowledge and competence, organizations are seeking cost-effective methods of training and development that not only provide just-in-time training but also, and possibly more importantly, compress the time required to acquire these new and updated skills.

Given the considerable investment being made in ICT by organizations as they integrate their staff into their own worldwide business networks, it is not surprising that they are also looking for more effective ways of deploying that technological infrastructure so as to develop the competencies of staff.

However, while there is clearly an increasing business imperative for training and development, there is also an expectation on the part of staff that they will receive good quality development opportunities plus the possibility of training and development utilizing technology in new and exciting ways. The rapid development of multimedia technologies, particularly in the computer games and entertainment fields, has direct spin-offs here. The enhanced graphics capabilities and virtual reality offer new and exciting opportunities for training and development.

However, the introduction of technology into the learning process raises some significant challenges to established practice.

First, there are questions about the educational benefit of interactivity with tutors and fellow learners as compared to computer based learning. Alongside this issue are also concerns about how technology can effectively support a variety of learning objectives and approaches. Furthermore there are questions about the extent to which organizations want to adopt learner-centred approaches rather than focusing on prescriptive approaches to achieve tightly defined organizational objectives.

The debate about lifelong learning raises issues about the integration of personal learning and competency development. But at the organizational level the greater concern may be about how the organization can be held together within the global context. Can technology be used to support the global enterprise including effective dispersed operations? Can the management of knowledge be tied into personal and organizational learning and, if so, what investment in technology is needed to support this?

Perhaps the greatest challenges facing those involved in managing training and development across the dispersed organizational network is how to deploy technology effectively to ensure a competent workforce is capable of meeting the ongoing challenges facing the business.

Learning approaches and IT support

Not only has technology evolved significantly over the past two decades, but our understanding of the ways in which learning takes place has also developed. Initial work on learning focused on observable changes to behaviour as evidence of learning having taken place. The changes were brought about through the presentation of stimuli that elicited a desired response. This behaviourist approach to learning was seen to be transferable to the use of technology and there has been a proliferation of computer based training (CBT) programmes developed as a result. These break down learning objectives into small incremental steps, provide drill and practice procedures and finally include a testing mechanism to establish that the required outcomes have been achieved. This instructionist approach in CBT is seen as appropriate to specific skills training programmes where routines, processes and procedures have to be learnt and where basic skills such as numeracy have to be developed.

Learning theorists, however, have also taken great interest in what occurs in the learner between stimulus and response, i.e. what cognitive processes take place and how they might be enhanced or made more effective. The ways in which the learner can be encouraged to move information from short-term to long-term memory and the mechanisms for stimulating the recall of existing knowledge in order to 'encode' new information is seen as central to the cognitivist approach to learning. Computer assisted instruction (CAI) and computer assisted learning (CAL) are directed at supporting such an approach by encouraging the transfer of new information into long-term memory.

Cognitivist and behaviourist approaches take a view of learning as being something that an instructor presents to the learner and hence the instructionist model. However, there is increasing recognition of the significance of the role of the learner themselves in building their own knowledge and understanding. Motivation, individual learning styles, prior knowledge, experience of knowledge sharing and peer group learning and the learning context are just a few of the many variables that the learner brings *to* the learning situation. This view of learning, referred to as constructivism, is especially relevant to adult learners and to 'everyday' learning as it occurs outside the more formal or structured learning environments of the classroom or lecture hall. It can also be seen as supportive of the acquisition of effective working practices.

Central to the constructivist approach to learning is the shift in emphasis from a teacher-centred to a learner-centred focus. The 'empowerment' of individuals can be seen to be taking place in all spheres of life, especially in the business sector where flattened management structures require the sharing of knowledge more widely to inform decision making. App roaches based on constructivism may fit well with new organizational forms. As our knowledge and understanding of the learning process has increased, so the potential for reaching learners outside the more traditional academic approaches has also developed. Generally, adult learners are now assumed to learn most effectively when:

- Use is made of 'authentic' learning tasks seen as meaningful by the learner.
- Use is made of discovery learning methods where the learner constructs his or her own understanding, rather than instruction by the teacher or computer package.
- There is an emphasis on learning how to learn and solve problems rather than learning facts.
- There is support for collaborative learning and problem-solving.

The social context in which learning takes place and the value obtained from learning within a group is also recognized as an important element of the learning process and particularly important for adult learners. Group learning occurs when members of a group share information with each other with the objective of supporting each other towards the completion of a shared goal. In collaborative learning the group learning process is moved one step further in that group members not only share information with each other but actually take responsibility for each other's learning. Computer based GroupWare products, such as LotusNotes, can be specifically tailored to support this type of learning, irrespective of whether the group is able to meet face to face or not. Indeed, the 'store-and-forward' feature (asynchronosity) of these applications, because they give users freedom of choice in time and place, is especially attractive to both distributed learning providers and to work based project teamwork between globally dispersed team members. In addition, video conferencing and application sharing through enhanced video links can eliminate the barriers of time and location.

While the technology available to learning and training providers can address many aspects of the learner's needs, the role of the 'instructor' remains central to the success of the learning process. However, in developing the more complex learning environments designed to support both collaborative and individual learning, the role of the instructor becomes that of facilitator. For many trainers, not only is the medium for delivery changing with the increasing use of a wide range of technologies, but their role within the process is also changing. As we have seen in relation to learner-centred learning and collaborative learning, the focus is on the learner. Learners are no longer seen as empty vessels to be filled up with the knowledge and understanding passed to them from the teacher. Their learning route is one of both personal development and of constructing their own knowledge and understanding.

Beyond interactivity

We have seen that an approach based on the behaviourist theory of learning seems to be suited to the acquisition of certain specific skills and might provide a cost-effective solution in some instances. However, an understanding of the processes of learning is likely to lead to a sounder basis for instructional design.

Computer based training programmes based on this learning theory normally offer self-contained learning opportunities and learning materials would normally be designed to provide 'interactivity' within the package itself. Such interactivity may take the form of self-administered tests of comprehension with routings through the programme determined by the answers given. By this means the learner will be directed through a personalized instructional route as the machine responds to the level of knowledge shown by the learner at any point in time. The pace at which the learner progresses will be carefully controlled by the machine and be determined by the level of learner mastery of the subject matter at each step. The technology platform can contain a wide variety of media including simulations to make the learning process stimulating, realistic and rewarding. Encouragement to progress through the programme results from the satisfaction gained at progressing through each stage. However, organizations, if they are to become knowledge intensive and self-regenerating, need their employees to acquire a deeper level of understanding in areas which may not lend themselves to instruction via computer based training even where it has internal interactivity built in.

The process of organizational reinvention is dependent upon constant questioning of assumptions underpinning current operations and strategies. This is a process that needs to take place at all levels within the organization and requires learning that is much more demanding of individuals as well as of the system that supports the learning process. Learners must be given the opportunity to test new ideas and concepts in an organizational context, develop an understanding of what is possible, set personal targets for development and change, and carry out regular and fundamental reviews of progress. This is a process that requires 'rich' communication in a questioning environment. Such communication is not currently possible within computer based training programmes but rather depends upon human interaction.

Yet technology does have a place here. Developments have made it possible to conduct our communications across barriers of time and space. For example, video conferencing, and to some lesser degree, telephone conferencing can make debate possible as can electronic means such as Internet and electronic 'GroupWare' such as LotusNotes. These technologies, however, cannot fully compensate for a face to face meeting. Each of these technologies reduces the set of modalities available to learners and tutors to communicate with each other. For example, auditory, visual, non-verbal and para-verbal is missing to some degree when any technology is deployed and the extent of loss will depend upon the nature of the communications possible with that particular technology. In using any technology for communication the nature of the interaction is changed and therefore the overall quality of interaction is affected.

The media vary particularly in the extent to which the transmission of values, interests, personal commitments and other similar features, known as media richness, is possible. For example, the use of electronic communication in an asynchronous mode is well suited to an exchange of information such as questions and answers but is less well suited to a discussion aimed at, say, resolving personal conflict.

Asynchronous communication removes spontaneity and is inappropriate if used in a traditional way. That said, electronic communications can enhance the learning experience when direct contact and face to face interaction is impractical and in this way it can improve the quality of that learning experience compared to that which would otherwise be possible. And with careful design, exciting new and different types of experience using the combined potential of media and technologies are possible which may well accelerate the learning process, compensating for some of the loss associated with modality reduction.

The effective facilitation of this process is, however, critical to the success of deep level learning and the need to provide such facilitation in an 'online' environment is especially demanding. The nurturing of 'online' discussions, the encouragement of peer support and query, closure and summary of key learning points and the development of an awareness of the learning activity as a process in its own right are all now part of the facilitator's role. For many trainers and tutors this means not only re-skilling in terms of the technology but also retraining in terms of the ways in which they can most effectively support learning.

Designed to meet learning needs

While there are many learning programmes being developed in specific technology formats there is much value to be gained from an integration of the various technologies. Presenting information through a range of different media, to support a variety of learning styles, to cope with cultural and other differences amongst the learning group, and to suit a multiplicity of learning objectives can result in a more effective learning experience. However, the choices are such that the courseware designer can be overwhelmed. Balancing cost considerations, accessibility issues, media application and selection and pedagogic design is a complex process requiring high level skills. Trade-offs invariably have to be made between initial investment in training materials and ongoing costs in learner support during their use. To be successful in engaging learners in the process where the only form of interactivity is within the programme itself, the quality of the learning resource has to be much higher than where tutor or trainer intervention is planned. The flexibility and responsiveness of the trainer will always far exceed the capability of the technology-based solution. And more importantly the tutor can bring an infinite number of approaches to challenge the learner's understanding. The costs of this intensive activity can, however, be reduced where the learner gets support from a learning group and where the tutor is communicating with the group rather than with each individual – a solution made possible with GroupWare technology.

Other considerations at the design stage include accessibility for the learner, the acceptability of the technology to the target group, the learning curve for mastery of the technology, the costs of servicing the system (tutor, administration and technical support), the overall management of the service and the limits to growth in the support system.

In approaching the overall design of the learning environment value for money will also be a major concern. The initial costs of creating computer based resource materials can be estimated with some certainty. Their likely effectiveness is much more difficult to predict. Often in considering the support of learners using technology the costs of the infrastructure are fairly easily established but this represents just a small fraction of the total costs of establishing a support system. The specific design of the learner support system needs careful attention to detail, but much of the cost is in getting the system working effectively including the training and development of tutors and trainers in the techniques of online facilitation. Technology can also be deployed to support the learning organization. Many large organizations are exploring the concept of the corporate virtual university to take advantage of their technology infrastructure to deliver training and development on a just-in-time basis by bringing together staff into a learning community. By sharing perspectives and expertise learning can be built around problem solving and change management. Such universities offer different ways for users to engage with the information they need in order to develop understanding of issues and concepts. This gives learners options to suit their particular learning need at the point in time. Such options may include self-contained CBT material with or without tutor support, a networked learning community with access to the Web for technical information to support the learning process, but high levels of electronic tutor facilitation or structured learning events with periods of self-study using computer based resources with occasional face to face tutoring. The possibilities are endless as technology develops and in many ways its use seems to be limited only by our imagination.

Conclusion

As organizations seek to meet the challenges of the information society, they will seek to match their own training and development needs with the opportunities they have access to, at a cost which provides good value for money. This proposition would appear to be sound and difficult to refute. However, we have tried to demonstrate that technology is opening up more choices for course providers and that this is increasing the complexity of decision making. Returning to first principles, it is clearly necessary to start from the vision and aims. Too much hype is attached to the potential of technology without enough consideration being given to basic design considerations. The starting point for design must surely be the learner's needs and an understanding of the learning process. While some topics lend themselves to computer based training in its various forms, interactivity, if restricted to that which is afforded within the package itself, is unlikely to provide for the deep learning required for much of the development needs of organizations.

The costs of face to face interactivity are high and limit the possibilities of just-in-time learning. So alternatives will have to be deployed for many situations. If medical surgery can be undertaken with the specialist located thousands of miles from the patient it does not seem beyond the bounds of possibility that learners can also be tutored remotely; and they can. However, it is at a cost – and that is the loss of modality and with it media richness. By using GroupWare technology, including products available on the Web, groups can interact within a learning community and these developments open up new and challenging possibilities for the learner.

Further reading

Brookfield, S. (1986), *Understanding and Facilitating Adult Learning: A Comprehensive Analysis of Principles and Effective Practices*, Milton Keynes: OU Press.

Draper, S. (1994), 'Constructivism, Other Theories of the Teaching and Learning Process, and Their Relationships', Discussion paper: Heriot Watt University.

Harasim, L., Hiltz, S.R., Teles, L. and Turoff, M. (1995), 'Networks for Higher Education, Training, and Informal Learning: Exemplars and Experiences', Chapter 3 in *Learning Networks*, Boston, MA: The MIT Press.

Kaye, A. (ed) (1991), *Collaborative Learning through Computer Conferencing: The Najaden Papers*, Berlin: Springer-Verlag.

Knowles, M. (1988), *The Adult Learner. A Neglected Species*, Houston, Texas: Gulf Publishing Company.

Laurillard, D. (1993), *Rethinking University Education*, London: Routledge.
Mason, R. and Kaye, A. (eds) (1989), *Mindweave: Communication, Computers and Distance Education*, Oxford: Pergamon Press.

Part Five

Evaluation – a constant theme for training and development

In this final section of the handbook you will find chapters that have a common theme relating to evaluation. Just because they are situated at the end of this handbook, however, does not mean that evaluation issues only need to be considered once training and development interventions have taken place. All the authors here make the point that evaluation is critical to the planning stage, in setting standards, as well as having a focus on outcomes.

The last chapter is, however, meant as an endpiece for this handbook. In it Eddie Obeng highlights where education is today as well as illustrating why it has to change. His 'New World' perspective challenges trainers and educators to face up to the fundamental transformation that is going on in business and to embrace the opportunities of the virtual world into which we are heading.

Chapter 33

Evaluating training and development

Peter Bramley

My intention is to make this chapter both practical and theoretical; to offer readers advice on how to carry out evaluations and why to carry them out in the way described. The chapter includes many of the things that I have learned over years of evaluating training and development activities. Experience gained from carrying out evaluations has sharpened my sense of what is practical and what is not; talking to others and reading about their work has broadened my understanding of the theoretical base. However, my central belief has not changed – it is that evaluations should be useful and actually used.

What about your views on evaluation? What sort of process do you think it is? Does it include asking the participants how interesting and challenging the programme is? Or perhaps collecting views on how effective it is? Then again, maybe it is about making a decision on whether the training event has met its objectives, estimating whether the benefits are worth the investment or finding out the extent to which the identified needs have been met? Could it be that it is all of these things?

My guess is that some of you will say 'all of these', but although this may be desirable it is seldom practical. Carrying out an evaluation takes time and if the time is to be well used, it is necessary to focus the evaluation on a purpose. The first stage then, should be to make some decisions about why you want the information and how you are going to use it. That should tell you what you need to collect.

Some way of grouping types of information into categories can help. A framework which many have found useful is that proposed by Kirkpatrick (1959). Four levels are described:

- *Reaction:* assessing what the delegates thought of a particular training or developmental event.
- *Learning:* measuring the learning of principles, facts, skills and attitudes.

- *Behaviour transfer:* measuring changes in aspects of job performance.
- *Results:* assessing changes in criteria of organizational effectiveness.

Some have criticized this framework on theoretical grounds (mainly that the categories are not discrete) but it has stood the test of time, which is always a good estimate of practicality. I have discussed evaluation at the 'results' level at some length in other places (Bramley, 1986a; 1986b; 1998) but it is rather outside the scope of a handbook on training and I do not propose to review this area here. Instead I have used the other three levels to structure this chapter. At each level, I have listed possible purposes for evaluation and thus the information which needs to be collected to meet those purposes. This will provide a practical framework which can be used to plan evaluations.

Reactions

The reactions of participants to a training or developmental event fall into two main categories: whether they liked it and whether they think they can use some of it. These opinions can be gathered during or after the activity and can be used to meet a number of evaluative purposes.

To improve the quality of the programme

Reactions are valuable for this purpose, particularly during and after the first two or three times the programme is offered. The perceptions of those attending the activity, on how well it was run and the extent to which it met their expectations, will often add information to the opinions of the tutors and organizers. Experience shows that, after the first few times, little new information is gathered. Further collection of reactions, if these are to be used to improve the quality of the programme, is only necessary for new activities or when the target population changes.

What information is needed here? Ratings of each of the sessions can focus on interest, pace, difficulty and usefulness. Such ratings are often collected at the end of the programme, but are much more useful if collected during it. Changes in timing and emphasis can then be introduced to improve the quality of the event.

The information can be collected by using simple questionnaires that ask for opinions on, say, the way the session was and how it could be improved or short interviews which can ask participants a range of questions such as what they hoped to get out of the programme, whether it is meeting expectations and what has proved most useful.

To make sure that they enjoy it

The 'happiness sheet' has had a bad press because it has often been the only form of evaluation used. When it is the only form of evaluation, the implication is that it will, on its own, serve a number of evaluative purposes. However, this is untenable as we know that this kind of reaction measure is not suitable for predicting the amount of learning on the programme or the likelihood of behaviour change at work as a result of attending the programme. The research (e.g. Alliger *et al.*, 1997) shows that good reactions do not predict the amount of learning any better than poor reactions nor are they any better at predicting the amount of behaviour change after the programme. Should we then dispense with these assessments? I think not. While it is true that good reactions do not predict very much, bad reactions to specific events can result in poor opinions of the general training provision.

There are many ways in which one can assess whether the participants liked the programme. The most common method is the use of questionnaires with questions such as:

- How interesting, stimulating, challenging etc. the sessions were.
- The suitability of the style, the methods and the pace 'for helping me to learn'.
- The best three things and the worst three things.
- The quality of the staff and the teaching accommodation.
- The residential accommodation, the food, the housekeeping.
- The extent to which they have achieved their objectives in attending.
- Whether they would 'recommend the programme to others doing my kind of job'.

It is also possible to hold review sessions (on how things are going, whether people are getting what they want, whether there are any administrative problems) and these may be more useful than end-of-course questionnaires as they allow the possibility of doing something positive while the programme is still running.

To focus on the utility of what is being learned

Opinions about how useful the learning is do, to some extent, predict the amount of learning and the amount of behaviour change after learning (Alliger *et al.*, 1997). Perhaps what we think is useful correlates with what we actually use. It is also possible that utility reactions are influenced by the participants' perceptions of the workplace and the constraints in it for the application of new ideas and ways of doing things. As the intention of most forms of training is to help people to increase their effectiveness in the workplace, a focus on utility during the learning activities should help.

One way of achieving such a focus is to ask the delegates, at the end of each day, to write down two or three things, out of what has been discussed (or learned) during the day, that they think will be particularly useful at work. Some sharing of this with the tutors and with other delegates gives a good feel for how the programme is going. Even better, delegates can use these daily notes to produce an action plan for what they intend to do when returning to work. Such action plans are a powerful method of focusing on utility and they also help the transfer of learning into behaviour changes.

In summary, the assessment of positive and negative reactions can serve a number of evaluative purposes. Opinions on enjoyment may predict very little but trying to gain positive reactions is a sound political strategy. Opinions on utility can predict gains in the amount of learning and, to some extent the amount of behaviour change. However, there are better ways of measuring learning gains and much better ways of assessing behaviour changes.

Learning

The assessment of the amount of learning during a programme can provide useful evaluative information. The gain in knowledge or skills made by the participants is an estimate of the efficiency of the learning situations. The level which they have reached at the end of the programme may well predict whether they have the necessary ability to do a particular task. Again, it is necessary to decide the purpose before planning the gathering of information. It has also long been necessary to demonstrate knowledge and skill to obtain a professional qualification or an educational one like an MBA. However, quite a number of activities, particularly management development ones, are run without any explicit attempt to discover what the participants are learning. I find this unsatisfactory, as the evidence from a wide range of learning situations is that participation does not equal learning.

The purposes in evaluating learning are as follows.

To improve the quality of the programme

The basic information needed here is the average amount learned during the programme. To assess this, one needs the starting level of each participant and the level achieved at the end of the programme. Those who have very little knowledge or skill at the beginning of the programme will have more to learn than those who have some pre-knowledge so the actual gain made will differ.

To estimate the efficiency of the programme as a set of learning situations, the gain ratio should be calculated from the following formula:

$$\text{Gain ratio} = \frac{\text{post-test} - \text{pre-test}}{\text{possible} - \text{pre-test}} \times 100 \text{ per cent}$$

Thus the actual gain of each participant (post- pre-test scores) is calculated as a proportion of how much there was to learn from the programme (possible score – pre-test). The average gain ratio across the group is a measure of the efficiency of the programme; an efficient programme should have an average of higher than 70 per cent. Where the figure is lower, it is often worthwhile splitting the group into two – those who had virtually no pre-knowledge and those who had some, and then recalculating the gain ratios. This often reveals that the programme is efficient for one group but not the other and thus implies that the target population should be split and the programme run at different speeds for the two groups.

The principle of using gain ratios is sound. However, the use of gain ratios is only practical when what is being learned is readily measurable. Where this is not the case, some estimate has to be made on the basis of situations which show when the delegates are thinking differently, or tackling problems differently.

End-of-course tests can also provide useful evaluative material as they reveal areas where the understanding of the participants is good and not so good. If one takes the view that the customer is always right, this means that some of the programme is not reaching some of them. This information can be used to review the structure or pace of particular parts of the programme. However, on their own, end-of-course tests do not provide sufficient information to assess the efficiency of the programme unless the participants can be assumed to have no previous experience in the area. Those who have some experience may well score high on end-of-course tests without attending the programme.

Check that they have learned enough to do the job

The basic information needed to do this is a thorough task analysis of the job requirements. This should enable the tutors to construct simulations of job tasks which capture the key elements. If the tasks simulated actually represent the key result areas of the job, then satisfactory performance on them will show that the trainee has the necessary ability. Research shows us that performance on key tasks predicts ability to succeed at a higher level. The identification of the key tasks or areas of competence will involve extensive discussion with those who are said to be doing the job well and their managers. A useful approach for this is to carry out critical incident interviews of when things went particularly well or badly and then analyse the content of the interviews for key aspects.

The quality of the analysis is important as there will be various levels within the tasks. At the basic level, individual pieces of knowledge or skill are needed; at a higher level, these are combined into procedures; in the job it is likely that each situation will need some analysis to discover which procedure seems most likely to be appropriate. Teaching people to follow procedures will not prepare them for selecting which procedure to use. The participants will need to practise this in a variety of situations.

It is relatively simple to set up performance tests of technical skills where the trainee makes most of the decisions about what to do and how to do it. With interpersonal skills of the type needed by supervisors and managers, it is not so easy. Role-plays in workshops will help, but the work situation is likely to be rather different in a number of crucial areas. Good practice may involve role-plays off-job and then attempts to use the new methods on-job, followed by discussions off-job about how it went.

To predict the future use of learning as behaviour change

Assessment of learning during or at the end of training is often used to predict future use of the knowledge or skills. However, care is necessary as, in many situations, learning is not a good predictor.

Where basic skills have been over learned so that they become automatic, the result is a high level of positive transfer. For instance, in the early stages of learning to drive a motor car, gear changing is a procedure which requires much thought and attention. Transfer of the skill from one lesson to another, a week later, is usually poor. However, after a number of driving lessons the movements involved in gear changing have been practised so many times that they do not need any attention, they have become automatic and a largely unconscious part of carrying out the task.

More commonly, time in training is short and learning is not a good predictor of what people will do after training. The research shows that performance tests are slightly better predictors than written tests but that neither can be relied upon.

The problem is that performance is not just a function of ability. The literature on performance management shows us that:

Performance = (some function of) Ability × Motivation × Opportunity

Measuring the ability to do something is not the same as measuring performance. When people are not allowed to do something or are discouraged from doing it, there will be no performance. My conclusion would be that if you want to know whether people are using the learning or whether their performance has improved as a result of the learning, you need to measure performance.

Behaviour transfer

The third level in the Kirkpatrick hierarchy is the assessment of whether levels of performance have improved. In principle, this is no more difficult to measure than learning. What one needs is a detailed breakdown of the behaviours of interest and pre- and post-programme measures. In practice the measurement becomes more difficult because few are willing (or able) to develop and use the necessary lists of key behaviours. With reactions and learning we can focus on the individuals within the training environment and discover what it is that we want to know by observation, collecting opinions and testing. This is harder to do with performance in the job context. The motivational and opportunity variables in the little equation above are not as easy to measure as ability.

As with the other levels, there are a number of purposes for evaluating changes in behaviour and these imply different kinds of evidence.

Did the programme meet the identified need?

Here we need a checklist of desirable behaviours and a system of measuring the frequency or quality of these before, and after, the developmental activity. For instance, take those organizations that are attempting to change their management style to a more consultative one in order to facilitate the development of junior managers. How would one set about evaluating such a programme?

The first, and most difficult stage is to define 'consultative management' as a list of things that middle managers are expected to do. This might include:

- *joint* target setting and reviews of progress
- holding team meetings and *discussing* priorities
- accepting responsibility but *delegating* authority
- asking for views *before* making important decisions
- *discussing developmental* opportunities with subordinates
- *coaching* and guiding rather than telling.

The second stage is to translate these into a set of measurable behaviours and then for the junior managers to be surveyed on whether these behaviours have been observed. Should they have the opinion that the behaviours of their managers are not consultative then some change in style might be seen to be desirable.

An alternative approach is to identify the key competence areas for managers and to assess performance against these as a starting baseline against which to measure changes in behaviour. The most comprehensive assessment will be a combination of the views of supervisors, colleagues and subordinates – what has become known as 360 degree feedback. If this process is to meet needs for greater effectiveness there needs to be a clear link between the competence areas selected and job performance. This implies that the competence areas must represent the key results areas of the particular job.

From time to time it is also necessary to assess how well the change process is going and thus what needs to happen next. Essentially, the evaluation establishes 'where we think we are now' and thus makes possible informed decisions on 'what we should be doing next'. Evaluation for this purpose is a process of asking the important stakeholders what they have to say about the intervention that is positive and what aspects they feel negative about (i.e. their *claims* about the programme). A summary is made of their opinions and the degree to which there is consensus is emphasized. A skilled evaluator is needed to establish which of the claims are strong and important.

Strong claims have the following characteristics:

- They include comparisons – to programme goals, over time, with other groups.
- They include replications – different groups, more than one run of the programme.
- They are based upon multiple sources – quantitative and qualitative.
- They have, to some extent, been collected by people who are not responsible for the delivery of the programme.

Important claims are those which:

- affect large numbers of people;
- provide a solution which can be sustained over time;
- save money or indicate an improvement in efficiency;
- have an impact on achieving desirable outcomes;
- imply a model or approach that could be used by others in other situations.

This kind of evaluation is very interesting to do and has great strengths where there are multiple objectives and where the key stakeholders (often the power brokers in the organization) are likely to have different perceptions of what is happening and why. The intention is not to attribute causality (the traditional view of evaluation), but to gain a sense of the value of the programme seen from a number of different perspectives.

Increased effectiveness as a result of the programme

The major challenge here is to establish what increased effectiveness means and how it might be measured. In some individual cases, the demonstration of skills learned is synonymous with increased effectiveness. For instance, returning from a course on how to use WordPerfect with the ability to carry out effectively a whole range of functions which were difficult before the programme, could be rated a success.

In other situations, where improved effectiveness of a part of the organization is being sought, a much broader approach is necessary. One way of doing this is to convene a group of managers to carry out an 'impact analysis' to discover just what 'effectiveness' means. The managers should have some awareness of the aims of the programme, but need not be closely involved. They are asked to list the three most important purposes for the programme as seen from their perspective in seeking greater organizational effectiveness. Each purpose is written on a 'Post-it' and these are collected and clustered by the managers themselves. They are then ranked in terms of importance and the managers are asked to decide how the achievement of the important purposes can be measured.

It is very difficult to establish that a particular programme, intervention or activity has actually caused the differences in effectiveness which have been measured. This is largely because of the complexity of factors which affect performance. Trends in the organization can increase levels of performance through factors which have nothing to do with the programme. It is also the case that people improve with experience whether or not they are trained. To control for variability in these one needs a careful piece of research.

One practical approach to assessing increased effectiveness is to use the action planning process. If the participants develop action plans during the programme which include goal statements and expected times to completion, these can form the basis of follow-up evaluation. The evaluator discusses with each participant, and, where possible, the line managers, the actions which have been completed. The saving in cost to the organization or the increase in efficiency in the department where the person works can be compared to the cost of attending the programme.

To identify blocks to changes in behaviour

Another purpose of evaluation might be to identify obstacles which are hindering the application of the learning. A number of studies have shown that the context in which people try to introduce new behaviours is crucial.

The key study is that by Rouiller and Goldstein (1993). They described a nine-week training course for assistant managers in a fast food chain and the extent to which these managers used the knowledge and procedures taught on the programme. Learning was measured on the programme and transferred behaviour a few weeks after it. The latter was measured by a list of 92 behaviours which were expected of those who had attended the programme (things like: checks deliveries, makes sure that the product is in good condition, makes sure that the oldest product is used first, makes sure that trays are carried for customers who need assistance). The 'transfer climate' of each of the restaurants to which these assistant managers were going was also measured. The 112 items for the climate measure were derived from some 300 critical incident interviews and were grouped into eight scales. These were:

- The extent to which goals were set and by whom.
- How like the behaviour scale the normal behaviour of managers in the restaurant was.
- Availability of equipment used on the programme.
- The extent to which the assistant managers were allowed to handle problems.
- Positive feedback on behaviours used.
- Negative feedback for not doing the things they were supposed to.
- Punishment by ridicule for using the learned behaviours.
- No feedback because existing managers were too busy to notice what the new person was doing.

All of the scales contributed to the measure but the important finding for us was that the amount learned in training only predicted 8 per cent of the behaviour transfer scores, whereas the climate for transfer measure predicted 46 per cent. Now this is not a surprise to those of us who have been saying that the role of the line manager is crucial in transfer of learning as motivation, encouragement and opportunity all contribute to performance. What is new about it, and therefore important, is that it tells us exactly what the line manager should be doing to encourage the use of the new skills and knowledge. It also provides a set of scales to measure the extent to which these things are happening.

It is worth remembering that evaluation is carried out to meet a purpose and one might argue that the work is only worthwhile if the findings are used. According to Leviton and Hughes (1981), four aspects which might have an important effect on the utilization of an evaluation are:

- The relevance of the findings to decisions which need to be made.
- The amount of communication between evaluators and users.
- The plausibility of the evaluation results.
- The amount of user involvement in the evaluation.

This should alert us to a political aspect of our work. Evaluations often imply asking for changes to be made and some thought must be given to how this is to be done and who needs to be involved.

Conclusion

Evaluation, as it has been described in this chapter, is a process of collecting information. The information to be collected is that thought necessary to meet a particular purpose. It is not economic and indeed not feasible to evaluate something from all perspectives. It is, therefore, important at the outset to decide why the evaluation is being carried out. The 'why' will determine what information needs to be collected.

Information at a number of levels can be collected to meet a particular purpose. Some care is needed as, in general, information about lower levels (i.e. assessed reactions to the learning activities or measures of amounts of learning) does not predict changes at higher levels. If the evaluation is intended to discover whether the participants do things differently or perform better after the learning, then the evaluators need to define and measure these criteria.

Further reading

Alliger, G. M., Tannenbaum, S. I., Bennett, W., Traver, H. and Shotland, A. (1997), A meta-analysis of the relations among training criteria. *Personnel Psychology*, **50**, pp. 341–358.

Bramley, P. (1994), 'Using Subordinate Appraisal as Feedback'. Paper given to the 23rd International Congress of Applied Psychology, Madrid. Copies available from the Department of Organizational Psychology, Birkbeck College, University of London.

Bramley, P. (1996a), *Evaluating Training Effectiveness,* 2nd edn, Maidenhead: McGraw-Hill.

Bramley, P. (1996b), *Evaluating Training*, London: IPD.

Bramley, P. (1998), 'Evaluating Effective Management Development', *International Journal of Training and Development* (in press).

Goldstein, A. P. and Sorcher, M. (1974), *Changing Supervisor Behaviour*, New York: Pergammon Press.

Guba, E. G. and Lincoln, Y. S. (1989), *Fourth Generation Evaluation*, London: Sage.

Kirkpatrick, D. L. (1959), 'Techniques for Evaluating Training Programmes', *Journal of the American Society of Training Directors*.

Latham, G. P. and Saari, L. M. (1997), 'The Application of Social Learning Theory to Training Supervisors Through Behavioural Modeling', *Journal of Applied Psychology*, **64**, pp. 239–246.

Leviton, L. C. and Hughes, E. F. X. (1981), 'Research on the Utilization of Evaluations: A Review and Synthesis', *Evaluation Review* **5**, pp. 525–548.

Patton, M. Q. (1997), *Utilization Focused Evaluation*, 3rd edn, London: Sage.

Rouiller, J. Z. and Goldstein, I. L. (1993), 'Transfer Climate and Positive Transfer', *Human Resource Development Quarterly*, pp. 337–390.

Chapter 34

Employee development – budgeting and financial control

Ed Moorby

The key skills and competencies required of today's employee development (ED) practitioner are wide indeed. They typically include identifying training needs, programme design and delivery, administration and evaluation to name just a few. Sometimes, however, the question of how employee development practitioners obtain and control financial resources is overlooked and this chapter will address this important issue.

The approach taken will assume that the organization in which the employee development is taking place has been established for some time and that budgetary routines, of some description, are in use. It will also implicitly assume that an employee development function, of some size, already exists.

An established ED function will, of course, have one important dynamic that needs to be mentioned at this stage and that is inertia. Vested interests will have supported much of what has taken place. For example, the patron of a management centre will often be a strong advocate of its use and therefore its funding. One of the skills of managing the funding of employee development is undoubtedly that of understanding the role of political power and sponsorship in the allocation of resources.

In this respect the chapter will review the critical aspect of presenting plans in appropriate language and linking development to business strategy. It will then consider ways of creating the training and development plan and budget and identifying costs and benefits. Finally it will take a look at managing the budget.

Using the language of business

If we want a reminder of why the appropriate use of language is so important, we need only look at the process of selling. A key principle that most experienced salespeople work with is to focus on helping the buyer realize the benefits of what he or she needs to buy. An essential factor here is to put the selling proposition in a language that the buyer can understand. Thus 'blue sky' products such as holidays or pensions highlight the enjoyment and security elements respectively of the buyer's future.

Some of the elements of the language that the ED professional has to feel comfortable in using with finance are gross profit, net profit, loss, shareholder value, cash flow, bottom line, corporation tax and margins. The basic proposition in business is that for any investment the shareholder should get a return. In the marketplace this becomes a competitive return or a return that is acceptable to the stakeholders.

The employee development officer/manager usually has to request funds from the financial function and line management which might otherwise become residual profit. For example, if the net margin on a product is say 5 per cent and £1000 is allocated to employee development, the sales or line function will have to achieve an income of £20 000 to provide this funding. The real challenge to the employee development function then is to convince their customers of the advantages of investing in employee development and releasing their staff for employee development activities before any clear, tangible and quantifiable benefits become apparent. This is where it is essential to link development activities with business activities. For example, as we have seen over the past few years, an untrained financial adviser can attract severe penalties for mis-selling. Equally, a hospital pathologist can create major difficulties for a hospital if poorly trained staff make mistakes in analysing samples. However, on the positive side, staff in call centres, for example, may attract more repeat business once they have been through effective training programmes.

The point here is that it is essential to present proposals for funding and expenditure that will readily make financial sense to the financial function while also clearly addressing the needs and interests of the wealth creating departments. Thus a case for specific aspects of training in branches of a retail bank will need to demonstrate how it is anticipated that branch performance will be improved.

Linking business strategy and employee development

To be successful, employee development has to be an integral part of the business strategy and must understand and buy into the values and aspirations of senior management. In this context the employee development function needs to be part of a process which is based on a clear and shared vision for the organization. It can then become a key and valued contributor to the development of the detailed strategic plan which will be required to deliver the vision. Its main task, whether the function consists of one training officer or a department of a hundred specialists, is to identify and deliver the development options that ensure that employees can achieve the detailed strategic aims of the organization. The basic approach required here involves a combination of analysing business plans to identify development requirements and keeping close to senior managers to identify with them emerging development needs.

A business vision such as linking England and France by the Channel Tunnel would provide an interesting example of this process. Employee development for the large number of activities involved would span areas such as project management; developing tunnelling skills with specialized equipment; enabling English and French train drivers to communicate with each other; operating the tunnel crossing safely; a whole range of marketing skills; the development of a management ethos which embraces private sector values in a sector that has been traditionally state controlled and a host of other activities.

The employee development function would need to integrate its activities with the business and technically driven programme to ensure that the right skills were available when they were needed.

Creating the development plan

The process of identifying needs and specifying ways to meet these needs is at the heart of the employee development specialists' competence and this handbook contains extensive coverage of issues relating to this process. Suffice it to say for the purposes of this chapter, any training and development plan will need to be expressed in clearly quantified terms that lend themselves to conversion into financial amounts.

The choice of each component of the development plan should be carefully considered against cost effectiveness criteria. It is usually sensible to ensure ownership of the proposed plan by involving the key players in its development. For example, a plan which assumes a widespread implementation of, say, action learning may be more likely to gain acceptance if senior management have had the opportunity to discuss the approach with senior colleagues from other organizations – real comrades in adversity. It can also help when one or two senior divisional managers have achieved real success in overcoming problems using this approach. When this is the case and the financial review of overall budgets then takes place, the management team is far more likely to be inclined to commit resources to such development.

A final point worth identifying in the context of budgeting is the power of inertia. Much of what is proposed for next year may be a repeat of last year. Induction training, safety training, graduate induction, first appointment training for managers and supervisors are examples. The past will provide a guide for the future in these types of expenditure. Also, it is in these areas of 'repeat' training that cost-effectiveness improvements should be rigorously and continuously sought.

Identifying costs

This section will consider a number of perspectives regarding the cost of the investment in employee development and readers are encouraged to identify data specific to their situation. When you have read this chapter, sit down and confirm for yourself the amount your organization spends on training. How does this compare with others? What is your cost per training day? Has it increased or decreased since last year and what are you looking to achieve?

One of the most convenient indicators when it comes to costs is to compare the percentage of payroll spent by your organization with that spent by competitors in the same sector. It can also sometimes be helpful to compare with other sectors, for example in the financial services arena, you could compare between banking, insurance, building societies and food retailers such as Tesco or Sainsbury.

What is obviously important is to compare like with like. The gross payroll is stated annually in most organizations' Annual Report and provides a conventional and comparable platform. Expenditure would typically include salaries and employment costs e.g. National Insurance and pensions, the running costs of training facilities, expenditure on outside facilities and travel, the cost of external training, the cost of using information technology, the capital costs incurred, the cost of educational courses and the cost to the organization of any national initiatives it supports.

The percentage of payroll spent on training might vary from something near to zero to as much as ten per cent. Many organizations will spend in the range of two to four per cent. This would be a typical figure in sectors that are not involved in high-technology research or where the nature of the product demands extensive training. An airline might spend in the range of six to eight per cent because of the high cost of pilot training. Sectors such as health and education, with the very high cost of entry training, could also be expected to spend a relatively high percentage of payroll on training. An indication of how your organization's expenditure compares with others in your sector might be obtained directly from colleagues, through discussions at trade associations or educational institutes and by regular reading of industry magazines which, from time to time, publish extracts from surveys on training expenditure.

There are also a number of useful indicators which can be used to monitor and estimate elements of the budget. The following indicators provide a guide as to how you might analyse your own situation using current and specific data.

Cost per day of training

This compares the total expenditure on training per annum with the total number of days training per annum. The resulting cost per day can be used as a guide in budgeting, as a comparison with the cost of external training and as a measure of the trend in costs on a year on year basis. Clearly, if it can be reduced in absolute terms, i.e. after allowance for inflation, it can be a positive selling point in budget discussions. It can also, arguably, be used to demonstrate cost efficiency improvements in the delivery of training. It is an overall figure which may include both internally and externally provided training, the changing use of computer managed training and an evolving balance between formal and other types of employee development such as coaching and mentoring.

Average training days provided per member of staff

This compares the total number of training days provided per annum with the total number of employees. A figure in the range 1–5 days per employee might be typical. By multiplying this figure by the number of staff employed and the cost per day of training, the total budget allocation can be derived. Thus an organization with 1000 employees that provides an average of 3.0 days of training per employee at an average cost of £200 per day would spend some £600 000 per annum on training.

These three variables combined with the employee development plan provide a sound basis for establishing the approximate size of the budget.

Internal vs external training costs

It is useful to compare regularly the cost per day of internal training with the average cost for one day of training from an external supplier. Two figures are useful here. First, where a supplier will give a price for a group of, say, 15 attendees; second, when you compare this cost against the cost of one or two individuals attending 'public' courses.

Training days delivered per trainer per annum

This figure compares the total training days delivered per annum with the average number of training staff employed over the year. Such a figure has to be used with care. It is affected by the number of events, the duration of the events and the attendance at each event. However, it is usually necessary to estimate each of these variables when producing the budget. The plan itself will also usually include elements such as computer based training, educational courses and any combination of the dozens of training approaches described elsewhere in this handbook.

The actual preparation of the budget requires the following steps:

- Identify what elements of the plan will follow on from the previous year.
- Identify what new initiatives will be required to meet the business plan.
- Determine what training methods and approaches will be used.
- Specify what volumes of activity will be required.
- Identify how the employee development will be delivered e.g. training courses, CBT, action learning and what resources will be required e.g. training rooms, technologically based resources, employee development staff.
- Convert this data into financial statements under appropriate cost headings.
- Provide narrative justification for the budget identifying contribution to the business plan together with a clear statement of the cost involved using appropriate accounting conventions for the specific organization.
- Convince senior management of the merits of the case in the budget.

Once the budget is approved, it is essential that all those employed in the employee development function understand what the budget means in day-to-day as well as strategic terms and, furthermore, that they are motivated to deliver the strategy for which the budget represents the financial statement.

Managing the employee development budget

The employee development budget is essentially a plan for the year which identifies the probable cost of implementation. In the same way as any other plan it is essential to monitor progress and to adapt the plan as reality unfolds. It has been said that no plan survives contact with reality and the most appropriate way to stay in control is to produce regular statements of actual expenditure against what was planned for the period. Management can then concentrate on taking the appropriate action on variances. The process basically works as follows:

1. The first step is to ensure that the budget is based on sound foundations. Discussions take place with internal customers about the future in which projections from the past year are essential ingredients. A thorough analysis of the business plan in association with line colleagues can then identify new elements or changes which require employee development in the budget period.

Some organizations use an approach called 'zero-based' budgeting. This involves starting with a clean sheet of paper each year. Every activity included in the budget and the associated costs then have to be justified. This approach is rigorous but highly recommended. It can be taken further as a philosophy of management where all expenditure is questioned continuously. A useful way to encourage ownership and accountability in larger organizations is to operate each subdivision or section of the employee development function as a 'cost centre' or, if possible, as a 'profit-centre'.

2. The next step is to ensure that the information being used is accurate and timely. To achieve this it will be essential to integrate the employee development plan with the monthly budget reports. A close collaboration with the finance function is essential to ensure that costs are allocated correctly to mutually understood cost codes. It can also be useful to line up the employee development cost review process with the accounting reporting timetable. In a large organization with several employee development managers, a monthly management meeting scheduled for a few days after the monthly budget progress figures become available, can ensure that adverse variances can be identified and acted on where necessary.

3. A review and analysis of variances, be they positive or negative, should be followed by prompt action. It may be necessary during the year to add or delete elements of the employee development plan as business needs evolve. This may require redeploying staff or cancelling programmes later in the budget period. Experience has shown that it is useful to have an informal target of achieving a final expenditure that is a half to one per cent below the agreed budget. It is certainly not advisable to advise the finance function in the last budget period that the budget will be overspent as such an overspend would, in effect, come straight off the bottom line.

Conclusion

As indicated at the start of this section, budgeting and financial control are essentially management activities. Employee development practitioners need to 'run a tight ship' and to achieve this it is necessary to be close to the business planning process and the business managers. The process requires a balanced integration of employee development skills, a business focus and an understanding of financial estimating and budgetary control.

Further reading

Harrison, R. (1989), *Training and Development*, London: IPM.

Moorby, Ed. (1996), *How to Succeed in Employee Development*, 2nd edn, Maidenhead: McGraw-Hill.

Reid, M., Barrington, H. and Kenney, J. (1992), *Training Interventions*, 3rd edn, London: IPM.

Chapter 35

Performance management

Trevor Bentley

The nature of performance

There is a paradox and contradiction existing when we talk about performance. Is what we see people doing called performance, or is it the outcome of their efforts?

If we believe that what we see people doing is performance then we can measure it by looking at how well they are doing what they are doing. This is a competency based approach to measuring performance. On the other hand, if we believe that performance is the outcome of what people do, then we have to measure it by measuring outcomes, and the degree of competency displayed or not displayed is less important.

So here is the paradox – we need to be competent to perform, but competency does not in itself result in performance.

If we take an output approach to performance then there are three important elements to consider – expectations, outcomes and results.

- *Expectations* are those things that we anticipate will or, we think, should happen. If I am a performer and I know what is expected of me I have something to aim for and a basis for measuring my performance.
- *Outcomes* are the things produced by my efforts to meet expectations. They are the outputs of my performance. The skills and methods I use to produce my outputs may be less important than the quality of the outputs themselves.
- *Results* are the impact that my outcomes have on the environment in which I am performing. They are the results of the outputs I produce – for example satisfied customers.

You will notice that there is nothing in these comments about performance that is concerned with competencies. The paradox is that it does not matter what my competencies are – if I do not meet these performance criteria *I have not performed*. Here is the performance 'gap': between what I am apparently capable of and what I achieve in terms of meeting expectations, producing outcomes and achieving results.

Critical performance factors

There are five critical factors that determine the extent of the performance gap.

1. *The environment*   The environment in which we perform is very important in supporting our efforts. It can cover many aspects of the workplace – our colleagues, the facilities we have access to, the premises and so on. For example, in order to foster improved customer service many banks have redesigned the 'front office' to be a more welcoming and hospitable place. Attention to the environment in which people are expected to perform is part of the process of bridging the performance gap.

2. *The conditions*   The conditions under which people perform can help or hinder. If the conditions involve pressure because the office is short staffed performance will suffer. If the conditions demand an over punctilious attention to a particular code of behaviour and there are fixed rules and procedures to follow then again performance will suffer. On the other hand, if the prevailing conditions allow people to use initiative and explore their potential then performance will improve.

3. *Personal desires*   One aspect of performance that is often overlooked by management is the personal desire of the individual to perform. All kinds of approaches have been tried in the attempt to motivate people to work harder, or perform better. Money, status, prizes and recognition have all been used yet the underlying and critical factor is still whether people want to do it or not.

4. *Personal state*   If I am physically unwell and/or psychologically affected in some way I am not going to perform very well. How we feel varies all the time but we are expected to perform at the same high level regardless. Placing more pressure on people who are not in a fit state to deal with it actually worsens performance.

5. *Personal competence*   Of course people do need to have the competence to perform at the expected levels. It is important to know what levels of competence are needed for what is expected. With this information it is possible to pay attention to enhancing competencies accordingly. However, simply improving competence does not necessarily lead to improved performance.

Measuring performance

Performance is not measured by 'what we bring' (competencies) or 'what we do', but by 'what we produce'. It is the outcome and the results of our efforts. This 'output focus' is fundamental to creating an effective performance management system.

Using an input focus of 'what we bring' and 'what we do' does not lead directly to improved performance and only serves to take the spotlight away from what we should be measuring. Imagine measuring the performance of high jumpers by the way they run up and their competency to leap, rather than the height they clear.

However, stating that the focus is on 'what we produce' is of little value if it is not clear 'how' it can be achieved and measured. This depends on finding answers to four questions.

1. What is the output (outcomes and results) of the activity?
2. How can the output be measured?
3. Can the outputs be directly related to inputs?
4. How can outputs be improved?

So we need criteria for measuring outcomes and results. These can include the following.

Performance indicators

Performance indicators are a way of combining measures of performance output to indicate the current level being achieved. If it is possible to produce a single performance indicator for an activity, then it might also be possible to monitor this continuously and provide feedback so that action and behaviour can be adjusted to optimize performance. Cars, for example, have a fuel gauge that measures the contents of the fuel tank and a speedometer that indicates the speed and a mileometer for the distance. By combining this information it is possible to display a 'performance indicator' of fuel consumption. With this information drivers could adjust their driving to optimize fuel consumption.

If a particular activity has as a measure of performance the numbers of customers served and time spent per customer, it would be possible to devise a performance indicator that displayed this information.

Establishing standards

Standards are the desired or intended levels of achievement that can be set for performance measures and performance indicators. We might set standards in customer service of, for example, 15–20 calls per hour and a customer spend of £30–£50. Of course setting standards is never easy, set them too high and people are demotivated, set them too low and poor performance becomes acceptable. If we set standards as a range of performance then it is possible to take account of variations in the five critical factors that will affect performance and still ensure high overall levels of performance.

Standards and targets

There is a great deal of misunderstanding and misuse of the terms standard and target. A standard as described above is a range of desirable and/or intended performance. A target is something to aim for and could be set above the standard range.

It is important that performance standards are set not only for measures of volume of outputs, but also for the quality factors attached to the activity concerned. The aim should be to create a situation where people are able to focus on outputs and to have measures and indicators for that output that are meaningful and achievable.

So the components for performance assessment are:

- expected outcomes and results
- performance measures and indicators for each
- performance standards
- targets (where appropriate)
- actual performance achieved
- nature of the critical factors.

With all these components it is possible to assess the extent of the performance gap and to have some ideas about the contributing factors. This in turn leads on to action for improving performance.

The performance management cycle

Working and performing is part of a continuous life cycle. As we travel along this cycle, and as we learn from our experiences, the way we travel changes. We apply what we have learnt to our present activity so that we influence our future outcomes .

The performance cycle describes one view of how we do this and can be represented as a wave, the crest of the wave being our action and performance and the troughs being time for reflection and learning.

The cycle invites the involvement and participation of everyone concerned. From establishing expectations to appraising success the whole cycle is one of co-operation. It entails discussion and agreement about expected outcomes

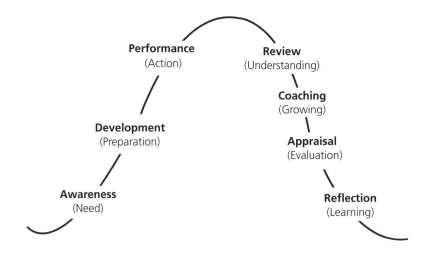

Figure 35.1   The performance cycle

and targets and, though people may feel stretched and challenged, it should provide them with a sense of involvement. In a supportive environment this is likely to lead to significantly improved performance.

The focus of the performance cycle can be described as 'achieving success through others'. Managers cannot make people perform. When the pyramids were built the slave masters used starvation and whips to make people work. Later the Romans realized that half-starved and half-dead slaves were pretty rotten performers so they used the promise of good food and wine and other vicarious pleasures to motivate their slaves to perform.

Today the use of economic whips and emotional starvation still exists. However, more enlightened organizations recognize that people who are well rewarded and emotionally fed outperform those under the threat of economic sanction.

One basic requirement of the performance cycle is that people own their performance. It is true that there are many factors outside the control of individuals that impact on their performance. These external factors do not change the nature of the ownership of performance. Racing cyclists who fall in rainy conditions can blame the rain and the slippery surface, but at the end of the day it is still *their* performance.

Awareness

The awareness stage is important in the performance management cycle because it is here that decisions are made that will become the basis for measuring success. Performance plans should be challenging and achievable and set as part of a two-way dialogue that seeks to reach agreement and acceptance of the plans by managers and staff.

There are four tasks in the planning process:

1. Defining performance outputs in terms of *outcomes* and *results*. Imagine that the activity being measured is chopping logs, the outcome will be a supply of chopped logs and the result will be a warm home. If the person chopping logs is doing it for someone else then the outcome would be the same, but the result for the log chopper might take the form of wages.

2. Agreeing *improvements* in current performance levels. The focus here is how can outputs and results be improved? For this to happen it is important to select the area of performance and to look at all the critical performance factors to see where people can be supported to make improvements. Overall improvement is unlikely to occur unless the detailed improvement area is identified and worked on.

3. Agreeing a specific *focus*. So far in the planning process everything has been output focused. This is very important because it concentrates attention not on what people do, but on what they produce. It focuses on performance rather than on competency.

4. Agreeing the *expected range* of performance. The fourth step in the planning process is to agree the expected range of performance included in the plan. Using a range for a performance indicator shows what is considered acceptable, so that above the range is high performance, below the range is low performance. It enables both challenging and achievable expectations to be agreed.

Although we have not focused on what people do it is clear that what they do and how they do it impacts directly on performance. The extent to which people are given 'freedom with responsibility' in the way they work can be, and often is, a precursor to high performance. People need to know what aspects of work they are responsible for and the extent of the freedom they can exercise in meeting their responsibilities.

Development

Most people want to be high performers and with the right support most can succeed. For development to succeed people need:

● To have their personal *aspirations* taken seriously. An aspiration can be defined as, 'a strong desire for high achievement'. It is something that all high performers have. People need to be encouraged to have aspirations and when they do their aspirations need to be taken seriously and supported.

- To be *challenged* in all aspects of work and life. Most high performers seek out challenging situations and activities. People need to be invited to take on tasks which they find challenging and at the same time they need to be supported in a way that helps them to succeed. Nothing breeds success more than success.

- To be provided with *opportunities* for development. We all need opportunities to develop. Some we can create for ourselves in our own time, others we need to be allowed the freedom and time to explore. We need others to support us in seeking out and responding to opportunities.

- To have clear development *objectives*. Development objectives need to be built into performance plans. These have to be realistic and have immediate as well as longer-term benefit. Development objectives might include:
  - ways in which I want to improve
  - my development actions (assuming anything is possible)
  - the training I think I need to succeed.

- To believe in our own *potential*. Why limit yourself? We are all unlimited in our potential. However, there are factors in life that we have to acknowledge as limiting our realization of our potential called 'potential inhibitors'. They include: lack of self-belief, lack of belief in others, lack of opportunity, lack of support and lack of commitment.

Performance

Being aware of what is happening during performance is an important part of the development process. Reaching a state where skills are so finely honed that people can operate with 'unconscious competence' happens because they have been acutely aware of what they are doing during their development.

All performance is a development opportunity if we focus on what is happening. Sometimes the repetitive nature of what we are doing and our lack of interest, i.e. going through the motions, has little if any developmental value.

Review

The performance review is an essential stage in the performance management cycle and is designed to maintain both performers' and managers' motivation and commitment. Performance reviews are important for four reasons:

1. They are instrumental in keeping everyone's focus on the performance plans.
2. They provide an opportunity for dealing with difficulties that might be preventing people from performing at their best.
3. They provide managers with an opportunity to acknowledge the progress performers are making towards achievement of their performance plans.
4. They provide an opportunity for dealing with changing circumstances.

During the performance review all aspects of performance should be considered with the emphasis on outputs. The focus is on improvement and achievement, not on finding fault or criticism. Of course everyone encounters difficulties from time to time and these need to be discussed openly and honestly but the performance review is not the time and place to deal with matters of discipline.

Coaching

The primary use of performance reviews is to help people build bridges towards their performance plans. The key to building performance bridges is to build effective supports that will allow people to progress at the speed and distance appropriate to their desires and capabilities. Pushing people to jump across 'performance gaps' will lead to fear and resistance. When people are pushed they only see the depth of the chasm and the dangers they face. Bridge building is all about encouragement, support and taking small steps forward.

Coaching is an important ingredient here. Coaching does not involve giving advice or telling people what to do. On the contrary, it is an approach to personal support that helps people to focus attention on those areas of their performance where there are opportunities for improvement. By asking 'awareness-generating' questions and by observing and commenting on performance, the effective coach is able to provide the kind of feedback that highlights and hones their client's performance

Appraisal

Performance appraisal is the area of performance management where the focus on performance is the hardest to maintain. More often than not the appraisal turns into an assessment of the individual rather than their performance. It is often exacerbated by the one-way nature of many appraisals, where managers tell performers what they think of their performance and/or of them. The competency approach to performance further clouds the issue by looking at how well people do what they do rather than on what they produce.

The whole appraisal process and its outcomes are largely dependent on managers adopting an open, honest and consultative approach from start to finish. This is a simple model, or framework, that people can follow to make their appraisal meetings a success, and surprisingly to make them more time effective. It consists of:

1. asking open questions
2. listening attentively
3. reflecting back what is heard
4. responding appropriately.

The model encourages performers to share their thoughts and feelings with other people. By using this consultative approach appraisers can manage the meeting without controlling it and be powerful without disempowering performers.

Appraisal meetings are, or should be, a two-way dialogue. It is the performers' responsibility to fully understand, accept and take ownership for their performance.

Reflection

Because the appraisal stage of the performance management cycle links directly with the awareness and planning stage of the next cycle the reflection and learning stage can get rushed.

This does frequently happen. However, performers should have time to:

●   Reflect on their appraisal and what they have learned about their performance.
●   Enjoy the acknowledgement and recognition that they receive for their achievements.
●   Think about how they want things to be different in the future.
●   Focus on how they can improve their performance.

After a period of time they can then move more confidently to the next stage of the cycle, having gained some sense of satisfaction from the completion of the previous cycle.

Performance reward

All performance brings reward in some form or another, from a deep feeling of self-satisfaction to the rapturous applause of an appreciative audience. Generally speaking there are five main forms:

1. *Satisfaction*   Perhaps the highest level of performance reward is satisfaction with a job well done. Much of this must come from people themselves who know what they are capable of and know when they have delivered their best shot. The environment and conditions can support the chance for satisfaction, but they cannot create satisfaction. It is the other performance factors of personal desire, personal state and personal competence that lead to satisfaction. When everything comes together, when people are not deflected from performing at their best, then they can achieve satisfaction.

2. *Recognition*   Being recognized as a high performer is reward in itself. Knowing that others know that you are a high performer brings with it a sense of self-worth that increases confidence and probably competence. However, recognition has to be handled carefully and must fit in with the culture of the organization.

3. *Appreciation*   Appreciation is not as public as recognition and yet it is just as powerful an element of performance reward. Appreciation can be given frequently for the smallest and simplest aspects of performance. From a simple 'thank you' to a more formal memo or letter, appreciation indicates that performance is being noticed and appreciated. Giving appreciation is one of the most important parts of a manager's job.

4. *Status and position*   Obvious examples of meeting these needs are through the use of high sounding titles and status symbols such as large and/or flashy cars. Promotion and advancement are seen as an indication of high performance and competence. So there is also a form of recognition in meeting status needs.

5. *Pay (financial reward)*   The issue of pay, all forms of financial reward, is treated in a wide variety of ways. Some put it at the 'lower' level of need and downplay its importance as a form of reward. Others make it the primary focus of reward systems. However, there is no doubt that pay is a very important and central part of performance reward and many attempts have been, and are being, made to design pay systems that can be seen to be linked with performance. Of course, not everyone reacts in the same way to the different elements of reward. The mix of performance reward elements can and will vary from person to person. The desires and needs that individuals have are reflected in the way that they look at performance reward systems. The best systems are those that recognize this variety and do not try to force a particular ranking on everyone.

Linking pay and performance

Few subjects give rise to more heated debate than that of linking pay and performance. When employers suggest it, the immediate reaction of employees and their representatives is: 'they want to pay less money for more output'. And when employees and their representatives suggest it, it is because: 'they want more money for less output'. What a sorry state of affairs it is when people cannot sit down together and arrive at an appropriate and meaningful way of linking pay and performance so that everyone can benefit.

However, for the vast majority of people working as employees for organizations pay has only a rather tenuous link to their performance. It is in this particular context that so many problems arise. Links that do not work include:

- profit sharing that is too remote from the individual to have a clear and calculated link with what that person actually does and produces;
- bonuses paid for 'doing well' which are only vaguely related to performance and are mostly decided at the whim of management;
- schemes that link pay to the subjective opinions of managers which are widely mistrusted because they are usually manipulated by management according to some predicated standard distribution of ratings.

For the link between performance and pay to work effectively five things are needed:

1. The reward has to be calculated and paid close to the actual performance.
2. The decision on the amount has to be objective.
3. Rewards must be clear, i.e. if A is achieved then X will be paid and not manipulated by management.
4. People must be able to calculate what they will earn for each level of performance they achieve.
5. Rewards must be paid as soon as the performance is achieved.

Freedom with responsibility

People work harder and better when they do it for themselves than they ever will when they do it for others. It is the exercise of choice and desire which signals freedom in the workplace. Freedom for people to operate more independently in terms of when, how and, sometimes, where they work can be a significant spur to performance. For this to happen they need to display their willingness and ability to take full responsibility for producing the outputs that are expected from them.

Such freedom that people earn in their work falls within certain boundaries, beyond which they will only operate with the agreement of colleagues and management. As trust grows and the capacity for responsibility increases, the boundaries can be extended. In this context boundaries are seen less as limits and more as 'territory' demarcations. They indicate where one person's responsibility ends and another's starts. This is very important in ensuring good relationships. People learn to respect others' boundaries and in return have their boundaries respected. In this way freedom can flourish within personal 'territories'.

When we are free to pay attention to all the factors that play a part in our performance and free to decide how we are going to perform, then and only then will we be able to do our best. This link between commitment, freedom and personal power is crucial. When we are doing what we are doing because we are choosing to do it then we call upon everything we have to perform at our best.

With this commitment and motivation also comes the responsibility for what we produce and for the consequences of our actions. When we meet barriers to our performance, if we have the freedom, we can tackle them creatively and find ways to overcome them or to circumvent them. Without the freedom and the responsibility that goes with it, the barriers become excuses for poor performance. Freedom, responsibility and performance are inextricably linked. None can exist without the others. In combination they are formidable.

Further reading

Bentley, T. J. (1996), *Bridging the Performance Gap*, Aldershot: Gower.

Bentley, T. J. and Clayton, S. (1998), *Profiting from Diversity*, Aldershot: Gower.

Cooper, R. and Sawaf, A. (1997), *Executive EQ*, London: Orion Business Books.

Heider, J. (1986), *The Tao of Leadership*, Aldershot: Wildwood House.

McCallum, C. (1993), *Appraisal Training*, London: Kogan Page.

Parsloe, E. (1993), *Coaching, Mentoring and Assessing*, London: Kogan Page.

Redman, W. (1994), *Portfolios for Development*, London: Kogan Page.

Schaef, A. W. and Fassel, D. (1990), *The Addictive Organisation*, San Francisco: Harper & Row.

Whitmore, J. (1992), *Coaching for Performance*, London: Nicholas Brealey.

Weisinger, H. (1998), *Emotional Intelligence at Work*, San Francisco: Jossey-Bass.

Chapter 36

Assessment and development centres

Julie Hay

Assessment and development centres are events during which participants undertake simulations and other activities and are observed and assessed against a set of criteria. The term 'centre' is somewhat misleading as it dates from a time in the past when large organizations tended to dedicate a specific location; it has now come to be the label regardless of the venue.

Although not everyone uses the same definitions, most assessment centres are focused on providing information on which selection and promotion decisions can be based whereas development centres use the results to devise development plans. It is also possible, and quite common, to run a centre for both purposes.

The original assessment centres were run by the War Office many years ago as a quick yet reliable way of identifying who had officer potential. The method was picked up by the US military, and subsequently by US industry. Eventually it migrated back to UK industry. Much research was conducted in the USA by AT&T, who assessed people and then kept the results secret for years in order to check the validity of the assessments. This and later research has confirmed that assessment centres are indeed a reliable way of identifying potential.

Assessment centres

An assessment centre is a method of predicting future performance by using simulations and other techniques to measure a candidate's ability to handle future responsibilities. Because it looks at future, rather than past or present performance, a centre is particularly suitable for establishing who has capabilities that they have not been called upon to use so far. It is particularly useful, therefore, when people are about to move into a different kind of work, such as into supervision or management for the first time.

397

The usual process is:

1. Identify the criteria associated with successful performance (this may of course require considerable research into competencies).
2. Select simulations and other appropriate ways to measure candidates (again, this may require research to be confident of a good match).
3. Select assessors, who should normally be the people who are responsible for judging performance at the target level, i.e. who will appraise the candidate should they be given the new responsibilities.
4. Train assessors – so they know the activities and the assessment process – and ensure they will assess consistently with each other.
5. Run the centre, during which assessors observe participants as they engage in a series of activities and collect evidence to assess them against the agreed list of criteria.
6. Pool the various assessments and any other information (e.g. test results, personality profiles).
7. Optionally provide feedback to participants.
8. Use the results as a guide when making selection, promotion or succession planning decisions.

There are several key principles, or ethics, that must apply if a centre is to be fair and valid:

●   The simulations and other activities must represent the future tasks and responsibilities – this should include matching the environment and working conditions (for example, there should not be a time limit on a task that could normally be taken home overnight).

●   Simulations should, however, be based in fictitious organizations or situations – if you use familiar circumstances participants are likely to give learned responses or copy what they have seen others do. For example, someone with an ineffective manager may nevertheless act in the same way because they believe this is what the organization wants.

●   Performance in one simulation should not be dependent on or influenced by performance in another (for example, poor decision-making at one stage should not mean some candidates are disadvantaged at a subsequent presentation of their ideas).

●   There must be multiple assessments – assessors/participant combinations are rotated so that several assessors see each participant. This counteracts the risk of having an incompetent assessor.

●   There must be separate assessments – to avoid bias the assessors should not discuss their opinions with each other until the end of the programme.

- There must be multiple opportunities to display competence – because people often behave differently in different circumstances, there should be overlap between activities so participants have more than one chance to demonstrate what they are capable of.

- All participants should go through the same experience – they should have the same workload, undertake activities in the same order, where this might be significant. A common mistake here is to have one participant do a presentation after a break while another comes immediately into their presentation from another activity. The first participant has the opportunity to relax beforehand; the second does not.

Development centres

Development centres are run in a similar way to assessment centres, although the focus is on producing feedback as a guide to future development and training needs. Thus, a development centre is still a series of simulations and related activities, with multiple assessments against a predefined set of criteria. In many cases, a developmental aspect is included within an assessment centre anyway and participants are given detailed feedback about their results and helped to draw up development plans.

However, development centres may also be run to assess current, rather than potential, performance. When this is the case, peer assessors are often used. This has the benefit of reducing the cost, as peer assessors tend to have lower salaries than senior assessors do. They are also likely to be better able to find time for the centre, especially as they will in turn be being assessed during the event. Another key advantage to peer assessment is that it has greater impact on individual participants, who will often believe and act on feedback from colleagues but would have doubted or ignored it if it came from their manager.

Unlike a pure assessment centre, where participants are given no feedback until the end (and sometimes not even then), development centres are often designed so that feedback can be given after each activity. This allows participants to incorporate it as they go along. If the feedback reflects lack of a competence, the participant can at least begin thinking about the sort of behaviour they need to use even if they cannot yet display it. In this way, a development centre may be similar to an experiential training event.

The key principles for development centres are similar to those set out above for assessment centres, with some significant additions if peer assessment is used:

- Participation must be voluntary. People cannot be 'forced' to assess their colleagues; nor will the centre function well if participants are unwilling to accept feedback from each other.

- The results must be 'owned' by the individual participant, who decides how much to share with management. Without this protection, peer assessors will be unlikely to offer genuine assessments about the weaknesses of their colleagues (unless they want to become unpopular!).

An amendment to the principles may also be needed whether peer or senior assessors are used:

- The activities may be selected to reflect the current rather than promotional level of tasks and responsibilities. For current level assessment, it may still be useful to include tasks that are not currently within the remit of the participant. For example, the same *level* of work within a department might involve attendance at meetings even though a participant might currently work in a section where meetings are rare.

Typical content of a centre

In order to reflect the current or potential range of tasks and responsibilities, a centre is likely to include simulations such as:

- *Meetings*   These may be with or without a chairperson, with or without in-built conflict of aims, with or without an element of negotiation or influencing rather than simply giving information or directives, and as a team or as a collection of individuals with different priorities.

   It is sensible (and kinder) to start a centre with a conflict-free meeting so that participants have a chance to get to know each other and settle in. A meeting where participants are given conflicting briefs is better run a bit later; otherwise participants will expect the whole event to be contentious!

   If you want to assess chairing skills, you will need to arrange it so that each participant has the opportunity to be chairperson; you will therefore need a number of meeting topics.

   Beware of assessing a participant who has been expected to chair the first meeting of the centre – they may be far more unsure of the process than someone who takes the chair after seeing several others do so.

- *Presentations*   These are given with or without an element of persuasion, to a group or to an individual such as a senior manager who needs briefing. The group may consist of other participants and/or assessors, or may be a specially created audience. A range of topics will be needed if participants are to see each other's presentations – otherwise the last candidate has a major advantage.

- *One-to-one activities*   These include selling or negotiating, dealing with customers or clients, counselling or coaching someone, conducting appraisals, handling disciplinary or grievance interviews.

- *Written activities*   These include dealing with in-baskets of correspondence and messages, producing reports, minutes or briefing papers, or maintaining notes during specific periods of the centre.

- *Planning and organizing activities*   These require participants to comprehend information, determine priorities, plan what to do and how to monitor it. Participants may be provided with fictitious teams and projects to see how they organize them.

- *Contingency activities*   These deal with interruptions and changes in priorities.

Where activities require the presence of someone other than the participants, these can be role-played by professionals, by the assessors, or by others who are unconnected with the assessment process.

Other activities that are typically included within centres are:

- *Tests and questionnaires*   Such as for knowledge, ability, aptitude, intelligence, personality, team or leadership styles, occupational fit. It is essential that these are professionally chosen and administered to ensure they are valid contributions to the assessment process. There should be a proven link between any test results and the competencies that are being assessed.

- *Interviews*   These may be with assessors or with other professionals. For example, assessors can usefully interview participants to discuss how they handled a written activity; this will provide valuable extra information that often cannot be ascertained from the written notes alone. Interviews to explore candidates' previous experience and/or career expectations will also add to the process. Psychologists may interview participants as part of the process of administering and interpreting psychometric questionnaires. Participants may bring information with them for discussion, such as 360 degree feedback or their appraisal results.

Choosing the criteria

Centres provide a valid and highly credible source of information about candidates. It is therefore essential that the criteria against which they are assessed are truly associated with successful performance. If the wrong criteria are used, the process will systematically lead to the wrong decisions – and the impact on the organization may not become apparent until it is too late.

There are basically two ways of selecting a suitable competence framework: use an off-the-shelf list or research your own. The key factors for either approach are:

- What does effective performance look like? You will need to identify some effective and less effective performers so that you can compare their behaviours and identify those associated with success. Note that these may not be the 'textbook' answers – in real life it is rarely that simple. Note also that a 360 degree perspective adds accuracy – what seems effective from below may not even be evident to those above, and what colleagues think is important may be different again.

  Identifying key competencies is, of course, even more difficult if you are creating a new role. In that case, you may have to settle for collecting as many views as possible and then carefully monitoring the results.

- How will assessments be made against the criteria? Good assessments are based on observable behaviour or results and not on interpretations. The criteria therefore need to be stated in behavioural terms that will be understood and applied consistently by different assessors. This needs to be checked even when you have identified in-house criteria; people often use identical words in different ways. For example, integrity has been found to mean variously: working long hours without being asked; never being caught out in a lie; and wearing a suit and tie to meetings. The problem of meanings will be even more acute if you use a list of criteria developed elsewhere.

The benefits of centres

There are a number of significant benefits that arise from running assessment or development centres:

- They generally lead to significantly better decisions than would be made through interviews or where they are based on past performance.

- They are seen as 'fair' by candidates, who therefore feel the organization has treated them reasonably even if they do not get selected or promoted as a result.

- They have high face validity, particularly when managers are the assessors – so the final assessments are readily accepted by line managers.

- They provide the organization with up-to-date information on current and/or potential capabilities on which to base development activities and succession planning.

- They give participants an opportunity to demonstrate their real potential – especially important if they have been discouraged or misunderstood by their present manager (assessment centre stars are sometimes the same people that are regarded as troublemakers by their bosses, because they show characteristics such as decisiveness that are unwelcome in junior roles).

- They provide the organization with the chance to identify potential that has been deliberately or unwittingly hidden.

- Involvement as assessors leads to increased skills of observation and assessment against factors which are directly related to performance.

- Assessors learn skills at giving feedback, participants (and their managers if appropriate) learn skills in listening to and using feedback constructively.

- Participants and assessors become more flexible because they are exposed to new ways of tackling familiar tasks.

- Identifying the criteria forces an organization to investigate and focus on the behaviours that are really linked to effective performance.

- The work involved in the various stages of designing and running centres signals that the organization is committed to developing its members.

Disadvantages of centres

Although the benefits may well outweigh the disadvantages, there are still a number of drawbacks to consider:

- The most significant of these is cost, particularly in terms of time taken to:
  - research the criteria
  - design or choose the simulations and other activities
  - brief all concerned
  - train the assessors
  - have participants and assessors there throughout the programme, which is unlikely to take less than one day and may well take three days plus another two days for the assessors to pool their results
  - and yet more time for feedback interviews that may also involve the managers of the participants.

- Additional problems may arise due to career or development aspirations being raised. Participants may subsequently become demotivated if promotions or training opportunities are not available and those who are assessed highly may leave the organization for better prospects elsewhere.

- Those who receive poor assessments may also become demotivated and need support to come to terms with their results – it can be very discouraging to be forced to accept our limitations.

Introducing a centre

The following is an overview of the key steps in introducing an assessment or development centre:

Making the decision

- What do you want to achieve – the best possible selection decisions or identification of potential so you can initiate development activity? Or is it participant-focused, so that people will recognize their own development needs?
- Who will the participants be? How will they be selected for attendance? Beware of allowing managers to choose as this often defeats the purpose of having a centre.
- Before you commit to a significant investment in centres, check how else you might attain what your organization needs. Will any of those be more cost-effective or culturally acceptable?

Selecting the criteria and the activities

Will you research your own or use an off-the-shelf set? How will you ensure that these are truly relevant for your organization, now and in the future? Will you need a steering group and if so, who should be in it so you get a broad spread of opinions?

Involving others

- Who will need to know about the centres? How will you brief and enthuse line management? How will you brief and reassure employees (and their representatives)? How will you encourage employees to opt to participate/or what will you need to tell external candidates?

- Who will be the assessors? How will you train them – so they understand the activities, can observe and assess, give feedback, discuss development options with participants and their managers?

- How will the results be used? Who will have access to the results? How will you ensure that results are used only by people who understand the assessment process? How will you avoid outdated results being referred to at some future time? What are the links to other systems such as appraisal and training?

Administering the centre

- Who will be competent to administer a centre where you may have as many as 16 participants and 8 assessors, all operating to individual programmes, with masses of documentation to be distributed, completed, copied and collated?
- Who will chair the discussion at which assessors pool their assessments? This will need to be someone competent to ensure all assessor views are noted, particularly if some assessors are more senior or more vocal.

Using the results

- What arrangements will you have for feedback to candidates? For internal participants, what involvement will their managers have? (For example, the assessor might meet manager and participant to discuss strengths and development needs – preferably without sharing any ratings as managers tend to confuse these with current performance appraisals.)
- What systems will you need to ensure results are used only for agreed purposes, and how will you ensure they are destroyed once they are out-of-date?

Evaluation

- To evaluate the programme design, ask participants and assessors about:
  - the realism of the simulations
  - the range of activities
  - the perceived relevance of the criteria
  - the accuracy of the feedback.
- To evaluate the centre itself, wait a few months and then ask:
  - how selected candidates are performing in the job
  - how feedback was used
  - what happened to the development plans
  - what assessors and participants feel they learned from the process.
- To evaluate the use of centres in general, observe:
  - how the approach has impacted on the organizational culture
  - whether people are taking more responsibility for their own development
  - whether assessors are now more skilled at assessing performance and encouraging development generally
  - and whether morale has improved.

Some practical tips

- Have programmes ready for varying numbers of participants – for the inevitable day when they do not all turn up.
- Identify standby assessors – for the equally inevitable day when *they* do not all turn up.
- Analyse assessor ratings so you can identify and retrain or drop the ones who fail to use the whole scale, or operate on halo/slipped halo mode (i.e. give all high, all low or all average ratings).
- When participants 'deny' the feedback, let them – we all need our defence mechanisms at times. Give them the feedback in writing so they can think it over later.

Further reading

Ballantine, I. and Povah, N. (1995), *Assessment and Development Centres*, Aldershot: Gower.

Stewart, A. and Stewart, V. (1981), *Tomorrow's Managers Today*, London: IPM.

Woodruffe, C. (1990), *Assessment Centres: Identifying and Developing Competence*, London: IPM.

Chapter 37

Using psychometrics in management development

Michael Gregg

Surveys suggest that over 70 per cent of major UK based organizations use some form of formal assessment to both select and develop their managers. This chapter will highlight why these techniques have become so popular, review the various approaches organizations can take and illustrate when and where techniques should be used.

Gaining competitive advantage

After decades of empty statements in annual reports about 'people being our best asset', employers really are beginning to believe that their employees will make the difference to their future competitiveness. Most senior managers today accept that one of their most pressing objectives is to have the right person in the right job. That reasoning has two implications. First, it means being able to recruit the right person in the first place. Second, it means developing them to fit the requirements of the job. In order to do both effectively, organizations need effective assessment methods.

There are sound business reasons for this approach.

- As corporations look for ways to improve efficiency every part of the business structure comes under scrutiny, especially human resources (HR) and training. Today HR must show that it understands the needs of both the business and the individual and that it has the means to deliver people who have the right skills sets. This implies a rigorous testing system to match candidates to vacancies and identify development needs in current staff.

- There is no other way. In the past – before downsizing and delayering were part of business vernacular – middle management served as a convenient testing ground from which to choose the future leaders of the business. Now that those layers have been stripped out organizations have no alternative but to rely on assessment methods to select senior managers and identify the areas where they need to develop further skills.

● In a job market where high calibre candidates are a scarce resource there is more reason than ever to make sure the right candidates are being selected. At the same time, it is prudent to assess and develop existing employees before going down the expensive recruitment route.

Assessment tools for development

Testing and assessment is nothing new. Indeed, we have records from ancient China which highlight the written tests and verbal creativity standards that civil servants were required to take.

Today, however, assessment tools are used not only in selection but as part of the development process of individuals in the workplace. They attempt to produce detailed information on an individual's knowledge, skills, abilities and motivations – all in relation to a job or role they are asked to undertake.

So, how do organizations in the modern age use psychometric assessment for developing their managers? There are three different approaches.

Pen and pencil tools

First, there are a number of paper and pencil psychometric tools that are aimed specifically at the development market. For example, many people will have experienced the Belbin Team Roles questionnaire in which individuals answer a series of questions to determine their preferences to undertake specific roles in a team environment. According to Belbin these roles capture all the major activities involved in successful team performance. Preferences are categorized under a series of labels, e.g. 'completer/finisher', 'plant' (the ideas person), 'chairman' and so on, and once people have identified their preferences, team tasks are often undertaken with teams being made up of various combinations of roles.

Another traditional psychometric tool used in development is the Myers-Briggs Type Indicator. This measures an individual on four separate scales – Extraversion/Introversion; Sensing/Intuition; Thinking/Feeling; and Judgement/Perception. Scores on each scale allow respondents to be categorized into one of 16 psychological types (e.g. ESTJ, or INFP). Proponents of type theory argue that different psychological types have both strengths and development needs. The output from the questionnaire is used as the basis for both exploring these development needs and planning how they can be tackled.

Personality questionnaires

Second, is the use of the broader based personality questionnaires. Indeed, the use of personality measures to assess and develop managers in the workplace is currently experiencing a renaissance. There is now a general consensus among both academics and practitioners alike that measuring personality, using the 'Big Five' factors, is the best way to gather such data in both selection and management development. This is because instruments based on this schema capture all the main areas of normal personality and are regarded by most as technically superior than more conceptually based models. So, what are the 'Big Five'?

The 'Big Five' have their origin in statistics rather than in psychological theory. In other words, regardless of the theory of personality put forward by designers of personality inventories, an analysis of the responses of those that complete such questionnaires suggest five major trends or factors. These are:

1. *Emotional stability* which measures individuals on a scale ranging from nervous and moody through to calm and self-assured.
2. *Surgency* which describes people on a scale from quiet and unassertive to active and outgoing.
3. *Warmth* which measures people on a scale from hard-nosed and tough to tactful and sensitive.
4. *Conscientiousness* which describes individuals on a scale from impulsive and careless to conscientious and conforming.
5. *Openness to experience* which measures people from narrow and unimaginative through to curious and imaginative.

This structure is not new. Indeed, psychologists in the 1930s were commenting on this factor structure of personality, suggesting that the relatively simple model above did indeed chart most of the territory of normal personality. However, it is only recently that inventories based on the structure have come to the fore. Among the leaders in the field is the Hogan Personality Inventory (Hogan and Hogan, 1992). This is a 206 item questionnaire taking 20 minutes to complete. Hogan argues that responses to the questionnaire focus on how someone presents himself or herself to the world. Thus, rather than being a self-report, the results are more about self-presentation, and as such, are about a person's reputation. Reputations dictate the course of our careers and according to Hogan, if we can measure accurately a person's reputation, we can predict the extent to which they will be successful in their working lives. So, do the results from such an approach justify these claims?

Evidence to date, both in the United States and in the UK, does seem to lend credence to Hogan's position. Indeed the results are impressive. Evidence has been produced from a wide range of industry sectors and across a number of organizational levels that predictions made through using such techniques are very good predictors of job performance. Furthermore, the accuracy or validity of those predictions are probably greater than those obtained by the more 'conceptually' personality measures and may even rival the validity obtained by assessing behaviours through such techniques as Assessment Centres.

However, using personality questionnaires in development has both advantages and disadvantages. On the plus side personality inventories are relatively inexpensive. Once trained to the British Psychological Society's 'Level B' standard, users of such inventories can produce data on an individual for a few pounds. They are also quick and easy to administer. The Hogan Personality Inventory takes 20 minutes to complete and modern expert systems can produce interpretive and feedback reports in seconds. Standardized and objective scoring methods ensure that, at least in terms of data collection and measurement, all respondents are treated equally. Face validity is also high. Widely used across industry in the UK, and accepted as an integral part of assessing individuals in the workplace, those who complete such questionnaires rarely question their purpose. Combined with normative data enabling an individual's scores on the scales to be compared with a similar population, and evidence to suggest little or no adverse impact on ethnic minorities, such techniques do have many advantages.

Personality inventories do, however, have a downside. First, it is often argued by many leading psychologists that personality becomes 'set' in one's twenties. It follows that if these inventories are used with people older than this, one is measuring relatively unalterable characteristics. While this might be important in selection, such a view might call into question their use in management development. There is a strong argument when assessing for development to suggest that if one cannot alter or develop the individual on the construct that is being measured then why measure it? At the very least, it will make feedback to the individual difficult. Second, such data are eminently fakeable (although whether people *actually* fake them is more open to question). Third, the very fact that data are being gathered on five broad dimensions of underlying characteristics puts an upper limit on the richness of data that can be gathered on any one individual.

Behavioural assessment

The third approach is that of behavioural assessment. Although relatively expensive and 'resource hungry', techniques such as assessment centres that include job simulations (e.g. interactions, in-trays, group discussions, formal presentations) have much to offer in the training and development arena (see Chapter 36). This is because, rather than attempting to look at underlying characteristics, they look at competencies. These are descriptions of clusters or groupings of behaviours, motivations, and knowledge that relate to job success or failure. In other words they are the things individuals must demonstrate to be effective in a job or role.

Those who support this assessment tradition argue that, if one can present an individual with some of the problems faced at work – such as dealing with customers, coaching subordinates or analysing data – then measuring how an individual behaves in such circumstances is the best way, not only of predicting future job performance, but also of producing development plans which can help managers address their own specific needs. Undoubtedly less fakeable than personality data, assessment centres also provide a richness of data that can be used to help individuals change the way in which they approach their jobs.

So, how do these claims stand up to scrutiny? Undoubtedly, such techniques have a long and illustrious pedigree. Modern assessment centres and related assessment techniques have been with us, in one form or another, for many years. Throughout this time they have consistently provided impressive data to suggest that they predict individual strengths and development needs as well, if not better, than any other technique available currently. They are used widely in government, the military, and in industry both in selection and, more recently, as a central plank in management development. The quality and quantity of information regarding strengths and development needs available to both the organization and the individual is indeed comprehensive. In short, behavioural assessment techniques provide a richness of sound psychometric data which are unavailable through measuring personality data.

The way forward

Both personality and behavioural assessment have their use in management development. However, much of the work in both supervisory and management development, by its very nature, concentrates on changing individual behaviour. Remembering the fact that personality measures stable characteristics, behavioural techniques are likely to lead the way if one is to emphasize the things that can be changed. Indeed, such an approach is already popular in the UK. The use of assessment centres, or their more palatable cousins, development centres, is prevalent across industry to identify potential among existing employees. In addition, behaviourally based assessment is used to audit management strengths, help succession planning, and help individuals in the organization both identify development needs and put development plans into action.

It is increasingly argued by those in the field that personality data has a limited role to play in management development, except in the area of executive assessment. When assessing senior level executives or directors it is important to collect not only behavioural data, but also to assess the personality of the individual in relation to effective performance, the likelihood of 'derailment', and the motives, values and work preferences of those being assessed. Given proper guidance in the interpretation of the results, those assessed can use personality data as supplementary information when making sense of overall development centre feedback. So, what does the future hold for the two perspectives? Certainly, the emphasis on the 'Big Five' has provided a much needed tonic for those who support the use of personality assessment in the workplace. Validity data are impressive and they can add to our understanding of individuals working in organizations. However, that validity does seem to have reached a ceiling. If the 'Big Five' approach is the best, and there are technically sound inventories like the Hogan Personality Inventory to measure them, what else can be done? Should practitioners and organizations rely on test developers to produce more of the same and invent even better inventories? Or should they be improving and refining their use of behaviourally based techniques?

The answer is to continue to improve our capability and understanding on both fronts, at least in the short term. In the longer term, predictions of this nature are more unreliable. However, in a recent presentation Paul Barrett (1998) argued that:

> Behavioural (outcome) classification is already an implicit part of many personality questionnaires in that many tests ask individuals about the situations they prefer, or the behaviours in which they prefer to engage. They do not measure dispositions, but observed 'outcomes' of whatever cognitive processes are at work in an individual in order that the behaviour can be generated, then classified.

Given what we are taught about personality this may seem surprising, but many leaders in the field of 'Big Five' research would agree with him. If this is the case then behavioural assessment, backed up, and corroborated by, structured, personality assessment (which can help an individual assess and interpret that data) may be the way forward. The only challenge then, as Barrett points out, is how best to go about collecting, measuring and interpreting these behavioural data. From a psychometric perspective, that is an entirely different issue.

Using assessment for development: ten tips for the trainer

If you are contemplating using standard tests and questionnaires you should:

1. Get qualified at 'Level A' (ability tests) and 'Level B' (personality assessment) – but plan carefully before you embark on training. Both courses are generally five days and are run by most major test publishers and by numerous Chartered Occupational Psychologists. 'Level A' is a standard course and the same material is covered no matter what you go to. Details are available from the British Psychological Society in Leicester. 'Level B' is a different matter. Each test publisher trains on their own questionnaire so if you want to use the Hogan Personality Inventory you need to be trained by the publisher. If you then want to add the Myers-Briggs Type Indicator to your toolkit, you will need to attend a shorter (two-day) conversion course with the publisher of that instrument. Again details are available from the British Psychological Society.

    If you choose to use behavioural assessment a number of things need to be considered:

2. Choose a target job that people need development for. Ask yourself questions such as … where is the most need? Where will I get most commitment from the organization? Where will I get least resistance?

3. Carry out a competency analysis, either yourself or by employing outside consultants.

4. Design a series of simulations which are designed to trigger the behaviours associated with successful performance in the role.

5. Train assessors to observe, record, classify and rate behaviours.

6. Pilot the centre to ensure that everything works smoothly.

7. Conduct the first centre and produce a list of strengths and development needs for each participant.

8. Set up a system to tackle each individual's development needs.

9. Keep the momentum going. Experience in many organizations suggests that this is the most difficult part of the process. Most identify development needs successfully, but then lose momentum in the development phase because other organizational pressures intervene. These organizations that have been successful have generally incorporated development needs into an individual's key results areas (KRAs), thus ensuring that progess is monitored and checked.

10. Once the process is working successfully, choose another job or role and repeat the process.

Further reading

Barrett, P. (1998), *Science, Fundamental Measurement, and Psychometric Testing Paper, presented at the BPS Test Users Conference*, Brighton.

Hogan, R. and Hogan, J. (1992), *The Hogan Personality Inventory Manual*, Tulsa, OK: Hogan Assessment Systems.

Chapter 38

The future of management development and education

Eddie Obeng

The preface

For the past four years I have been living, full-time, an experiment called Pentacle The Virtual Business School. There have been two purposes for this experiment. First, it has been an attempt to operate according to the concepts and principles of the New Business World which I have been teaching and consulting on as a business educator. Second, and more ambitiously, it has been an attempt to completely re-invent the management development industry.

This chapter is based almost entirely on first-hand experience and through projects I have conducted with real clients. Although much of the client work is of a strategic nature, and therefore confidential, I have nonetheless drawn out a level of detail that I believe will be acceptable to the reader. More pertinently, however, the approach the company has taken to its work allows us to claim that here we have a model of what management development might become in the years ahead.

The New World of management development

There are a number of drivers behind what I have termed the New World approach (Obeng, 1997a). In terms of management development these can be seen in the following trends:

- A drive for a less parochial, or a more transnational, view on courses and programmes.
- Fewer opportunities for managers and executives to spend prolonged periods away from their work.
- A demand for real-life business wisdom, skills and application in addition to concepts and models.

- A demand for cross-functional issues-based programmes of learning.
- Organizational demand to encourage managers and executives to 'take ownership' of their own learning.
- Probability and recognition of learning through courses.
- Company focus and tailoring of courses and also individual tailoring of programmes as opposed to the traditional 'sheep dip' approach.
- Organizations starting to build their own databases of 'good' management developers and to 'cherry pick' tutors to run in-house business courses or insisting on specific faculty members participating in business school courses run on their behalf.
- Loss of profitability of MBA courses as supply has outstripped the demand.

So how is it that the traditional providers of management development are not in a position to respond to these trends? Let us look at them in turn.

The operating models for business schools and management colleges have remained unchanged for 30 years. Research is still mainly via the case study route – collect data on several organizations, present proportional data, or study one organization in detail over a period of time and create a case study. Case studies have also remained the key method used in the classroom. The use of complex live exercises or computer simulations acts as a peripheral activity often taking up less time than outdoor exercises or site visits, where these are incorporated.

You can argue that this approach has been extremely successful but with the demand for greater value and real-life business wisdom it is not hard to see where the business schools and management colleges are failing to perform. For example a re-engineering project that I was involved in during the mid-1990s showed that at one major management college 40 per cent of the internal process steps were 'ad hoc' or individual dependent. And of the 13 major processes only three related in any way to money making. Furthermore, there was no relation between activities and value to customers.

Many management consultancies have also been going through a relatively lean time, and they have been under increased pressure from their clients to follow-through, help with implementation and in some cases to leave behind some of the learning they gained during assignments.

This might well be possible apart from the fact that the management consultancy model usually revolves around experienced partners being supported by a young army of MBA/ junior consultants. Much of the profitability of such organizations derives from the ability of their corporate brands to stretch like an umbrella to shield and allow inexperienced consultants to be deployed at significant fee rates for significant numbers of hours. Unless the client wishes to pay additional costs for the transfer of learning, the experienced consultant is quickly moved on to the next assignment. Furthermore, since most consultants are not trained as tutors or educators they seldom have the skills and processes for transferring learning effectively.

Independent trainers are the third main providers of development and education. Typically, they compete either on cost or by offering a tailored or localized consultancy service but essentially the model they are following is the same as in the schools and colleges. Indeed, they are often past employees of those very institutions.

What organizations themselves are demanding, however, is a middle ground – they want help in implementing realistic strategies that can be developed and can be implemented by their management teams. And it is this New World that I will be outlining here.

The New World environment and virtual cyberspace

With hindsight all these trends and their effects are attributable to the existence of what I call the New World (Obeng, 1997). But what is the nature of this world and what are its rules?

Few people today argue with the assertion that the pace of the world is increasing. Just consider the combined effects of customer expectations, high speed financial markets, increasing regulation and legislation, technology and the increasing pervasiveness of communication. If most organizations were to chart all the various parameters they have faced over the past decade it would probably look like Figure 38.1.

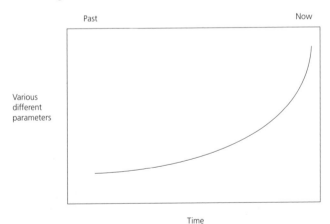

Figure 38.1   **Various parameters that most organizations face over a decade**

Interesting, but so what?

How about if I asked you to think about how fast your organization learns. That is the time from when it sees something, understands it and knows what to do about it. Take some time to think about this and note I said *your* organization, not you. Think about what limits the rate at which your organization learns. Is it the people at the top? Is it the speed or rate at which information about external events, such as customer demand changes, filter into the organization? What is it? For most organizations a couple of decades ago, the speed of learning was limited by the person, invariably a man, at the top. If they were a smart Henry Ford or Thomas Watson Jr., the organization could learn faster than their world changed. If they were not that smart they might get an initial foothold but eventually competition and change would weed them out. We will only concern ourselves with the smart ones which includes your organization as well. So over the past decade what has happened to your organization's ability to learn? Could you represent it graphically on to Figure 38.1? You may have started with your learning rate higher than the change of the parameters. But what happens next (see Figure 38.2)?

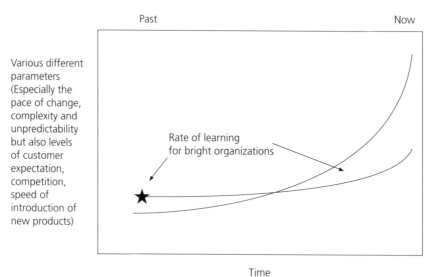

Figure 38.2   Mapping rates of learning onto organizational change

Do you agree? So now you are thinking, 'If there is a gap between the two lines the trick is to close the gap'. 'In fact,' you think, 'if only we could close the gap and put the learning curve *above* the change curve we would be in control again. We could run our organization from a position of knowledge.' You have probably concluded that, 'The aim is to learn faster, to create the learning organization and then all will be well. We will once again be able to learn faster than the world changes'. 'No!' I exclaim. 'Wrong!' Why wrong? Because it is now a different context. Learning faster would only encourage you to accelerate the pace of change.

Before we move on I would like to explain the differences between the two environments – the one in which you can learn faster than the world changes versus the one in which the world changes faster than you can learn.

If you lived in a world where you could learn faster than the world changed, how would you feel? What would you value? What would the same good rules of thumb be for making money? How would you organize people?

Now, consider what would alter if you lived in a world which could change much faster than you could learn. How would you feel? What would you value? What would the same good rules of thumb be for making money? How would you organize people? See? They are not the same. In fact, in most instances they are diametrically opposite. And the names, nicknames, I use for these two environments, as if you had not guessed, are depicted in Figure 38.3.

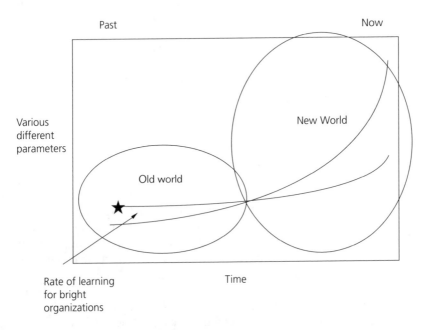

Figure 38.3   Introducing the New World

Built into the New World is a phenomenon which we have not experienced before. This phenomenon has created an environment, a space, which not only obeys different laws, but is probably already bigger than the 'real world' environment we currently live in. This phenomenon is 'cyberspace'.

To most of us, making a phone call no longer seems miraculous, something special, and yet it represents one of the biggest changes in interaction we can now exploit. You see, once upon a time, two people would meet in a room or on a path and have a conversation. We could say where they met and had their conversation. It was obvious! It was in the room or it was on the path. However, now if you phone someone up, exactly where is the conversation taking place? Is it at your end? Or at their end? Or both ends? Or perhaps it happens at both ends and also in-between and is not really in a place at all? This room, this space, where your conversation takes place, is cyberspace. It is the place where electrons and software applications live. We, us humans, live in touchspace – the world where we can physically touch each other. We interface with cyberspace through the earpiece of the phone, through the computer screen, television, and fax. So now we have the choice of interacting with two environments, *touchspace* and *cyberspace*.

Cyberspace is already bigger than our physical world, containing enough information to fill several lifetimes of learning. (Just think how long it would take you to read everything on your computer.) In cyberspace everything moves at the speed of light. Concepts we are familiar with, density, gravity, smell do not apply. The interconnectedness of people, cultures, trade and ideas creates surprising emergent outcomes. And most important of all it fixes the speed of change and interaction well above the traditional rate of learning for most organizations. This is the New World; a world where you are more likely to describe the time it takes to travel to a meeting in Amsterdam than the actual distance you travel. A world where events in customer or financial markets on the other side of the globe can deal devastating impacts instantly, or provide tremendous opportunities.

So far, most of us touchspace creatures prefer to have our information available in touchspace. We even claim not to be able to read things off a computer screen. We like to print things out so that we can touch and feel them. As cyberspace grows it makes less and less sense to bring anything into touchspace at all. It makes far more sense to instead peer through the peephole into cyberspace, or to listen to the sounds it broadcasts than to keep moving information in and out of it. Cyberspace manages information much better than touchspace. And in cyberspace the concepts of volume and density do not really exist. Why handwrite a letter, type it up, print it out, fax it for an immediate response whilst posting another copy for legal coverage? Why receive it the other end on fax paper, collect it from the fax machine, walk down the corridor to the room of the person who needs to see it and then place it in a pile of other touchspace artifacts and paper? Why read it and then purchase a large grey metal box with drawers into which the piece of paper is stuffed alongside several thousand others? And why then reply, by reversing the entire process, when you could have typed it straight into a digital format and sent it directly to the person you want to receive it? Bizarre! Generations to come will laugh at us.

If cyberspace exists, it exists in our minds. Just as both people in the phone conversation thought the conversation existed because it exists in our minds, it exists as we perceive it and only as we perceive it. It exists only so far as it interacts with us in touchspace. Cyberspace is a world which has the effect of being real but actually only exists to us when we perceive it in our minds. It is a *virtual* world (see Figure 38.4).

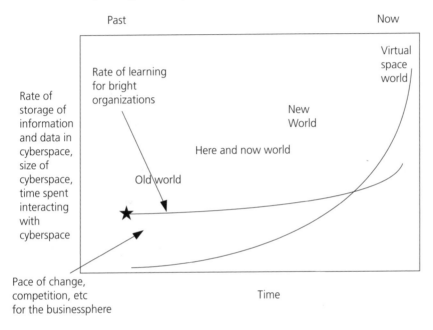

Figure 38.4   Cyberspace as a virtual world

In a New World environment as information becomes more available in an appropriate format and as we begin to understand how to utilize the multi-interactions of virtual space world, training replaces supervision as the key route to getting the desired outcome.

As a result this New World works to different rules. Knowledge, skills, ideas, values and competencies will only have a shelf-life for as long as they allow us to influence the future. This forces us to have to learn about a greater range at a faster speed.

So how do organizations respond to these new conditions? With our focus still on management development we can endorse the following set of operating practices:

Continuous learning

The concept of continuous learning was invented as part of the way out of the issues facing business education. The diagram in Figure 38.5 summarizes the shift in emphasis away from knowledge provision to a continuous model based around knowledge and skills and application in the real business environment.

Local learning

The local learning concept is simple. The additional 'contact time' required from continuous learning is delivered at the participants' place of work, in their own (not course) time, with participants focusing on issues that affect the business directly. The net effect of a reduction in the time spent on general (and often irrelevant) case studies, time and cost saved in travel, and the increased focus on work that primarily affects business performance is a powerful incentive.

Furthermore, the concept of local learning differs significantly from distance learning. Local learning has the following characteristics:

- The point of view imposed is from the executive's desk. 'What do I need to know/do in order to be more effective with delivering our strategy?'
- Solutions evolve and are created by the executives.
- Follow-up and follow-through are by tutors and other executives. Executives and managers may mentor and tutor each other.
- Explanation of complex concepts best understood through dialogue must be immediate or soon.

Virtual space

Local learning work is also dependent on the concept of 'virtual meeting space'. Virtual space is the use of cyberspace through GroupWare (software which allows several people to share knowledge and work on the same information at the same time) to create an area with access by course members and tutors where issues and problems can be openly discussed and resolved. Tutorial support is provided on subjects as required and involves the invitation of tutors to join the space. This in turn requires a virtual faculty or virtual tutors.

VIRTUAL BUSINESS SCHOOL

BUSINESS WISDOM
– Ownership is shared between mentor and delegate
– Feedback is via new communication media and is continuous

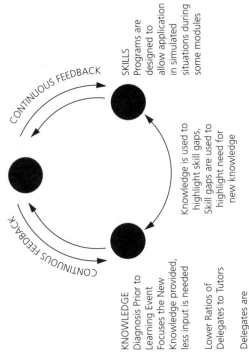

CONTINUOUS FEEDBACK

CONTINUOUS FEEDBACK

SKILLS
Programs are
designed to
allow application
in simulated
situations during
some modules

Knowledge is used to
highlight skill gaps,
Skill gaps are used to
highlight need for
new knowledge

KNOWLEDGE
Diagnosis Prior to
Learning Event
Focuses the New
Knowledge provided,
less input is needed

Lower Ratios of
Delegates to Tutors

Delegates are
encouraged
to Share Knowledge

TRADITIONAL BUSINESS SCHOOL

BUSINESS WISDOM (real life application)
– Ownership is with delegate
– Organization might hold some responsibility for course projects
– Feedback is infrequent

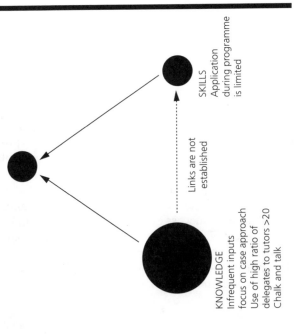

SKILLS
Application
during programme
is limited

Links are not
established

KNOWLEDGE
Infrequent inputs
focus on case approach
Use of high ratio of
delegates to tutors >20
Chalk and talk

Figure 38.5   The continuous model of learning

Virtual faculty or virtual tutors

Virtual tutors have:

- A clear understanding of the New World philosophy to ensure that concepts and advice are in line with each other in spite of them being physically separated and the fact that they may never have met.
- Access to cyberspace.
- The encouragement to think and teach cross-functionally.
- Participation only so long as the quality of their work lasts.

Furthermore, it is not enough to use tutors in the same old world classroom/ workshop way but instead learning approaches have to be created which match the demands and needs of the executive or manager who lives in the complex New World situation. These new learning approaches have to be used in addition to, rather than instead of, the 'classroom' method and provide learning effectiveness and productivity in the areas where classroom/workshop activity are less effective. They also beg for the creation of 'virtual worlds' where real-life problems of thought, behaviour and action can be learnt about, tested, and planned for application.

Such virtual worlds come in many different forms. Some exist in cyberspace, but many others exist only in touchspace, ranging from virtual reality environments through to 'canned' projects with real-life organizations where the learning from a course or workshop is applied to someone else's environment.

The experimental method

The New World approach has many significant advantages over traditional approaches. Notably it is first hand and the effects can be viewed directly rather than after post-rationalization and there is transparency in the objective and purpose of the action. The project approach has also proved very valuable here. The approach of using projects as much as possible makes it much easier to notice and evaluate the effects of decisions and actions taken within the business. Many projects are pragmatic because they involve spending real time and money in real time and this helps to focus thinking and ensure they are influenced towards success even when the initial thinking or planning may have been incorrect. This means that there are fewer outright failures than would be expected with a non-interventionist approach.

And the approach has worked in practice. In published benchmarks we have found there are significant benefits as follows:

Ratio of variable costs to fixed costs	Traditional 1:8	Virtual 3:1
Ratio of educators to support team	Traditional 1:5	Virtual 6:1
Ratio of knowledge input to skills and application (hr)	Traditional 4:1	Virtual 1:2

Solutions to real business problems

Management development has to focus on delivering business benefits. This requires that managers in the New World establish actual or potential cause-effect relationships in a business situation and that programme delivery is innovative.

This means utilizing both touchspace and cyberspace in order to provide 'continuous learning'. Why both? Well, you will inevitably find that although it is possible to operate effectively and almost completely in cyberspace, many executives and managers are unwilling to trust, in cyberspace, people they have not previously met in touchspace. This makes the group working aspect of cyberspace very difficult.

The spectrum of programmes you may want to consider are represented in Figure 38.6:

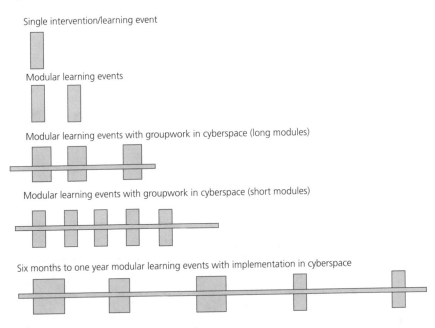

Figure 38.6   **The spectrum of learning programmes**

Our own experience also shows the need to have modules that provide both learning and accelerated team development. The cognitive and emotional roller coaster is a design method which allows participants to move from unconscious incompetence to conscious competence while at the same time becoming more emotionally engaged with the learning and each other. This allows effective operation of learning in cyberspace.

The use of cyberspace and touchspace is decided based upon the model below which has been previously published (Intranet and Web-based training IQPC 25 June 1997).

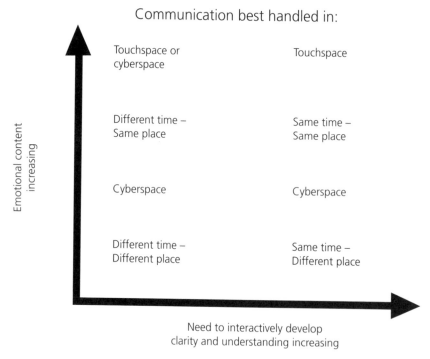

Figure 38.7   **Using cyberspace and touchspace**

New World development in practice

New World management development is already here and leading organizations are already using it. We have developed programmes with organizations including Alcan, Lotus, Motorola, Glaxo Wellcome, Nuclear Electric and SmithKline Beecham who are utilizing this thinking across many areas of management development including:

- new business creation
- process re-engineering
- project management
- leadership development
- virtual teaming
- culture change
- information strategy
- international finance.

Specific learning approaches that we have used to deliver effective learning in some of the above areas include the following:

- Columbus the Virtual Reality Business Game. Most business games and simulations force a context on the player. This often limits the ease of transfer back to work. Columbus was created on a Superscape Virtual Reality platform. It allows the player to enter and interact entirely with the environment and to explore the outcomes first hand and in real time. It is based on the New World rules: make time fit, fair = different and unlearn everything.

- The E-coach. Our electronic coach concept is based on the New World rules fair = different and go virtual. It is a coaching package which either speeds up or slows down or follows long or short cuts depending on the skill level of the person being coached.

- The 'live' project. Our live projects are designed to match current situations and have included working with general practices (NHS), solicitors and hospices. Projects have also obviously been carried out directly inside client organizations themselves.

- Scenario-based learning through simulation. By collecting the strong emergent patterns of situations we have created scenarios which can be navigated by executives to allow them to 'see the future'.

Conclusion

For those managers whose responsibility it is to forward plan or who want to be sure they can take advantage of New World management development they need to consider the following:

- That executives/managers have the skills and capabilities to use IT.
- That they manage stakeholders in the IT/IS departments and gain their early support.
- That they use common/platforms e.g. Lotus Domino or direct Internet Web page access as a primary route in order to minimize internal IT support issues.

- That they ensure participants agree ground rules on how the shared virtual space will be used and managed.
- That they agree confidentiality limits to prevent participants from being reticent about what information they share.
- That they carry out reasonable training on how to use the virtual space. The concept of e-mail is well understood but not that of shared space.
- That tutors respond regularly to requests.
- That tutors regularly make requests of managers/executives.

This chapter has focused more heavily on the education and learning side of New World organizations. In reality, operating the business side is just as, if not more, difficult. However, through Pentacle The Virtual Business School we have shown that it operates effectively and profitably and I believe that this model will become a cornerstone for next century management education and development.

Further reading

Kelley, K. (1994), *Out of Control. The New Biology of Machines*. London: Fourth Estate.

Obeng, E. (1995), *Making Re-Engineering Happen*, London: Financial Times Pitman.

Obeng, E. (1996a), *All Change!*, London: Financial Times Pitman.

Obeng, E. (1996b), *Putting Strategy to Work*, London: Financial Times Pitman.

Obeng, E. (1997a), *Achieving Organisational Magic*, Pentacle Works.

Obeng, E. (1997b), *New Rules for the New World*, London: Capstone Publishing.

Waldrup, M. (1992), *Complexity*, Harmondsworth: Penguin.

Index